A WALK ACROSS AFRICA

A WALK ACROSS AFRICA

James Augustus Grant

A General Books LLC Publication.

CONTENTS

1

SECTION 1

A WALK ACKOSS AFEICA:
  DOMESTIC SCENES FROM MY
NILE JOURNAL

CHAPTER I.
EMBARK AT PLYMOUTH FOR THE CAPE|MADEIRA|RIO DE JANEIRO|
SIMON'S BAT|SAIL FOR ZANZIBAR|CAPTURE OF A SLAVE VESSEL AND
500 SLAVES|LAND AT ZANZIBAR ON THE 108TH DAY AFTER DEPARTURE
FROM ENGLAND.

On the 30th of April 1860, Captain Speke and I embarked at Plymouth on board
H.M.'s steam-ship Forte, 51 guns, bearing the flag of Admiral the Hon. Sir Henry
Keppel, K.C.B., and commanded by Captain G. W. Tumour. Generally speaking, few
persons care to hear details of a voyage to the Cape, although, in a frigate with 640
souls on board, a greater variety of incident as well as interest might be expected than
in an ordinary sailing-vessel. Eight days passed smoothly; on the ninth day we gladly
stepped on shore to enjoy the bright island of Madeira, with its scented shrub-
    2 RIO DE JANEIRO.

beries, which, though hotter than the temperature on board ship, were exquisitely refreshing and delightful. Here, for some days, dances, picnics, rides, walks about the picturesque ravines, and cricket-matches, formed the chief occupation. A farewell waltz was danced on board ship, and the deck was like a brilliant May-day, crowded with ladies wearing gay sashes inscribed with the name of our good ship Forte. Our next fete vas on the Queen's birthday, when the poop was grace- iully hung round with large silken colours, and the Admiral gave a bountiful entertainment. The crossing of the Line was duly commemorated in the old nautical style, with douche baths, and effective applications of steam-hose in the hands of joyous young middies.

The lottery as to the hour of arrival at Rio de Janeiro was won by the only lady on board ; and on entering the magnificent bayla most lovely sightl we were saluted by a perfect storm of cannon and music from the Brazilian, French, and American men- of-war lying off the town. On landing, the mule carriages, the dingy sallow look of the people, the dazzling displays of jewel&ry, and the artificial flowers made from the feathers of gaily-plumaged birds, particularly struck us; and a drive to the botanical gardens to see the avenue of betel-palms, and a walk to the neighbouring woods, deepened the interest of Rio. As cholera raged in the town, several parties took steamer to the head of the bay, passing richly-foliaged islands in their course. Hence, forty miles of rail, through swamp and forest, brought us to the foot of mountains, which we ascended in omnibuses drawn by four mules, passing on the way others, handsome

MAN OVERBOARD. 3

animals, laden with bales of goods for the interior. The drive was most interesting, every curve in the Simplon-like road unfolding fresh beauties. Tree- ferns, the papau, and air-plants of every colour, clothed the hill-sides. At dusk we reached Petro- polis, a hill sanatorium, where we remained two or three days, enjoying its many natural beauties and the fine cool air.

Embarking again at Rio, the day after we left shore our attention was arrested by the cry of " Man overboard!" The life-buoy was slipped and the cutter lowered. We saw the poor fellow struggling with the buoy, and then disappearing; but he was picked up, and the ship stood on her course again, the whole taking place in less time than I have taken in mentioning the fact. Oddly enough, the hero of the scene got a fortnight's salt-water grog for having been in some forbidden place when the accident occurred. During the night of the 22d June, the tramping, rushing to and fro, and shouting of commands on deck, told there was a storm, and sleep was impossible. Sixteen hours afterwards, the sea still raging in striking magnificence, and the ship running along at eleven knots, the cry was again heard " Man overboard!" and every one sprang to his feet. Such was the discipline that, from the time I first heard the alarm till *I* saw the boat lowered in charge of two of the officers, Wilkinson and Gye, only two minutes elapsed. The man is seen clinging to the buoy; in the dusk of evening he is lost sight of; the boat also disappears; the suspense is painful; " burn a blue light;" the boat nears the ship; every one holds his breath, till at length the simple words, " All right, sir!" convey joy and gladness to

4 CAPE MOUNTED RIFLES.

all. The hardy English tar who had caused such excitement, actually assisted in rowing the boat back to the ship. We, of course, had our storm off the Cape la midnight scene; and though we had four boats washed away, our mainyard sprung, and water rushing wildly through our cabins, the noble ship bore the strain most gallantly, anchoring the following day, 4th July, in Simon's Bay.

Sir George Grey, the Governor of the Cape, whom the Forte was conveying to his seat of government, was a true friend to our expedition, and evinced the deepest interest in its progress. By his influence we obtained a grant of $300 from the Cape Parliament to supply us with a dozen baggage - mules. Two honourable members, who formed the minority, when the question was put, sagely remarked that " It was nothing to them *where* the source of the Nile was; every one knew it was south of the equator;"l not a bad guess ! In the Governor's body-guard, when he called for volunteers to cross Africa, there was not even this minoritylnot a dissentient voice was heard ; all wished to go, and we selected tenla corporal and nine privates of the Cape Mounted Rifles. When paraded for our inspection, they reminded me of the Goorkas of India. On the 16th July two teams of beautiful bays pulled up at the Admiral's house, Simon's Bay, where we then were, conveying these ten volunteers, who sat in the open four-wheeled vans looking very smart with their red caps, much to the envy of some Forte marines, who would have liked to go with us.

The embarking of the unmanageable mules was kindly effected by Mr Wilkinson of the Forte; and hav-

MULES. 5

ing bidden adieu to all her officers, we sailed that night for Zanzibar in H.M.'s steam-ship Brisk, 16 guns, Captain De Horsey. Sir Henry Keppel and Staff, on a tour of inspection, were also on board. The first night was one of intense discomfort. We were shut up within the walls of a screen-berth 10 feet by 10, the cots bumping against each other, a rolling sea, and half-a-dozen mules kicking and neighing in their misery all night long, and directly overhead. The officers, however, were extremely kind, and their wardroom so cheerful, that we soon forgot these midnight annoyances. Every morning a man named Long, a sailor, who said " he knew how to manage mules, as his mother kept a team," would report that the mules were " all alive." This was very superfluous news, for we had been hearing their music overhead all night. Often at dinnertime Long would take the favourable opportunity of exercising his mules about the deck, and giving the middies a chance of a ride. At roll-call of a Sunday, some of the names of the crew sounded very oddly. For instance, three Kroomen dignified themselves with the titles of " King John," " Soda-water," and "Prince of Wales;" while my servant answered to the name of "April." He was a jet-black man, and one of the " Tots" (Hottentots), whose first essay as valet much amused us. I had never had pillow-slips on board, and he, thinking that I ought to possess them, found one for me the first night in the shape of my empty clothes-bagla feat most creditable to his ingenuity and sense of cleanliness. On the 27th of July this same gentleman, while in Delagoa Bay, landed in green velvet shooting-coat, tight jockey-trousers, and neat regimental caplquite a *swell* in compari-

" TURTLE-TURN1NG."

son with his master; but though he was considerably blacker than the natives there, and very probably came originally from the same stock, he told me that he did not understand a word of their languagela curious instance of negro affectation. These Delagoa men were the first genuine Africans I had made acquaintance withlbright-witted apparently, slim, and very ugly, with a wild avaricious look, eating and drinking anything you chose to offer them, and scrambling for the fag-ends of your cigarslall in strong contrast to the gentle Hindoo. What surprised me was, that near their conical grass huts they kept pigs, which are rarely seen near an Indian village. The breed was a very good short-nosed black kind. Two vessels in the harbour, manned by East Indians, were pronounced by the " Prince of Wales," and others who boarded them, to be fitted up for slaves; but the Portuguese governor assured us that no slaver had visited Delagoa since the last English man-of-war was there a year ago. This did not remove our suspicions, for the flat-roofed houses in the bazaar had every appearance of being receptacles for slaves.

On the night of the 1st August the Admiral indulged us all by landing on the uninhabited coral island of Europa. He was the first to " turn a turtle," and in low water capsized and sat upon the animal all alone, while a jolly middie, named O'Rouke, ran for help. The beast was so strong that he was carrying the " light weight" out to sea by the use of his flappers, which acted to some purpose on the making tide, and on the Admiral's legs in particular. The doubtful struggle lasted an hour and a half, when some sailors came up and towed the vanquished turtle ashorel

SEWING-SCHOOL AT MOZAMBIQUE. 7

weight, 360 lb. The birds here were so tame and insensible to danger that the men were able to knock them over when on the ground with sticks and stones. Four living turtle were brought on board and placed on their backs, with a swab each as pillow. When the ship was at anchor they were lowered with a rope attached to them, and swam about playfully below the stern of the vessel, coming to the surface for air every thirty seconds. The butcher, while killing one by cutting its throat all round and opening holes in its groins, remarked that its thick blood felt " cooler than a sheep's," and I observed it to be two degrees less than the atmosphere (78). He also entertained the common belief that turtle will only die at sunset.

On the 7th of August we lay off the wooden pier of the island of Mozambique, an extinct coral formation. Here Speke and I were able to converse, in their native tongue, with Indian traders living away from their wives and families, whom they had left behind in India. We saw an interesting sight at a ship-provisioner's: in his back premises we found a sewing-school of negro boys and girls, presided over by a black sempstress; the boys were on one side and the girls on the other, Quaker fashion, all very neat and orderly, and engaged in making shirts. Farther on, in a dirtier quarter, women stood at a millstone grinding wheat, while others were alongside sifting it. One, a handsome gypsy-looking girl, had through her upper lip a large button of wood, which she sucked into her mouth most adeptly, in order to create a laugh and coquet for money. The cooks and henmen were of a lower grade ; and two lads, who also begged hard, were in chains,

8 CAPTURE OF A SLAVER.

having a rod of iron between their ankles. They probably were recent investments, and could not be trusted at large. But what shocked us most deeply was seeing a poor woman brutally struck across the chest by her master, a black half-caste Portuguese, for attempting to - go out without leave. Such are some of the vicissitudes in the life of a slave!|submission may obtain kind treatment, but even this is not always sure.

The Portuguese troops in Fort Sebastian have Hin- dostanees amongst them, and they observe the pleasing (Spanish ?) custom of doffing their caps during the "beat off" at sunset, and I understood from a sentry that they paid this respect also to the rising sun. The governor dined with the Admiral. He was in plain clothes, and wore a star. His crew of ten negroes had to wait in their boat during the operation of dinner. They were in man-of-war costume, and, remarkable enough, the head-dress was a black Highland bonnet with crest.

On the 10th of August a slave - vessel, Sunny South or Manuella, was captured with upwards of 500 slaves on board, 75 of whom were women. The scene they presented of nakedness, despair, disease, and hunger, was too loathsome to describe; while, to judge from the ham and preserves I saw with Long, our mule attendant, who had been sent on board and made good use of the opportunity, the captain and officers must have fared well. The crew were brought on board the Brisk for the Admiral's inspection. All came willingly, with the exception of one or two, who were a little rusty, requiring the assistance of one of our big marines to bring them

ARRIVAL AT ZANZIBAR.

to order. They continued smoking till stopped by the stern discipline of the ship's corporal, who received and ranged them in formal line to take their names. Eventually they dispersed over our ship, and, after some days, might be seen working quietly with the other sailors. The slaver, one of the fastest and most beautifully - proportioned vessels ever put together, went to the Mauritius, losing 105 of the poor starving creatures during the passage, and was afterwards wrecked near the point at which she was captured.

At Johannah Island (about 12 S. lat.) we stayed four days taking in coals. To a rambler or lover of picnics by clear brown mountain-streams, margined by a most luxuriant flora, I know of no such charming spot within the tropics. Its harbour, however, is a dangerous coral basin or lagoon.

On the 17th August the island of Zanzibar came in sight; also four smaller isles, looking like great arks whose bows and sterns hung bushing over the waters. The island has a low appearance. The town, running along the shore for a quarter of a mile of flat-roofed warehouse-like buildings, is not imposing, its mud fort-towers and the flags of four consulates being the only prominent objects. The bay is perfect, and we anchored close to shore in seven fathoms, this being the 108th day since we departed from England.

The greatest heat encountered|and it was felt to be excessive|was when in 16 S. lat. at Mozambique, the medium temperature in the shade being, on the 7th August, 78. Lat. 37 S., long. 21 E., on the 22d of June, after a storm during the night, shows the lowest

10 AMUSEMENTS ON BOARD SHIP.

recorded medium temperature, namely, 46. Many a pleasant hour was whiled away during the two voyages |shooting, band-playing, rubbers at whist, amusements with the various dogs,|Tawny, a clever collie ; Ossian, a deerhound; and Lumpua, a retriever, &c.;| sketching and photographing, drying botanical specimens, and picking up daily instruction in nautical observation.

2

SECTION 2

CHAPTER II.

ZANZIBAR|THE SLAVE-MARKET|CLIMATE AND PRODUCE OF THE IS-
LAND|TRADE AND SHIPPING|DECAPITATION OF TWO MURDERERS|OUR
PARTY PROCEED TO THE MAINLAND OF AFRICA.

After anchoring at Zanzibar, the Brisk had complimentary salutes from the men-of-
war in the harbour| namely, the Sultan's, the French, and H.M.S. Lyra. Next morning
at eight the Admiral had a special salute from one of the Sultan's frigates; and again,
as he put his foot on shore to attend a durbar, another waa given in honour of our
country|our ships returning each and all.

Colonel Rigby, an officer of the Bombay army, H.M.'s Consul, entertained us with
true Indian hospitality during the thirty-nine days of our stay; and his exertions greatly
contributed to our getting away so quickly. He, having passed in six languages, acted
as interpreter at the durbar, where the Sultan was most affable, shaking hands with all.

Though the streets of Zanzibar are too narrow for a wheeled carriage, and the
supply of water deficient, everything looked clean and neatly kept; and the shop-

12 ZANZIBAR SLAVE-MARKET.

keepers, chiefly Indians, were respectful even to a painful degree, rising as we
passed them. The bazaar is very abundantly supplied with vegetables, fruit, and dried

fish; little butcher-meat, but liquor-shops abound, and water has to be purchased|the best quality being carried fully a mile from a hot spring, which bubbles from under rock, and tastes unpleasantly warm. Men in the marketplace have an odd way of hawking about their goods for sale. Goats, carved doors, beds, knives, swords, &c., are all paraded up and down, and their prices shouted out. The market for human beings is a triangular space surrounded by rickety huts, thatched with cocoa-nut leaves; and the parties of slaves (negro men and women brought originally from the interior of Africa), on being exhibited, are guarded by men with swords. Some of the unhappy groups sit calmly in the marketplace, looking very clean, well fed and dressed, but with a depressed anxious look, saying to you with their eyes, " Buy me from this yoke of slavery !" It is a very striking though most humiliating sight to observe one of the Zanzibar rakish-looking crafts (felucca-rigged) arrive from Ibo, on the mainland, crammed with naked slaves for the market|all as silent as death. The Arab owners, gaily dressed, .stand at the stern, and one holds the colours, in seeming defiance of the British Consulate, as he sails past. The price of slaves was low in I860|only $3 each; and many Arabs would have taken less, as Colonel Rigby had released upwards of four thousand, who became independent, living in a newly-made part of the town, and gaining a livelihood by fetching water and selling the produce of the island.

The Sultan was most polite in sending riding-horsesThe Sultan's Stud. 13 to any gentleman who might request them from his stud of Arab descent. Colonel Rigby's horse-attendant took me to the spot. The *menage* consisted of some forty horses and mares of Arab blood|twenty of them packed so close in line under a long shed that it would have defied any one of them to lie down. They stood upon an incline of wood six inches higher in front than behind, with heel-ropes so tight that the poor animals could hardly raise their feet; many of their tails shaved to the bone, others snipped round with scissors; not a sound one amongst them|broken knees, greasy and gummy legs, mangy skins, bags of bone; and the outer one of all such a skeleton that I listened to ascertain whether he breathed. Certainly the mares looked more comfortable when picketed in the morning in the open yard upon sand, and tied loosely by the head, with nose-bags full of grain; and the picture around them of domestic animals had much the appearance of a home farmyard.

The climate of Zanzibar is very relaxing, owing to the humidity of the air, a great amount of rain falling during the year. The rain comes down in plunges, pelting showers, or like squalls at sea, and in the intervals any bodily exertion is attended with profuse perspiration and lassitude. I may mention that we. pitched camp on the 13th September, for our Cape Mounted Rifles, on a rising ground near a pond behind the town, where they remained upwards of ten days. On the 28th, when on the main coast of Africa, three of these Tots were struck down with fever, a fourth was seized soon after, and then a fifth|all on the same day. Speke and I did not sleep in that camp, and our health was not affected. Colonel Rigby men-

14 ATTRACTIONS OF ZANZIBAR.

tioned a similar case of the Assaye men. Twenty-six out of sixty who slept inland were attacked with fever; those who had taken quinine recovered, while those who had not died. From this it would appear that risk attaches to certain constitutions from sleeping inland, away from the sea-breeze; although, on the heights of the island, where the soil is a rough red grit or friable clay, I should not anticipate danger. But on these elevated spots there is this disadvantage, that no water is procurable; even in a well forty feet deep I observed there was none.

To one wishing to enjoy good health I would prescribe this recipe : Reside on the shore ; be in a boat by sunrise; row to any point on the island, or to the exquisite living formations of coral; walk home between the hedgerows, amongst beautiful clove or mango groves; enjoy the refreshing milk from the cocoa-nut; observe the industry in the fields, the snug country- houses of the Arabs; examine the " diggings" for copal; look at the men washing the elephant-tusks on the sea-shore, or at the immense variety of crazy craft lin short, keep active, and you will find that there are many worse climates than Zanzibar.

The island has two crops of grain yearly, and four of manioc, which, with dried shark, is the staple food of the people. They cook it in every form, making also flour of it. One has only to walk of a morning along the roads leading into the town, to see the productiveness of this beautiful island. Negro men and women laden with mangoes, oranges, plantain, sugar-cane, grass, cocoa-nut, manioc, yams, sweet potato, Indian corn, ground-nut, &c., go in streams to the market. The return of these crowds is, in con-

FKUITS AND VEGETABLES. 15

trast, utterly ludicrous. Nothing do they then carry but a stick over their shoulder with a cut of stale fish hanging from it; and one wonders at the extreme poverty of the people in the midst of such abundance. Besides the above products, cloves, cotton, bajra, sorghum, dall, coffee, tobacco, sessamum, grass, nutmeg, red pepper, betel-nut, catchoo-nut, jack-fruit, papau, almond, pomegranate, and the castor-oil plant, were all seen growing. To remark upon a few :|The mango-tree, met with everywhere, is splendidly umbrageous, more lofty than the variety seen in Indian topes, and not so brittle. It yields two crops yearly of stringy fruit; but there are better sorts, such as those from Pemba Island, to be procured. The clove- tree is planted in rows 20 feet apart, and after it has grown to the height of 30 feet, it seems to die, as if from the effects of ants. Cloves have diminished immensely in value ; what cost 25 dollars twelve years ago can now be purchased for one dollar; consequently the agriculturists do not replace the dying trees. The spice was being gathered by men on tripod ladders on the 6th September. Cotton we rarely saw. The cocoa-nut is the most common tree in the countryl the husk, we observed, being used as firewood, and a capital salad is made from the crown of the trunk. The Arabs allow their slaves to cultivate the manioc or "mohogo" gratis, under the cocoa-nut trees, in payment for gathering the harvests of mango, cloves, &c. The growth of the ground-nut is very curious, creeping close to the ground, with a yellow flower and leaf resembling clover. On the flower withering the pod goes underground, where it matures. The coffee- tree grows luxuriantly, and the sugar-cane is very

16 TRADE.

fine; pomegranate does not seem to succeed. The boundaries of farms are often marked by the castor- oil bush.

Miserable-looking camels drive the oil-press. Cattle do not thrive, though upon the neighbouring island of Pemba a small breed succeeds. Few butchers' shops are seen:

the natives adopt the vegetable and fish diet, not being able to afford meat. Goats, when castrated and stall-fed, become very heavy, and their meat is considered a great delicacy by the Arabs.

Trade has considerably increased at Zanzibar. The shipping consists chiefly of large native craftlthirty to forty from Bombay, Muscat, &c., and but three or four ships from Europe and America. The merchants have their Exchange, if the place they daily meet in may be designated by this title. Here human beings, money, ivory, copal, cloves, cloths, beads, rice, cowries, opercula, and goods from all quarters of the world, change hands. The largest single tusk we saw at Zanzibar weighed 165 lb.; length, 8 feet 7 inches ; greatest circumference, 1 foot 11 incheslall of the purest blue-tinted soft ivory. It belonged to Mr Webb, the American consul. He had also an enormous hippopotamus tusk, nine inches greatest circumference, and turning, like the horn of a Highland ram, once and a half round. As the tusk increases in size, a corresponding rise takes place in its value per lb. Tortoise-shell fetched 15s. per lb.; for hippopotamus ivory there was then no demand in Europe.

Several stirring events occurred while we were at Zanzibar. Once the Brisk got information of a slaver, but on sailing in search could find nothing of her.

BRAVE CREW OF BLACKS. 17

Again, after she had left, the Sultan requested Speke to take one of his ships of war and capture a slaver at Panganee; but this also proved a fruitless chase; and as we were anxious to return to the preparations for the march, we left the Sultan's corvette at sea and proceeded homewards, at 10 A.m., in an open boat of ten oarsldistance to Zanzibar, 40 miles. We pulled till 5 P.m., found the current carrying us to the Indian Ocean, and put in for the night on a coral isle.

Our brave crew of blacks, the same class of men who subsequently accompanied us upon our expedition, started again at four in the morning, rowing, off and on, till we reached home at eight that evening. The rowers accomplished this great feat without a grumble, singing the greater part of the way, though with nothing to cheer them for the two days but a few biscuits, sweetmeats, and oranges. Who can fail to admire such spirit! But we have the same class of African, when roaming amid his native wilds free from all control, committing murder without scruple ; and an illustration of this came under our notice here. Dr Roscher, a German gentleman, while exploring near Lake Nyassa, was murdered in 1859 by natives who coveted his scientific instruments. The sultan of the country, justly indignant, sent four men to Zanzibar to stand theirtrial for the murder. Two were condemned, and suffered decapitation on the 23d August. I was present, going to the execution with the " sur- rung" or boatswain of the British Consulate, who cleared the way for me to get near the two men. They squatted outside the fort wall with perfect composure, naked from head to foot, except a waistcloth; neither

18 DECAPITATION OF TWO MURDERERS.

tied nor handcuffed, and guarded carelessly by a few jesting soldiers. The Sultan's order to proceed with the execution not having arrived, a considerable delay occurred, during which the most intelligent-looking of the two prisoners stated to me that he had committed the act when in a state of unconsciousness! A jail official here announced that the Sultan wished the sahib to give the order, and I informed Colonel Rigby of the circumstance. He at once saw through the timidity of the Sultan, and said, as the sentence had been passed weeks ago, he could give no orders about it. Returning to the place of execution, where both men still sat, we found the mob had increased. An Arab boldly asked me, " Why should two men suffer for one white?" On my remarking that " Sooner or later the men must suffer|the sun was broiling over the poor creatures' heads|would it not be charity to go on with the execution?" the reply was, "They are mere animals, and have no feeling." Still no one would give the order. Again the Sultan was applied to. A rush was now rudely made on the crowd by half-a-dozen handsomely-dressed Arabs, brandishing their shields and swords. I thought it was a rescue, but kept my place; and it appeared they only wanted to get up to the prisoners, around whom every one laughed heartily at the momentary panic. Here one of the guard with whom I had been conversing laid hold of my arm, and, followed by a noisy drummer, the prisoners, and mob, we pushed on for a dozen yards, and stopped in an open space where some cows were lying. A twig of grass pinioned each man, and they were made to sit on the ground,

EXECUTION SCENE. 19

speaking calmly, while the crowd, all crushing around, joked as if at a holiday rout. Another delay occurred; no one had given the order. On being asked, " Might it commence ?" I replied, " Yes, certainly; proceed." The executioner at once took his place, drew his sword, weighed it in his hand, threw up his sleeves, and slipped his feet out of his shoes, while the dense mass all seemed breathless. The executioner was a small man, respectably dressed, looking like an Indian " Nubbeebux." The prisoners sat three yards apart, one slightly in advance of the other. The foremost was then ordered to bend his head, when, with one stroke, the back of his neck was cut to the vertebrae; he fell forward, and lay breathing steadily, with his right cheek in his own blood, without a sound or struggle. The executioner, after wiping his sword on the loin-cloth of the dying man, coolly felt its edge. The other victim had seen all, and never moved nor spoke. The same horrible scene was again enacted, but with a different result; the man jerked upwards from his squatting position, and fell back on his left side, with no sound nor after-struggle. Both appeared as if in a sweet sleep; two chickens hopped on the still quivering bodies, and the cows in the open space lay undisturbed. I left the spot, hoping never to witness such another scene; but I had the satisfaction of feeling that justice was carried out, and that had I not been present those murderers would have escaped punishment, owing to the effeminacy and timidity of the Sultan of Zanzibar. Their accomplices, each with a cleft log on his neck, were taken to witness the bodies: they were to

20 CROSS TO THE MAINLAND.

have a free pardon, and to be sent back to their homes.

We had now a great deal to do in preparing for a three years' journey, in taking observations and working them out. For the benefit of photographers, I may mention that the " developer " succeeded. It was given me by Mr Apothecary Frost, E.I.C.S.

The Sultan very kindly ordered that we should proceed across to the mainland of Africa (only forty miles) in his corvette, the Secundra Shah, commanded by Captain Mahomed Camese. We sailed on the anniversary of Havelock's entry into Lucknow, the 25th September. The wind was ahead; our crew, a rough set of African lads;

sandbanks were about; and after splitting our maintop-sail, and many oaths (strange to say, in English) from the native commander, trying to put things to rights, we put back for the night, anchoring close to where we started. The commodore, an Arab gentleman, came on board to see what accident had happened. He remained in charge, and early next morning, taking us as far as Choomba Island, returned in an open boat. The passage to the seaport of Bagomoyo was made in ten hours, but before we could land there was a row of three miles' shallow water, near the end of which two fine stout fellows came splashing through the water, shouldered me from the boat, and bore me like a child, *nolens volens,* in triumph over to the dry shore. These were our own " Seedee boys," or Africans, and they gave us a warm greeting. Everything was reported by Sheikh, the Arab in native charge, as ready for a start. We tried to march on the 1st October, but the trashy

THE MARCH DELAYED. 21

bazaar|all its flints, fish, rice, grog, and sixpenny accordions, not worth more than ten pounds|had too many attractions for our men; and we did not get away till the following day, after having drunk success to the expedition in a bottle of Colonel Rigby's champagne, and seen our kind host into his boat on his return to Zanzibar.

3

SECTION 3

CHAPTER III.

JOURNEY TO KAZEH, 500 MILES IN THE INTERIOR|ESCORT AND CASU-
ALTIES ON THE MARCH|CROSS THE EAST AFRICAN CHAIN INTO UGOGO|CLIMATE
AND DISEASES OF KAZEH|AGRICULTURE AND PRODUCTS|WILD ANIMALS,
BIRDS, AND FISH| FOUR NATIVE RACES, THE WAZARAMO, WASAGARA,
WAGOGO, AND WANYAMUEZI.

On the 2d of October 1860, we started from Bago- moyo on the East African coast
for Kazeh, 500 miles in the interior of Africa, latitude 5 south. The party consisted of
the following:|

Captain Speke, commanding.

Grant, second in command. Corporal, Cape Mounted Rifles, butcher. Private "
William," bugler and cook.

Middleton, Speke's valet.

April, Grant's valet, cook, &c.

Lemon, useful generally.

Reyters, fiddler.

Peters.

Arries.

Jonsen.
"Jacob "Adams.
Said bin Salem, native commandant .
Bombay, factotum, interpreter.
Baraka, commanding Zanzibar men, interpreter.

CASUALTIES OF THE EXPEDITION. 23
Rohan, interpreter, „ .
-,-.. ' / I Pnvate servants and
Fry, do.,
Uledi, valet, j
Mabrook, valet, donkey-man.
Three or four women.
Sixty-four Seedee boys,) Carrying our Mt and
115 porters of the interior,) barter.
Eleven mules carrying ammunition.
Five donkeys to carry the sick.
Twenty-five Belooch soldiers escorted us for the first thirteen stages, and we had
the under-mentioned casualties during the journey:|
Private Peters dead;
Five other privates sent back sick ;
About thirty Seedees deserted;
One discharged;
113 porters deserted;
Eleven mules and two donkeys dead ;
Fifteen out of twenty goats stolen ; and
Our native commandant, the Sheikh, *hors de combat.*
The daily stages have been so well and so fully described by Captain Speke that I
shall not dwell upon them, but merely mention a few incidents descriptive of our life
in the interior, and the fauna we observed. To accomplish this distance of 500 miles
in 71 travelling days, of from 1 to 25 miles per day on foot, took us all the months of
October, November, December, and twenty-five days of January, struggling against
the caprices of our followers, the difficulties of the countries passed through, and the
final desertion of our porters.

There being no roads, merely a rough track, no beasts of burden nor conveyances
of any kind in the country, our whole kit was put into loads of 50 and 60 lb. each,
without lock or key, and the porters paraded up and down with them a whole day
trying24 Cries Of "bomah" And "posho."

their weightla ludicrous scene of confusion and squabbling. Their captain, distinguished by a high head-dress of ostrich plumes stuck through a strip of scarlet flannel,
seeing all ready, led the caravan in single file with great dignity during the march.
The pace was never more than three and a half miles per hour. When the captain put
down his load for as many minutes as he thought necessary, the rest, a gang of naked,
woolly-haired negroes, with only an airy covering of goat-skin in front, would also
stop and refresh themselves with pipes, snuff, grain, dancing, and singing choruses.

Generally there was an argument to settle how long the march should continue; and many were the excuses found for a halt, no water ahead being a common one. Once camped, and the loads stacked amidst cries of "Bomah !" or ring-fence, and " Posho !" or food, the first concern with every one was to receive his day's wages, consisting of either a portion of cloth or one necklace of beads, while we retired to tents seven feet square, which were generally sheltered under a tree, with the kit and natives all round us, a motley crew. If we had that day arrived at the headquarters of a sultan, an officer would call saying his master must have so many cloths, with various other articles, and he must himself have so many more. Strong arguments and menaces would follow, and it sometimes took several days to the conference, as the sultan would be reported absent, or, more often, tipsy. However, once settled, if no porters absconded, we were free to proceed on our journey. I may here remark that nothing can exceed the noise and jollity of an African camp at night. We, the masters, were often unable to hear ourselves talk for

THE RIVER KEfGANI. 25

the merry song and laughter, the rattle of drums, jingling of bells, beating of old iron, and discordant talk going on round our tents. No Hindoo dare be so rude in your hearing, but an African only wonders that you don't enjoy the fun.

We passed through three distinct countriesǀ Uzaramo, Usagara, and Ugogo. Now at Kazeh we were in Unyamueziǀtranslated " Country of the Moon." Our interpreters had been Africans speaking Hindostanee, and seemed to learn the dialects as they went along, their native Kisuahili tongue being to them a useful basis. The four countries were not governed by one king, but divided into provinces, each from 20 to 30 miles across; and each had its despot ruler, the terror of travellers, who were forced to pay whatever tax was demanded without reference to any scale. The aristocrats or chiefs lived in no greater luxury than the poor, although they had a revenue from fines, taxes, a tusk of every elephant killed or found dead in their province, and the produce of large herds of cattle and of farming.

On leaving the coast our path ran up a broad, flat, dry valley of grass and trees for twenty marches. At the ninth stage, from a ridge of rising ground composed of small pebbles in rotten sandstone, we saw distant hills to the north-west, and had a good view of the sluggish, winding Kingani, which we did not altogether lose sight of till the thirteenth march. We crossed the East African chain at an elevation of 4750 feet, and got into Ugogo, a plateau without a river, and its " neeka" or deserted land requiring abundant rain to make it look at all green. These hills were tame in general outline ; the flora also was poor. We

26 ACCLIMATISATION FEVERS.

next hailed with delight the country of Unyamuezi, where water was abundant, oozing from under rocks on the surface or from outcropping rock; and there was a pleasant confiding air of homeliness and repose in the people, so different from those worthless races we had found such trouble in passing through.

The climate, with wind behind us on the march, was cooler and less creative of thirst than that of India. Our dress was an English summer one; no turbans were necessary; the evenings were delightfully cool; the sun seldom set in a haze, and one morning of mist, the 24th January, was the only one we had. At night, feeling quite secure from attack, we never slept in our clothes, but covered ourselves with from one to five thin blankets, according to the elevation. During the last week of November, previous to the regular rains, our camp at Ugogo suffered from heavy north and west gusts of wind, which set in at 9 A.m., or from dust- storms lasting two or more hours. In December the rain for the time would almost crush our little single canvass tents, but it afterwards imparted to the air that delightful freshness of the " cold season" in the Punjab. Fine, however, as this country appeared to us, nearly all suffered from an acclimatisation fever, which rapidly undermined our strength. The five Tots were sent back from its effects; all were martyrs to it, suffering from pains in the head, eyes, and limbslague, perspirations, drowsiness, startled sleep, and delirium. The only remedies in our power or skill were calomel and jalap, quinine, the first thing in the morning, and strong soup or hot grog when in store. The following is the report, 27th October

GUN ACCIDENT. 27

1860, and about the same number of men were in hospital every morning:|

William, 10 laud., 2 quinine.

Middleton, 10 jalap, 2 calomel.

Lemon,

Corporal, I

-i / 2 quinine each.

April, '

Jacob, /

Rahan, 2 pills coL ; Speke dressed wound.

This does not include the doses given to natives in camp, who had the greatest faith in the medicine- chest, often sitting round us as it was administered, and asking for the dregs of the glass ! We had an amputation case. The men were practising with their rifles at a suspended bottle, and Rahan blew off one of his middle fingers, and came bellowing with rage into camp, saying, " Look here what I have suffered by being induced to come upon this horrible journey! My life-blood is running," &c. He had evidently been drinking. No time was to be lost. I thought from the first that I should have the operation to perform, and Speke requested me to do it. I overcame the feeling of reluctance, and asked for a knife. The Sheikh's razor performed a beautiful flap operation, taken from the inside of the hand, and covering the knuckle. Bahan shrank at first from it, crying out most lustily, and abusing us and Baraka for having brought this misfortune upon him. At last he said, " Go on : do it." When half through, he pulled away his hand, and gave a tremendous scream; but with great coaxing the affair was finished; and, without having tied up any arteries, in a very few days he had the use of his hand, and recovered his temper.

We never could understand the disease that was

28 MULE DISEASE.

fatal to the mules and donkeys. Speke and our Tots would have known a tzetze fly had they seen one, and we therefore concluded that their deaths must have been caused by their eating deleterious grasses, for they lived on what they could themselves pick up, having neither corn nor hay. Here are the notes on one case : "30th Dec. '60. I Mule (the last red one) swollen all over the body for the last two days; breathing thickly; discoloured water oozing from the body; on making incisions, blood and water came freely ; not relieved; half of tail cut off; no blood, only water came; on pressing the body with thumb, the impression remains. Miracle if he recovers "|which he never did. The donkeys had much more spirit than the mules. We lost only three out of five during the march, though overladen with bundles, pots, and kettles. The wild zebra and donkeys mingled and fraternised by distant neighs.

Some of the daily incidents seemed so strange and interesting to me that I noted them rather fully, and think a few quotations from the Journal now and then may not be unacceptable. Extract: " 8th Nov. '60.|Peters reported ill yesterday; teeth clenched, eyes rolling, body rigid, pulse 120 ; wouldn't speak; had been asleep in the sun. I recommended bleeding. To-day he had ridden the march on a donkey, but could not sit up; had to be lashed to the beast. He now lay on the ground seemingly unconscious, his stomach violently heaving. At 3 P.m. the caravan was under way again. Lashed Peters on the saddle like a Mazeppa ! Fever still upon me." " November 9th.| ' The man is dead,' said the corporal, while we were busy painting. We were all shocked. He had died

FUNERAL OF PETERS THE RIFLEMAN. 29

calmly without the knowledge of Ins comrades. I had fever to-day." " November 10th.|Funeral, 5 A.m. The body sewed up in an American cloth; carried in a blanket, four Tots with a corner each. The corporal, Speke, and myself formed the procession, the corporal carrying a hatchet and two sword-bayonets to extend the grave if necessary. Found only a grave one foot deep, and partly filled in with grass. Hatchets and bayonets were used, and we got a place large enough. I read the service, and afterwards returned to camp. Sketched a ' Goodae' tree. Had fever, no ague, but mind wandering; very drowsy; disturbed rest. All the niggers exceedingly jolly|singing, playing bells, horns, drums, &c."

At our first camping-ground by the coast there was not a drop of water to be seen|a sad calamity! But Bombay, an old traveller, and always ready-witted, relieved the minds of the Tots by telling them that a well would be di|lf after the camp had settled down a bit, which lite$lly was the case. While near the Kingani|a truaj&frican-looking river, with its tall reed edges|weniiad abundance of water, but mawkish. It was a'white, muddy, sluggish stream 40 to 50 yards across, with steep clay banks 16 feet above the water, and winding so much that no steamer could make its sharp turns. Canoes ferried it. One well, or puddle, a short distance from this river, made our plated spoons quite black, and turned blue test-paper red. In Ugogo the wells were from 11 to 15 feet deep, of bluish clay upon rock, the water nitrous, and nearly the price of beer. Sometimes, when there was no water for thirty miles, a small quantity would be carried in. gourds, where, from the shaking and heat,

30 CULTIVATION OF THE GROUND.

it soon became nauseous or insipid. Our Zanzibar Seedees have a very polite custom: when they see any one of the camp arriving fagged, done up, and parched with thirst after a long march, one's thoughts perhaps running on displays of fruit in shop- windows, ices, or lapping water in a stream, they run out, like good fellows, to meet you with a drink. Let it be hot, bitter, or black as ditch-water, thirst is allayed; and, on looking to see whence the luxury came, you observe the men standing in a miry pool, like dogs on the 12th of August, while the poor birds, disturbed by the intrusion, wait their turn in the trees overhead.

There is not a plough in the country; a broad hoe answers equally well. Men with small axes cut down the forest; the trees and rubbish are burned; the long-handled iron hoe, chiefly in the hands of the women, turns over the light soil; and the seed is dropped into a hole made by the woman's toe, and covered up. Manure is seldom used; six months' fallow would seem to be its substitute. Fields close to villages occasionally get manure, or red clay heaps are spread over the dry, drifting sand-soil of Ugogo. We had no opportunity of seeing the reaping. Copal holes are only found between the coast and the African chain of hills. The country produces chiefly sorghum, bajra, sweet potato, and Indian corn, with tobacco, pumpkins, a small quantity of rice, manioc, ground-nut, and grains mentioned in Appendix to Speke's book. Mushrooms grow wild, and are eaten considerably. Tomato is not eaten. Tamarind, figs, honey in hollowed logs placed up trees in the forest, rich and good. The chief staff of life is stirabout,

CATTLE AND FOOD. 31

made from the sorghum, and from this grain they also produce a coarse, intoxicating, thick liquor, tasting like wort. In Ugogo they manufacture small pillars of salt by evaporation, but it is dirty in colour, with a disagreeable bitter taste. Fowls, eggs, and goats were occasionally brought into camp to be bartered for cloth, tobacco, or beads, as there was not a coin| copper, silver, or gold|that they would take in exchange for their produce.

We met with no cattle, except those collected for export at the coast, until we had proceeded twenty marches into the interior, at which point, and farther on, we saw a small humped breed, the prevailing colours being white and red|the bulls with large humps and small horns. The goats were of the ordinary short-haired sort, never used as milkers; and sheep, though rarely seen, were of the " doomba" or fatty-tailed variety, the size of a year-old Leicester, costing nine yards cotton stuff. Small bandy-legged brindled dogs followed the Wagogo.

Food was not abundant. As it was the dry season, we had to trust to chance and our rifles. One night our entire dinner consisted of two ears of Indian corn, eaten with salt; nothing besides, neither bread nor rice. Bombay very kindly, in the middle of this repast (which was laid out on our " service " of reversed tin lids placed on the tops of wooden boxes as tables), went and brought a cold grilled chicken, very small, and awkwardly flattened out . Though our hunger prompted us to accept the offer, we declined with many thanks. But, while sitting rather silently over our empty tin covers, he again appeared, having foraged five live chickens|thus securing for us not

32 THE RHINOCEROS.

only that night's supper, but food for the next two days. Our supplies of grain frequently ran out in camp, but the sportsman need never starve in the country we passed through; for although we could not always find large game, there were sparrows, doves, or guinea-fowl to be had; while persons who do not sport may take note of the herbs gathered by the natives, and live upon them at a pinch. The spirit of our men sank, and a deep, gloomy silence hung over camp, when we had no grain, and continuous days of bad sport with our rifles. Not a man would obey orders; they refused to march, and discipline had to be upheld in several instances by inflicting corporal punishment for the crime of stealing cloth to buy food. One Seedee, a powerful fellow, roared for mercy during the flogging, and disclosed to us who had been his accomplice in the theft. He was therefore excused the third dozen of lashes, and carried away bound, to be expelled from camp next morning.

We foraged zealously for the camp, and succeeded in giving to every one a little meat. The black rhinoceros would rarely charge, even though he saw us standing close to him; but they always afford considerable excitement by the feints they make, and by their deep hoarse grunt. Their ears were often torn and their tails mutilated, apparently in consequence of their fighting with each other. Our whole camp ate heartily of the rhinoceros; but the flesh, though sweet, requires very sharp teeth. Their young would seem to have great affection. Wounding a large female one night, I next day traced her spoor for four miles, , and suddenly came on her squatting like a hare in her form, with her back towards me. There was a great

ZEBRA-HUNTING. 33

deal of whining or puling near the spot, which I took to be her dying cries. Advancing cautiously, a different rhinoceros cocked its ears at me, and I felt for an instant at a loss which to fire at: both barrels from " Blanshard " went at my new *young* friend, who rushed off crashing through the underwood, and I only then saw that the poor old lady was cold dead, and she proved so heavy that three of us could not move her. It was the young one weeping over its mother that caused the plaintive cries I had heard.

Zebras seen cantering in open forests of bare-poled trees without a vestige of underwood, form a beautiful sight; they can be stalked very easily, and, unless made aware of danger by antelopes feeding with them, they will turn round and stare at you, some even advancing a few paces, like the wild horse of Thibet. When I first heard the cry of the zebra I took it for the call of a bird, with a little of the donkey at the end; but, listening for some time, and seeing the animal, I would describe it as a half-bray, or cross between a foal's and a donkey's call. They are perfect in symmetry, and barred jet black to the very hoofs, which are large, wide, and well cared-for by nature's farrier, the grass in the forest. Two of our Tots would not eat them because they had never eaten horse-flesh; but everyone else was glad to get "five- year-olds," or even " aged" ones, though of all wild animals I considered it the worst food, tasting so very strong. After the tongue or any portion of the meat had been boiled, it smelt of a stable, and caused instant disgust and nausea. Cut in long stripes, sun- dried, and toasted in ashes, was the only way of making the zebra flesh lose this flavour. Had we had any

34 WILD ANIMALS.

salt, probably pickling it might also have answered. The paunches were in several cases lined with clusters of maggots, a disease known amongst sheep in this country.

Buffaloes gave Speke some dashing home-charges; but though I sought them everywhere, I never had a shot. Their meat was as fine as that which any English butcher can produce|the men eating of it day and night as long as it lasted. Brindled gnu is equally good, but far more beautiful in the field. Fearfully shy, they look at you for an instant only, then scamper off, lashing about their switching long tails; and after giving a short spurt, they turn round again, take another furtive glance, and then bound madly away.

Giraffe are such wary animals, their heads peering over the tops of the acacias on which they feed, that only one specimen, a bull, was shot. This was done with a Lancaster ball through the heart, and I thought the latter small in proportion to the size of the animal. On asking for the head to be brought for preservation, I found that the Wezee porters had cut the ears off, and were already frizzling them for dinner. The hairs of the tail are so stiff, thick, long, and such a handsome black, that the natives value them very much for stringing bead-necklaces. It being a thorny acacia country, our men benefited by the giraffe's thick skin, which they converted into excellent sandals. For days afterwards, as they passed to windward, the odour of a menagerie was unmistakable.

Lions were fired at once during a moonlight march; others were heard both day and night making short coughing noises, but never " roaring like a lion." They

WILD ANIMALS. 35

kill cattle, and, if trapped, are carried lashed in a litter as royal property to the sultan. Tracks of the elephant were numerous in Ugogo. Here we saw some hunters, Mukua, from the Lufigi, with long "Tower" flint-muskets, looking as perfect as when new. With these they watch the elephant at night by solitary pools of water, and fire a volley into him ; but they consider that the best place to strike him is just in front of the ear orifice. Eland, hartebeest, black antelope, &c., and several smaller species, were shot or observed in our constant pursuit for specimens. There is a charm about the bark and spring of the startled saltatrix, a chamois-sized antelope, or when seen standing proudly on the face of the shelving rock, that reminded us of the goorul or chamois of the Himalayas. Their fore-feet hoofs are immensely long in the heel, enabling them to cling to the rocks. The hirax, or coney, basking on the rocks, is also very interesting: he is about three times the size of the hare. We saw very few of the latter; they were the same colour as the English, but smaller, with ears disproportionately large; they seemed to run more like rabbits than hares. Lungoor and monkey we seldom met with; the latter are hunted for their skins by the common pariah dog in Uzaramo, but the natives do not eat them. Squirrels occasionally cracked nuts on the forest-trees: they were of the usual size and beauty, most difficult to " twig," and having a white longitudinal stripe running down either side. There were weasels, brown ferrets, small foxes with black muzzles, and red foxes, jackal-sized, white-chested, with the perfect bark of a dog, and extremely graceful, with elegant dark brush. Mangy-coloured, impudent hy-

36 WILD ANIMALS.

enas prowled and howled round the camp, much to every one's amusement; they are such wary, cunning beasts that only one was shot, and our men had no delicacy in carrying it into camp for examination and dissection. In India private servants would refuse to touch such a piece of carrion.

The ugliest monster is the wild boar|head narrow and long, with four warty protu-berances, and the skin between the two tusks as broad as it is between the eyes. The mane is immense, but behind it there is little or no hair; however, nothing looks prettier or more like a race of Arab horses than a herd in full flight going across the forest with erect heads and straight-up tails. We saw a crocodile, the colour of a tiger, lying on the bank of the Kingani, where the spoor of hippopotamus was visible. We came across very few chameleons or serpents, but saw a puff adder 2j feet long, with abruptly short tail and four fangs. There were many species of lizards; one twelve inches long, very handsome, with vermilion head and shoulders, and bright-blue body. Shooting two of these amongst some rocks cost us twelve cloths, as I was told that I had encroached on sacred ground. Rats, bugs, and musquitoes seldom gave us trouble. During rain, frogs and crickets were deafening. Insects and white ants (eaten by natives) seemed to enjoy themselves by attacking us and the candle at night; and small yellow butterflies, apple-green underneath, fluttered in suspense over the edges of little puddles.

Of birds of song there were remarkably few: a species of lark on the coast had a short sweet note. Of game-birds, the ordinary guinea-fowl, weighing 3$ to 3$ lb., was the most common, and ate deli-

BIRDS AND TRAPS. 37

ciously after being kept two days. Early in the morning they roost lazily in tall trees, and in the evening they may be found near cultivations, chasing insects or grubbing up sweet potato. We killed one rare species, red round the eyes and on the throat, having a standing-up purple collar of loose skin, a ridge of ostrich-like black feathers from the back of the head to the nostrils, weight about 3 lb., and in running it seemed to have a more compressed body than the ordinary species. There is something peculiar about the shape of the " merry-thought," which differs from that of a fowl. The best-flavoured bird we found was the florikan, which has a rough gritty call; but few were shot, as they were extremely shy. Green pigeons are handsome, and after they have fed on the wild fig, no bird looks plumper on the table. Rock-pigeon, snipe, quail, plover, and several species of partridge, we shot occasionally; also a very pretty species of pin- tailed dove found in Ugogo. Pigeons, generally white, and not differing from those at home, are sometimes kept as pets by the villagers. Of ostrich we saw only one gang on the bare plains of Ugogo, where the natives make handsome wreaths of their plumes; and among the other birds seen were crested cranes, hawks, a solitary raven or two, a few parrots, but scarcely any crows. The natives capture all these beasts and birds by means of pitfalls and nooses. The former are cut like a wedge, most disagreeable to look down upon, eight feet deep, and but one foot across the top, which is coyly covered over. The nooses were formed of an elastic bough, stripped of its branches, with the noose hung perpendicularly, neatly concealed and placed in an antelope-frequented track. Diminutive traps were

38 FISH-CATCHING.

set for partridge, quail, &c.; and if intended for soaring birds, the noose is laid on the ground horizontally. The animals are struck with spears and killed, and are eaten by all; while the tendons are made into bowstrings, the horns used as charms, and the skins rudely dressed for wear.

Fish are rarely met with. On the coast, women standing in a circle up to their waists in the sea use their cloths as nets, and encircle small fish. Stake- nets in the form of the letter U, turned in at the apices, were seen. In the interior, upon the clear, gravel-bottomed river M'gazee, a party of fishers were seen wading down the stream, the men leading with hand- nets, while boys in their rear thrust spears into the holes in the banks. A number of slimy-looking fish, 18 to 20 inches long, had been caught, and were slung by their heads to a cord tied round the waist, surrounding the wearer like a Highland kilt. The four native races were as follows:| I. *Tlie Wazaramo.*|A smart, dressy (though nearly naked), well-to-do-looking people, with a most self- possessed air, and fond of ornaments in beads, sea- shells, or tin. Their heads are covered with wool, elongated with bark fibre into hanks, and their bodies smeared with an oily pomade of red clay, which soon soils their only covering|a cloth wrapped round the loins. The dress of the women is slightly longer, but they leave the neck and chest uncovered. Their arms are spears, and bows and arrows, with a few flint-guns. As they do not allow strangers to camp within their villages, we saw few houses, but those into which we were admitted were very tidy, with mud-and-wattle walls and thatched roofs. The appearance of these

WAZARAMO VILLAGERS. 39

people was prepossessing. The attentions of the men to their women were very marked. A man might be seen in a field performing the office of hair-dresser to his lady-love; or, spear in hand, he would join a party of women going to draw water, pitcher on head, and escort them lest any of our camp should fall upon, steal, or seduce them away. A very pretty girl and her beau were coaxed to sit for their likenesses, and went away with a smile; but two hideous old women screeched at the pitch of their voices because they got but one necklace of beads as payment for sitting before the camera. This partly exhibits the boisterous nature of the people: they killed a European named M. Maizan, and I have no doubt that it was only the warning guns fired by our Belooch guard every night that prevented an attack, for which, however, we were not unprepared.

The villagers *en route* turned out to see the white men; amongst them, during a single march, we saw two albinos, one of whom had black woolly hair. Again, of an afternoon, we considered it an extraordinary occurrence if our camp was not thronged by people, curious and well-conducted, some bringing their produce to barter. Women would sit at our tent-doors suckling their infants while cracking jokes at our expense. We saw no places of burial, but by the roadside the skeleton of a traveller lay; and also at other places single tombs, with large dolls of wood or some broken bowls of delf, standing as *immortelles* at one end of the graves, which were those of Seedees from Zanzibar. The only superstitious observance we noticed was in a field at the foot of a tree; a grass model of a hut was erected for the rain-god, as our

40 SPORTING COUNTRY.

men told me, and called, as usual, a " M'ganga." The worst features in this Wazaramo race are, that they will give travellers no aid, and will pounce upon stray men. They are polygamists; their only faith is belief in the "black art;" and though residing on the borders of civilisation, they have no curiosity or ambition.

II. *The Wasagara* population live such an outcast life on the tops of their conical hills, above the path of the traveller, that we saw little of their manners or customs. Parties from the coast attack them, to capture their people and cattle; and as we were considered of this class, our followers had great difficulty in getting supplies. We also suffered from a set of coast slave- hunters, who gave orders-that we were not to be supplied with anything, because we had come into the country to put down slavery.

However, it being a sporting country, we were more or less independent. Guides were got with difficulty, but a short, sharp fellow took me over a very fine range of stream- beds and shady spots for buffalo and rhinoceros, showing great cleverness and intelligence as a tracker. We met with nothing but beds of lilac convolvulus in the woods. My guide's chat, and his archery at a leaf ten paces off, beguiled the time very agreeably. He made me laugh at his sultan, Senga, who had fourteen wives; but he himself, he said, could not marry until his present wardrobe was increased, it consisting only of what he then wore|a rag round his loins.

III. *The Wagogo.*|We did not enter their oblong, walled villages, but I have a distinct and vivid recollection of the people. Among them were smart, wiry, active young fellows, who would make first-rate recruits. Their woolly hair, elongated by working into it

INQUISITIVENESS OF THE PEOPLE. 41

hanks of bark fibre, flew in the air as they ran; beads were at times strung on, or an ostrich-feather waved about their heads; their ear-lobes were distended by a plug of wood, &c. Their arms were five-feet-long spears, knobsticks, and oblong shields of leather; dress generally a small loin-cloth. With a gourd cup they drew water from their wells and filled it into earthen " gurahs," similar to those in India. Women carried their children on their backs in a skin, with cross supporting-straps; and boys brought music out of a stringed bow attached to a gourd as sounding-board. We were so mobbed by the people in camp that a ring of rope had to be placed round our tents; but this only increased their inquisitiveness. When told to go away, and not keep peeping under the canvass of our closed-up tents, they laughed, telling us the ground we pitched upon was theirs, and that they could take our guns and property from us if they chose. A porter of ours accidentally broke one of their bows; this was immediately turned to account, and a demand made for something ten times its value. I shot a lizard at some curiously outcropping rocks, and was told I had hurt their feelings, and must pay for my folly. Previously to firing I had thought of the Indian superstition as to sacred spots and marks, and examined the place well; but seeing no trace of them, I reckoned this fine had no connection with any such traditions, but was knowingly imposed on us in the way of extortion. They told us we must not have lights out at night|alluding to Speke making his observations. Like all Africans, if they gave us any information a present had to follow. The settlement of the tax was a most harassing affair. The sultan, after receiving all

42 THE WANYAMUEZI.

he had demanded, said the cloths were not suitable to his rank|" you have better ones than you gave me, and my head wife must get some." In short, he so bullied us by threats of attack that our main stand-by of porters, 113 "Wezees," were frightened into the dastardly act of deserting us at the most critical part of the journey.

IV. *Wanyamuezi.*|The 115 porters we left the seaport with were of the class of the Wanyamuezi, and we had good opportunity for observing their habits and character. They were average-sized, slim-limbed negroes, many of them with handsome counte- nances and incisions of caste above the cheek-bones; they were dressed in goat-skins hanging loosely in their front from the right shoulder; most of them with a shabby small bow and a couple of arrows; a few of the better sort had flint-guns, which they carried awkwardly at the long "trail," and pointing to the men behind them.

They are frank and amiable on first acquaintance, eating or taking anything from your hand, singing the j oiliest of songs with deep-toned choruses from their thick necks and throats, but soon trying to get the upper hand, refusing to make the ring-fence round camp, showing sulks, making halts, or going short marches, treating with perfect contempt any message sent them even to sit apart from your tent, as the smoke of their fires, the odour of their persons, and their total want of delicacy annoy you. All these grievances my companion bore with great patience, and often got the offenders into humour by suggesting a harangue at night, to be delivered by their captain. On an animal being cut up into shares one day, they so far forgot themselves as to dash

THEIR WOMEN. 43

upon it with the utmost rapidity, and bore *oft* the whole from our Zanzibar men, who were left in vacant amazement without redress. On killing a goat, I observed they never spilt a drop of blood, but smashed its head with a stick or stone. Out shooting they were invaluable as guides, first-rate spoorers, and never at a loss for anything: a pipe would be made by putting a grit of clay an inch or so into the end of a tube of bark. "Duncan's *smoking* mixture" they preferred stuffing as far as possible up their noses. When an animal was shot they always stole the fat. They had extraordinary knowledge of edible roots and herbs, and under almost any circumstances would not starve. They had no particular superstitions or sacred days, either in the week or year. They were intelligent and amusing enough, but had no claim to honour or honestyl113 of them, although handsomely paid, deserted us, carrying away a considerable quantity of property. Perhaps they treated us in this way in consequence of having been badly paid by Arab traders on former occasions.

A few of their women accompanied us: quiet, decent, well-conducted, tidy creatures, generally carrying a child each on their backs, a small stool and et ceteras on their heads, and inveterately smoking during the march. They would prepare some savoury dish of herbs for their men on getting into camp, where they lived in bell-shaped erections made with boughs of trees.

4

SECTION 4

CHAP TER IV.

SOJOURN AT KAZEH, LAT. 5 S., LONG. 33 E.|PROVINCE OF UNYANYEMBE|CROPS CATTLE, ETC.|MOOSSAH, AN INDIAN

TRADER, HIS WIVES, ATTENDANTS, AND COWHERDS THE

WATUSI | DISASTROUS EFFECTS OF WAR | MOOSSAH'S ACCOUNT OF THE NORTHERN KINGDOM.

We were delayed here for fifty-one days on account of the falling rains, the flooded state of the river ahead, and the impossibility of getting porters to move at such a season, when grain was not procurable. Our arrival was hailed with great delight. Moossah, an excellent friend of Speke's, several Arabs and many followers, all in holiday attire, came out a mile to welcome our ragged - looking Indian file. Guns were fired, yambos and salaams with shaking of hands followed, and we were lodged once more under a hospitable roof.

The country is surrounded by low bare hills, which every morning till eight or nine were obscured by an unhealthy coloured mist, filling the wide valley where we lay. There was nothing to cheer the eye|no river, no trees: it reminded Speke of the Crimea. Rills ran here and there through grass, and opened out on

REMEDIES FOR FEVER- 45

white sand: one of these, collecting in a pool, formed the drinking water of the inhabitants. Scarcely a man amongst us escaped fever. We arrived on the 25th of January, and by the 1st February several were laid up. My first attack lasted seven days, the 2d, 4th, 6th, 7th, and 8th terminating in headaches every morning. After twelve days another sharper attack, with delirium at night, but no ague, lasted three days. The third and least severe came on fifteen days afterwards, with drowsiness and profuse perspiration, and terminated in three days. All suffered from after-weakness in the limbs; some from blindness of one eye, the eyelid much inflamed and drooping, accompanied with excessive watering; or no inflammation of the eye, but total blindness of it, and no disease or scale observable. Acute pain rarely accompanied this complaint. Our men ascribed their bad health to not having got accustomed to the water of the country. The natives had no efficient remedies for preventing the recurrence of fever, but took pinches of a pounded plant or wood to cure their headaches, or cupped themselves in the following curious manner: A man put some beeswax into his mouth, applied a small cow's horn to cuts made in the temple of the patient, exhausted the air by suction, and with his tongue shut the hole at the end of the horn with the wax. We had only one fatal case. Quinine and applications of blistering tissue behind the ear and on the temples partially restored health and eyesight. During our stay the prevalent winds were the E., N.E., and S.E., but the coldest were the westerly after rain. The mornings were foggy, the grass dripped with the night-dew, which interfered with

46 CLIMATE AND AGRICULTURE.

Speke's observation of the stars by dimming the instruments. The days were often dark and hazy; pelting showers beat down from the N.W., but we sometimes had a fresh English morning, with a clear sky, a N.E. wind, and temperature only 69 at 9 A.m. We had no striking or beautiful sunsets like the equatorial at sea, but in the evening the flowering grasses, gorgeously lit up by the rays of the setting sun, had a singularly fine effect; .and such evenings were often followed by a few dry days, and a temperature of 82. This hot weather occurred when, at the short twilight, the sun appeared to set in the east, and the whole sky was an arched illumination. On an average we had rain two-fifths of the time we halted, and the greatest fall noted in twenty-four hours was two inches. These African rains we did not find followed by the disagreeable steamy or muggy feeling experienced in India; all was cool and fresh after them. We had thunder and lightning, but rain did not always follow. This province of Unyanyembe has nearly four months of rain, commencing in the end of November, and winding up with the greatest fall in February. As soon as the soil of sand, or black spongy mould, has softened, the seed is dropped, and by the 1st of February all is as green as an emerald. The young rice has to struggle for fifteen days against the depredations of a small black caterpillar, green underneath. It is a precarious time for the agriculturist; for if rain does not fall the crop is lost, being eaten close by this insect. Women walk in the fields, with small hand- picks, loosening the soil, clearing it of weeds and worms. There is only one crop in the year, and all the cereals known in Zanzibar are grown here. Cotton

SUBURBS OF UNYANYEMBE. 47

was considered by an Indian resident to be as fine aa that grown in Kutch, but he said they had no use for it, merely burning it as wicks. As the previous year's corn had been consumed, the poorer classes gathered the heads of a wild grass *(Dactyloctum Egyptiacum),* and prepared it for stirabout by sun-drying, beating on the rocks, and rubbing it into flour on their flagstones. They also fed upon mushrooms, growing amongst the rank " dub" grass, after drying, roasting, and peeling them. They were five inches in diameter, and sienna-coloured. Another variety was white, and half the size. All the cattle and goats in the country seemed to have found their way into the folds of the Arabs, and had been captured in a war still going on between them and the native population. The surrounding country is devoid of game, but within a long day's march a forest was visited, where various antelopes, giraffes, lions, and a few elephants might be met with along the valley of the Wallah river. The scales of an armadillo were seen worn as a charm, three inches across, and striated or lined at one end. Our men had a superstition that the person who found a live armadillo would become a king|meaning, I imagine, that it was so rare. However, we came upon a pet one at 3 N. latitude. About the cultivations near the village no singing-birds are ever heard, but the plumage of those seen is often very brilliant. Flocks of beautiful little birds, with black bodies, golden- tinted scarlet heads and backs, peeked at the ears of corn; or in the rice-fields the favourite of the Cape farmers, the "locust bird," black, and looking like a curlew when walking, went tamely about. Crows, with a ring of white round the neck, were seen in twos

48 MOOSSAH, AN INDIAN TRADER.

and threes. The matting in the houses was full of bugs, or ticks, which pestered one while seated at night, causing considerable irritation.

It is not a country for ivory, the natives seldom if ever bringing any for sale. Grain was so scarce that slaves could be purchased for two fathoms of calico. One day a naked native passed us in charge of three Seedees armed with spears. They had found him stealing, and offered him for sale. No one would purchase him, and he was taken to the sultan, who would, as Moossah said, either spear him, keep him as a slave, or allow him to be sold. Slaves from the northern kingdoms of Uganda, &c., were considered the most valuable, just in the same way as many persons consider a country girl the best servant. They were held to be more trustworthy than men from the coast, made excellent servants, and were famous at killing or capturing wild animals. The most esteemed women were of the Wahumah tribe from Karague; they resembled the Abyssinians.

Let me give the reader some idea of our life here. Moossah, an Indian in whose house we resided, was a fine benevolent old man, with an establishment of 300 native men and women round him. His abode had, three years ago, taken two months to build, and it was surrounded by a circular wall which enclosed his houses, fruit and vegetable gardens, and his stock of cattle. The lady who presided over the whole was of most portly dimensions, and her word was law. Moossah sat from morn till night with his " foondee," or chief manager, and other head servants within sight, receiving salutes and compliments from the rich and poor at the front or *gentlemen's* side of the house,Moossah's Household At Kazeh. 49

while the lady presided over the domestic arrangements of the interior. We had full access to both, and no house could be conducted with greater regularity. At three o'clock in the morning, Moossah, who had led a hard life in his day, would call out for his little pill of opium, which he never missed for forty years. This would brighten him up till noon. He would then transact business, chat, and give you the gossip at any hour you might sit by him on his carpet. To us it seemed strange that he never stopped talking when prayers from the Koran were being read to him by a "Bookeen," or Madagascar man. Perhaps he had little respect for the officiating priest, as the same reverend and learned gentleman. was accustomed to make him his shirts ! After a mid-day sleep, he would refresh himself with a second but larger pill, transact business, and so end the day. The harem department presented a more domestic scene. At dawn, women in robes of coloured chintz, their hair neatly plaited, gave fresh milk to the swarm of black cats, or churned butter in gourds by rocking it to and fro on their laps. By seven o'clock the whole place was swept clean. Some of the household fed the game-fowls, or looked after the ducks and pigeons; two women chained by the neck fetched firewood, or ground corn at a stone; children would eat together without dispute, because a matron presided over them;lall were quiet, industrious beings, never idle, and as happy as the day was long. When any of Moossah's wives gave birth to a child there was universal rejoicing; the infant was brought to show its sex: and when one died, the shrill laments of the women were heard all night long. When a child misbehaved, we white men were pointed

50 Moossah's Head Keeper.

at to frighten it, as nurses at home too often do with ghost stories.

The most important functionary about this court was the head keeper or foondee, who had been a slave all his life, and now possessed a village with a farm and cattle. His daily duty was to sit within sight of his master. On Speke calling to see his collection of horns, and extract a bullet from the leg of one of his slaves, the foondee made us heartily welcome. Stools were placed, and in gratitude for the operation he produced some ripe plantain, and showed us about his premises. He also took us to one of his favourite shooting-grounds, where he certainly knew how to make himself comfortable. His servants had constructed for him a most luxurious waterproof hut with broad stripes of freshly-cut bark, and a capital bedstead of boughs. At night five fires were kept burning round him to keep off the musquitoes. The grate was most original: three stout pegs of green wood driven into the ground, forming an equilateral triangle, answered every purpose of an iron utensil, and on it a frying-pan, made of bark, frizzled mushrooms and meat to the chief's satisfaction. By his own account, he had shot many a lion from trees; and during the march to and from Zanzibar with his master's property, he, with a staff of under-keepers, used to supply the porters with rations from wild animals, which plan saved the expenditure of bead-money. He had many sporting stories. The lion, he said, seldom killed men; but, not long ago, one had jumped the wall of the building and killed five cows, two of which he dragged over the walllthe natives fearing to impede his course.

Moossah's Watusi Cowherds. 51

Moossah's cowherds were a very interesting set of peoplelso well-featured, tall, and generally superior to the Africans, that I took great interest in them. They were

Watusi from Karague. There were ten men and women, all with woolly hair|the men leaving a crescent of it unshaved. Their gums were blackened with a preparation from the tamarind-seed, powdered, roasted, and mixed into a paste with blue vitriol, and afterwards heated until fit for use. Their ornaments were large solid rings of brass upon the wrists, and iron rings, in masses, on their ankles. In walking they carried a bow and arrow, a staff, and long- stemmed pipe. The women were of a large stamp, with fine oval faces and erect figures clad in well- dressed cow-skin from above their waists to their small feet. Their huts were quite different from any we had seen, being shaped like the half of an orange, and only five feet high, made of boughs, and covered with grass very neatly. There was but one door; the hut had no chimney, the smoke finding its way through the light grass roof. I observed a portable Indian " choolah " or fireplace inside the hut, which was kept tidily floored with hay.

These Watusi are a curious and distinct race. Previous to milking the cows in the morning, they wash themselves, their teeth, and their wooden milk-vessels or gourds with the urine of the animal, as they consider there is some virtue in it, afterwards using fresh water for cleansing. They are allowed half the milk, and Moossah had his half milked into his own clean vessels in the morning at eight o'clock. It took the milk of two cows to fill one good-sized tin teapot. A cow's value was four or five dollars, though a first

52 WATUSI MODE OF SALUTATION.

class one would cost double, or $2. Men milked them into a large crucible of wood or gourd in an open yard; the hind-legs were tied above the hocks with a thong of leather; one of their handsome women sat on the other side with a bough beating off the flies, and with a stick to keep away the calf which stood at its mother's head, a boy sometimes assisting. Should the calf die, its skin is stuffed and placed before the cow, otherwise she refuses her milk. The Wanyamuezi look with great respect on this people. When two of them meet, the Wezee puts both his palms together, these are gently clasped by the Watusi, a few inaudible words are repeated, and they pass on. The form of salutation when a Watusi meets one of his women senior to himself is gentle and pleasing; he places his hands on her arms below her shoulders, while her hands hang by her side.

The way in which an African leads a goat or cow is different from the manner in this country. The fore-leg of the goat is held up by the man, who walks briskly along as if he led a child. An unruly cow is never tied by the head: a man walks behind it, having hold of a rope tied tightly round its hock; this plan seems to subdue or *Rar&yfy* the animal most completely. For several days after our arrival, different Arab residents sent us presents of eggs, some coffee, a fatted cow, rice, or a goat|a very pleasing custom, which was intended as their call upon us. We in return sent each a handsome cloth, which they valued very much. This friendly ceremony over, they freely asked our advice when necessary.

For two years, since the death of the chief of the country, the people of Kazeh had been fighting against

DEATH OF SNAY, AN ARAB CHIEF. 53

the real heir to uphold the puppet appointed by them in his stead. They had killed 300 natives, seized all their cattle and goats, and lost two Arabs and sixty slaves. A severe defeat occurred while we were there, Snay, the chief Arab, and six others, with followers, being killed. A panic ensued, and Speke was requested to patch up a peace by inviting the rebel Manua Sera into Kazeh to attend a conference. "Once," they said, " at our mercy, we can murder him !" We were shocked at hearing this, but Moossah assured us that it was no uncommon occurrence with them. The news of their defeat was brought us by a man who may be allowed to tell his own story :|" I was one of five in charge of cattle ; the rebel himself killed three of us; and as I never fight, but run, I threw away everything, and saved my life by coming here." He had a very good sword by him. " Where did you get that sword ?" " Oh! it belongs to an Arab who was killed; I picked it up."

It seems that Snay was a very brave fellow, who in the midst of every fight whipped his slaves to prevent them from running away; but this time they got dispersed after plunder: he was left unprotected; and being old and too proud to run like his slaves, he fell a victim. After this severe defeat many plans were proposed for affording relief. "The single cannon must be sent in the morning." Moossah was tired of assisting them. " The Arabs stick at nothing; they had expended twenty barrels of his gunpowder and lost him five slaves; a beautiful gun of his was lost by his late partner Jaffir in this last fight. Jafiir had just been killed, and yet they still ask for aid !" So with true Indian parsimony he despatched

54 DEPOPULATION FROM WAR.

five slaves to the war, with only ten rounds of wrought-iron bullets each, to fight the powerful rebel chief!

This long-continued war had driven the natives of the country away from the Arab settlement; the bazaar supplied almost nothing|only one tobacco- shop and one or two depots for grain; the most common iron-work could not be made. The villages around had no inhabitants but the sick, aged, dying, and starving, or idiots. We were told not to walk out alone, as a man had been killed the previous month; the country had been made dangerous, and the people were getting exterminated. But when one of our men cut through his hut and ran away one night, having been suspected of theft, Moossah said with confidence, " The Wezees will not harm him, neither will they give him shelter; he'll be found;" and so he was, rifle and bayonet untouched. All the natives were Hywans|that is, unable to count, write, or tell their own ages. Some practised medicine, giving one of our men, who suffered from weakness in the limbs after fever, a black ointment made of roots. The black art of the Damars and the chipping of the Oovamba's teeth are practised here, as noticed in An- dersson's Travels. During the illness of the late chief, witchcraft was suspected to be the cause. A fowl was placed in the hands of the suspected, dissected by a seer, and verdict given accordingly. Similar fancies, differing only a little in detail, long prevailed in the Highlands of Scotland, a very common form being to bury a black fowl in the exact spot where a person had been first seized with illness. Moossah had never heard of fowls being thrown up in the air to discoverMoossah's Account Of Karague And Uganda. 55

the sorcerer; and but one woman was killed to be placed in the grave with the old king.

Our exploration of the northern kingdoms enabled us to ascertain how far the mass of information gleaned from our good friend Moossah was correct . I can honestly say that, though he had never visited Uganda, his hearsay, on the whole, was a marvel of accuracy:|"The Egyptian river flowed from the Lake Nyanza. Copper and gold are found in Uganda. [We discovered neither, however.] The king alone wears clothes, killing all others who do so. He keeps slaves, and has 3000 women. The people have 100 each, and the youngest fellow 10 to 20, whom they steal or kidnap in war. The Karague people live entirely on milk diet, yet they are men fit for war. M'tezia, the king of Uganda, is a ' boorra admi,' bad man; but being great friends with Rumanika (of Karague), he will send you from 300 to 400 men to escort you. Smallpox is rife in Uganda yearly. The king has Zanzibar guns. At Uganda and Karague the sultans do not, as in other countries, claim one tusk of the killed elephant. Karague people carry about grog in calabashes; one sort being an intoxicating, fiery liquor, the other mild and good. Rhinoceros (white) are numerous. The king of Uganda makes people kneel in front of him, commanding them not to expose their skin or feet before his 400 or 500 women. The reed-grass huts of Karague and Uganda are so high that strong fires may be burned in them. Musicians of every sort there; king has five clocks sent him

At Kazeh I understood that Moossah had never travelled farther than Karague; but I observe that Speke, in his Journal, states that Hoossah (or " Musa," *as* he writes the name) had reached Uganda.

56 DEPARTURE FROM KAZEH.

from Kazeh. At Karague they have three crops yearly of murwa and sorghum. King of Uganda has a menagerie of 200 wild buffaloes; will give as many cheetah (leopard) skins as you like. The Wa- humah of Karague have the most enormous arms, bodies, and legs; cannot walk; always rest on their elbows and knees; hands and feet very small; good noses and fair skins. Karague sultan cannot write, but sends a string of bark-cloth with knots upon it corresponding with the number of elephant-tusks sent." All this exciting information made us eager for a move, but Moossah kept delaying. However, by the middle of March we had finished maps from observa-. tions, made collections, boiled thermometers, inspected newly-purchased presents for the kings ahead, sketched, written reports and letters to wait any chance opportunity for the coast, and recovered from sickness. The rivers would soon be fordable, and a fourth of our porters had arrived; the remainder dreaded coming to us, as war was waging. We pitched camp on the 15th, and marched north without Moossah on the 16th March 1861, leaving the bulk of our kit behind, in charge of Bombay. In return for Moossah's hospitality, Speke gave him five hundred dollars and a beautifully chased gold watch made to order by M'Cabe. We experienced one great privation here, never receiving letters from home; but, odd enough, those despatched by us reached their destination.

5

SECTION 5

CHAPTER V.

JOURNEY TO UKUNI|DIFFICULTIES AT STARTING|PICTURESQUE COUN-
TRY|ATTACKS OF FEVER|TREES AND FRUIT|MODE OF MAKING BARK-
CLOTH|NATURAL HISTORY|NATIVE CLUBHOUSE|DANCES AND GAMES|DESCRIPT
OF A SULTAN| WOMEN OF THE COUNTRY|SLAVES IN IRONS|RELEASE OF
A SLAVE|NATIVE COOKERY|THE NEGRO ON PARADE.

However great was our desire to push on with the journey, we could not impress
the Africans with this feeling. Porters would be ordered, and two days afterwards
you found no one had gone for them. A general panic had seized the natives that the
plundering Wa- tuta race were on the wing. The villages to the north were busy making
defences, or a report had reached them that the Arabs had killed two of their clan;
how, therefore, could they take service with *us,* who might do the same ? Everything
seemed to be against us; they would accept no bribe. None of the slaves of the Arabs
would take service, though offered it, first by Baraka, and then by Speke in person,
who walked 80 miles to induce them to accompany us. Ultimately we moved off by
detachments, and accomplished 90 miles, with 110 men's loads, in 75 days.

58 ROUTE TO MINEENGA.

To describe this country and its inhabitants, I devote the present chapter.

The whole route was fine; never once did we lose sight of trees, wooded hills, or valleys, while water was everywhere abundant. The forest was what might be called " Donkey or Zebra forest"lbare-poled trees and no underwood. The hills, now close, now distant, were richly clothed and exceedingly graceful, reminding me of the Trosachs. Grey rocks looked out in fantastic shapes from amongst the trees. Huge blocks lay one over the other, or abruptly ended a range of hill. The valleys had been cleared by the axe, the wild grasses were most luxuriant, and palisaded villages were often met with. We had not to leave the path in order to pluck the Indian corn. Our way led from one valley to another, or threaded the green forest, which rang with the songs of our followers. Generally the road was of fine sand, which, when lately washed by the rains, was loose and yellow. Once it crossed a quicksand, the only one I recollect seeing in Africalvery shaky and waterylalong which a patch of rice grew. Two streams running west were forded; the Gombe, twenty yards across, there only 4 feet deepland with no current, merely a gentle flow of mud-coloured water; its banks well wooded and shelving : our men shouldered us across, but there were some rickety canoes made of bark lying on the left bank. The other we crossed at night in two channels running also west, but said to be dry one half of the year, although now it was breast-deep, with a current that nearly bore me down in my weak state. Attacks of fever came on about every tenth day, lasting eight and ten hours, with from two to five days of

CAPE RIFLEMEN OBLIGED TO RETURN. 59

nausea and fevered brain. Speke, who had been so long in Africa, was not subject to them, but our men were constantly laid up. One died, and the poor Cape riflemen were such martyrs to fevers and sore eyes, that they confessed they could not stand the hardships of the journey, and were sent back to Kazeh, saying they were sorry they had come so far. We were told that smallpox was the most fatal disease in this part of the country, but we saw no cases. The general elevation of the country is 3400 feet, rising gently up to the low ranges of hills everywhere around. It is more open than Unyanyembe. Mists rarely lie, except on the hill-tops after rain. The greatest fall measured was three-fourths of an inch in half an hour, after a storm, which burst overhead with fearful concussions of thunder at 3 P.m. of the 13th April. This may be described as the grand *finale* to the rainy season. Every morning the dews lay heavily, and a S.E. wind blew, but the coolest breeze was when from S. by W. The daily temperature inside a hut was 78 to 80 at 1 P.m. During the day the sky was generally clear, with a fierce sun; but the air in the mornings and evenings was deliciously cool, a fire at night being cheery and comfortable. No dust-storms troubled us, otherwise the open huts would have been uninhabitable. Drinking water was always sweet and refreshing. At Mineenga a copious spring gushed out of the shell of a tree lying level with the earth in the centre of a rice-field. This was the well of the village; from its position it was considered a phenomenon, and was looked on with veneration, as it afforded cool water the whole year roundla rare blessing.

60 FLORA OF MINEENGA.

The flora was new and interesting; but we were amazed at not seeing better crops, as grasses with pendent panicles grew luxuriantly ten feet high. The surface-soil, however, was very lightlmerely the washings of the hill-sides brought down in a stream of red clay grit. In this tract of country we came upon groups of palms, not met with since we left the coast: they were converted into many uses|fences, thatching, firewood, and uprights for building, &c. Toddy also was occasionally extracted. The fruit hung down in rich, large, tempting clusters, at the mercy of any hungry traveller. We observed several of these palms, with their leaf-stalks still remaining on the tree, to be the support and life of a species of ficus, growing like a parasite, luxuriantly healthy, its roots not near the ground, but forming a complete network round the stem of the palm. Tamarind-trees, so umbrageous and beautiful in outline, were numerous. There was also the rumex, from ten to twelve feet high ; and the tree, a ficus, whose bark affords the Waganda their clothing, was here seen for the first time. The bark is taken off in stripes, according to the size they can get it, then damped and beaten by heavy wooden hammers till pliant, and afterwards sewn into a sheet the colour of chamois-leather, but much thicker; the outer bark is thrown away. Near the villages a few scrubby bushes of cotton were grown upon mounds made by white ants. Looms of the rudest construction converted the produce of these into a hard, very stout, heavy cloth, about four or five feet in size, with one- fourth of it a black border, and worn by women only. Sessamum grew in ridges with the sorghum; its oil, and that extracted from the ground-nut, being used

HARVEST SCENE. 61

by the natives for smearing themselves from head to foot, giving their skins a handsome colour, like the gloss on polished marble. To vary the colour, some red clay is added. The sorghum is sometimes affected with a black blight, but the natives do not think this any deterioration; all goes into the mill. They live upon Indian corn, ulezee, and sorghum, made into flour by rubbing the grains between stones as a house- painter pounds colours. Their vegetables are sweet potato, and the leaves, flowers, anjl fruits of pumpkins; and they brought us daily ground-nuts, tobacco, and fowls for sale. On the 3d of April the rice-harvest was being gathered in; but we perceived no traces of irrigation as in Egypt. Abundant rains gave an ample crop. The reapers consisted of negro women and girls, who sang pleasantly, though the scene was marred by the sight of a gang of men-slaves, heavily ironed together by their necks, with some superintendents, gleaning. Those who had small knives cut the stalk four or five inches below the grain, and held it in their left hand till the hand was full, when it was placed in a huge tub of bark lying in the field. In this way a three-feet-high stubble was left standing, to be trodden down by cattle. The thrashing of the rice was novel. A quantity of ears was placed upon a cow's hide, slaves in irons were made to work it with their toes and feet, and winnow it in the wind; and after being thoroughly sun-dried upon a clear space of cow-dunged ground, it was fit for the process of shelling in the large pestle and mortar. If a considerable amount was to be thrashed, a bludgeon answered the purpose of the negroes' feet. The stubble would afterwards be turned over with powerful long-handled hoes,

62 PRICE OF PROVISIONS.

beds of the soil made, and the suckers or offshoots of the sweet potato planted there by bands of twenty or thirty villagers, shouting and singing the whole time. If our Seedees had to clean rice in the wooden mortar, a dozen hands would set about the work of two. It could not be done without those who worked beating time with the pestle to their song, the lookers-on clapping hands and stamping with their feet. The work and song never ceased till the rice was pounded almost into dustIsuch joyous, reckless creatures are these simple Africans! Yams are grown upon mounds of earth placed all over a field, the branches of the plant trained up a stick, or more commonly allowed to crawl over the ground. They do not attain a great growth. Grain is housed under the eaves of stack-shaped huts, or a clustered mass of Indian corn may be seen suspended from the bough of a tree, as exhibited in the illustration of "Unyamuezi harvest," in Captain Speke's Journal.

Provisions were all remarkably cheap upon this route. A fat cow was purchased for four fathoms of calico; another full-sized cow, and four small goats, were got for eight fathoms; a single sheep was dear at two fathoms; but three small goats were a bargain at the same price; a donkey was offered for fourteen, but he would have been dear at half the amount. For a fowl, one native demanded a charge of gunpowder, and would not sell it for anything else; another native led in a goat to camp, saying if we repaired his old flint-musket we should have the animal; he refused to bargain for anything else. For two quarts of impure honey, ten strings of common beads and a fathom of calico were asked, but not given. Milk was not

CATTLE AND WILD ANIMALS. 63

always to be had, the people being afraid to keep herds of cattle, as they would attract the plundering propensities of the wandering Watuta race. Milk sometimes cost three strings of beads per pint; twelve measures of rice, one fathom of calico; sweet potatoes were one-tenth of the price they brought at Zanzibar; a basinful of ground-nuts or a load of wood cost but one string of ordinary beads. In short, our men lived luxuriously on their daily allowance of one string of beads per man. The people preferred keeping a few milk-cows, being more productive than oxen, which were rarely met with, except one or two fattened up to a large size on purpose to be killed on the visit of a neighbouring sultan, or to celebrate some success in war. After the cattle have been brought in at night, a quantity of rubbish is allowed to smoke and smoulder in the centre of their fold. It was amusing to watch how each animal took up its nightly position, never altering it, and thoroughly enjoying the smoke, which prevented it from being annoyed by insects. The sheep were very stupid-looking animals, small, and wanting in rotundity. Their colour was either white and black, black with white, or a bay brown; no wool, but crisp hair; their tails tapered off from a broad fatty base. The head was the only handsome part; and two pieces of skin hung from the throat, as is seen in the long-eared breed of goats in India.

Of wild animals we shot none on this route, though, away from the cultivations, the spoors of buffalo and antelope were seen. A herd of ten elephants had passed through the district, eating up the sorghum crop, but no one went after them. The skin of a leopard was brought us for sale. Its spots were jet black

64 BIRDS.

upon yellow ground, and shone almost like a mirror. At this season of harvest the crops were favourable for concealing lions; and after a native had been killed by one, we were recommended not to go out after sunset . When travelling at night, the natives move quickly in bodies, blowing cow-horn trumpets, which sound wild in the stillness. While we were at Mineenga three men were chased by a pair of lions, and just as the last man reached a hut, he was picked off by a horrible man-eater. I went to see the spot. There were the tracks of the poor victim when knocked down and dragged, and where his blood was first spilt; farther on, blood lay in quantities, as the body had been trailed along; but of the body itself only a small bit of bone was left. The incident had happened just after sunset, said to be the most dangerous time.

Here Speke shot and brought in a load of four large black geese, weighing 9 lb. each, having curious horny spurs to their shoulders, and taking to trees on being wounded. Farther south I had seen the same kind flapping their wings and pluming themselves between showers on rocks in the bed of a stream, and I took them for cormorants. Their wings were white outside and black under. The natives came in numbers to see these birds, such a load of them never having been seen before. The wing-feathers were converted into head-dresses, but the meat was rej ected. Flocks of wild pigeon and varieties of small hawks were constantly seen about the groves of palms. We shot numbers of the former, but they were not good eating, though plump to look at: a large red wattle surrounded the eyes; their plumage was extremely pretty; wings and rumps blue, with one white bar across their black tails :

UNYAMUEZI VILLAGES. 65

shoulders and elbows chocolate-coloured; feathers of the crop forked; and legs grey. The crested crane is a slaty black or blue colour, the size of a heron, with shorter hackles. His head is very handsome, the contrasts of colour being beautiful. He has a black bill, a top of rich black feathers, behind it a straw-coloured bunch of four-inch-long fibres, having a few black featherlets near their roots; a chalky-white bare skin on the cheeks, and a hanging scarlet wattle underneath, with quantities of beautiful blue down on the rump; his call at night when roosting is harsh and grating. Fish weighing three and four pounds were occasionally caught by our men in pools, but the natives would not eat them, as they had not come out of the sea. However, with the addition of eggs, we thought these mud-fish *(Malcambara)* as good as any we had ever tasted.

The villages of the country are fortified by high palisades; many of them are of immense strength, having a broad dry ditch, a quickset hedge of euphorbia, a covered-way, and then a palisading. Sometimes a very good attempt at a bastion of mud is made, to give a flanking fire of arrows. Outside, opposite the only entry of one village, an old hoe was stuck on a mound, and protected by an awning of bark cloth: we were told this was to repel the evil eye. To give a. general idea of these villages, I may mention that, on entering at the low doorway, you see before you an avenue of

palisades; to the right and left sets of houses are similarly railed off. Until lodging had been obtained inside the village, we rested with our kit at the " iwansa " or club-house. It was a long room, 12 by 18 feet, with one door, a low flat roof, well blackened
    66 UNYAMUEZI DANCE.
with smoke, and no chimney. Along its length there ran a high inclined bench, on which cow-skins were spread for men to take their siesta. Some huge drums were hung in one corner, and logs smouldered on the ground. The young men of the village gathered at the club-house to get the news. They smoked, pulled out each other's eyelashes and eyebrows, filed their teeth, and cut their marks of caste on the face or temples. Dances would take place in the space in front of it, either by day or night. The regular Wezee dance is as follows:lA strip of bark or cow-skin is laid on the ground, and a line of men, the tallest in the centre, stand on it; the drums commence, a howling song joins in, and with hands on their haunches and heads bent down, they thump in unison with their feet. Female spectators look on silently from behind, and men in front join in the chorus. A shout of laughter, or burst of admiration, winds up each dance, and never was there a more truly primitive scene of joyous riot. Our Seedees had a much better performance, which they went through to the music of their voices, hands, and feet. Two stood in the centre of a ring, kicking high at one another like Frenchmen, clapping hands and dodging about most ingeniously, while the mob sang a lively song, clapped hands and stamped, all keeping perfect time, and enjoying it with the most thorough good-humour. They also had a favourite teetotum game. Two sides were formed facing each other, and all sitting on the ground. Each had before him a stump of Indian corn and a teetotum of gourd in his hand. The object was to knock over with the spinning-totum the adversaries' stump, and the efforts on each occasion caused immense merriment.
    EAELY MORNING SOUNDS. 67
In a Wezee village there are few sounds to disturb one's night rest: the traveller's horn, and the reply to it from a neighbouring village, an accidental alarm, the chirping of crickets, and the cry from a sick child, however, occasionally broke upon the stillness of our nights. Waking early, the first sounds we heard were the crowing of cocks, the impatient lowing of cows, the bleating of calves, and the chirping of sparrows and a few other unmusical birds. The pestle and mortar shelling corn would soon after be heard, or the cooing of wild pigeons in the grove of palms. The huts were shaped like corn-stacks, supported by bare poles, 15 feet high, and 15 to 18 feet in diameter; sometimes their grass roofs would be protected from sparks by "michans," or frames of Indian-corn stalks; there were no carpets; all of them were unswept, and dark as the hold of a ship. A few earthen jars, made like the Indian "gurrah," for boiling vegetables or their stirabout, tattered skins, an old bow and arrow, some cups of grass, some gourds, perhaps a stool, constituted the whole of the furniture. Grain was housed in bandboxes of bark, and goats or calves had free access over the house. The goat-skins worn by the Usagara natives differed from their neighbours in Unyanyembe, being neatly dressed, so as to leave an edging of fur upon them. The cotton-cloth of the country, or a piece of soiled calico, generally covered the loins of the women. We saw here a man wearing the skin of a new antelope, the Nzoe, afterwards discovered in the Karague Lake.

A description of one of the sultans will suffice to give a general impression of the appearance, manners, customs, &c., of the three Wezee clans we had passed

68 UNYAMUEZI SULTAN.

through, keeping in mind that this dignitary was the finest specimen we had seen, and was supposed to be enlightened, though he did not know his own age, could neither read, write, nor count beyond ten, and had no names for any day of the week, for any month, or for any year ! After we had been about a month in his district, Sultan Ugaleel*i. e.,* Stiraboutlarrived at Mineenga on the 21st of April, and was saluted by file-firing from our volunteers, and shrill cries from the women. He visited us in our verandah the day following. He looks about twenty-two years of age; has three children and thirty wives; is six feet high, stout, with a stupid, heavy expression. His bare head is in tassels, black hanks of fibre being mixed in with his hair. His body is loosely wrapped round with a blue and yellow cotton cloth; his loins are covered with a dirty oily bit of calico, and his feet are large and naked. A monster ivory ring is on his left wrist, while the right one bears a copper ring of rope pattern; several hundreds of wire rings are massed round his ankles. He was asked to be seated on one of our iron stools, but looked at first frightened, and did not open his mouth. An old man spoke for him, and a crowd of thirty followers squatted behind him. Speke, to amuse him, produced his six-barrelled revolver, but he merely eyed it intently. The books of birds and animals, on being shown to him upside down by Sirboko, the head man of the village, drew from him a sickly smile, and he was pleased to imply that he preferred the animals to the birds. He received some snuff in the palm of his hand, took a good pinch, and gave the rest to his spokesman. He was led to look at my musquito-curtained bed, and on moving away

UNYAMUEZI WOMEN. 69

was invited to dine with us. We sent him a message at seven o'clock that the feast was prepared, but a reply came that he was " full," and could not be tempted even with a glass of rum. The following day he came to wish us good-bye, and left without any exchange of presents, being thus very different from the grasping race of Ugogo.

The arms of the people consisted of spears, bows and arrows, and leather shields shaped like the figure 8. Boys in the villages were fond of practising war, by pelting each other with Indian-corn stumps, using leather shields of defence.

We had daily visits from the women of the country, who came in parties. They were copper-coloured and flat-featured, and wore round their necks a profusion of pendent bead necklaces of the colour of the mountain-ash berry; their ankles were concealed with masses of wire rings. For hours they sat silently before us, smoking, nursing, and shampooing the limbs and necks of their infants; some wore the heavy cloth of the country, others had soiled robes of calico. Young girls, many of them with pleasing faces and plump round figures, wore merely a diminutive cloth about their loins, and infants had a fringe of beads. These women were rarely accompanied by men, but on Speke having taken a woman's likeness, the husband requested him to write his (the husband's) name on the picture, so that the people of England might know whose wife she was ! We saw some decidedly handsome N'yambo girls on this route: their men attend upon cattle exclusively, while they stay at home doing household work, cooking, coquetting, and showing *oft* their beautiful feet and ankles. Two, in

70 WAHA WOMEN.

the bloom of youth, sat by us with their arms most affectionately twined round each other's neck, till asked to sit apart that they might be sketched. The arms were at once dropped, exposing their beautiful necks and busts, quite models for a " Greek Slave." Their woolly hair was combed out and raised up from the forehead and over their ears by a broad band from the skin of a milk-white cow; this contrasted strikingly with their transparent light copper skins.

The Waha women are somewhat similar, having tall, erect, graceful figures even without crinoline, and with intelligent features. They are looked upon as an inferior tribe to the Watusi (described at Kazeh), though wearing the hair bound up, and having naked arms, &c., similar to them; but their cow-skin coverings from the waist to the ankle are different, being of a yellow-ochre colour. We put up one day at the settlement of a trader, Sungoro-bin-Tabeeb, of whom we had heard a good deal, as he travelled always in a double-poled tent, and kept sixty wives, who lived like goats inside his tent. We saw five of his women; one was a Hubshee, or Abyssinian, whose appearance disappointed us. Her mouth was large, and, though fair for a negress, and with distinctly bridged nose, she was a poor specimen of her race. Another was of my favourite caste, always distinguishable by their intelligence and easy, polite manner| a Watusi, a beautiful tall girl, with large dark eyes, the smallest mouth and nose, thin lips, small hands, &c. Speke said she much resembled the Somal; her noble race never will become slaves, preferring death to slavery, and they refuse to touch fowls or goats. It was to be regretted that she had not a better

SIRBOKO OF MINEENGA. 71

husband, for Sungoro had been in jail for robbery, committed by order of his Arab master. His master, however, by way of compensation, left him his ill- gotten wealth.

Two years previous to our arrival in this district, the wandering Watuta, whose women are said to use the bow and arrow, treacherously inviting up their enemy, had come in thousands to plunder cattle from the villages; but after fighting against the sultan for five days and losing three men, they left, not being able to make way against the muskets of a See- dee named Sirboko. We lived for some days with this excellent man, who was most anxious to get back to Zanzibar, but the sultan would not hear of his departure; because, in return for his having protected his country, he had made over to him a considerable tract of land, on which he was expected to reside for life. This was a rare instance of generosity. While living in his clean, comfortable, thatched bungalow, waiting for porters, Sheikh Said communicated to us by letter from Kazch that we had better get on with our journey as fast as we could, for the Arabs there had meditated putting us to death, believing that we were the accomplices of the rebel chief Manua Sera! However, on our friend Moossah taking a solemn Mussulman oath that neither he nor we were thus guilty, the affair was supposed to have blown over, but they would not allow Moossah to join us. Since poor Snay's death Mohinna was the chief of the Arabs, and had taken offence at us, probably because he was requested not to beat so brutally his women-slaves, who one day came weeping and wailing to us at Kazeh for protection. The result of our good-natured

72 SLAVES IN CHAINS.

advice was that, though he promised he should not again offend, the poor women got another and more severe beating, and were put in the stocks to prevent their coming near us to complain. The class of Arabs we met were certainly a most degraded set, and instead of improving the country had brought ruin upon it by their imperiousness and cruelty. All traded in slaves, whom, for security's sake, they were often obliged to treat harshly. At Mineenga, we met several parties or gangs of slaves in chains, and my thoughts reverted to the happy village-life in our own country, a pleasing contrast to such painful and revolting scenes.

Clad each in a single goat-skin, the slaves kept themselves warm at night lying near a fire. Never is the chain unfastened day or night. Should one of the number require to move, the whole must accompany him. All ate together boiled sweet potato, or a spinage made from the leaves of the pumpkin plant, and were kept in poor condition to prevent their becoming troublesome. One day a woman-slave, on seeing our cook casting away the head of a fowl he had just killed, picked it up, and gave it to a poor convalescent slave, who grasped it with the eagerness of a dog. Any meat or bones left over from our dinner were always given them. A small lad, whose ears had been cut off" (probably a Uganda boy), watched or accompanied the slaves, and treated them, I thought, with unfeeling coarseness. A sick slave having recovered, it was the boy's duty to chain him to his gang again, and it was grievous to see the rough, careless way he used the poor emaciated creature. Beyond bringing in firewood for themselves

RELEASE OF A SLAVE. 73

and cleaning corn, they were not much worked. The sole object of the owner was to keep them alive, and prevent their running away till sold at the coast. Ten men and five women had lately deserted, chains and all, from Sirboko, so that he did not approve of taking off their irons ; " the birds would soon fly if he did." They looked generally sullen and full of despair; but might be seen dancing, and even riotous at times, till a word from the earless imp of a boy restored order. One amongst them was of a cannibal race to the N.W. of the Tanganyika. In appearance he did not differ from the rest, but he was laughed at for his cannibal propensities, which were not entertained by them. Another who had been five years in chains was heard by Speke to say that " life was a burden to him ; he could stand it no longer." We had observed him to be a good fellow, the leader and conductor of his gang, and we released him from bondage; his chains were struck off with a hammer while he lay calmly with his head on a block. Once on his feet, a freed man, he did not seem to believe the fact; but when attired in a clean sheet of calico by Baraka, he strutted about, the pet of our Seedees, and came to make us his best bow. His life had been hazardous, as proved by the spear-wounds in his body; he had been captured by the Watuta, who cut off several of his toes, and also some of his toe-nails. This man never deserted us the whole journey. It was his good fortune to reach Cairo, with the character of a faithful servant; and if any of his companions attempted to assault his benefactor Baraka, he would instantly fly to defend him.

The curiosity of the people was sometimes trying to our tempers; but it was excusable, as they had never

74 THIEVES.

seen white men before. There was not the slightest privacy even inside our tent; they were certain to peer in. Sitting in the open air under a tree was tried, and succeeded best, for they saw you till they became tired of looking, or at your laughing at or mimicking them. Every one, except an old woman, was easy to manage. She would pester you with questions you didn't understand, didn't mind being laughed at, and would not leave till led away by some villager who took compassion on us. Another woman was most anxious to see my feet. " What had I under my shoes and socks? She had never seen such coverings." I told her she could not be gratified till the evening, when I would take them off. The men were generally fawning, very inquisitive, and fond of putting their arms round Bombay's neck to try and get him to give them some present. Little satisfied them ; and though we had all our kit without lock or key, we never suffered loss by theft in a Wezee village. At Sirboko's, thieves came one night, were caught, beaten, and dismissed. Exactly one month afterwards they again came, carrying away a tin case with clothes and writing materials, seven ivories of Sirboko's, &c. &c. Our Seedees were as active as policemen, flying about the whole night with torches, looking for the stolen goods, and at break of day they found the tin case, minus some things, including four tusks. To recover the rest a quack doctor or Mganga was sent for, an elderly-looking man, and he found the whole, except an ivory and a flannel shirt, in a couple of days. The thieves, in fear, had placed the articles at the doorway of the village. Our men were most excitable creatures. If a cow- attempted to break out of the village by jumping fences

SEEDEES AS SERVANTS. 75

and defied capture, they never thought of calming her, but all would arm with guns, spears, swords, and sticks, and chase her down till stupefied with fear. If they had been behaving badly, it did not prevent them from asking to have a cow given them ; and on being refused, they never sulked, but took it out of you some other way by studying their own wishes, comforts, and wants in marching, halting, eating, drinking, or stealing whatever they pleased, and at night giving us the benefit of their laughter, shouting, and riots or howling, in imitation of a Wezee who has smoked bhang. Our cooks (Seedee boys) were most difficult to teach, though they had learned a little from the Cape men, who had always done this duty. The only idea these black roughs had of cooking for themselves was to stick a wooden skewer into a piece of meat and scorch it over the ashes, or make stirabout. No great *cuisine* could therefore be expected. Being anxious on one occasion to get some soup after a fever, and knowing the larder to contain only a wild duck, I asked Eehan, " Could you get me some soup for breakfast ? I cannot eat meat." " Yes." " What!" said I, " out of a duck ?" " 0 yes." Thinking him a clever fellow, I gladly consented; but bis soup was only a thin watery stew, placed before me with the most perfect complaisance. Again, at 7 P.m., he came up asking would I like some dinner? He had not thought of preparing even a boiled potato. Such were the men we had as cooks for our entire journey. On the march a party of them tried, by holding out for three days in not accepting their rations, to extort double allowances, on account of the price of provisions; but finding it of no use, they quietly submitted. Again, they told us our donkeys

76 SEEDEES AS SOLDIERS.

would not live long if they were made to carry beef; and this I believe was only a device to get the meat themselves.

When detained for want of porters at Mineenga, we taught our men the sword exercise for an hour every afternoon. They were apt at learning, did remarkably well, and enjoyed it very much, though kept strictly to it for the time they were out. Not understanding discipline, if a shower of rain fell, they thought themselves at liberty to run off our parade-ground; and when I brought a cane in my hand, they could not resist a titter, thinking I had brought it to enforce orders, and not merely to show the sword positions. On the coast we had taught them the platoon exercise and target practice, but they never would take care of their ammunition, ramrods, or stoppersialways firing them away. On the arrival of a detachment, salutes of welcome must be fired, and always, on new moon being visible, each one would try to be the first to fire his gun. But with six months' drill and strict discipline, we saw that a negro could be made into a good light-infantry soldier; and if he only becomes attached to his officer, there is no more devoted follower in the world.

On arrival outside a Wezee village, generally a set of armed men would meet us, bounding on the grass, running in circles, making feints at our caravan, either in delight, or in attempts to frighten us. A shot in the air would cool their courage, though our porters on hearing it would sometimes drop their loads and fly in fear, but speedily returning when reassured. Men were in abundance in the country, and if a solitary one ran away, he could always be replaced. For

FOREST GUIDES. 77

instance, a father saw his son carrying a load in our caravan; he led him angrily away, and we soon got another. But to collect one or two hundred we found a most difficult task: they are as fickle as the wind. A wave of a flag will attract them, while one misplaced expression will send them away discontented. They higgle pertinaciously about their hire; and after they have been induced to accept double wages, they suddenly change their minds, think you've got the best of it, and ask for more, or more commonly disappear.

One of the most pleasing sensations in going through an immense forest is suddenly to come upon the traces of man. The Wezee experience this, for, in their forest south of Kazeh, they erect triumphal arches with poles, over or by the side of the path. These they ornament with antelope-skulls, having the horns, or with elephant-dung, bones, bows, or broken gourds. It cheers the traveller, and gives fresh vigour to his wearied limbs, for he knows that camp and water are never far distant, and that the trumpet of the caravan leader must soon sound the welcome "halt." In travelling through these forests, the Unyamuezi rarely loses his way, as he is accustomed to range in woods, and to mark his route either by breaking boughs or noting the position of the sun.

During my fifty-five dajTs' detention at Mineenga, Speke had been away for sixteen days at Kazeh trying to procure porters by means of the Arabs. The third day after his return, the 18th of May 1861, I inarched northward with a detachment of forty loads, making for Ukuni. He picked me up on the 21st, and I again went on alone, and reached it on the

78 BLACKSMITH AT WORK.

27th. The Journal of the last two days may perhaps possess some interest to the reader, as it introduces him to Ukulima, the sultan, in whose place I was detained one hundred and nine days. It is as follows:| *"26th May.*|Speke keeps the larder well filled. Last night, three guinea-fowl and a large tree-goose. I went early amongst the Watusi; handsome people, beautiful rounded small heads, prominent large eyes, thin noses, rather compressed upper jaws; all so clean and trim; no resemblance to the dirty Wezee, who are coarse and mannerless in comparison. They make their own baskets of osier-like twigs, with a sharpened spear, and work with their feet very neatly. They got a cow down by pulling its hind-legs to a post, and then carefully washed its eye, which had been injured. The blacksmith was working amongst them making wire anklets from long rods of iron; bellows very small, of wood, with cane handles, which a man worked up and down. The hammer was a massive mason's chisel: they worked squatting. A whole family were very curious to hear the tick of my watch. The fighting Watuta had one open-field combat with the Watusi, and obtained a victory over them; both are afraid of each other. I see that the slaves of the Wezees are very well dressed, and treated with great kindness, never doing but what they choose: quite different from slaves at Zanzibar, where, as Bombay tells me, they would be made to work all day, and, by some, be made to steal all night . The orthodox custom at Zanzibar is five days' labour for master, and two days' for the slave himself. Rehan (the new cook) came to say ' there was no grease to roast with.' ' What are you to roast ?' He pointed

MARCH TO UKUNI. 79

to his breast. 'You ought not to roast a brisket.' He brought a tongue, hump, and double brisket, smelling, all of which had been boiled yesterday, and now he wanted to roast the brisket already done.

'"27ih.|Bombay and I march with 38 porters to make a start of it to Nunda, in Ukuni, and to see Sultan Ukulima. Distance was eight miles through a very pretty country, with rocks jutting out fantastically, and lying now and then one on another; cultivation all the way. Sighted the village when within a mile of it; quantities of spring water coming down from a rocky height to our right. After we had entered the first milk-bush enclosure, there were several cleanly-swept windings. Village nearly empty. A heavy old man sitting on a stool with half-a-dozen men round him, induced me to say ' Yambo;' he returned it, and I went looking for a house. Came to the palace, a very high round hut, smelling strongly of goats and cattle. I asked permission to live here, and the old man, who proved to be the sultan, said, 'Doogoh yango'|'Come along, my brother.' Sweeping out the verandah of goat-dung, my bed was soon made. The sultana, a fat, fair, gentle old lady, welcomed me with both hands as if I had been her son. She was so surprised at the bedding as she sat upon it, and everything she saw, saying ' Eeh, eeh !' and nodding her head: indeed, all were surprised. Bombay got some pombe"; the drunken old sultan himself carried a basket-cup of it. He drank first (through a straw), and then I had some, and very good it was. Then he drank again, and I drank again, laughing heartily. People in hundreds came. I went to sleep, though

80 PEOPLE OF UKUNI.

drums beat all day in honour of the arrival. Their politeness was remarkable; they retired as I sat down at meals. Milk very dear, and got with great difficulty. Lads excited with drums, jumping in the air, and flying about. Did not see old man for the rest of the day; he was in a state of pombe"! "

6

SECTION 6

CHAPTER VI.

VILLAGE LIFE AT UKUNI, MAT 27 TO SEPTEMBEE 12, 1861|THE COUN-
TRY WELL CULTIVATED AND WOODED|THE SEASONS, WINDS, ETC.|BLIND
MUSICIANS | FOOD OF THE NATIVES | WOMEN AT HARVEST|COINAGE
AND MANUFACTURES | FLORA OF UKUNI|DOMESTIC AND WILD AN-
IMALS|SINGULAR CEREMONY WITH A DEAD LION|ATTACK OF ANTS|
SULTAN AND SULTANA OF UKUNI|AFRICAN WOMEN ARE GOOD MOTH-
ERS|DRUM MUSIC|SUPERSTITIONS|SYSTEM OF BROTHERHOOD.

To commence with the country around, I may state that its general elevation above
sea-level is 3260 feet. All the lands run southwards, and are cleared for cultivation,
while the low hills are well wooded, their ridges capped with huge masses of rounded
rock, some single blocks forty and fifty feet in height, balanced on each other, or
forming gorges and passes between one valley and another. The village of the smaller
sultan of Roongwa, seven miles to the N.W., has some remarkably pretty landscapes
in its neighbourhood. Upon gently-swelling lands gloomy peaked masses of granite
rise amidst the dense foliage, reminding one of a baronial castle at home, with its
parks and clumps of trees. Sometimes large water-

82 THE SEASONS.

cavities are seen in those boulders; one contained sweet pure water in a basin fifty feet in circumference and six to eight feet deep, which had been worn out by the crumbling of ages.

During the months of June, July, August, and twelve days of September, we had but one or two slight showers of rain (in July), which were preceded by dull cloudy weather every night, that prevented our seeing a comet in the constellation of Ursa Major. The sun rose and set in a haze, which obscured the sky for 40. During the day, unless the regular S.S.E. wind blew very hard, a veil of mist lay about. This wind from the S.E. was very unhealthy, making every one sneeze, and giving hard coughs and colds. It generally began about 8 A.M.; but by the 12th of September it changed to a more easterly direction, and brought with it beautiful clear weather. The June mornings were piercingly cold, and at night the naked boy who looked after the calves might always be seen sleeping with his head pillowed upon them to keep himself warm, and our Seedees would lie out for the night with a sheet-covering, and a blazing fire at their backs. By the end of June the trees had shed their leaves. Nothing but evergreens were interesting in the forest; the grasses had been burnt; the fields lay in fallow baked in the sun, or were of powdered dust, where cattle had trodden: the aspect was decidedly wintry. In August the trees began to bud, and the grasses, where they had been set on fire, were sprouting with fresh leaves. I have alluded to the S.E. wind being unhealthy|not a man of us escaped it. Speke suffered most dangerously from its effects while separated for three months from me. His

DISEASES. 83

heavy cough had been brought on by constant anxiety, and by his walking about the country trying to persuade men to lead, or proceed with us in our journey northwards. My fever came every second day from the 29th of May till the 4th of July, lasting six hours, making me feel weak and tottering. In July I had colds, discharges of mucus from the nose, and a large abscess burst|all of which staved off fever for a time; and I had only one or two attacks, of nine hours each, during the two following months. In the intervals of fever I generally managed to go for a stroll with my gun to shoot a dove or guinea-fowl for the sultan or myself. Of ten Seedees who formed my body-guard, servants, &c., only half were generally fit for duty, or, perhaps, four in ten, at this S.E. wind season. Their complaints were of the chest, cough, fever, abscess, ulcers, and venereal (the *social evil* was evident every evening in the frequented part of the village). Our medicine - chest was at every one's service, but some Seedees applied to an old-lady doctor, who, instead of cure, brought tears and screams from them whilst applying her remedies to ulcers, bandaging them up with cow-dung and leaves to exclude the air. To cure headaches, the men cut their temples and rubbed in a paste of gunpowder. Blood would scarcely appear, but the mark was indelible, and the cure said to be complete.

The diseases observed amongst the inhabitants were swollen legs, resembling elephantiasis, itch in children, scales on the eyes, a few smallpox-marked and blind people, one harelip, and a shrivelled infant without a thumb. One blind man used to visit periodically, and, without even the guide of a dog, knew every turn in

84 BLIND MUSICIANS.

the village; he was welcomed everywhere, as a smile for ever played upon his lips. By moonlight he would stand singing for two hours at a time with a crowd of a hundred people, men and women, the sultan amidst them, all round him, joining in a chorus of almost devotional music. He had the power, by placing his hand to his mouth, of sending the deep, pleasing tones of his voice away to a distance, which gave delight to every one, the women in particular showing approval by a shrill peculiar falsetto noise, which they make by tapping the cheek or shaking the lower lip with the forefinger and thumb. Another blind man, deeply marked with smallpox, gathered the village boys around him and taught the songs of their country, while he beat time with his foot . They have several fine national airs.

Their funeral ceremonies are simple enough. Chiefs, and most of the respectable classes, are buried under the floors of their dwellings, or more commonly in cattle-sheds; while witches and slaves are thrown into the jungle without interment. I observed one of the latter lying, tied with his face to a pole, in long grass, with some rags round the waist; the limbs were trussed up much in the same way as an infant lies asleep.

Though residing in the verandah of the chief house of the M'teme or sultan, or in the most central part of the village, I rarely saw any men at their meals, unless when assembled round pombe". They seemed to take pot-luck at any hour of the day, and at any house where the signs of eating were going on|getting a boiled sweet potato here, a drink of pombe " there, or a snack of beef as a rarity. Women were more regular

THE SULTAN AND SULTANA. 85

in their living. The lady of my house, seated on a wooden stool in the open yard, had always some guests to dine with her, generally women of her own age and some little children, and never by any chance did her husband, the sultan, eat with her on these occasions. The food|some boiled sweet potatoes|would be brought on a wooden tray, and placed on the ground by a servant-maid, who knelt on one knee, or a bowl full of pombe" would be presented in the same way. The sultan had seven wives. Each had her own separate house and establishment, which he visited daily, though at night he always slept in a place not much larger than himself, surrounded by charms and lions' paws. He lived almost entirely upon pombe", drinking it three or four times during the day, commencing as early as seven o'clock, and ending the day, if he was not already stupefied, by having it at supper- time. He was a very hale, healthy-looking old man, apparently about seventy, and most active in his habits. Different houses in his village held daily " receptions " for him, when he presided, and he was the first to taste the bowl of beer. The female population drank separately, and were presided over by the sultana. The liquor took five days of preparation: the grain (sorghum) had to be cleaned, ground, soaked, boiled, generally with cow-dung as firewood, allowed to cool, and was drunk, without filtration, in a fermenting state, out of bowls neatly made of grass by the women. With honey added it was tolerable, but without it the beverage was coarse and heady to a stranger. Our men were constantly tipsy; but the natives who fed upon it had a healthy appearance, and rarely became drunk. Their active early habits conduced to this result,

86 HARVEST AND FOOD.

for all of them were in the fields before sunrise gathering the crop, or were doing varied works inside their enclosures. The women on the 3d June were clipping with a knife the tops of the sorghum, putting them into baskets, and carrying the whole on their heads to the village, where the grain, after being thoroughly sun-dried, was thrashed out by lines of men with long- handed rackets, as seen in the illustration, " Unyamuezi Harvest," of Speke's Journal. They sang and beat the grain to a chorus, winnowed it in the S.E. breeze, divided it into shares, and by the 1st of July all was housed for the year; and porters, had they chosen, might have gone with us to Karague, but they preferred tasting the new year's grain. After the harvest, the poorer people were allowed to glean the potato, ground-nut, and grain fields, glad to have some refuse, as, should the previous season have been a poor one, they must have lived upon dried potato, or what wild herbs they could pick up. Our Seedees, all of whom except ten were away with Speke, could not afford to purchase a cow or goat, and they felt the want of meat considerably, but not to the extent that a European does. My gun almost daily provided a guinea-fowl or pigeon, and the Seedees lived upon stirabout or fish; while, clubbing their daily rations, they could afford to purchase a fowl, or by doing some office for the natives, such as sewing, &c., they always secured friends. The coin we at first used was rose-coloured beads, called " goolabee." These were great favourites ; and when exhausted, the price of everything rose to double|in fact, the new coinage of sea-green beads, or " magee bahr," was refused point-blank; they wouldn't circulate. Pure whites, " Kanyera," were tried; they also failed.

COINAGE AND MANUFACTURES. 87

Indian reds, or " Kudunduguru," were utterly refused, as only taken in uncivilised northern countries! " Kutu'mnazee," cocoa-nut leaves, at last passed muster, and milk was procured for our tea. It was a regular strike in the market. All this rubbish of beads was merely the equivalent to coppers. Silver was represented by webs of unbleached calico, 30 to 32 yards long, 1 yard wide, and weighing 10 lb., stamped in blue, " Massachusetts Sheeting." The man who got this stamped portion|" Keerole," or looking- glass, as they called it|was thought a considerable swell, and took care to show it across his loins. Sovereign coinage consisted of coils of brass and copper wire, thicker than that used for telegraphic purposes, and converted into bracelets by the natives. The blacksmith is never allowed to work inside the village, perhaps because he has ample space outside, and it is considered safer|not that his caste prohibits it.

The nodules of ore are generally smelted in the forests, and brought in a lump to the smith, who, ,by means of stone anvils and stones as sledge-hammers, converts it into a long rod; and finally, by a hand-vice, and grease from a small pot he carries, it is tied between two posts and drawn till it becomes a thread. It is now fit, after being once heated, for being twisted neatly with the finger and thumb round a few hairs from the tail of a cow, or the thicker hair of a giraffe. In this state it is worn in rings ornamenting the ankles of men and women, fifteen of them costing one string of beads, value a halfpenny, and fifteen copper or brass ones being double price. Iron hoes, adzes, grass-hooks, small knives, pincers, &c., are all made up by the

88 ABRUS SEEDS.

natives in the above rude way; and this is the extent of their knowledge in ironwork.

The women have no needlework. The men, if they make a web in the loom, sew it all themselves; but the former are very neat-handed at working in straw and matting. They grind the corn and attend to the house. There is no fine earthenware, such as cups and plates, in the country; 'they are not requisite. Straw or wooden ones suffice to hold water, beer, or vegetables; and European pots and kettles are represented by earthen gurrahs, like a sphere with a slice off it. Salt is extracted from the soil, as practised in Uhiao, and is considered better than that taken from the ashes of plants.

The forest at this dry season did not afford any amusement in its flora : everything was in a dormant state, and fev or no flowers could be gathered, except some jasmine-scented bushes in the stream-bed; the beautiful little seeds of the abrus peeping out of their open curled-up pods, and the plant twining delicately round a small tree; some thorny bushes of a vermilion flowering-shrub, and large umbrageous trees of the ficus order, used for bird-lime by the natives ; several sweet plums now ripe, but nearly all stone. The most useful tree to the natives here is the Miombo; it makes a brilliant fire, and lasts the whole night, just to suit the African, who luxuriates in its heat. Most of the trees are bare-poled, admirably adapted for palisade purposes, and seldom heavier than can be carried by two men. The wands from the Miombo, a kind of banyan, afford the natives the fibre which they attach to their wool. Its manufacture is simple : split the wand longitudinally, separate the inner from

DOMESTIC ANIMALS. 89

the outer bark, and chew it well till the next wand is ready; use soon blackens it. Every tree and fruit has its separate name and use in this country.

The sultan owned three hundred milch cows, yet every day there was a difficulty about purchasing milk, and we were obliged to boil it that it might keep, for fear we should have none the following day. This practice the natives objected to, saying, "The cows will stop their milk if you do so." The calves drank most of it. Butter, except when rancid, we could not procure, the people using it for smearing their persons. They seldom had butcher-meat for their dinners, preferring to economise their cattle; and on my informing them that a cow lay in a neighbouring jungle with its leg broken, and ought to be cared for, a party, headed by the sultan's son, went at night, killed the animal, and brought over the carcass. It had belonged to another village. They kill all their animals with bludgeons, hunting them down through lanes and amongst houses. The goat's head is twisted; it never is killed as is done in this country, because it is thought the skin would thereby be injured for wear. The dogs are no better than the pariahs of India, and quite as prolific; a favourite, which was fed by me daily, had twelve pups, two of which were drowned. Pet pigeons, of the ordinary dovecot sort, flew in circles round the village, or would evince alarm at the sight of a large bird.

We met with no new wild animals here, and killed no lions. The natives used to trap game by means of nooses and pitfalls, and the lads of several villages would assemble with dogs, horns, and spears, to have a battue of the different forests|partridges, hares, coneys, and sometimes antelopes, being the result. In

90 WILD ANIMALS.

my morning walks (I could not leave the property for a single day's shooting) after guinea-fowl, when they had become so wild that a rifle was necessary, I once stumbled across two full-sized rhinoceros; both attempted to run up to me, but at 20 yards' distance turned off, showing their full lengths, hobbling in their canter like little pigs, the leader with cocked tail. A steady aim at the shoulder had no effect, and in case he might charge, I looked for my shot-gun, but my two followers were in full flight. They had observed the animals, and had been calling out to me to take care, but allowed me to go right upon them without a stalk. We tracked, and found that the two had separated. All animals wander so, that you never know which to keep in your hand, the gun or rifle. I was fortunate in knocking over with shot a light bay hornless female antelope, which was new to me: it had four white cuts across its saddle, the spinal ridge and inside of legs white, spotted sides, and tail a tuft of long hair. Altogether I was proud of my prize, as there was nothing whatever in the larder. My single follower made many excuses that he was not able to carry it home, but I assisted till close up to the village, when I was ordered to go and ask whether the sultan would allow it inside, my attendant saying, " Wezees generally have an aversion to it." "M'weeko"|*i.e.,* "it's not customary;" "it's a 'phongo,'" "never eaten," &c. Disgusted at having wasted two charges of English shot upon it, I thought there was a chance for me through the sultan. He looked surprised, and flew into such a rage, that the men round him had to explain|" If you eat it you'll lose your fingers and toes, get scab all over, and if it has spat on you the part will be-

WILD ANIMALS. 91

come a sore." I begged that the skin might be allowed inside the village ; no, not the skin even, nor its tail, so I could only sketch the animal. By-and-by a native caravan, carrying loads of salt, arrived, and the men were glad to get it to eat. Our Seedees said it was called the "bawala"in their country, and was never eaten; but to look at, it was as nice as any antelope I had ever seen. The smaller animals were N'geeree, a pig which the Wezee is very fond of: wells are dug by them in the forests. Another animal of the same size, but which it is not customary to eat, is the N'grooweh; and from the description given of it, it must be an antelope, having no tusks, but teeth like a goat and hair like a buffalo. There are also wild-cats, deep brown, and barred across|very bold, fearless-looking creatures. Troops of that beautiful little animal the mongoose, which becomes so tame in the house, we saw searching for water: they are called "goozeeroo." Their dark bodies are barred across to the -tip of the tail. On one of them being wounded by a bullet, another commenced to tear it with the greatest viciousness.

Lions and lynxes are considered the sole property of the sultan, and form part of his right and revenue. When carried in, lashed on a frame on men's shoulders and placed at his door, drums are beat, the women shout, great excitement prevails, and a dance usually takes place about the carcass. I had the curiosity to measure the length of one lion, and found it was three steps from the root of the tail to the nose, and in passing round it I was said to have subjected myself to a fine of two fathoms calico; but this I refused, and never did pay, because I had not stepped over it. The putrid

92 WILD ANIMALS.

flesh is cut in pieces, and boiled by the sultan in person. All the grease is preserved as valuable magic medicine, the tail and paws are hung over his doorway, and the skin, skilfully pegged out in the sun to dry, is prepared for the sultan's wear, as no one else dare use it. The colour of a young male lion was a pale ochre, with distinct dark spots on his hind-legs. The lynx is even more highly prized than the lion, though only the size of, and a little heavier than, an English fox, with a stumpy, short, curled-back dog-tail, and tips of hair to liia black ears. He has immense, powerful, thickly- formed little arms, great length of body, and is said by the natives to kill even the lion and buffalo. This I believe, for he gives one the idea of bull-dog courage. He is said to watch his prey from a tree. The colour of the lynx is a dusty red, indistinctly spotted ; a perfect cat's head; white round the eyes and underneath the body. The ceremony observed on the arrival of either a lion or lynx is curious :lThe sultan, sultana, and the sultan's wife next in rank, sit on stools placed in the open air, with the dead animal in front of them, the crowd all round, squatted or standing. A small lump of serpent-dung is made into a paste with water upon a stone. Spots of this white ointment are placed by the sultan's own hands upon the forehead, chest, tips of shoulders, instep, and palms of hands of himself and the two wives, and drums and dancing continue afterwards for some hours. The serpent-dung is supposed to have the charm of bringing plenty, or " bur- kut," to a house, because it gives many young. No one but kings may make use of it.

Vultures always hover where a dead body is thrown out of the village into the grass. This did not prevent

BIRDS AJSD FISH. 93

the natives from making use of their feathers, or those of the adjutant, for head-dresses on occasions of merriment, or on the march. Another bird of prey is a slate-coloured hawk, possessing a powerful flight, quite able to knock over a guinea-fowl, and altogether of noble appearance. Of eating-birds, there were three species of partridge, a few quail, the florikan, blue wild-pigeon, guinea-fowl, and a knob-nosed duck . The "k'engo," tree-partridge, resembles the painted one of India, has yellow legs, beautiful plumage, and weighs about a pound; the natives trap them in nooses of hair. The "kewtee" or "naenae," only half a pound in weight, is a very plump little partridge, found in open places, scratching and scraping the ground like a hen; and in colour it is almost the same as the quail. It has reddish legs, with a button-like pearly spur. A third kind of partridge is the " qualae:" it is more common than the others, and has a handsome blue full plumage and red legs, with sometimes an appearance of a double spur. The most game bird in plumage was the florikan, weighing from 1 to 2 lb., and forming even better food than the Indian species. A few parrots, a long-tailed bird of paradise, with the most graceful airy flight, some handsome yellow birds, about the size of the blackbird, and others with black bodies and white primaries, taking languid, short flights, were the most remarkable we saw during a morning or evening walk.

Our Seedees killed nearly all the fish in the country. They were caught by raking the still, waist-deep pools in the stream-bed by means of a hurdle of sticks. The large 20-pounders were often left for another day, but a good load of fifty smaller fish was generally brought

94 FEROCIOUS ANTS.

in to be split up, dried over the fire, and kept for consumption. Two species, the " makambara " and " go- go," were usually takenlthe former and largest is scaleless, large-headed, and lank-bodied ; the latter is only f Ib. weight, and resembles a stickleback.

Eats, fleas, and ants very often made our nights miserable. The calves alongside broke through their pens, and roused every one, while an alarm of " seafoo," or ants, and " bring a light," would be shouted by our Seedees. In a moment these vicious insects fixed upon our skin, biting and clinging like leeches till killed in their death-grip, and it became a desperate case for us whether we turned out or they turned in! A line of burning charcoal was placed to scare them away, and then you could again recline without further molestation or after-effects. But what was to be done to prevent their return the following night like an invading army ? The sultan very properly would not allow the reckless Seedees to place charcoal round his house during the night, but he had about a hundred goats brought in, and kept there three nights and days to pollute the place and make it obnoxious to the ants, and this was found to be an effectual remedy for the time. These ants are no larger than ordinary ones in England, but bite with the greatest ferocity.

The description given of the sultan at Mineenga will answer for all the natives in the " Land of the Moon," *i. e.,* " Unyamuezi." They are a sottish and unambitious race, even the best of them, though by no means incapable of improvement. My friend Ukuli- ma of Ukuni was a fine old fellow, although he had his failings. As I resided in the verandah of his best house, the inside of which was occupied by the

CHILDISHNESS OF THE SULTAN. 95

old sultana, some goats, and female servants, he passed or saw me daily, always saying "Yambo," or, if in extra good-humour, calling me "Doogo yango," brother, or even "sultan." Constantly, till I was tired of him, would he sit by me in my iron chair, greasing it all over, and playing the fool in various ways, such as opening the medicine-chest, helping himself to quinine, which he would put in his beer, or give it to a neighbour, to have a laugh over its bitter taste. Lucifer-matches he delighted in seeing lit, though afraid to light them himself. One day he felt dissatisfied because I would not give him magic medicine, and when he left, he with great difficulty put on my thick shoes, strutted about the village with them, and collected all the little boys as he trailed his feet on the ground. If a pigeon was shot, he would be most childish in begging it of me, saying, "Go and shoot another, as I want two." If this was not done, he would not be content with the one, but leave it in a pet, saying, tauntingly, " There will be pombe " to-morrow." My Bible, sketch-book, or the book of birds, he would turn over, smiling at each new leaf or picture, and asking what it meant. When he saw that I never asked a fee for the medicines given to his wives or followers, he thought I must have some object in it, and redoubled his little kindnesses ; or, as I was so friendly, he would suggest that I should give him a recipe by which he could distinguish friends from foes ! He inquired anxiously why we were going on to Karague ; we should get killed. " The people there plant their spears in your foot, and demand,' What do you want?' You must return to the coast, and I will send my own son in charge of you."

96 EXTRACT FROM JOURNAL.

All this was very good; but, on the day of our departure, having already received and expressed satisfaction with the presents from Speke, he showed his true character by demanding a separate present from me. He so far forgot himself as to seize two cases of ammunition and a gun, and drove my porters out of the village with his stick. Poor old man ! some cloth and beads sent the following day softened his anger, and my effects were allowed to leave his dominions. He was much respected in the country, and most of the neighbouring sultans visited him with great formality. On these occasions my guns were asked for to fire salutes. The procession would be headed by spearsmen, then followed the lady visitors carrying gourds of pombe", drums beating furiously, shots, sham- fights, &c.; and the sultan would ask me to join in the dance. After a time I was called upon by the strangers, and every book, box, blanket, &c., was minutely scrutinised by them.

On the morning of the 8th June, my journal remarks :I" A.m., One shot knocked over two guinea-fowl la blessinglnothing to eat; people pleased at seeing them. No fever. Sultan still here : whole village at pomb ; had a potful sent me, but cat turned it over. Bombay and Rehan asleep all day. Called for dinner at usual hour, fire black out; asked for the roast-fowl of the morninglRehan had eaten it. Took all this philosophically, and got two fellows to prepare a guinea-fowl by *1* P.m. Not many drunken men aboutlall asleep." A batch of tall Watusi men paid me visits; my umbrella was much fancied by their chief. He offered me his pipe for it; and, finding this was not enough, he brought me another day an iron

THE OLD SULTANA. 97

hoe ! To get rid of the subject, I asked him to sell me his forefinger, and said that twenty cows wouldn't buy my umbrella, which at last made him understand my meaning, as they value everything by cattle. The natives had great faith in the "Wazoongoo," white men. Our very paper, which they called "pupolo," was considered by some to have virtues; but we hadn't much of it to give, having had no communication with England for nearly a year.

The custom of the Arab in this country is to take presents for everything he does, and the same idea was formed of us. For instance, if a gun had to be repaired, a bullet to be extracted, an old sultan to be cured of dimness of vision, or the split lobe of an ear to be mended, for any of these services a cow or cows were at hand to be paid when the task was finished. When slaves were brought us for sale and declined, they could not understand our indifference to such traffic, but would turn from us with a significant shrug, as much as to say, " Why are you here, then ?"

Every morning the sultana and myself met, cordially shaking hands and asking how the night had been passed; previously to this her grandchildren had been in to her bedside, bidding good-morning. Every respect was paid the old lady by her family and by the lower classes, who stooped, knelt, or twice clapped their hands as they met Her. She was active like her husband, an excellent housewife, gave herself no airs, but still maintained her dignity. She might be seen nursing an infant, kindly carrying it about on her back, or at times shouldering a log of firewood. If I had refused pombe" from her husband and son, she would bring me a cupful, put it to her lips, and with

98 WOMEN OF UNYAMUEZI.

a gentle, ladylike curtsy, ask me to accept it; refusal would have been boorish. Her old eyes were getting dim, and on her hearing that I had made up some wash (from filings of zinc), thinking in her ignorance it might have a virtue for impaired vision, she begged for a little. On our getting to Cairo, some beads and trinkets were sent her ladyship *vid* Zanzibar, which it is to be hoped have ere this reached her.

The women, through my servants, soon found out that I had a looking-glass. They took it into then- hands, and held it there, continually looking at themselves, but it was evident they were not altogether satisfied with their appearance. They busied themselves with field operations, even using the flail, and at night a band of them would meet to dance in the moonlight. Their manner was to twist their bodies, stamp, and sing, till, exhausted by their antics, they paused to breathe and laugh. Two quarrelled one day, and came at last to blows, striking out like men, and drawing blood, but they were separated by our Seedees. They are very masculine in several respects; two of them accompanied me as volunteer porters when going to join Speke, and were even more inveterate smokers than the men. Their entire dress was one cloth wrapped round the loins from below the breasts to the calf of the leg, below which, down to the ankle, were immense masses of brass or iron wire rings, as before described. The head wool, dressed with an oily preparation, looked as if they wore a scalp of shining black beetles, among which were interspersed hawthorn-berry-coloured beads or rings of brass; others wore their hair in tassels, with seed-charms, &c. Necklaces of beads, brown or rose- coloured, adorned their necks; they had no rings on

WOMEN OF UNYAMUEZI. 99 '""''

their toes. Men often allow the nail of the small finger to grow long. The meeting of two women of unequal rank is a pleasing sight; the inferior sinks on her knee, and droops her head, while the other lays a hand on her shoulder muttering something. Both remain silent for a moment, but on rising they chat and gossip. The curtsy is also observed by them. When the wife hears that her husband is about to arrive from a journey to the coast, she dresses herself in a feathered cap and in the best costume she possesses, and proceeds with other women in ordinary dress to the sultana's, where they sing and dance at the door.

These Wezee women do not practise much tattooing, merely making three lines on each temple, and perhaps a line down the forehead reaching to the bridge of the nose; but some of the Watusi females were observed to have their shoulders and breasts very handsomely tattooed to imitate lady's point-lace in front, and crossed like a pair of braces behind. The waists were also marked in the same way. They prepare their dress of cow-skin to look like thick Irish frieze-cloth : a needle teases the leather fibre into this appearance, and "the turn-over part at the waist is made ornamental by strips from the skins of variously- coloured cattle. I have understood that some East African women live in the forests as much as fifteen days before the expected birth of a child, having a hut erected for them. This practice was not observed here, but the children are as fondly cared for by the mothers as in any part of the world, and not an instance is known of one of them selling her offspring, even when tempted to it by famine|they would sooner die. The boys practised many manly games as seen in

100 SKULLS ON THE PALISADING.

our *own* gymnasiums,|such as jumping over sticks |shooting, with bolted arrows, partridge or pigeon, or teaching small birds to sing|making model guns out of cane, going off with a trigger and having a cloud of sand for smoke|copying our double-barrelled guns, and making them, with nipple, hammer, trigger, &c., out of mud, with cotton for the smoke. They had also made cross-bows; and generally they evinced great powers of imitation. Seeing the ingenuity of the little fellows, we could not help longing for the happy day that should introduce amongst them more valuable improvements.

The habitations of the country have been described in the previous chapter. It only remains to add that there were no wells in the villages, water being carried from distant springs|that the dust was very annoying from the dances, &c.|that ground-nuts were not allowed to be roasted inside the bomah|and that outside the village human skulls and skeletons of hands (those of enemies killed in action) were stuck on the tops of the highest trees, or fixed on poles at the top of mounds. When the boundary of the village was to be enlarged, bare-poled trees for palisades were carried from the forest by Watusi, crying like jackals. On putting them into position, skulls of animals (or human), broken stools or baskets, land shells, &c., were stuck upon them.

On the 27th of June we had cries of "War, war!" In an instant the place was alive, and thirty poor- looking creatures, each with a bow and from four to six arrows, rushed out of the village, followed slowly by the sultan, carrying two spears. All got upon a mound, looking in the direction whence the noise proceeded. A party from a distance here joined them, and after

AN OPEN COURT. 101

skirmishing and larking in the grass, all again turned into the village to have their pombe " ! There was a second attack on the 4th July. The people of a M'salala village had captured some cattle. A few men with short-handled hatchets, spears, bows and arrows, all the "troops" that could be spared, paraded under the command of a red-robed leader; in ten days they returned all alive and safe, reporting the death of six of the enemy, and bringing the trophy of one head, which was stuck upon the palisading over the eastern gate, with the face to the zenith. Great rejoicing and pomb$ took place in the evening.

On the 17th, at 1 P.m., a dance took place for an hour, after which a court assembled on the same ground to hear evidence regarding the M'salala war. In the centre space lay the tusk of an elephant. Only the sultan and his wuzeers or officers sat on stools. The women were most attentive listeners to the speeches, and all was marked with the utmost decorum. For an hour the sultan addressed the crowd, sometimes stopping to think, and pulling out hairs from his face with iron tongs. There were bursts of laughter at his jokes, and when he had finished, a general conversation began. A wuzeer now spoke very sharply, and after each of his sentences there was a great clapping of hands and assent of " hums." Two of the crowd then delivered addresses, which were received with a single "viva," and the court abruptly broke up. Except the ridiculous part of pulling out the hairs of the sultan's beard, there could not be a more impressive or orderly court. It again assembled two days afterwards: the tusk still lay in the space, and was presented by the chief of M'salala

102 IMPEDIMENTS TO TRAVELLING.

in token of submission to the court's decision against him. Thus, by simple arbitration, ended their war of four-and-twenty days, which had entailed no greater loss than half-a-dozen men.

A great talk and excitement was caused on the 4th August by the discovery of a man throwing a pair of human hands into a bush in the forest. As he could give no satisfactory account of himself, and was suspected of murder, he was at once made prisoner, but unfortunately he made his escape. It seems to be the established/ rule here, that when such trophies are proved to be those of war, the chief of his village kills a cow and gives a feast. This was sufficient for the prisoner, and for many others, no doubt, to commit murder, and it was the only case I heard of that created any very great sensation amongst the natives.

Owing to such incidental circumstances, trade and travel are very much impeded, as single individuals can never with impunity move from one district to another, and are sure to be plundered, if not murdered. Two of our men fell behind upon one occasion, when their guns were at once seized, and to recover them it was necessary to pay a tax of two fathoms of cloth, after which the men were allowed to pass on. War causes retaliation in every direction. A M'salala caravan on its way through Ugogo from the coast was plundered by the natives. The latter on their part attributed their ill fortune to the Arab traders, who had brought war on the country, and to revenge themselves they seized the property of an Arab trader passing through their territory, and meant to treat all foreigners visiting them with the same rigour, until the *lex talionis* was fairly vindicated.

AMUSEMENTS OF THE NATIVES. 103

The sepoys of the sultan consisted of about twenty idle young fellows, who tried to dress jauntily, and were the fast men and pick of the place. If an order had to be conveyed from one of the sultan's villages to another, their word was law. If an escort was necessary, they were employed, and when war broke out they collected levies all round the country from their own class or from poorer natives. None of these soldiers would deign to carry a load for us; they were, in their own estimation, the life-guardsmen of the state, consequently led an idle life, playing at pitch-and-toss, bao, beating the drum, &c. Without coins one would imagine that pitch-and-toss could not be played; but has not bark got two sides ? Circles of bark were used, also a few leaden discs pitched in the air, while the gamester clapped his hands and let the discs fall upon a cow-skin placed on the ground. My wonder was how they fell so fairly on the skin, and also that the game was not known by our Zanzibar men. The stakes were bows, arrows, arrow-tips, and ankle-wires; the counters were made of pieces of stick. Bao is a coast game, played by two, with a board having thirty-two cups or wells in it, and sixty-four counters of seeds, called "komo." The sultan sat down with any one he could get to play this rather skilful game.

Every large country has its own style of drumming; that of Unyanyembe was more musical than the jumble of drums here. The conductor had always the largest drum; the rest watched him for the time, while at his feet a little black youth rattled as hard as he could, without ceasing, at a wooden trough. If the noise of it was not heard, the music lost its stirring

104 SUPERSTITIOUS FEABS.

effect! The drums were of wood, three to four feet high, and slung on a beam at a convenient height; the sticks were twelve inches long. At these dances the head men were present to preserve order, and to prevent, as much as possible, the use of spears or arrows in their antics. On the arrival of a distinguished guest, such as the son of the sultan, who owned a neighbouring village, a roll from each of the four drums was given in succession, and as he entered the place every one hid in his house from shyness. If a lion or a culprit was brought in, the "assembly" was beaten furiously. Single taps at short intervals, and gradually increasing to a roll, were given in a case of murder, at five in the morning, and again an hour afterwards. The previous days had been, night and day, celebrated by incessant drumming on the part of a dark set of wandering beggars or gypsy lads, richly necklaced with beads, to commemorate some event which appeared, from the scant information I could obtain from my interpreter, to be celebrated once or twice in three years. This, if true, shows that they mark a period, announced by gypsies, whom I observed but twice during my stay at Ukuni.

Of religion, idols, Sabbaths, or holidays they have none, but of superstitious fears and beliefs they have an ample store. On the occasion of the arrival of Speke with a detachment at a village, the natives shut their doors against him, and for three hours inhospitably kept the party in the sun. They had never before seen a white man, nor the tin boxes that the men were carrying; " and who knows," they said," but that these very boxes are the plundering Watuta transformed and come to kill us all ? You cannot beSultan's Daughter Possessed. 105 admitted." No persuasion could avail with them, and the party had to proceed to the next village.

Three stones, placed in a triangular form, surrounded the dwelling-house of the sultan of Ukuni, and within them it was believed no harm could ever happen to him, even if a gun were fired at him. One of our men sitting on one of these stones, jumped off, as if stung, on being told of the sacred character of the place.

The ceremony of driving out an evil spirit, or " Phepo," is elaborate and curious. The sultan sits at the doorway of his hut, which is decorated with lion- paws. His daughter, the possessed, is opposite him, completely hooded, and guarded by two Watusi women, one on each side, holding a naked spear erect. The sultana completes the circle. Pombe" is spirted up in the air so as to fall upon them all. A cow is then brought in with its mouth tightly bound up, almost preventing the possibility of breathing, and it is evident that the poor cow is to be the sacrifice. One spear-bearer gives the animal two gentle taps with a hatchet between the horns, and she is followed by the woman with the evil spirit and by a second spear- bearer, who also tap the cow. A man now steps forward, and with the same hatchet kills the cow by a blow behind the horns. The blood is all caught in a tray (a Kaffir custom) and placed at the feet of the possessed, after which a spear-bearer puts spots of the blood on the women's forehead, on the root of the neck, the palms of the hands, and the instep of the feet. He spots the other spear-bearers in a similar manner, and the tray is then taken by another man, who spots the sultan, his kindred, and household. Again the tray is carried to the feet of the possessed, and she spots with

106 BLACK-ART CASES.

the blood her little son and nephews, who kneel to receive it. Sisters and female relatives come next to be anointed by her, and it is pleasant to see those dearest to her pressing forward with congratulations and wishes. She then rises from her seat, uttering a sort of whining cry, and walks off to the house of the sultana, preceded and followed by spear-bearers. During the day she walks about the village, still hooded, and attended by several followers shaking gourds containing grain, and singing " Heigh-ho, massa-a-no," or " masanga." An old woman is appointed to wrestle with her for a broomstick which she carries, and finally the stick is left in her hand. Late in the afternoon a change is wrought; she appears as in ordinary, but with her face curiously painted, her followers being also painted in the same way. She sits without smiling to receive offerings of grain, with beads or anklets placed on twigs of the broomstick, which she holds upright; and this over, she walks among the women, who shout out" Gnombe !" (cow) or some other ridiculous expression to create a laugh. This winds up the ceremony on the first day, but two days afterwards the now emancipated woman is seen parading about with the broomstick hung with beads and rings, and looking herself again, being completely cured. The vanquished spirit had been forced to fly !

Black - art cases were duly tried, and generally ended in conviction. A cowherd who had sold me some fish died very suddenly; one of his two wives was suspected of having poisoned him; and being tried, she was convicted and condemned. She was taken to the dry bed of the stream, her arms tied behind her, and was killed by having her throat cut

CASE OF ADULTERY. 107

from ear to ear. No hyena touched the body, which still more confirmed the belief that she was guilty; for my Seedee cook said, " Has not the hyena the soul of a man ? does he not know your thoughts when you determine on shooting Vnm ?"

On the 10th of July my servant asked permission to go and see the uchawe". I accompanied him to the outside of the bomah (village fence), where a woman and lad lay on their faces with their arms bound painfully tight, and writhing in torture. Poor creatures ! they met with no sympathy from the jeering crowd, but the ropes were slackened at my request. They had been apprehended on suspicion of having bewitched the sultan's brother, who lay sick for fifteen days, and unless they could work off the magic spell they must die. The lad said, " Take me to the forest; I know an herb remedy." On the seventh day from this scene (during which the lad was outside the village, and the woman kept by the sick patient in the stocks) the former was killed and the woman released. I went to see his body the following day, but the hyena (I was told) had taken it away. Nothing remained but blood and the ashes of some hair by a fire. Could they have tortured him by burning ? A case of adultery was punished in the most horrible manner, too painful to describe minutely. They had no Divorce Court! The strapping young fellow who had found his way into the harem of the sultan, was tied to railings, stripped, certain parts of his person were smeared and covered with rags, then set fire to by the sultan in person, and he was dragged to the fire outside the village; but before he could reach it, assigais from the hands of the son

108 MAKING BROTHERHOOD.

and daughter-in-law of the sultan pierced his neck and chest, and he was drawn out by one leg like a dog through the gate. The woman who committed this act came in fear to me at night, saying, " Give me protection : it is said I am to be killed for stabbing the adulterer." Though for the moment I detested the woman, I endeavoured to calm her by saying my guns would be her protection, and my men should sleep in her house.

On asking her " Why did you soil your hands with such a deed ?" she replied, in the most animated way, " Oh, did I not glory in it! did the fellow not come to my bedside one night making propositions to me, and I never could get hold of him since ?" The following day she, as usual, wished me good-morning, but I shuddered to think that so handsome a woman and so kind a mother, with four beautiful children who must have seen all, could have committed such an act. The woman who had offended was a middle-aged good-looking person. Nothing whatever was done to her, though she had once before been the cause of a man's death under similar circumstances. Previous to this event she would come often to look at herself in my mirror, but afterwards I did not see so much of her.

Several of our men made brotherhood with the Wezees, and the process between Bombay and the sultan's son, Keerenga, may be mentioned. My consent having been given, a mat is spread, and a confidential party or surgeon attends on each. All four squat, as if to have a game at whist; before them are two clean leaves, a little grease, and a spear-head; a cut is made under the ribs of the left side of each party, a drop of blood put on a

CAUSE OF DELAY. 109

leaf and exchanged by the surgeons, who rub it with butter twice into the wound with the leaf, which is now torn in pieces and strewn over the " brothers'" heads. A solemn address is made by the older of the attendants, and they conclude the ceremony by rubbing their own sides with butter, shaking hands, and wishing each other success. Ten rounds of ammunition are then fired off; a compliment from each of the four drums is sounded, and they parade the -village all the afternoon. This was the form observed by the Wanyamuezi. An Uganda lad, the magician of the sultan, made brotherhood with Rehan, the cook, by cutting marks on his chest and rubbing in the fat of lions. This young wizard of Uganda, with his bamboo tube, could blow away all the enemies of the sultan, or, if persuaded to go out shooting with you, a second blast from his trumpet would make the animals of the forest stand before you! The last of their unintelligible customs I shall mention, was that of a number of men amusing themselves by running fast through and about the village, singing, at every third or fourth step, " Queri" or " Hairy," and " Queri Mahamba." I had seen the same custom across country, outside the village; and on the nights of this great stir, dancing would also take place.

To give a description of the difficulties and disappointments we experienced for nearly four months in procuring men to carry our luggage, would be tiresome. I shall only mention a few instances. Speke was away sixty miles in advance of me with a portion of the property : neither he nor I could proceed a step ; we were like two planets compelled by a fixed law to preserve our distances. He resolved on making a flying march

110 WE SUCCEED IN MARCHING.

to Karague, in the hope of sending me relief from thence. Our own Seedees mutinied; they would not hear of this plan, as the country of Usui was dangerous,lit was certain death to accompany white men, who were considered sorcerers of the deepest dye, and they insisted that we had not enough of presents for the chiefs. Speke, ever active, to my utter surprise, walked back the sixty miles to announce this failure to me. " What has happened? I thought you were in Karague!" What was to be done? Our beads and cloth were running short; *my* sultan would not give us a man. Unyanyembe and the Arabs must be appealed to, and carpenters might be got to proceed to the south end of Lake Nyanza, make a raft, and so escape the danger of Usui. This plan was carried out with success. Speke returned on the nineteenth day from the Arabs, having, in going and returning, accomplished a journey of 180 miles. He had ordered from Zanzibar a fresh supply of bartering goods, of which we heard nothing till our arrival in England two years afterwards. The raft scheme had been dropped, and he had brought with him trusty guides and interpreters for Uganda. Here more than a month elapses; his guides desert, his men are more mutinous than ever, and Bombay is on his way for new guides, as his master is struck down with illness, which I knew nothing of for twenty-seven days, and had no prospect of seeing him. Suddenly a party of coast men arrive from the north, saying, " Every chief there waits you; go on, get porters; the road is clear;" so, after days of obstinate resistance and final outbreak by my old sultan, on the 12th September I was able once again to be on the move to join my companion.

7

SECTION 7

CHAPTER VII.

UKUNI TO KARAGUE, SEPTEMBER 12 TO NOVEMBER 25, DISTANCE 200 MILES|COMMENCING THE JOURNEY|ATTACKED ON THE MARCH|THE WATUTA RACE|THE COUNTRY BETWEEN UKUNI AND KARAGUE | "WA-TERFALL | VOLCANIC MOUNDS|THE KING OF BIRDS|THE WANYAMBO|THE WA- LINGA, OR WORKERS IN IRON|A NATIVE BEAUTY|LANGUAGE OF THE COUNTRY.

Karague ! how charmed we were to get there; its fine hills, lake scenery, climate, and, above all, the gentleness of the royal family, were all in such contrast to what we had experienced elsewhere of Africa and Africans, that, if surrounded by our friends, we should have been content, for a time at least, to take up our residence there. But before describing the country, the thread of our narrative must be taken up to show what had to be undergone to reach this haven. In September 1861, when preparing to move, I found that before a start could be made on an African march, particularly after a long halt, there were hundreds of annoyances unknown in other countries. No one believes you wish to move till a display is made of your beads, by counting them out, stringing them, and

112 EXTRACTS FROM JOURNAL.

packing up the loads. The sight of these rouses the sultan : he, his family, and all the people of the place, begin to pester you for presents, and you would give worlds to be away from such intolerable bullying. Half your number of porters at last being collected to receive their pay, a momentary suspense takes place : the first man hesitates to accept the hire he had agreed for; each man strives to lay the responsibility upon another; but as soon as one accepts, instantly the rest scramble for it. Here are some extracts from my Journal previous to the march :|

" *8th September.*|Attempt to push all the engaged men ahead with their loads, in charge of Said, but fail . and half the day is lost by the native procrastination. Said no better than the rest of them. After a long day of it, started off 40 loads and three donkeys ahead to first march, where they will wait for us. Ten paid-up porters not present. One says, 'My wife is ill; I return my hire:' another, 'My father and mother won't allow me to accompany you.' I chastise him ; he puts himself under the protection of the sultan, and bolts, leaving his hire of calico blackened by one day's wear. A third will not go because I refuse him the leadership. Last night my men returned from searching for porters, saying, ' None will go unless you give them four times the usual hire.'

" 9.|Three of my men have been away all day, and have not brought back a man. Wezees had promised to come, but I have no faith in what they say; others ask triple hire. Twelve loads sent out by men of the advanced camp.

" *Wth.*|Cannot see a prospect of marching from here. Ordered Manua to Roongwa for porters; saw

EXTRACTS FROM JOURNAL. 113

him at night. 'Have you been for porters ?' 'Yes, there and back.' I laughed at this cool assertion, and asked, 'How many did you get?' 'Four are coming in the morning.' This was too much, as all the Seedees satisfied me that he had never been out .of the place ; I therefore ordered him to receive two dozen. Rehan (cook) said, ' / won't give it.' ' You must,' I said; but ultimately the matter was settled by Manua running away, all the Seedees after him! (Manua afterwards became a great friend of mine, as he knew the names and uses of every plant and tree in the country.)

"*llth.*|Yesterday sent a note to Speke, but find the bearer did not start, because he had a Wezee lady in tow. Verily these Africans are a self-pleasing and most trying set. Two men off for porters. My leader reported sick. Manua (the man I ordered to be flogged yesterday) not to be found. Four porters arrive, but won't start till to-morrow, as they feel tired!

" *12th.*|Start three loads; fourth man not present ; he had gone away to sleep in another village. Ten men came in from camp ahead to carry away my remaining traps. Sultan demands a present, but on consulting my men, we all agreed that as he had already got eight fathoms of cloth, a large quantity of beads, some gunpowder, and had lost four cows placed in his charge, no more was necessary for him. At this decision he struck my porters and drove them out of his village, and seized some cases of ammunition and a rifle. The quarrel was made worse by the drunkenness of my chief interpreter, Rehan, who in this state threw his gun and accoutrements at my feet, spat upon one of my men, and gave his

114 EXTRACTS FROM JOURNAL.

support to the sultan. After bearing these insults, and seeing the powder, &c., recovered, I walked outside the village and sat down, feeling sick, sore at heart, and exhausted from the detestable strife, but thankful to God that I had so much command of temper. A servant reported that he and another must sleep that night with their loads in the village, as security for my paying some cloth and beads. Anything to get away, and I marched to my advanced camp, eight miles off, regretting that I had not bid adieu to the sultana.

" *13th.*|Sent back the cloths to the sultan by Uledi. So jolly and civilised-like to have a note brought me by three or four Seedees from Speke, wanting me up sharp! Uledi returned at sunset, having satisfied the sultan. Said, Rehan, and Baraka sent word they would be up in the morning ; so like an African's system of procrastination, winning the mornings and evenings from us, and saying the day is too hot to move.

"*1ith.*|March three miles to a wretched village. A number of men hanging on for hire; one man promised for Karague, and backed out of it because I frightened him by writing his name down. Tried to make an afternoon march, but no one would stir; besides, three loads were behind.

" *15th.*|Under way outside the village by six A.M.; eight loads still on the ground, no porters to carry them, and loads in the rear belonging to men sleeping in other villages. Every day seems to be won from me. Countermand the march till the afternoon; a panic had struck the porters. The Watuta are at the next ground from camp. I took the chief porter,

WE ARE ATTACKED. 115

walked there and back, 20 miles, by 3$ P.m., and found this much-dreaded tribe had left that morning. "*16th.*|Having aroused my camp, a noisy conversation soon began with some strange armed men, who had been sent by Sultan Myonga to insist on my visiting him with my caravan; but as I saw yesterday that his residence was completely out of my route, and as Speke had laid down that no further present should be made to him, his 'soldiers' were told this; but, at the turn to their master's village, they planted their spears in defiance, and dared us to proceed by any but their way. We laughed at them, and held on our road for seven miles, when out of some thick cover came a howling of voices. I was about the third from the head of my Indian file, when a troop of about two hundred, with assigais, bows and arrows, burst upon us, springing over the ground like cats. Passing the van, apparently without any intention of molesting us, or ' showing their colours,' no one stopped even to look at them; but of a sudden they broke in upon the centre of our line, and, with uplifted assigais and shouts, frightened the porters to give up their loads and fly, if they could escape the hands of the ruffians who were pulling their clothes and beads from them. Seeing my goods carried off, I tried, without bloodshed, to prevent it; for they were too numerous to attack, as I had but one of my gun-men and two natives. On searching for others, I found Rehan with rifle at full cock, defending two loads against five of the men. He had been told by Manua that he was ' a fool to think of the loads; fly for your life !' but the property, he said, was his life. On making for the village of the Sultan Myonga to seek redress, I was

116 OUR PORTERS DESERT.

told not to fear; all would be returned me: ' to go and reside in the village of his son, where all would be brought.' On proceeding thither I found that the natives had dressed themselves out in the stolen clothes of our men. I felt like a prisoner; my bright hopes were wrecked; and they all laughed at me as I stood amongst the mob of insolent marauders jeering and exulting at their triumph. Very little at that moment would have set things in a blaze; but though honour was dear, the safety of the expedition was so also, and one false step would have endangered it. They threatened, presenting assigais at my breast; but though I was defenceless, my rifle in its case resting harmlessly on my shoulder, they did not venture to strike, but scattered over the place.

Fifteen of my 55 loads were returned during the day; 15 of 56 porters reappeared; two "VVezees were reported killed, but instead of finding even a trace of them, I came upon three others concealed in the grass with their loads. Myonga was said to be infuriated at his people; he had cut off the hand of one of his men, and promised that all, except the property of my porters, should be restored. The following night the sultan sent, saying everything in his possession had been given up, but by my account there were still wanting six bead-loads, some cloth, my teapot, looking-glass, basin, pewter mug, a saw, a goat, &c. Every load was partially plundered; our most private keepings had been ruthlessly handled; and cases were destroyed by rocks and stones in trying to break them open. My porters, who had received their full hire to Karague, deserted; the march was delayed ; and we had all been dishonoured. On making

NEGOTIATING WITH MYONGA. 117

this representation to the sultan, he expressed great sympathy at first, saying,' Your property will all be restored, and you shall have men from me to convey your goods to Karague.' This was a mere ruse. In four days after the attack I was in a position, by aid sent me from Speke, to march ahead; but the Wezees said, ' If you attempt a forced march, and leave without obtaining the sultan's permission, we will run away.' In reply to my request to be allowed to leave his country, saying I was satisfied with having recovered so much, he very coolly replied,' I want no present from you, but must have your Seedees with their guns to aid me in an attack against a neighbour of mine.' But though two of my men volunteered to go, intending to escape from him during the night, the proposal seemed preposterous; and, to settle the affair, a scarlet blanket was taken from my bedding and sent to the sultan, along with some other cloths. These were returned contemptuously, with a message that I must aid him with men and guns. The Seedees would not hear of my going to see this ruffian of a sultan, neither could they manage him themselves; their remonstrances and pleadings had become stale. The natives in the mean time were boisterous, refusing our bead coinage. I tried to make use of my rifle in the jungles, but failed to get anything. In my rounds I only saw the brutality of the people towards travellers in pouncing upon a party of four women and two men, demanding their bows and arrows, which I saved by interference. Again, the coarse fellows struck so brutally a donkey which Speke had with him on his former journey to Lake Nyanza, that the animal, then in foal, died. For this no re-

118 IN TREATY WITH MYONGA.

dress could be obtained, because the offender was said to belong to a different village. But how were we to get away from these annoyances, which were exhausting to one's strength and patience ? Our porters began to desert, saying, what was the use of staying therel there was nothing to eat ? I was almost driven to giving up a gun or more, as I had seen the country traversed without them; but on reference to Speke, who lay prostrated with sickness twelve miles from me, I was told on no account to give guns, but to settle the tax, and join him at any sacrifice. Some Seedees under Bar- aka, who had a great deal of native bluster about him, arrived with a bound and dash, bringing Speke's message ; and having armed himself and a dozen followers with ten rounds of ammunition each, Baraka went to the sultan, carrying an offer of forty fathoms of calico and ten wires of copper. The chief did not see why he should be treated so stingily! ' Other men of his rank get much handsomer presents; he merely asks for twenty coloured cloths, no guns, but he must have four barrels of powder, and don't forget the gentleman's blanket!' To settle the matter, as we had been delayed seven days, one case of gunpowder, double the quantity of cloth, the scarlet blanket, and a bundle of beads were sent sorrowfully, but in the full hope of success. No ; we could not leave his country till one case of powder was given; so the case was rendered, and his men were requested to take it to him. They then got up a noise because a box of percussion-caps had been taken out, and before going to their sultan they requested each a cloth for their trouble. Baraka again went to appeal; the box of caps was not wanted; the men were rebuked; one goat was given by the sultan

THE WATUTA OR ZULU KAFIRS. 119

to Baraka; and we marched that afternoon, the 23d September, having been detained seven days, with wounded feelings, and with every howl of the exulting natives sinking deeply into our hearts.

Some remarks upon the Watuta race may not be out of place here. They had lately been assisting Bolaema, a chief of the district, to defeat my friend Myonga, and had succeeded in capturing thirty of his cattle, and striking terror into the country. Although we never saw one of the tribe, we came upon their deserted camps, and had two men amongst our followers who had once been taken prisoners by them. To these two I am chiefly indebted for the following information. Their M'foomoo, or sultan, MTookoolla, has his headquarters at Malavie, a province bordering on the north-west shore of Lake Nyassa. A brother of his, called MTumbareeka, has wandered north to Utambara, and there formed a royal residence. They seldom go themselves in search of cattle and slaves, but send their wuzeers or officers, with several thousand followers, roaming over the country, leaving nothing but waste behind them. If they find a village without cattle, they demand slaves instead, never giving up the siege till some tax has been extorted. Some cases are told of their besieging a place for months, with their superior numbers encircling the village to prevent escape; those who were so fortunate as to break through this Watuta cordon being looked upon by the country afterwards as having had a charmed life. The only race in the south that ever mastered them, and can pass through them, are the Wabeesa, living to their west. We had one of these people in camp, a young lad, so bold that he would

120 THE WATUTA OR ZULU KAFIRS.

show fight against our strongest follower. Men from the coast are sometimes found to enter their camp fearlessly; but, as a rule, every race in the interior is in continual dread of their arrival. They have large boats, with which they navigate the Nyassa lake, landing and making raids on the people of Nyassa and Uhiao. The pure race adopt the costume of the Kafir in their extraordinary coverings; but as they are made up of many who love a life of freedom, or had been captured from villages in childhood, the race must be a very mixed one. Their arms are two or three very small short spears, which they never throw, but, with a leather shield in the left hand protecting their own bodies, they close upon their foe; and, if he resists being captured as a slave, stab him. We once were encamped in a village when, at night, the drums beat the alarm‖tap, tap, slowly, increasing to a tremendous roll. This was to warn all that the Watuta were on the move in the vicinity, and might take this village on their way; however, they did not come to it till some days after we had left it, when the people got warning and escaped. We saw their camp in a circle of fence, completely surrounding a village, at a distance of 200 yards. Forked sticks were stuck in the ground to support the cow-skins which their women carry to shade them during the day from the sun. Most comfortable beddings of grass lay on the ground; or, when long in one place, their huts were a half-orange shape, very low, and surrounded by a fence made from the euphorbia, which is imagined to be poisonous, and only fit for the use of the Watuta.

The chief Myonga, who plundered my caravan, and

OUR SEEDEES STRIKE FOR DOUBLE PAY. 121

the eight or ten other petty chiefs whose country we had to pass through afterwards, were not a whit better than the Watuta, and the wonder is they did not take everything from us. It was only because they feared being shot or bewitched, or come down upon by their neighbouring chiefs, that they desisted. When one is known to possess wealth, obtained by tax or by plunder, jealousy and quarrels are the certain result. We no sooner heard the vile sound of the war-drum to collect the natives, and intimidate our party into the settlement of the tax, than our porters would desert; and when the drums beat a "receipt" for all demands, and we were free to move out of their clutches, our Wezee porters would get up a row with us, and demand more cloth, thus causing us to suffer as much annoyance from friend as from foe ; and often they would run away in a body as soon as they got what they wanted. Nothing we could devise seemed to succeed, till their bows and arrows were seized, and they had got so far on the journey that going back through these boisterous races to their homes without arms would have been as bad as death to them. One trouble over, we had others: our Seedees, who had been engaged and paid at the British Consulate of Zanzibar to accompany us, struck for double pay and increased allowance for rations. Their complaints were calmly listened to; and when it was told that they might leave our service but lay down their arms, they surrendered them, but thought better of it the following morning, and only three of them deserted. These constant drains upon our resources had one good effect‖they lightened our baggage; and after the enormous tax levied by the sultan and under-

122 A WATERFALL.

chiefs of Usui, we were far in the interior at Kara- gue, with certainly not enough of beads to last us six months.

The first sixteen marches from Ukuni were through very pleasant undulations of tall soft grass and umbrageous forest-trees, spots here and there being cleared for cultivation, and capable of yielding gram for one or two thousand travellers throughout a season; On getting into Usui the watershed had changed; all ran to Victoria Nyanza. Our path crossed three or four escarped hills, tailing gently off to lower ground in the north. About Lohagattee there was picturesque scenery. Delightfully wild rocks and crags interspersed with trees overhung the valleys, reminding one of the echoing cliffs over the Lake of Killarney. A waterfall, too, added a rare charm to this part of the journey. The water fell upon hard, black, volcanic-like boulders of conglomerate, in a cascade of two cubic feet from the top of the escarpment seventy feet in height. Amongst the spray beautiful ferns and mosses grew in great luxuriance, recalling many a ramble at home for plants and objects of natural history; but though crabs were about the water, no land-shells were found. The natives came into camp asking why the fall had been visited by the white man. Did he mean to stop the water that supplied the whole valley, by turning its course or drinking up its waters ? Their chief, we heard, when rain is required, goes through a propitiatory ceremony at this spot to bring it in abundance; but as this year rain had fallen at its usual season, their fears were easily calmed. The rain-doctor had put out his magic instruments under a tree by the 20th October, and expected it abundantly at new

CRYSTAL WATER. 123

moon, fifteen days afterwards, when his year would have expired. He begged for a piece of paper to assist him, and on getting half a sheet of foolscap, said he would prefer paper written over! From the 26th of September, and during October, we had very pleasant showers and slight thunderstorms. At new moon, on the 2d November, as the doctor predicted, we had a heavy wind-storm, with pelting rain ; but by the 5th, *our* magical horn, the rain-gauge, had worked its charm and stopped the rain ! When in low ground, or where water was lying near the surface, the mornings were so cold that gloves would have been a comfort. During the day the sun was oppressive, but in the shade, with a N.E. wind generally blowing, it was agreeably cool. Water was everywhere abundant the first half of the journey, in wells dug outside the villages, and in the boggy dips which drained the country to the north in the latter half. For the first time in Africa, we got clear crystal water bursting from under the hard stratified rock of the parallel ranges of Usui; and whether it was that the water was purer, that the season had changed, or that we were in a finer climate, the men suffered less in health during the months of October and November than during any previous time of the year. Speke was rapidly recovering from his dangerous chest complaint; and instead of my fever visits, I had only periodical nausea in the morning, occurring about every ten days during the march.

Geologically, the country of Uzinza has a great deal of interest, being broken up into so many varied forms. One day, from the path of splintered rock, you may contemplate the face of a long, bare, sloping hill, the surface of which is half rock half bog, giving it the

124 THE PLANTAIN FIELDS.

wild dreary look of a Highland moor in the heart of Africa, but with this difference, that a garden of plantain forms part of the landscape. Again, pick up a waluutAsized nodule of iron, covered with a rusty red dust, and think how rudely, how quietly, they turn it into a spear that glistens like steel! Again, see the long high escarpments, and wonder at the power that had raised them into such a position. The volcanic mounds in Kishakka, seen from the spur above Vi- hembe", were most curious, so many of them rising in one part of the horizon like mole-heaps on the earth's surface, some of their tops nearer us being sterile and of red grit, their sides strewed over with white quartz fragments; others clothed with pale green grass to their very summits, and dotted with trees sweeping down to, and shading with verdure, the valleys below. Their forms were saddle-shaped, horse-shoes, and frustums of cones; many were crowned with rock, and nearly all had stratified splinters bristling from their sides. The eastern slopes below the escarpments, where the debris lay, were more cultivated than the western rocky parts. The natives bestowed great care on their fields, hoeing them up by the 8th October for the expected rain, collecting the weeds in heaps with a forked stick, and burning them. Fields of plantain- trees were grown, each tree six feet apart. From the fruit a sweet spirituous wine is made, tasting somewhat like still hock, and quite as pleasant. The decayed leaves and stems of the plantain were allowed to remain on the ground to preserve the roots and soil from the heat of the sun, and afford nourishment to a crop of beans, " maharageh," peculiar to this country, and often grown in the shade of the trees. The

CATTLE AND GAME. 125

other crops seen ripening in November, were Indian corn and manioc; sweet potato was ripe and abundant ; sorghum, " M'tama," at that season, was scarce and dear; tobacco, fowls, goat, and cows were more expensive than we had found them in Unyamuezi.

The cattle looked wildly at our dress, and were here a different breedlnamely, the heavy, ungraceful, large- horned variety of Karague, without humps, and many of them probably from Unyoro, hornless, like the Tees- water breed, but bony and gaunt from bad grazing. All night the people allow their cattle to remain in the field, without any fence, standing round smouldering fires by their habitations. I observed at cow-milking time the skin of a calf placed in front of one cow, when she licked it all over, and while her hind- legs were tied with a thong, the milk was taken. In a goat that was killed, a black glazed ball of hair very much resembling its own was found inside: no cattle diseases were heard of. The manner our men had of getting hold of a vicious cow was quite African. A noose is laid on the ground, she is driven over it till by perseverance she is caught; or if she is to be killed, they chase her with a sword-bayonet, and either hamstring or break the bone of a hind-leg.

In the southern forests of Uzinza, hartebeest, eland, zebra, pig, and various species of antelope might be shot from horseback or on foot, as there is a wide range of fine country for them; but the greatest number and variety of animals I saw in Africa were in the valley of Urigi, which is the boundary between Uzinza and Karague; all the above animals, with the rhinoceros and giraffe, might certainly be seen any morning by the sportsman. The valley or plain is covered with

126 GAME-BIRDS.

four-feet-high grasses, is from three to four miles broad, and probably twenty miles long, evidently once forming part of Victoria Nyanza. We counted fourteen rhinoceros upon the plain below; they were so numerous that while marching they were often within gunshot, affording us excellent sport had we chosen to follow them up. Instead of being frightened, one of these rhinoceros walked up towards me till I whistled at sixty paces, which was close enough; but the bullet from one of the men's rifles only made him put a twist in his tail and trot off proudly over the grassy plain for three miles, tripping repeatedly, and halting for an instant to give himself a shake, as if he had been stung. No elephants were seenlit was too open a country for them; hyena were rarely heard; porcupine-quills were picked up in the woods; serpents, we saw few or none ; beeswax was never met with, though hives made out of logs were occasionally. Of game- birds the most plentiful was the guinea-fowl near the cultivations. The natives of Usui will not eat the fowl, but the Walinga, a class of people who work in iron and its nodules, have no objection. Florikan were shot; also a species of partridge quite new to me. I was attracted by their curious gait in running with their bodies thrown back : their call, too, was strange l"cock, cock, ko-cock," or "chick-a-chick, chick-a-chick," not unlike the Himalayan cheer-pheasant's voice; our Seedees called it the " Booee." Its throat and round the eyes were an orange red; one was double-spurred, and weighed 1 lb.

While delayed by the sultan of Usui for fifteen days in settling his tax, we found the above partridge amongst the bushes of the valley; also numbers of

SWALLOWS AND THE KING OF BIRDS. 127

pretty birds of no value except as specimens. We observed three fine species of swallow on the wing; the prettiest was entirely black, except on the forehead and under the lower mandible, where it was snow-white; a smaller was black all over, and both had forked tails, and frequented craggy ground. A larger species have red belly and chest, whitish throat, some white under the wings, long forked tail and general colour black, frequenting ground covered with brushwood. The smallest seen was black with white belly, red over forehead and under the lower mandible, with forked tail. Black birds the size and shape of robins flew from tree to tree; water-wagtails were familiar with our camp; creepers hopped amongst the bushes; smaller genera were in flights; and a peculiar-looking bird, with plain brown plumage and long tail, was shot amongst the rushes. Though mentioned last, our Seedees considered this the king of birds. He is called the " M'linda," and he moves escorted by a staff of little birds, whose duty it is, should a feather fall from the king, to tear it to pieces, thus preventing its being put upon an arrow. A similar tale is told with reference to the tippet-monkey, who is said to believe his handsome skin so much coveted, that when wounded he tears out all his beautiful long hair, to prevent your making use of it! The skin of the M'linda is as thick as that of a mouse, the feathers might be called hairy, the bill is stronger than a linnet's, and the feet are soft and red. Our men were much pleased during a march to meet with a bird they called the "kong-ot'a:" we were certain to have luck attending us when it was seen !

128 THE SULTAN OF USUI.

The most powerful chief on our route through Uzinza was Suwarora of Usuila Wahuma by caste, but a superstitious creature, addicted to drink, and not caring to see us, but exacting through his subordinates the most enormous tax we had yet paid. His chief officer or " sirhidge " was a Watusi; and when he called upon us dressed in the most ridiculous costumela woman's crimson cotton gown, a red- check turban, and " saharee " thrown round his shoulderslhe was treated with every respect, and got a chair. We had time to make his acquaintance. He was middle-aged, with a dissipated, reckless look, full of animated conversation, very black, with flat nose and prominent teeth. His legs were masses of iron wire, fitting as tight as a stocking. He had many favours to ask; he would like so much to have a pair of our shoes, &c. He had sent two men, bearing the royal rod of his " M'kama" or sultan, to convey us with safety into the country. He hoped they had done their duty, for no Arab had ever such an honour paid him. There were ridiculous stories going about regarding uslas that we were possessed of supernatural powers, that we killed all the inhabitants of the country we passed through, and that we took possession of all countries; but, on his consulting the M'ganga, these reports were proved to be false, and we were admitted into the country. He paid us a second visit, dressed in a much less gaudy suit; and while he sat, eating coffee from a little basket he carried, we suggested that the tax had better be settled soon; but he treated the matter with great indifference, saying, " Oh, don't press it; let it take its time ! My brother will arrange it the day after to-morrow, because I have

THE WANYAMBO OF USUI. 129

to go into the district to see some patients; and now I must bid you adieu." The previous night he had sent us a message that some handsome cloths would be acceptable if we would have the kindness to present them. We did so, and in return he gave us two goats, and we saw no more of him.

The brother of the sirhidge, a more morose person, now came into the field, and said, " Before I can even broach the subject of your arrival here to his highness the M'kama (sultan), I expect a present;" and so the treaty dragged its length for several days, till officers appeared in camp pronouncing the demand, with little sticks to represent each article. About five men's loads of copper were paid and carried away for the chief by our men. Although the tax was heavy, it was conducted in a gentlemanly, quiet way, and much quicker than we had expected, on account, it was said, of their fear to detain magicians longer in the country. The last extortion was, that guides must escort us to the frontier, and they had to be paid a load of copper between them.

The people of tlie country, generally called Wan- yambo, dress in nothing but goat-skins, the length and shape of the tails of a shooting-coat, without pockets or buttons; a thong of leather ties this smartly round the waist, right side uppermost, and is slackened on sitting down; this forms their entire costume. With a variously-shaped spear or a bow and arrow (sometimes poisoned), they looked very active, slim fellows, having a far greater air about them than the Wezee. A tuft of wool is often left on their crowns; sometimes the teeth are entire, or the two upper incisors filed inside, but none are ever extracted. Some of the

130 SHOOT THIEVES.

people cover the body and arms with artificially raised solid blisters, in circles, waves, or lines. Their address, when it suited them, was that of cringing politeness, showing great respect every morning; but they could also be boisterous and insolent. The Wasui race can seldom be induced to carry loads; but amongst them numerous Wezees, driven from their homes by the Watuta, reside, and the traveller receives aid from them. A M'sui will carry a load on his head, but not upon the shoulder. On coming into camp to see the novelties, all the better class had a gourd of pombe" in one hand, and generally chewed coffee-beans. Round their ankles was a profusion of wires, generally more upon one leg than another. One stranger I saw wearing round his neck a flat piece of stone, which I thought to be malachite.

In this country we were more troubled by thieves than we had been anywhere else. After sunset our porters when beyond camp were assaulted, and their cloth coverings torn from them. At night they made several attempts to get inside our ring-fence of thorns, and the thefts became so numerous that we had to shoot two or three found plundering. The people rather approved of our doing this, and complimented us on being so alert and watchful during the night. They seemed generally to be an industrious people, with comfortable " crofts" round their houses.

The Walinga are workers in iron, scarcely distinguishable in dress from the Wasui. Their furnaces are in the heart of the forest; charcoal and lumps of iron cinder (like a coarse sponge, and of a " blue bottle" colour) usually mark the spot; and four lads, squatting under a grass roof with a double-handled bellows each,

A WATUSI QUEEN. 131

blow at a live mass of charcoal which has the nodules of metal intermixed with it. In this calcining nothing else seems to be used, and the metal melts, descending into a recess, much in the same way as I have seen at the Cumberland lead-works.

One morning, to my surprise, in a wild jungle we came upon cattle, then upon a " bomah," or ring-fence, concealed by beautiful umbrageous large trees, quite the place for a gypsy camp. At the entry two strapping fellows met me and invited my approach. I mingled with the people, got water from them, and was asked, "Would I not prefer some milk?" This sounded to me more civilised than I expected from Africans, so I followed the men, who led me up to a beautiful ladylike creature, a Watusi woman, sitting alone under a tree. She received me, without any expression of surprise, in the most dignified manner; and, after having talked with the men, rose smiling, showing great gentleness in her manner, and led me to her hut. I had time to scrutinise the interesting stranger: she wore the usual Watusi costume of a cow's skin reversed, teased into a frieze with a needle, coloured brown, and wrapped round her body from below the chest to the ankles. Lappets, showing zebra-like stripes of many colours, she wore as a " turnover" round the waist; and, except where ornamented on one arm with a highly polished coil of thick brass wire, two equally bright and massive rings on the right wrist, and a neck pendant of brass wire,|except these and her becoming wrapper, she was *au nalurelle.* I was struck with her peculiarly formed head and graceful long neck; the beauty of her fine eyes, mouth, and nose; the smaJlness of her hands and

132 WOMEN OF USUI.

naked feetlall were faultless; the only bad feature, which is considered one of beauty with them, was her large ears. The arms and elbows were rounded off like an egg, the shoulders were sloping, and her small breasts were those of a crouching Venusla perfect beauty, although darker than a brunette ! Her temporary residence was peculiarlit was formed of grass, was flat-roofed, and so low that I could not stand upright in it. The fireplace consisted of three stones; milk-vessels of wood, shining white from scouring, were ranged on one side of the abode. A good-looking woman sat rocking a gourd between her knees in the process of churning butter. After the fair one had examined my skin and my clothes, I expressed great regret that I had no beads to present to her. " They are not wanted," she said : " sit down, drink this buttermilk, and here is also some butter for you." It was placed on a clean leaf. I shook hands, patted her cheek, and took my leave, but some beads were sent her, and she paid me a visit, bringing butter and buttermilk, and asking for more presents, which she of course got, and I had the gratification to see her eyes sparkle at the sight of them. This was one of the few women I met during our whole journey that I admired. None of the belles in Usui could approach her; but they were of a different caste, though dressing much in the same style. When cow- skins were not worn, these Usui women dressed very tidily in bark cloths, and had no marks or cuttings observable on their bodies. Circles of hair were often shaved off the crowns of their heads, and their neck ornaments showed considerable taste in the selection of the beads. The most becoming were a string of the

CAIRNS OF STONES. 133

M'zizima, spheres of marble-sized white porcelain, and triangular pieces of shell, rounded at the corners. An erect fair girl, daughter of a chief, paid us a visit, accompanied by six maids, and sat silently for half an hour. She had a spiral circle of wool shaved off the crown of her head; her only ornament was a necklace of green beads : she wore the usual wrapper, and across her shoulders a strip of scarlet cloth was thrown ; her other fineries were probably left at home. The women of the district generally had grace and gentleness in their manner.

The plump little negro girls who came about our camp, standing with crossed arms and looking very frightened, are never allowed to shave their heads till they get married, consequently the hair is in matted tufts or mops, very ugly, with a triangular or square space shaved on the crown: if ornamented with cowries, the black wool appears to more advantage. They are not allowed to wear the usual clothing of women, but have the skin of a goat, with the hair inside, round their loins, and so arranged that from the waist to the knee it remains open, exposing completely the right thigh. Not having lived in their villages, we could not see any of their customs. The chief of Usui's residence, entitled Quikooroo, was a set of grass huts, encircled by three concentric fences of thorn, the largest one being two to three miles round. The other huts in the valley had no fence whatever, except where planted round with a dense quickset of euphorbia, growing from twelve to twenty feet high. Sometimes by the pathway we observed cairns of stones, such as are found all over the world, and our leading porters generally threw their mite on the heap. In Hindostan

134 LANGUAGE AND DANCING.

they would be called " Peer ke jaggeh," places of devotion ; and our Seedees called them " M'zeemoo." A rock was also passed, on which our porters placed pebbles.

The language of the country was quite unintelligible to our menlI mean as spoken by the Watusi, who are the reigning race here; but they did not find it difficult to pick up some words and phrases. It was not so hard as the dialect of Unyamuezi, which they considered more "bharee" (difficult). If one Seedee wishes to address another by saying, "I say," or "Old fellow!" he calls "Somoh!" lif a Muezi, " Doogoh yango ! "lif a M'sui, " Kunewani!"lif a M'ganda, "Awange"h!" There is no similarity in these;

consequently, to speak to any M'ganda, two interpreters were at first necessary, until our men picked up some of their language; but in their numerals they were almost the same.

The style of dance at Myonga's seemed to be peculiar to the country. It was conducted, without arms or any rough coarseness, by moonlight, in an open space, all the lads and lasses collecting without music. A circle was formed, singing and clapping of hands commenced, and either a woman made her most graceful curtsy to a favourite in the crowd, and retired skilfully backwards to her place, or a young fellow bounded into the centre, threw himself into attitudes, performed some gymnastic feat, bowed to the prettiest, and then made way for the next champion or fair lady.

After I had joined Speke at Bogweh on the 7th October 1861, a letter was received by him from Colonel Rigby, the consul at Zanzibar, dated 31st

STRANGER VISITORS. 135

October 1860, advising the despatch of brandy, biscuit, and cigars, &c.; and that our letters were in another packet. We, of course, were delighted at receiving this newsla whole year had elapsed without any communication whatever from the outer world; but where were the letters and supplies ? " Oh, they must have been lost in Ugogo, where the Arabs had gone to fight!" Whatever was the cause, our letters were cut off from us for the period of twenty-seven monthsl viz., from October 1860 to February 1863, when we got to Gondokoro. We had consequently to content ourselves with the news of the countries around us. Stories from men who had seen snow on the top of Kilimanjaro; with accounts of a tribe to the south of it who rode on horseback, and a salt lake called Lebassa in that direction; or the appearance of a M'ganda, tall, stout, broad-nostrilled, seen for the first time, gave me a longing desire, from his manly and true African look, to reach his country. The dress of this people was formed of gaily-coloured goat-skins and bark cloths, well arranged, striking, and becoming; their accoutrements and drums were got up with neatness and simplicity ; their drapery perfectly concealed the whole body, except the head, feet, and hands; and once a strapping girl, of a tribe still farther off, was shown to us as an Unyoro. Having since then seen her race, known by the extraction of the lower incisors, I can state that we were not imposed upon.

In the next chapter will be described the country of Karague, which reminded me of the English Lake district. An Arab caravan, like our own, but of 250 loads, had got ahead of us, and having settled their tax with the Usui chief, the men were plodding on to

136 OUR TABLE-ATTENDANT.

the ivory and slave mart. In their file two men and a girl were in chains togetherlno doubt recent investments. Our Seedees, by their curious ways, continued to amuse us. Our table-attendant, Mabrook, or Burton's " bull-headed Mabruki," was a thorough African, so opposite to what an Indian servant is. Ever naked from head to waist (and looking gross with fatness), he would come up to " lay the table," whistling or singing, with a bunch of knives, spoons, and forks in his hand ; having placed the tin lids and pots at our feet, he would squat on the ground beside them and dole out our dinner. Should he have to clean your plate, a bunch of grass or a leaf is generally within his reach; and, if he has to remove the plate, he seldom returns without wiping his mouth.

He chaffs his comrades as he sits by you; and dinner over, you see him eating with your spoons and drinking out of the teapot or the spout of the kettle.

8

SECTION 8

CHAPTER VIII.

KARAGUE, NOVEMBER 25 TO APRIL 14, 1862|THE ROYAL FAMILY |
HABITS OF THE SULTAN RUMANIKA | CRUSADER-LIKE CUSTOM AT NEW
MOON|IDOLATRY|THE SULTAN'S BROTHERS |DESCRIPTION OF KARAGUE
AND ITS NEIGHBOURHOOD | ILLNESS OF THE AUTHOR|ENGLISH GAR-
DEN PEASE|MARKETS, COFFEE-TRADERS|EARLIEST INFORMATION RE-
GARDING THE NILE|THE TWO RACES OF KARAGUE, THE WAHUMA AND
WAYAMBO|THE PRINCESSES|ROYAL RESIDENCE|MUSICAL INSTRUMENTS.

The royal family of Karague consisted of three brothers and their families. Their
father, Dagara, had died about eight years previous to our visit. He had lived to a
good old age ; was almost a giant in height, with leprous hands, of theWahuma caste;
was esteemed a wise and sagacious prince, and was very popular with the people. On
his death, his body was sewn up in the skin of a cow, and placed inside a hut, with
several women and cattle, who were there all left to die and moulder to dust. The
question of succession was disputed by three surviving sons, and the test as to who
should ultimately rule was that some sacred emblem would be placed before all, and
whoever should raise it from the ground would become the reigning sovereign.

138 RUMANIKA OF KARAGUE.

Rumanika, not the eldest, was found to be the only one of the three competent, or who felt conscientiously that he could support the dignity of the position by raising this weight from the ground; consequently he was elected. From that time a younger brother, Ro- gaerah, became his bitter enemy, and fled to a corner of the province, taking with him a great proportion of the people with their cattle, as he was the more generous and the greater favourite of the two brothers. But Rumanika's mother had to be got rid of before he could properly hold the reins of government; and by some magic medicine she was killed, and he was declared " M'kama of Karague."

Although illness prevented my seeing so much of Rumanika as I should otherwise have liked, I could not but notice that he was the handsomest and most intelligent sovereign we had met with in Africa. He stood six feet two inches in height, and his countenance had a fine, open, mild expression. There was nothing of the African look about him, except that he had wool instead of hair. His dress was a robe of numerous skins of small antelopes sewn together, and knotted over one shoulder,with a loin-cloth underneath; or an Arab cloak or shawl of bark-cloth hung from his shoulder, reaching below the knee. Going about with nothing on his head, his arms bare, except common ornaments of beads or brass, with painted porcelain beads on his ankles, and carrying a long staff, he was altogether the picture of the gentle shepherd of his flock. His four young sons, of ages from sixteen to twenty-four, were tall, smart, nice-looking young fellows|quite gentlemanly in their manners, and very cleanly in their persons and dress. There

HIS WIVES AND FAMILY. 139

was a younger son, an infant, always kept at the royal residence, and not allowed out. The five wives of the king have been described by Captain Speke: several were of enormous proportions, unable to enter the door of an ordinary hut, requiring a person on each side to support them when moving from one place to another, and expressing great delight at any present the " Wazoongo " (white men) should send their lord and master. Their diet, and that of the sons and daughters, was generally boiled plantain or milk. They considered their existence depended on the latter article of food, and certainly they all throve admirably upon it|the sons were full of vigour, and the women were fat and healthy, though not prolific. On Captain Speke asking to be allowed to take a young prince to England for education, the cry was, " They had never been more than ten miles from home; how could they go?|there would be no milk for them|they would die." Probably they had also some dread that the lads would be made slaves of. All of them were very particular and fastidious as to their diet.

The sultan drank milk; thought the meat of goat and sheep unclean; would not eat fish, fowl, or guinea- fowl; rarely or never touched stirabout; and merely sucked the juice of boiled beef. He drank very little plaintain-wine, and was never known to be intoxicated. He had many superstitions; he would not drink out of the vessel that we or any commoner had used, and he combined the offices of prophet, priest, and king. As prophet, he would place the tusks of an elephant upright on the ground, fill them with charms, seal them, and predict rain, although his calculations were not always correct. As priest, three days after

140 KING'S FONDNESS FOR CURIOSITIES.

new moon, he sat concealed, all but his head, in the doorway of his chief hut, and received the salutations of his people, who, one by one, shrieked and sprang in front of him, swearing allegiance. His head on these occasions was wonderfully dressed, and made to look quite patriarchal, with a crown of beads and feathers, and a false white beard of considerable length, giving him the look of an Indian " khitmutgar" or Jewish rabbi He was very fond of curiosities, and amongst the collection he had obtained from Arab visitors were stuffed birds, an electric battery, looking-glasses, a clock with eyes in the cast-iron figure made to roll with the movement of the pendulum, &c. He expressed surprise that we had brought nothing to amuse him, so that all our ingenuity was put to the test in order to try and gratify his highness. A jumping-jack made of wood was sent him for his infant son, and he said he must have me make him one the size of life before I left the country. He had a three-pounder brass gun brought him unmounted from the coast; and on a picture being sent him, showing how we in India drag guns into action by means of elephants, nothing would satisfy him till he had ordered fifty men to cut down trees, to be made into a gun-carriage. I protested, saying, " You have no iron|no elephant; who is to make the wheels?" Here was a dilemma| a wheel to make before I could be allowed to join my companion, and nothing to make it with but a penknife in my pocket! Luckily my friend Rumanika was not pig-headed, and had compassion on me when it was explained to him that ropes of bark, and men to drag the gun, would not answer the purposes of iron and elephant.

HIS VENERATION FOR LIONS. 141

This sovereign several times came to call while I lay sick, one day bringing me a fish alive in a jar from the lake; this pleased me, as the Wahuma have a prejudice against fish. But his chief delight seemed to be in medicines and pictures. It was an anxious moment when our tent was emptied of all listeners, and *we* were pressed for a medicinal charm to bring about the death of his brother Rogaerah. Then, during the visit, the weight of the mercury, its reflections, &c., were looked at in amazement; the compass |"was there water in it?"|our shoes, our bedding| all were marvels. With the sextant he looked through at the sun without fear; and when consulted one morning by my servant about some strange large animals that came in at night to our camp, he recommended that the next time they appeared we should challenge them three times, and if no answer were received, to fire at them; for "depend upon it they were enemies sent by his rebel brother to lay a trap for him." Should they, however, prove to be leopards, they were not to be molested. For all leopards they have a great reverence, asDagara, the late sovereign, is believed to be still protected by them; and on an invading army coming from Uganda, this sultan had the power to send leopards to disperse them. Their skins are only worn by royalty or its followers. The sultan, on seeing the picture of some of his milk-carriers, sent for the sketch-book, turned out all idlers, and showed them to a few favourite servants about his family. His wives were quite clamorous about seeing them, asking why Rumanika had not been drawn. The back view of a naked young prince, enormously fat, with clotted long hair concealing his neck, gave them

142 THE KING'S BROTHER, M'NANAGEE.

great amusement, and they clapped their hands and laughed with joy at the resemblance to the original. All the princesses living in separate houses got jealous unless they saw the sketches, so that my servant was several times detained a whole day by them; and it became so fashionable to look at the pictures, that for days my camp was beset with people wishing to have their curiosity gratified. M'nanagee, the brother of the sultan, a man of six feet three inches in height, brought his favourite bow to be ornamented with pictures. There never was a prettier bit of stick; it was exactly his own height, of ash-coloured wood, bent merely at the ends, balanced beautifully, not a curve in it that could hurt the eye, and it was strung with the sinews of a cow. He could with ease throw an arrow, by giving it a high flight, 150 or 200 yards. Wishing to enlighten and amuse Rumanika, I sent him coloured pictures of our soldiers, and of men in ordinary costume; these he admired very much, but could I not show him how our ladies looked ? Certainly. Figures of three ladies were painted|one in morning costume, one at an archery meeting using the bow and arrow, and a third in ball costume. He immediately hung all up on the wall of his small hut; and on inquiring which figure pleased him most, the palm was given to the evening costume.

Whenever he wished to spend the day at a spot on the hill across the lake, where I think his father had been interred, he was carried in a basket, made of osiers, by four men. The band led the way with music; several hundred followers surrounded him; and if he was on the return journey, small fat boys, having their heads wreathed with water-lilies plucked

A BAND OF THIRTY-THREE DRUMS. 143

in the lake as they ferried over, danced and skipped up the hill the whole way to the sound of the pleasing drum and bugle band. His revenue was said to be one jar out of every three of plantain-wine; and all his guests coming from the neighbouring provinces had to be fed by the farmers around. It has always been the custom of Uganda, Usui, and Karague, that when any one of their chiefs sends messengers to the other, the royal bearers are free to settle where they like, and to provision themselves as they require from the stores of the people, no payment being ever taken for anything. Plantain is so common that nothing is said if a stranger is seen plucking a bunch from a tree; but at night many disturbances and frequent fights occur when a raid is made for goats. Stones fly, spears are thrown, and all is in confusion, if anything beyond a bunch of plantain is attempted to be carried *off.*

We were asked to witness a new-moon ceremony. This generally takes place three days after the first appearance of the luminary, and it was celebrated as usual by our men firing volleys in the air. The sultan assumes the priestly garb, and dons his long, false, white beard on this occasion. His whole body remains concealed behind a screen, and he has beside him his insignia of office, either a small drum, or an instrument which no one but himself can raise. The drums, generally thirty-three, are on the ground, in a line, each having a large white cross on its head|a strange Crusader-like custom. A man stands behind each, and the leader, with two small drums, is in front to give the time. On his raising the right arm, the thirty-three drummers do the same, then the left arm,

144 STORIES TOLD BY THE SULTAN.

and they gradually beat the drums quicker, till ending in a tremendous roll. This continues for three hours, with intervals, and is repeated the day following. A band of hand-drums is near the sultan's hut, giving lighter dance-music for the amusement of the boys and girls, who must make merry as the new- moon term comes round.

Rumanika was on excellent terms with the neighbouring kings of Uganda and Unyoro, often exchanging presents with them. He had sent to M'tesa of Uganda a book printed in English (" Kaffir Laws"), which we saw on getting to Uganda; and they would send to him for powder, cloth, &c., he being supposed by the chiefs living further north to have easier access to the coast. In return for these favours, or for the gift of a porcelain cup, or neatly-made ankle or wrist ornaments in brass or copper, &c., he would expect to receive ivory, cattle, or slaves. Curious enough, none of these kings had ever visited each other, consequently their ideas of foreign countries were very limited, and they believed any story a designing traveller might choose to tell them. Rumanika, for instance, expected to have seen us always dressed in white cambric shirts, instead of which we had no soap to wash our flannel ones! Was it true that we made doors out of his ivory ? He told us the road to the north was a most dangerous one; we could not march through it without 200 guns ! One race we should have to pass through were pigmies; others lived in trees, and seized women; dogs we should come across with horns, sheep with three horns, and men travelled about with a stool tied behind them. This last was partly true, for we found the Wagani carrying little stools on their arms; and

SUPERSTITIONS. 145

" those living in trees " may allude to M. Du Chaillu's gorilla!

We could not trace any distinct form of religion amongst this interesting race, but there were certain indications or traces of Jewish worship. A piece of copper, made up in the form of a grapple or anchor, two feet long, lay near the door of the sultan's hut. We were told this was to represent the horns of cattle, and had a sacred signification. It was placed upright in the ground on the occasion of the monthly festivities, and looked like what the Brahmins of India might have assumed as an idol. The cleanly huts of the Wahuma race reminded me of Indians; also the superstition of not drinking out of the same cup with you. The moon in its different phases was thought to laugh at us. A tree was considered the greatest object in the creation, not even excepting man. Lions protected the mausoleum of Dagara, the former sultan ! " No kingdom was so powerful as this; no one dare attack us! Lions guard us !" Captain Speke could not kill any hippopotami in the lake, because he had made no present to the invisible god, or " deo," who lived upon it; and the sultan of Unyoro could divide the waters of the lake with a rod!

A younger prince, M'nanagee, was equally tall and erect with his brother Rumanika, and he was even a greater prophet and priest. The natives had unbounded faith in his powers as a diviner. Daily did he walk to a stone on the face of the hill, or he might be seen going to visit some stuffed elephant-tusks placed in the ground within an enclosure, for the purpose of daily consultation with his gods. Although M'nanagee had these peculiarities, he was friendly 146 M'nanagee And His Sons.

and gentlemanly, always ready to give any information he might possess; rather formal at first, with a haughty air, but ever kind in getting us provisions, assisting in the knowledge of plants and herbs, and very modest in his requests for presents. His dress did not differ much from the people of the country; the usual short leather wrapper hid his loins, and a sheet of cotton check kept his shoulders and body warm. The head was shaved bare, and a strap, holding a charm, was tied round the back of it. Bunches of charms hung on his arms and from his neck and below the knee, and huge masses of wire were on his ankles. He always carried a long walking-stick, with a charm of wood tied at one end. A small boy, very fat, carried his chowrie, or fly-flapper, and a huge black pipe, the size of half a goose's egg, with a long stem. On paying me visits he was seldom accompanied by any one. His eldest son measured six feet five inches; but, though quite as gentle as the father, was not so good-looking, and seldom came to visit me. A younger one, not more than two or three years old, died while I was at Karague, rather suddenly, and the father mourned greatly for the child, crying most grievously. The body was buried, the sultan said, in an island on the lake, whereas his barber told me it was placed under rocks on the face of the hill. I am. inclined to think the former statement correct, as the islands in the lake are considered sacred ground; while the Wanyambo (the peasants of the country) deposit their dead in the waters of the lake. M'nana- gee had a firm belief in evil spirits. He knew them to be about his country, and felt certain as to the fact; but it was possible, he thought, for clever people

VALLEY OF URIGI. 147

like those at Zanzibar to confuse their designs for certain periods.

A third brother, to whom we had to make presents on our arrival in Karague, was named Roazerah. On sending a gift of a red cloth and some beads, &c., he asked what he could give in return. " Would a tusk be received ?" " No." " Would they like a slave ? " "No," said Bombay; "give them a couple of cows, that their men may have a feast." Though older than either of the other brothers, he could not succeed to the throne of his father, because he had been born before his father became a crowned king. In like manner, none of the princes at present in Karague can succeed to their father, as all were born while he was a prince.

The chief possessions of this family are bounded on the north by the river Kitangule. The valley of Urigi divides the kingdom on the south from Usui, and its total extent is from 3000 to 4000 square miles of hills, dale, and lake, standing at a general elevation of 4500 feet above the level of the sea. Entering it from the south, the hills, rising 200 to 300 feet above the valleys, are covered with waving grasses; a few trees run in lines with certain strata, almost with the regularity of plantations; and very often dense brushwood, the refuge of the rhinoceros, crowns two-thirds of their tops, or runs down the ravines or water-cuts to the valleys below. They have a very desolate appearance, all the habitations being in the lower grounds: a traveller is seldom met with. On the more precipitous hills, rock-fragments and jutting-out masses of sandstone-shingle lie at a steep angle on their slopes; and the path, of splinters from these,148 "little Windermere."

goes up and down, or makes long circuits to get round the spurs, seldom displaying any pleasing scene except the freshness of the young grasses after having been burnt. These reminded me of the "Emerald Isle," and when the view on reaching the residence of Ru- manika, the reigning king, burst upon us, all hardships and trials were forgotten and forgiven. As you stand on the greensward, you see, 1000 feet below you, and two miles distant, the sweetly-lying lake of Karague, " Little Windermere," reposing in oval form amidst gently-swelling grassy hills, so surrounded as to puzzle one to think where the waters come from, and where they make their escape. On its western shore, trees hang over its clear sweet waters; wooded islands dot its glassy surface, and a deep fringe of the papyrus borders its southern side. But the most interesting sight to us was looking away to the far west over four distinct parallel ranges of hill, with water (Lakes Kagaera, Ooyewgomah, &c.) showing here and there between them; and occasionally about sunset, after the foggy mists had cleared away, appeared a sugar-loaf mountain, known to the natives as " M'foom- baero," or Cook . It is the largest hill in the country, and caused, on first view, quite a sensation, attracting our intense admiration by its towering height. Two brother cones, but lower, lie to its left, and all are so steep, that the natives said few attempt their ascent, having to do it on hands and knees. Their distance from where we stood was calculated at fifty miles. Unfortunately they could not be reached, as they were off our direct route, and in a different kingdom, and many obstacles intervened; so that our

RAINY SEASON IN KARAGUE. 149

only privilege was *to* look at them when not veiled in mists, at sunset.

The capital of Karague is 1 40' south of the equator, within a complete belt of vapour the whole year round. Fruitful showers seemed to fall continually. There are no very marked seasons, as winter and summer. On the same day, sowing, gathering, and reaping may be seen, and from November till April the fall of rain increases or diminishes according as the sun becomes more or less vertical to our position. The natives had their reasons for knowing this also; for when asked, on the 2d December 1861 (when we were having abundant showers), " How long is this to last ?|when does your rainy season commence ?"|they at once said, " With the new moon," which corresponded with the time for the sun to return towards its more vertical position. Again, when asking them, " When have you your heaviest rains ?" the reply was, "At the time the Mohammedans call Ramezan," which is equivalent to our equinoctial period in March, when the sun crosses our zenith. A note about this time is as follows :|" 17th March 1862. The weather looks black, peals of thunder with lightning; 1.65 inches of rain fell straight and thick, with occasional hail, in one hour." The fall increased in quantity from this day till it reached its climax about the 10th of April, when it began again to decline. In December till January 7, the usual maximum temperature in a grass hut open to the south was observed to be 81, and the minimum 56, at an elevation of 5000 feet above the level of the sea. We had a great number of dull English

150 CAPTAIN SPEKE DEPARTS FOR UGANDA.

days, very few bright ones, never an Italian sky, as too many vapours hung about this equatorial region. The dews were heavy, and lay long, and the mould getting amongst plants was very disheartening to the collector, obliging him to discard many a souvenir. Brushwood was used instead of firewood, which was scarce and dear, otherwise the chilly mornings and nights might have been cheered by the watchfire. The country was luckily so hilly, that, though the rain dashed with the N.E. wind into the red clayey soil, making the hill-sides stream with muddy rivulets, one hour after the " pelt" all had run down, and a gleam of sunshine made the ground not unpleasant to walk upon. The health of the men did not seem to suffer from wet. Zanzibar people are accustomed to getting ducked. It keeps them occupied in repairing their grass huts, collecting firewood, and making merry over it, rather than causing despondency. With one case of ophthalmia, and a few of fever, there were no other cases of sickness amongst the half-dozen men left by Speke on the 10th Jcinuary, when he departed for Uganda, leaving me behind sick. At first sight this appeared to some persons at home as an unkind proceeding, leaving a helpless " brother" in the heart of Africa; but my companion was not the man to be daunted; he was offered an escort to the north, and all tender feelings must yield to the stern necessities of the case. " Strike while the iron is hot," applies to Africa more appropriately than to any country I know; another such opportunity might never occur, and had the traveller's determination of character been softened, and had he not proceeded without me at that time, we might never again I so little upsets theThe Author's Illness. 151

mind of an African chieflhave had the road opened to us.

The following account of my own ailments I give, not with a wish to parade them, but in order to convey information :IHaving had. fevers twice a-month, in December my usual complaint assumed a new form. The right leg, from above the knee, became deformed with inflammation, and remained for a month in this unaccountable state, giving intense pain, which was relieved temporarily by a deep incision and copious discharge. For three months fresh abscesses formed, and other incisions were made; my strength was prostrated; the knee stiff and alarmingly bent, and walking was impracticable. Many cures were attempted by the natives, who all sympathised with me in my sufferings, which they saw were scarcely endurable; but I had great faithIwas all along cheerful and happy, except at the crisis of this helpless state, when I felt that it would have been preferable to be nearer home. The disease ran its course, and daily, to bring out the accumulated discharge, I stripped my leg like a leech. Bombay had heard of a poultice made of cow-dung, salt, and mud from the lake; this was placed on hot, but it merely produced the effect of a tight bandage. Baraka was certain that a serpent had spat upon my legI"it could not have been a bite." Dr M'nanagee, the sultan's brother, knew the disease perfectly; he could send me a cure for itland a mild gentle peasant of the Wanyambo race came with his wife, a young pleas- ing-like person, to attend me. With the soft touch of a woman he examined the limb, made cuts over the skin with a penknife, ordered all lookers-on outside

152 RECOVERY FROM ILLNESS.

the hut, when his wife produced a scroll of plantain- leaf, in which was a black paste. This was moistened from the mouth and rubbed into the bleeding cuts, making them smart; afterwards a small piece of lava was dangled against my leg and tied as a charm round the ankle. Two days afterwards he found no improvement, and, having repeated some mystic words behind me, another charm of wood and goat's flesh was tied above the knee and round the ankle, much in the same way as a kind lady-friend in Scotland once sent me a string of soda-water corks to be worn at night as a cure for cramp ! Paste, very like gunpowder, was rubbed into fresh cuts, and this was repeated without any result, although the charms had been on for two days. M'nanagee, seeing his medical adviser had failed, sent an herb to soak in water and rub over the part; it had a very soothing effect, but did not allay the pain. He had seen me apply the leaves of the castor-oil plant as a hot bandage, and forbade their use a second time as being injurious, having given me a delirious fever, and causing a counter-action of profuse discharge of water from the limb. By the fifth month the complaint had exhausted itself; at last I was able to be out of the hut inhaling the sweet air, and once more permitted to behold the works of God's creation in the beautiful lake and hills below me. Never did I experience a happier moment! During this illness, the family at the palace were very kind in coming to sit by me; the young sons brought me plants in flower, birds' nests, eggs, or other things which they thought might interest me; while I sketched for them or their father, and sent a servant to get the news, and ask for the

VISITS OF THE NATIVES. 153

king every morning. Since Speke had left, there was considerable difficulty in getting supplies, and the sultan was not so kind in this respect as he might have been; but, African like, he had received his presents, and until more were given him he withheld sending goat, fowls, or other necessaries, which my men had to hunt the country for. One poor fellow lost his life in doing so. Two were together; the natives set upon them while bringing home loads of grain; they shot one with arrows, the other ran for his life, and slept all night up a tree, afraid to go near a village. On asking him, " Did you sleep ?" "0 yes, I tied myself with rope to the boughs, and slept several hours." The sultan sought for redress from the village, but all the people had decamped in fear. Several other natives paid me almost daily calls|officers, barbers, ivory-traders, musicians, &c., in whom a good deal of character could be observed. At night my few men would gather round their fire, and, particularly after having an extra allowance of plantain- wine, sing a ditty about my health. Frij on the single-stringed zeze or guitar would commence|" I am Frij, I am Frij; my brother Grin (meaning Grant), my brother Grin, is very sick, is very sick; well get a cow, we'll get a cow, when he gets well, when he gets well," to which the others would all subscribe in a louder voice, " Ameen," with the most perfect solemnity. My couch or bed, the height of a table, was formed of the trunks of plantain-trees covered with grass and blankets. This was roofed over with a low grass hut, having its gable end wide open to the south, where no wind blew from at that season. Much to the surprise of the natives, there was no fence round our encampment.

154 NATIVE CURES AND MEDICINES.

By day, dogs walked into our huts, and by night hyena often carried away our fowls. Indeed, while lying awake, one came sniffing with his nose in the air up to my couch, and ran sulkily away on my shouting at him. One cannot say whether he would have sprung upon me had I been asleep, but the precaution of a trap was taken for several nights following.

The most curious disease known in this country was a case of dropsy brought to be operated upon. Some days after having seen it, and declined the operation, a number of watery globules, the size of common marbles, were brought me upon a leaf, said to have been extracted from the person afflicted. This operation they performed generally without fatal consequences, and the disease was not uncommon. There were several leprous people, favourites about the court. One, an old woman, who saluted us with " Vihoreh," had flesh-coloured hands and colourless patches on her arms. M'nanagee complained of not being able to drink his usual fare of milk; and though his knowledge of herbs was very extensive, he could not cure himself. One of his favourite medicines was a preparation from the long roots of nettles found growing in the shallow end of the lake. These, I was informed, were used in decoction as purgatives. On my requesting him to give me his tapeworm medicine, it was obtained with considerable difficulty. The servant was told to go to a certain bush on the hillside, never to look back on his way thither, but to return without plucking the plant if he should meet a dog ! Through the kindness of M'nanagee, his nephews, and others, a species of frankincense and many interesting plants were examined and preserved.

KARAGUE. 155

The country of Karague rarely affords space flat enough for a single tent to be pitched, but there are thousands of acres now in grass which are perfectly capable of profitable cultivation. Captain Maury, of the United States navy, at the British Association meeting in 1863, stated his opinion that this region, from its equatorial position and moist atmosphere, would make an excellent coffee-growing country; and as many parts resemble portions of the Himalayas, where tea is grown, and there are no frosts at Karague, I think it is admirably adapted for the culture of tea as well as coffee. Wild grapes were occasionally gathered in the lower grounds, but no beds of gravel similar to those at home or on the Continent, where the vine flourishes in such luxuriance, are to be seen. A few clumps of wild date-trees grow in the valleys, but the natives are ignorant of the sexes of the trees, and never have any fruit. Sugar-cane is seldom or never grown. There are two heavy crops in the year|sorghum and plantain ; while pease (English garden), a species of bean or calavance, called "maharageh," Indian corn, &c., are grown at other seasons. All these we saw ripe or ripening, and fresh shoots of plantain were being set, while other fields were prepared for the heavier crop of red sorghum, sown in March. Then squads of men and women assemble, probably only one-fifth working at a time, the rest standing, lounging, and laughing. The men, with a hook having a three-feet-long handle, slash down the weeds, women hoe them up, collect the stones, clear the ground, and give it the tidy appearance of a garden. In February great care is bestowed upon the plantain, which affords one of the staples of life in this country throughout the year. Acres of

156 PRICE OF PROVISIONS.

it cover the hillsides, a rivulet sometimes dividing the field; the trunks are trimmed of the leaves which have been torn into shreds by the wind ; fresh shoots are planted; and the whole orchard is industriously superintended.

The natives asked us ludicrous prices for their products. Our beads, the manufacture of Venice, were of little value, from fourteen to twenty-five (size of pigeon-eggs) being given for a single goat, and a proportionate number for a cow. This our Seedees thought a great contrast to their native country of Uhiao, where a bucketful of flour, with a fowl on the top, could be obtained for one necklace of ordinary beads. But here the women were double the size round the waist that they were anywhere else, and they must have beads enough to begird them once before a goat can be parted with. They would refuse us milk and butter, because it was not their custom to sell them, and because we eat fowls, and the bean called maha- rageh; but on making them a present of several coils of brass wire (thirteen), we could procure a quart- sized wooden jar of butter. In November, grain is scarce. The natives brought salt to exchange for it; and on being offered meat instead, they have been known to refuse it, because the allowance was not so large and satisfactory to them as grain. When marching, the head-men of the villages had orders from their sultan to supply our camp with sufficient provision for the day. A quantity of sweet potatoes, some pumpkins, fowls, and a goat, were generally given, and a present of cloth and brass wire was made them in return. Plantain-wine was seldom presented: it seemed to have conveniently run dry on our arrival! English

TOBACCO AND PLANTAIN-WINE. 157

garden-pease were first seen in this part of Africa by Speke, and with the aid of the sultan we were able to lay in a supply of this delicacy, not in their green form, but dry and dead ripe, boiling and making them into a mash. They were grown broadcast in considerable quantities about Meegongo. Tobacco, ripe in April, we could always procure, but it was extravagant in price|six pipefuls of the finest description costing the daily ration allowance of one porter. The sultan smoked a very full-flavoured description in his large pipe. We tried to discover from an old man, his one-eyed tobacconist, the secret of its preparation; but he would not divulge it unless a handsome reward was given. It had a rich mellow aroma, more pleasant than any tobacco we had ever smoked; and whether it was from rubbing the leaf in his perfumed hands, using a secretion from the cow, or that honey was mixed in it, we never could discover. He would not allow that any ingredient was used|the tobacco when green was merely rubbed in his hands. In December beautiful granulated honey was offered for sale. Though there were few bees to be seen in this country, their produce was always procurable in small quantities, and it was of excellent though sometimes of highly flowery flavour.

Plantain-wine, called here "marwa," was made by every family that had an orchard of the trees. It is a sweet raisiny-tasting wine; if aerated, nearly equal to sparkling hock in richness of flavour. A quart could be taken with comfort, but after the third day it becomes dead, sour, and intoxicating; our men got so riotous from it that the sultan was requested not to send us the daily allowance of one gourdful.

158 TRADE OF KARAGUE.

Ridiculous scenes of drunkenness would sometimes occur. One Seedee with a gun would in his intoxication chase another through the fields; others with guns would fly to prevent bloodshed. At last the original offender would have so many guns pointed at him that he would surrender, and then his gun would be found not loaded !

The process of making plantain-wine in Karague takes generally from two to three days. A huge log scooped out, and looking like a canoe, is essential for a large quantity. It is tilted at one end, and dammed up with grass in the centre. Ripe fruit has clean grass put amongst it. A woman mashes all at the upper end with her hands or feet. The liquor strains through the dam, and is again strained with grass till clean. All the liquid is then placed for fermentation in the " canoe " freshly cleaned. Some burnt, bruised sorghum is placed in it; all is covered up from the air, and allowed to remain in the sun or near a fire for two or three days, when it is skimmed and fit for use. Wine is never exported or bottled, and probably not a drop of the brewing can be obtained after the lapse of only four days. All, even the youngest children amongst the peasants, drink it, carrying gourd- fills of it about with them wherever they go, as regularly as we carry our purses.

Of the natural products of the equatorial regions, such as slaves, ivory, salt, copper, iron, bark-cloths, coffee, and sugar-cane, Karague scarcely yields any, but it is a great depot for trade. Arabs and coastmen bring up beads, cloths, and brass wire, and meet people of all the nations around, and trade with them for ivory and slaves. Copper and salt are brought from

TRADE AND PRICES. 159

beyond Paroro to exchange for brass wire. N'kole is justly celebrated for its tobacco, though every hut here has its garden of it. Ruanda sends her painted matting, goat, salt, and iron wire, and requests the sultan, who drives a stiff bargain, to fix the price of each article las, 160 ankle-wires l a single necklace; a goat = twenty necklaces. The Wanyamuezi carry salt from their country to exchange it for the ivory brought by the people of Unyoro, N'kole, and UtumbL Bark-cloths are not made well in Karague : the people of Uganda, Kittara, and Uhia excel in them. They are sewn in four stripes, each a foot to 18 inches broad, and, when well greased by the Wanyambo, make a most comfortable, becoming square shawl to keep out the cold and rain. During the 1861 war in Unyanyembe (at 5 S.) a slave might be purchased for something under one shilling sterling, or, if estimated in beads, ten necklaces. If a number of them were brought up (as they have been in several instances) to the equator and beyond it, they would each fetch a frasila, or 36 lb. weight of ivory, equal to $12 in Zanzibar. This is one of the inducements for Arabs and Africans to speculate, but the instance is exceptional.

Trade encounters great difficulties in such a country, where there are no regular laws, no roads, no carriage conveyance, and the caravan is liable to losses from heavy taxes, desertions, and attacks. For instance, two traders, named Sungoro and Joomah, left Karague while I was there for the south with a considerable supply of ivory. On reaching the borders of the first province (Usui), they sent forward to ask the sultan's permission to pass through his country. A demur was made that the party was too strong, but they would

160 THE COUNTRY OF UHIA.

be permitted. When once in the chief's power, he demanded half their ivory as a tax. Provisions were very dear; they resisted, they complained, all to no purpose ; and they were told to cultivate the soil if they chose, but that they would not be allowed to depart till the demand was paid. Rumanika interfered and got them out of the trouble, otherwise they would have been detained there for many months. In Ugogo and Unyamuezi the chief claims a tusk of every elephant found dead or killed; he gets the tusk from the cheek that lies nearest the ground. There is no such law in Karague. Amongst the curiosities in tusks, we heard of one so large that it could not be carried to the coast, and that one elephant had been seen with four tusks! Both stories, like those about fences being made of them in some countries, are, of course, among the fables of the natives.

Between Karague and the Victoria Nyanza there is a country called Uhia or Mohia, whose people are traders to the north. They also bring coffee to Karague for sale in bundles covered with plantain-leaf, containing two handfuls, which they sell very dearly at one necklace of beads. It takes a handful to make a pint of very inferior coffee, as the bean, when the loose husk is taken off, is not larger than half a grain of rice. In this state the natives chew it as a sailor does tobacco. It is pleasant, inducing saliva, and leaving a comfortable flavour in the mouth. When our store of tea and coffee was consumed, we found this, when roasted and infused for drinking, a substitute, but very inferior, because the bean had not been allowed to come to perfection when it was pulled. The natives do not make use of it as we do, but refresh

THE NATIVES OF UHIA AND RUANDA. 161

themselves on a journey by throwing two or three beans, husks and all, into their mouths. Several of these Wahia traders were seen I sturdy, very black, middle - sized men, with bare, unshaven heads and beards. Their dress was a cow-skin, having the leg parts neatly rounded off, of a saffron yellow, and friezed inside, knotted over the right shoulder, and hanging to the middle of the thigh. This dress is sometimes worn with the hair outside : above it they generally wore a brick - coloured bark - cloth, well greased. Their ornaments were a sheep or goat's horn, tied jauntily with a strip of leather round their bare heads, and a few solid rings, crow-quill thickness, worn round the ankles. Their arms were differently shaped, as was their dress, from those 6f any race we had met with. The spear-shaft was six feet long, and the spear was heart-shaped, or like the ace of spades. Jumah, a coast-trader, called them a bad, unsafe set of people, probably because they were rivals in his business. He also abused the Ruanda people, because they refused to allow any coast-men into their kingdom, which, he said, was even more populous than Uganda. The specimens seen by us were merely men from its borders, who had come with produce by water in three days from the west. They were tall, lean men, with the shortest loin-cover of skin I ever saw; of the same pattern as, but even smaller than, those worn by the natives of Usui. The above native gentleman, Jumah, had travelled a great deal, had sailed on Victoria Nyanza, had attempted the ascent of Kilimanjaro, had made great friends with the king of Uganda, and said he could converse in at least ten different African languages. I begged to differ with him as to their

162 Jumah's Stories About Kilimanjaro.

being distinct languages; but he insisted that each was as different from the other as Baniani is to Hindoo. He was of East Indian origin, though he could not speak its language, and had acquired all the superstitious notions of the Seedee. However, .during my illness he paid me constant visits, afforded me a great deal of amusement, and was a kind, hospitable man. He told strange tales about the snow-capped mountain Kilimanjaro, which has since been ascended by my friend the Baron von der Decken, gold-medallist (with myself) of the Royal Geographical Society for 1864. When encamped at Chaga, Jumah could see it change colour "five times during the day. First it was white in the early morning, then changed into black, green, brown, and, lastly, scarlet, like a red blanket. He thought the colours were not reflections from snowithe sun was too hot for any to thereithey were stones! and he picked up several carnelian-coloured pebbles at its base. He and all Arabs firmly believe that the mountain can never be ascended by either black or white man. Though gold is there in abundance, no one dare dig for itla demon has possession ! Even Speke could not go up it, unless the devil should take fright at the face of a white man! He mustered courage one day, and determined to try the ascent, but he was struck with a huge swelling in both limbs, which disappeared as suddenly as it came. Was not this a caution ? and did it not show that it was possessed ?" Jumah was full of these tales, and of his brave fights with supernatural characters. Of Uganda he gave me a great deal of accurate information, describing the numbers of people who are daily killed there by order of the

TRADE IN IVORY. 163

king; and he thought if M'tessa were asked not to rule so cruelly, that a greater sacrifice would be the only consequence. " It was not from any love he had for destruction of life, as he was an amiable young man, but from its being the ancient custom of the country; and were it not done, the fear was that the people would become rebellious. Besides which, was not the country swarming with people ? did it not abound with food ? did they not love the king's rule, and prefer his sentence of death to a natural one, as being more princely ?" Jumah had made M'tessa a considerable present, which will illustrate the manner of trading in this part of the world. A gold-embroidered silk scarf or deolee, value $50, a " mucknuff," a gold-embroidered vest, two men's loads of blue beads, half a load of brass wire, a small tiara, value $1, and two flint-muskets without powder, constituted his gift. The king, in return, gave him 700 lb. weight of ivory (some of the tusks weighing 90 lb.), seven women, and fifty cows; besides which Jumah asked for his two guns to be returned. In receiving these he considered himself well repaid, as one-third belonged to himself, the rest to his master in Zanzibar. He had been trafficking for three years in this way without ever visiting the coast, and meant to remain another year, when he would have completed collecting 500 frasila, equal to 17,500 lb. of ivory. This mode of fair dealing is very different to what takes place at the Nile trading-marts to the north of the equator. There guns and bullets, in the hands of Nubians employed by European, Turkish, and Armenian masters, assist in capturing the herds of cattle used in paying porters and purchasing ivory. If a tax is asked, all that is

164 FIRST TIDINGS OF THE NILE.

given, as one of them told us, is the muzzle of a gun. It seems marvellous, therefore, that the Zanzibar traders who pay as Jumah did, or buy tusks at the market price of weight for weight in Venetian beads, can bring their ivories into the same market as the Nile men, who actually *pay nothing* for the tusk. But this is the explanation : although they have been purchased by plundered cattle, the master of those plunderers has to provide guns and ammunition; he has to pay the men, and also the freight of the ivory, and its duty to the Egyptian Government. These are the expenses which bring the price of Nile ivory up to that which is taken to Zanzibar. But on either the one or the other side of the equator no *honest* man would have a chance against the present field of traders, who do everything in their power to keep the country as a preserve for cattle, slaves, and ivory.

As our narrative has here touched on the Nile, I may as well mention what information we received regarding it from the many travellers coming to Kar- ague for the purposes of trade. On the 2d of January 1862, while Speke and I were together, we were thrown into a state of excitement by being told that a man had arrived from a country far away to the north, bringing tidings that "a party having guns which knocked down trees had been attacked by the Wagani race, one hundred of them killed, the most of their property seized and made over to one Kamarasi, a king." The extraordinary part of the story was, that the strangers had not left the country, but still occupied their ships, which were reported to be large enough to contain cattle. Our firm impression was, that this could be no other than Petherick, who had

FIRST TIDINGS OF THE NILE. 165

promised, when we parted with him in England, to meet or have boats for us in November 1861 and until 1862. ,Plans were at once formed to send him a letter, and Rumanika gave us every facility, as the king above mentioned was his connection, having exchanged sisters with him. Although this intimacy existed, nothing would induce Rumanika to allow us to march there till a reply had been received. We were to be kept for months in suspense, until Baraka, the bearer of the despatch, should return. Although we told Rumanika repeatedly that we expected boats on the Nile for us, on the receipt of this important information he would not allow us to advanceļit would not be etiquette toward the northern kings! Meanwhile the king of Uganda luckily sent a message that he was most impatient to see the white men, and as a story was got up that no sick people nor donkeys were allowed to enter his territory, I had to remain till sufficiently recovered to march. Speke left on the 10th of January; and Baraka, having bought the disguise of a nativela bark-cloth and spearlconsulted magicians to find out whether this march would be prosperous; he started on the 29th with several companions, and letters for the ships supposed to be Petherick's. These turned out to be a perfect mythl no such boats were there; the nearest point that any lay at was Gondokoro, a place known in Europe for thirty years. But the Nubian soldiers of M. de Bono had worked their way from Gondokoro by laud far south by means of their guns, and gave origin to the report we had heard. Feeling anxious about Baraka, my head man Frij went repeatedly to the sultan's brother, M'nanagee, asking whether anything had been

166 FROM KARAGUE TO LONDON BY WATER.

heard of him. No intelligence had actually been received, but M'nanagee had consulted his magic horns, and they told him that " Baraka was perfectly well, but his companion Seedee was suffering from a chest complaint!" M'nanagee was so confident about this telegraphing on his own part, that he said, " If it does not turn out true, 111 give you that goat." Months afterwards, on our reaching Kamarasi's, we were told that the man had been ailing slightly!

Of Speke I could hear occasionally by letter; his men were discontented at getting nothing to eat but boiled plantain; but they ultimately found out that there was nothing else to be procured in the country. He had crossed a body of water four hundred yards wide, running to the north. What a pleasure it must have been to him to come upon the first flowing waters of the Nile ! In a previous letter, dated 12th February, from the borders of Nyanza, he wrote saying he was to return for me in a boat along the lake. On mentioning to Rumanika that an Uganda boat was to arrive in his lake to convey the baggage and myself away, he replied, " It was all practicable except for two miles, at the Kitangule, where the river is shallow, and the boat must be carried." I added, that as the waters we then looked upon mingled with those in my country (alluding to the Mediterranean), the day might come when a traveller could go from Karague to

London and *vice versa* by water! Since saying this, we have discovered that cataracts are the only obstacle to this grand tourist route.

The cattle of this country resemble those we saw at Cape Town|all horn, with staring ribs. The sultan kept 400 of such animals at his residence on the high

THE CATTLE OF KARAGUE. 167

grounds. He had perhaps 10,000 more on the graz- ing-grounds on the banks of the Kitangule, where they had better feeding, and looked more sleek. Some horns were two and three feet long, and eighteen inches round the base. No use seemed to be made of them, unless by Seedees and Arabs, who converted them into powder-horns. At nine every morning" these 400 cows were trotted down the hill to their grazing-ground, sometimes accompanied by one of the princes, and they were walked back to be milked after dark, having been allowed to drink once at a trough of clay filled by an osier bucket from a well on the edge of the lake. Every tenth day the lanky creatures were driven down (at 7 A.m.) two hours earlier than usual, as they had to go farther, for the purpose of receiving a drench of brackish water some distance away. On the hillside by the path shallow pits are dug in horizontal lines, to allow water to collect there for cattle or wild animals. They are wretched milkers, only giving half the quantity of the plump small-horned breed of Unyanyembe. Two were set apart by the sultan for our use, as no one would drink from the same cow that supplied us; and whether it was that the animals were less cared for, or that they soon became dry, our supply of milk latterly became reduced to almost nothing. No doubt this was attributed to our bewitching the cows by boiling the milk! Daily, men carrying five or six prettily-shaped "chanzees" or jars of yellow wood, browned from use, slung from a stick on their shoulders, would pass my hut with milk for the palace. It was the staff of life|the children and women fattened upon it; and the butter, sometimes

168 PET DOGS OF KARAGUE.

of a good quality, but never rich, was used merely as a pomade on their bodies, to soften their skin-coverings, and as an external cure for everything. We had considerable difficulty in procuring any, because we ate it. However, a handsome present now and then would induce them to give us some. The sheep (lambed in the month of November) were a small species, without wool, generally white, and only half-a-dozen would be seen in a tract of ten or twenty miles. Within 200 yards of them we have observed the white rhinoceros grazing, looking like a solitary stack in the middle of a hay-field. We did not take the trouble to shoot him, because his flesh is worthless, and shooting interfered with the march. Sometimes our men fired, which made both them and the animal run in opposite directions. Every hut had its little flock of short-haired goats, whose skins were so valued as an article of dress that the natives could seldom be induced to sell them. One roan-coloured goat presented to us was fancied for its colour by the sultan, and exchanged, as he longed for it to assist in some ceremony.

There were pet dogs about the palace, used in going after small antelope and tiger-cats. The breed was like the pariah of India, leggy, with smooth red hair, but much more domestic, giving a paw, lying down quietly by your side, or always ready to walk with you, having been taught docility by the young princes. They are said to run after game by scent, but this we did not observe. This particular breed is always gelt, the natives believing that they are thereby rendered more keen in the pursuit of sport. One, a great favourite, answering to the name of "Keeromba"|a wild, beautifully-sounding, musical

CAPTURE OF A NZOWE ANTELOPE. 169

namelbecame much attached to our camp. To give an idea of the sport here, Speke bagged three white rhinoceros in one day, much to the delight of the native princes, who never will forget the enjoyment it gave them. They would not eat the flesh; but some Wezee porters|poor starved-like men, belonging to the Arab traders at Kufro|carried it away in enormous loads; but when seen by their Mohammedan masters, the meat was sent out of camp as being unlawful, not having been regularly killed. On our mentioning to the king that we had heard of an extraordinary animal like a goat living in the lake, he ordered his people to capture one. Canoes of logs, two paddles each, and 18 feet long, were collected to beat the papyrus rushes, driving the animal into the water, when he was chased (as we were told) and captured alive, care being taken by outside canoes that no crocodiles attacked the men while in the water. A procession of singers walked up the hill, passing our huts, carrying the live animal neatly lashed upon a frame of wood to the sultan, who sent him to us " fresh from the lake." He (a young male antelope) was very timid, and lay down with a rope about his neck for a whole day; but on a dish of water being presented to him, he dashed his head into it *aa* if he felt himself once more in his native element. As he seemed to pine, refusing his natural food|the tops of the papyrus|he was killed. His coat was of long, dirty brown, rather soft hair. His horns, from five to six inches long, were commencing to spire; the hoofs were of the true waterboc, immensely long, and widely separated; height more than three feet. This species of antelope is called "nzowe" by the

170 THE SPORT OF KARAGUE.

natives, and lives altogether on the borders of lakes.

We never heard of elephants while residing here. There are no forests for them on these heights and valleys. Hartebeest, and rhinoceros or "faroo," are the common animals of the chase. The former, called " nyamoera," in the rutting season become highly combative. Two stags fought in the plain with unflinching determination, calmly halting to breathe between each round. The force of every butt as their heads met, and as they fell on their knees, sounded distinctly, the energy and impetus of the attack sending their small bushy tails over their backs. After a battle of twenty minutes, one became the victor, and chased the other into and out of a herd of hinds, when I was obliged to leave the interesting chase. Several antelope were wounded this day, but they were very wild in the open plain of grass, and it required accurate shooting at 300 and 400 yards to bag one. Of other game animals there were several varieties of antelope. The mountain gazelle bounded very prettily over the bare hills, and did not seem very wild. Pigs were in the low grounds, and hippopotami swam in the lake. But Karague is not a country of sport; and although the sultan imagines that lions garrison the country, and mount guard over his father's remains, we never saw one, dead or alive. The natives told us that otter, called "gonejeh," of the ordinary colour, live in the lake, and that their king (concerning whom they have some superstition) is as white as an old man's beard. The manner in which a Wezee prepares a skin for wear is very simple, and seems perfectly efficacious. Straw is laid on the ground, the skin is

NESTING SEASON. 171

pegged out neatly over it till thoroughly dried by the sun into the state of parchment; it is then doubled and pressed in every possible direction, and a few integuments are pulled off. It is hand-rubbed, and smeared with grease, and then becomes fit for wear. Great numbers of moles, larger than English, were caught in our camp. Their fur was black or brown, and some were white. The natives seemed to make no use of them.

Of game-birds the most numerous are the guinea- fowl, the " boee" and " qualee" partridges. The natives shoot at long distances with their arrows, and must destroy great quantities of game. They also use springes, for during the march a small boy was met carrying on a string some birds he had caught . We said to him, "Come to camp|you'll be paid for them;" but he naively replied, " Catch me going to your camp ! you'd put chains upon me, and make me a slave." On the 10th of April a nest of guinea-fowl, " kanga," eggs were brought me ; this was in the middle of the rainy season; but they most probably breed all the year round. Small red sparrows were also picking up feathers ; and a nest made of one species of grass, with two unspotted white little eggs, was brought in, showing that incubation goes on at this season. On the lake there were varieties of duck, which came in flights every night about the beginning of December from the east, flying over our camp with the sound of a passing shell. An Egyptian goose, to us particularly interesting from its name and connection with the Nile, was shot by Speke, and sent to the sultan, who was more delighted with its splendid plumage than with the English table-knife, fork, and spoon he had

172 THE GROW USED IN DIVINING EVENTS.

that day been presented with. He, no doubt, had never seen the bird before, although it was shot by his own lake. We, of course, observed the rhinoceros- bird, which sits as calmly on the animal's back as a man does on the top of a coach; he is the size of a " mina " or a blackbird, and has black wings, with a grey or white rump ; they are partly gregarious, three being seen together; and they must feed upon the tics which infest the skin of the rhinoceros. Here we came across a new swallow skimming the grasses of the hillsides|black or dark-brown wings of a slate tinge, white belly, black ring at neck and round the rump, tail-feathers not forked but slightly convex, body sparrow-size, and not so fish-shaped as swallows generally are. The golden-headed and crimson- backed little finch perched here, as in Unyanyembe, on the stalks of the Indian corn near dwellings. Another bird had, as Speke described it, a black coat and plush waistcoat; its colours harmonised beautifully with the tree on which it sat, a thorny species of jasmine, then (December) in rich pink-and-white bloom. We had no songsters at Karague, but we had a " bugler," who had one very rich note. There never were more than from two to four crows (handsome birds, with a ring of white round the neck) seen together, and the natives like killing them, as they eat up the red bitter sorghum, and prevent the people from sowing the white or sweet variety. The crow was used here by the sultan as supposed to be useful in divining events. The crops are protected from the barn-door fowl by a barbarous practice|the toe-nails of the fowl are cut off to prevent them from scratching the ground. This is done also in Zanzibar, but here it first attracted

SNAKES, VERMIN, AND FISH. 173

our notice in consequence of the peculiar crippled gait of the poultry.

A snake was caught amongst the rocks, measuring six feet five inches; it was of a bluish-black colour. M'nanagee brought it in a wicker basket to show me. He said he had had it for three days, and meant to keep it as a pet. Although one of his men held it fearlessly by the neck, they were afraid to allow me to do so, because they called it poisonous; however, no fangs were visible. It was one of the few snakes seen in Karague. Rats were in swarms, and were very troublesome to the traders, stealing their beads and cowries in considerable quantities, and concealing them in their holes ; unfortunately we had no poison with us when asked for some by M'nanagee. This shows that the natives have no means to rid themselves of them; some pills of flour and pounded caustic were made up, but we never heard whether they were effectual. In the low flat valleys near the lakes, large grey-legged musquitoes bite through your socks and trousers, keeping your limbs in constant motion; but on the higher ground, where wind blows, we were never annoyed by any. The bee that produces the honey of the country resembles our common hive-bee at home; and although beautifully granulated honey was brought for sale, we observed no hives. It certainly is not a productive country in this respect lthe hills are barren of flowers. There are quantities of fish in the lake; but during my residence no fisherman was ever seen or heard of. Except one fish, the makambara, brought me. by the sultan as a curiosity alive in a jar, and a half-pound-weight macquareh, caught by a Seedee in the Kishakka lake,

174 THE YOUNG PRINCES OF KARAGUE.

we saw no fish, and the natives never eat them. The macquareh attains a great size, has immense large scales, no feelers, and a ridge of sharp-pointed fins along its arched back, and eats very sweetly. These notes must not be accepted as a list of what the country contains, but merely a notice of those which struck me as strange or interesting.

The population of Karague may be divided into two races: the reigning race or Wahuma; and the peasantry, who originally owned, and now cultivate, the soil, called Wanyambo, alluded to in the preceding chapter.

The king and his brothers, of the former race, have already been described; a few remarks on their Mo- heenda or young princes may be added. This royal class or caste have slight marks cut below the eyes; but they neither extract their teeth nor file them into any particular shape. Their diet of milk seems to make the men a tall active race, while the women get out of all proportion with obesity. The grown-up sons of the king (according to seniority) were Chun- dera, Kienj, Kananga, and Kukoko. First, Chundera, twenty-five years of age, was a smart active young fellow, about five feet eight inches in height, with a somewhat effeminate figure and expression of countenance ; he was fair for a negro, and except that his lips were rather thick, and that his wool was in regular pepper - corns, he might be taken, from his straight features, for a slim East Indian sepoy. He affected the dandy, being more neat about his loin- skin cover and ornaments than the other brothers. He lived a gay life, was always ready to lead a war- party and to preside at a dance, or wherever there

THE YOUNG PRINCES OF KARAGUE. 175

was wine or women. From the tuft of wool left unshaven on the crown of his head to his waist he was bare, except where decorated round the muscle of the arm and neck with charmed horns, stripes of otter- skin, shells, and knobs of wood. The skin covering the loins, which, with the Karague people, is peculiar in shape, reached below the knee behind, and was cut away in front. From below the calf to the ankle was a mass of iron wire; and when visiting from neighbour to neighbour, he always, like every Karague person, carried in his hand a five-feet-long staff with a knob at the end. He constantly came to ask after me, bringing flowers in his hand, as he knew my fondness for them; and at night he would take Frij, my head man, into the palace along with his " zeze " or guitar, to amuse his sisters with Zanzibar music. In turn the sisters, brothers, and followers would sing Karague music, and early in the morning Master Frij and Chundera would return rather jolly to their huts outside the palace enclosures. This shows the kindly feeling existing between us and the family of the sultan ; and although this young prince had showed me many attentions, he never once asked for a present. The second son, Kienj, was by a different mother (the sister of the king of Unyoro, I believe); he was six feet high at least, very black, and so ugly and disproportionately long about .the head, that we called him the "camel." He was a slow, stupid fellow, very simple, and a bumpkin in comparison with the others. Like his brothers, he was married, and had one child, but lived in the palace enclosure. Previous to my leaving he made bold to beg for my only umbrella, because his own was past mending ! The third son

176 THE WANYAMBO OR KARAGUE PEASANTRY.

of the family was so shy that he only came near me when told to sit for his portrait; and the fourth, Ku- koko, was such a pet, and was so nice-looking, that the father never went anywhere nor did anything without taking the young prince along with him. He was mild and gentlemanly in manner, and would come to us every day, putting out his left hand when wishing us good morning, and remaining to chat quietly for an hour at a time. After we left Karague we sent him a comfortable blanket as a reward for his attentions. Although none of these lads had more covering than a sheet of leather round the loins, it was so neatly put on, their ornaments were so becoming, their persons so bronze-looking, their gait so polite and *distingue,* that we quite forgot their nakedness ; more particularly when we saw the effect produced by pulling on a pair of white kid gloves upon Kukoko's hands, and seeing him strut away with the air of a Bond Street swell! Their food was chiefly a bowl of milk once in the morning; no grain, nor mutton, nor fish, nor fowl, but a small quantity of boiled beef or goat at night. They looked after the cattle belonging to their father, had M'koongoos, or agents of their own, who went to neighbouring countries to traffic for them; and so domestic were they that they never were known to sleep out of their own country.

The Wanyambo are the ryots, or peasantry. In the low grounds of Urigi, where there was a great deal of swamp at the very doors of the people, they are very black and rather lanky. All grease their bodies to prevent the skin getting dried in the sun, and smoke themselves with sweet fuel having a peculiar heavy

THE WANYAMBO OR KARAGUE PEAS ANTR Y. 177

odour. The Wakungu, or district governors, possess probably one sheet of calico, or a scarlet blanket, in excess of the skins usually worn by the people. The men about

Urigi seemed a depressed race, and though superior in position (being cultivators of the soil) to the Watusi, who tend cattle, they surprised me by their appearance of misery; this, however, may have been assumed. They have the sultan's orders to furnish all travellers with sufficient provision for themselves and followers free of charge; and in return for this a present is generally given of some coils of brass wire. Some of our Wanyambo porters showed spirit on the march by refusing to be led by an Unyamuezi. On this occasion it was alarming to see the fellows using their spears and arrows at one another; the whole caravan joined in the fray, which became a party one, and had to be settled by our men threatening to shoot them: one cut finger was the only casualty. Again, if a Seedee or two wandered away from camp amongst the Wanyambo, they were in some danger, for this tribe were so drunken and excitable that several instances of their boisterous nature proved serious to our men when out purchasing provisions. About the palace, however, they were very civil, constantly advising me as to my health, telling me to keep my weak limb shut up from the air, to eat plenty of meat, &c. They never carried arms when near the palace, neither did our men, which was different to our practice in the badly-governed district of Usui, where no one dare go about unarmed. The only weapon was a five-feet-long knobstick, generally carried across the shoulder; and in wishing good morning to a comrade the end of the stick was presented

178 THE WOMEN OF KARAGUE.

to be touched. The bows of Karague are the finest I have seen in any part of the world, 6 feet 2 inches in height, and of immense power; the arrows are about the length of the arm, seldom or never poisoned, with their tips shaped like a spear-head. There is no particular character in the spear : the handle is from six to twelve feet long, and the iron part indifferently made, the people prizing themselves more upon their bows. Guns are unknown, except amongst the princes. As has been mentioned, the Wanyambo are fond of carousing over drink, singing and chanting wild airs till early morning; but tottering drunkards such as we see at home are never met withlthe people have more self-respect. The food of those who possessed cattle was chiefly milk; others lived upon boiled sweet potato, the flour of Indian-corn or millets, and various calavances or beans. Meat they eat when they can get it, but fowls and fish are forbidden them, though the prince M'nanagee told me the Wanyambo would eat the former " on the sly."

The princesses have been well described by Speke, who had more opportunities of seeing them than I had. One I saw walking, enormously fat, obliged to rest every few paces, by sitting down or reclining in a stooping position, one hand grasping a long staff. When seated, her head was uncovered, the wool allowed to grow into a mop neatly tied off the face with a thong of leather, and having a bouquet of bird's feathers in the centre. The face was a handsome oval, with fine intelligent eyes, and the flesh of her arms, bare from the shoulder, hung down like a fashionable sleeve. They had few employments, their mode of life forbidding this, and most of them could not move

THE CHILDREN. 179

without the support of a person on either side. In some respects they reminded me of Hindoo women. In visiting us, the better class, from modesty or custom, had a shawl of bark-cloth covering all their persons except one eye, while they wore the ordinary friezed cow-skin from the waist to the ankle. They were very fond of pictures, the sultan always indulging them by sending my sketches for their amusement. They could make caps of cane stuffed from the outside with their own wool, like moss in a summer-house. Their children were very handsome, with large shining black eyes : the wool was never shaved off their heads nor cut till after marriage, and no covering was ever on their loins till the age of puberty, or even later. Boys and girls would come to look at us, careless or unconscious of their nudity, and chatting without the slightest shyness. A wet-nurse is provided for the infant prince or princess, who is generally suckled away from home, as was the custom amongst Highland families in the last century. Their after-diet is altogether milk : they are whipped into drinking and fattening themselves with it. No marriage ceremonies were observed, but on two occasions we saw a couple of women walk together without any followers, one of them hidden in bark-clothes ; and we understood that the veiled one was being conveyed to her betrothed. The dead of the Wanyambo, as has already been mentioned, are deposited in the lake, and princes alone receive burial on the island. On one occasion we observed inside a village enclosure two sticks tied to a stone, and lying across the pathway; and this was done, as we ascertained, to prevent people walking over the spot, as a woman had died there.

180 THE RESIDENCE OF RUMANIKA.

With respect to the habitations of the people, suppose that on the face of a bare hill overlooking a lake we place forty or fifty low dome-looking huts of cane, covered with grass; divide them into sets of twos and threes by screens and gates of cane; throw an embankment round the whole, and have a dense hedge of euphorbia trees on the top of the embankment, screening the view of the lake and the country around, and you have the Palace of Rumanika, containing his five wives, sons, four hundred cows and their calves, &c. Except a hut or two outside this " bomah," nothing but a curl of smoke in the valleys showed that there was any population in the country. Descend to the valleys, and you find neatly-formed huts of grass inside the plantain-groves. Their interiors are plastered for five feet with cow-dung and mud; the ceiling is of cane, blackened by smoke, for there is no fireplace. The temporary huts made for us by our Seedees were gable-ended, made of props from the meelomba or bark-cloth tree, and roofed over with grass and the decayed leaves of plantains, the whole made water-tight by India-rubber sheeting being placed on their roofslthe last a requisite which the traveller should never forget. The sultan generally received us in a tidily-kept hut, carpeted with the silky leaves of the papyrus, and loopholed in several places for visitors outside to make him their obeisance by clapping their hands and addressing him. Here, seated on his warm bedding, we chatted and laughed with him, paying long and pleasant visits, his majesty at the same time smoking his large black pipe. Screens of cane, placed as gates, prevented our interviews being interrupted, and permission was required

CRIME, HOW PUNISHED. 181

before any one could visit him or pass those barriers, where men always stood, like porters at the Government offices. The ordinary mode of salutation of an Unyambo or ryot of Karague, when he reached a circle of people seated, was to present the end of his staff to each acquaintance, who touched it, saying, " Verembe, verembe, verembe

kooroongee," *i. e.,* How do you do, how do you do, how do you do? are you very well
? The same answer would be given, and the same salutation exchanged, if two met
upon the road. To a superior they also hold out the stick, bnt it is only acknowledged
by a nod from him.

Crime was seldom observed or heard of, but the people had their distinct punishments, and traders had the protection of the sultan. A caravan of Moossah's was
plundered by the Urigi chief, who was at once arrested and made over as a slave, to be
dealt with at the coast as Moossah chose. The property lost or destroyed was doubly
repaid by the sultan in ivory, and the chief, in gratitude to Moossah for not making a
prisoner of him, promised a present of ten tusks every time his caravan should pass
through his district. I am indebted to M'nanagee, who judges all cases for his brother
the king, for the following list of offences with their punishments:|An ear is cut off
for adultery; if the case occurs with a slave or a princess, the offender is tortured, as
in the Ukuni case, and his throat is cut. Simple theft: kept in the stocks from two to
ten months. Striking and assaulting with stick: ten goats. Assault with spear, bow
and arrow: property confiscated, half going to the sultan and half to the injured party;
if the culprit has no property, he is put into the stocks. Murder : all pro-

182 ARAB PUNISHMENTS.

perty made over to the relatives of the murdered person, and the eyes of the murderer
gouged, or he is thrown over the precipice below the palace. If a husband comes upon
a case of adultery, he is permitted to kill the offender on the spot. Unnatural crimes
they regard with horror, but these are said to be known only amongst the "waeroo"
or slaves; so that the Karague laws are as strict as our own, and, without statistics, I
believe there is far less crime. The punishments at Muscat and Zanzibar, under Arab
government, were described to me by Frij, and are barbarous in comparison with the
code at Karague. For theft, the hand is cut off; if the property is recovered, the thief at
Zanzibar is buried in the seashore up to his neck, to allow the tide to reach him|a mode
of punishment that will remind the reader of the case of the alleged Wigtown martyrs.
Some silver and clothes were stolen from the sultan of Zanzibar, and the thieves being
detected were pulled up to the top of a flagstaff and thrown to the ground. At Muscat
the tongue of the thief is cut off, and owing to this severe punishment there are few
cases of theft. The Arabs are hard masters, and train their servants (several of whom
were with us) in a system of rigorous discipline. To enforce despatch, a master will
spit on the ground, and say to his servant, " If that dries up before you return with an
answer to my message, you'll get flogged."

Musical instruments were in greater variety in Karague than we had previously met
with, and the little plaintive native airs could be picked up and hummed, they were so
sweet and pleasing to the ear. There was stringed, wind, and drum music. Their most

MUSICAL INSTRUMENTS. 183

perfect instrument was the " nanga," of seven or eight strings; it may be called
national. In one of these, played by an old woman, six of the seven notes were a
perfect scale, the seventh being the only faulty string. In another, played by a man,
three strings were a full harmonious chord. These facts show that the people are
capable of cultivation. The " nanga " was formed of heavy dark wood, the shape of
a tray, 22 by 9 inches or 30 by 8, with three open crosses in the bottom, and laced

with *one* string seven or eight times over bridges at either end; sometimes a gourd, as sounding-board, was tied on to the back. Prince M'nanagee, at my request, sent the best player he knew. The man boldly entered without introduction, dressed in the usual Wanyambo costume, and looked a wild, excited creature. After resting his spear against the roof of the hut, he took a " nanga " from under his arm and commenced. As he sat upon a mat with his head averted from me, never smiling, he sang something of his having been sent to me, and of the favourite dog Keeromba. The wild yet gentle music and words attracted a crowd of admirers, who sang the dog-song for days afterwards, as we had it encored several times. Another player was an old woman, calling herself " Keeleeanyagga." As she played while standing in front of me, all the song she could produce was " sh," " sh," screwing her mouth, rolling her body, and raising her feet from the ground; it was a miserable performance, and not repeated.

Of wind instruments we had the fife and horn. The fife is more common with the Uganda than the Karague people. It is an 18-inch-long hollowed reed, about the thickness of a German flute, is held like a

184 Rumanika's Band Of Musicians.

flageolet, has a slit at the top, and six finger-holes. As the Waganda walk smartly along the road, with a light load on their heads, they often while away the time with this rude instrument, out of which some of them bring soft, sweet, flute-like music. The bugle they have is shaped like a telescope, and is made of several pieces of gourd fitting into each other, and covered with cow-skin. It is 12 inches long. An expert performer on this bugle can produce a whole chord, which is varied by the thumb acting as a key.

Drums are of different shapes, according as they are beaten by the hand or by a stick. The drum made for the hand is a 4-feet-long log, hollowed out in the shape of an inverted dice-box, open at the lower end, and covered at the top, which is 1 foot across, with the skin of an ichneumon. It is slung from the left shoulder, and played by tapping and stopping with the fingers. The thirty-three drums seen ranged in line at the ceremony after new-moon were of every possible shape, except round, which they all tried to be. They were trunks of trees hollowed out, and covered over with skin. Two copper kettle-drums had found their way into the collection. The sultan had an excellent band, of its kind, composed of 16 men, who performed several tunes before us. The instruments were 14 bugles and 2 hand-drums. Three ranks, the drummers in the rear, formed in front of us, and played, with great spirit and precision, bugle music in waltz and march time. While " trooping " they advanced, swaying their bodies very gracefully to the music; and as they neared us all halted except the bandmaster, who, as he played, being an active, well-made little man, advanced to our feet, kneeling

DISPUTE ABOUT A CHILD. 185

nimbly on alternate knees in time to the music. The drummers were energetic, smart, mirthful fellows; and their music, sounding so sweetly among the hills, was more pleasant than any performance I had ever expected to witness in Africa. It was called Unyoro music, but at Unyoro we heard none of it in consequence of the moroseness of the king. All the time we were at Karague we saw no dance worth noting; they did not seem much given to dancing, and the war-drum was never sounded. Long may this continue ! On such occasions the men take the field and the women beat the drums. An alarm of cattle having been captured was once spread, and the men rushed about in hot haste, armed each with a single spear and their faithful bow and arrows; but it proved false, and the bold Prince Chunderah was disappointed of a raid.

The only alarms we experienced were caused by the hyena or other animals stealing from us. Twice an infuriated mob came shouting into our camp, the voices of the women being above all others. A woman had a child, and two men fought for it. Each claimed it; the woman wouldn't give it up ; she couldn't settle the dispute; would the white man do it ? I was not for some time made aware of the circumstances; but my Seedee servant appointed himself arbiter, and, after looking at both the men and the child, decided who was the rightful father, after which they all scampered off in noisy confusion. A second case was soon after decided in the same way, but with a different result, for the man who lost the suit took his spear and threatened to stab the infant. The African, however, is more prompt in speech than in action.

186 RELIGION AT KARAGUE.

Of religion, the only approach to it has been mentioned in the various superstitions of the king and his brother, who made idols of horns filled with various charms. To these they appeal for aid against an enemy, for the blessing of health, for the discovery of men's inward thoughts, for rain, &c. In the event of a war or a journey, the mysterious horn was consulted as to the probable success of the expedition. Another belief is that certain animals are possessed of devils, but are in the power of soothsayers. We found that amongst the Wahuma kings it was lawful to cohabit with a brother's wife, or with his own sister.

They have no knowledge whatever of reading, writing, or arithmetic. A printed book to them was like a picture-book to a child; its leaves were turned over one by one carefully by the most intelligent, and immediately shut up by the more ignorant. For twenty years Arabs have been amongst them, but Mohammedanism has taken no hold of the king or his people. The country presents a wide field for commerce to pave the way for regenerating an intelligent race.

On reading the ten commandments to my Mohammedan friend Jumah, who dealt in slaves, ivory, &c., often complaining that his slaves were under no control, he shook hands with me after each commandment, saying how true and excellent they were, he believed in them all. " But do you practise them ? " I asked. " Read ' Honour thy father and thy mother,' and tell me how can the slaves honour their fathers and mothers if you tear them away from their families ?" " Oh, I am a father to them." " How can you be a father ? Are the affections of a parent not as strong in Africa as anywhere else ?" He felt theDEPARTURE FROM KARAGUE. 187

force of the argument, asked me to desist from pressing the matter, as it was not convenient to adopt these sentiments at present. He would return to Zanzibar, never again keep slaves, study the Bible, and go to England. I wished to believe that he said this in sincerity, for the conversion of one influential man in such a land would be of importance.

By the end of March 1862 there were some hopes of my leaving Karague to join Speke in Uganda. The king had sent an officer and forty of his men to convey me up to the kingdom I so long wished to see. Rumanika had received his presents of a Whitworth rifle, Tranter's revolver, Inverness cape, cloths, beads, japanned box, a compass, pair of binoculars, &c., to conciliate him; and he had acted the part of a kind friend in giving us all the information in his power. An Unyamuezi M'ganga, or priest, named Kiengo, was to join my party, but until he had completed his arrangements the march could not take place. The Waganda who had arrived for me were clamorous to get away, but they refused to carry the luggage ; and as Rumanika could provide no porters, three-fourths of it were left behind in his charge. Being unable to walk, I was placed in a wicker stretcher (April 14, 1862), and was trotted off on the heads of four Waganda. Wishing to shake hands with Rumanika, I ordered the carriers to convey me into the palace, but nothing would induce them to leave the pathlit was not their duty. My adieus were therefore sent through Kukoko, his favourite son; and I left Karague, its hills, lakes, and groves, feeling intensely curious about the next kingdom of Uganda, where I hoped to rejoin my fellow-traveller.

9

SECTION 9

CHAPTER IX.

THE UGANDA MARCH, APRIL 14 TO MAY 27, 1862|MARIBOO AND HIS UGANDA FOLLOWERS|RICH FOLIAGE|FERRYING THE RIVER KITANGULE|SUPERS AGAINST SOUNDING THE RIVER|VICTORIA NYANZA, A BOUNDLESS SEA|FINE COUNTRY BETWEEN KITANGULE AND KJTONGA|FLORA OF THE DIS-TRICT|INCIDENTS OF THE MARCH|LUNCH WITH UGANDA WOMAN|DISAGREEAB MARCH|THE GOVERNOR POKINNO|SUMMER-HOUSES OF THE UGANDA.

Having been detained at Karague for so many months, I was right glad to have a prospect in the end of March of getting away to join my companion. A party of Waganda, under an officer named Mariboo, arrived to take me as far as the Kitangule river, four marches, where large boats were said to be lying to convey me by the lake to Uganda. This, however, was not the case; no boats had been sent, and the journey of twenty-nine marches was performed by land, much to our disappointment, as Speke had previously been over it, and we missed the navigation of the Nyanza. Day by day the Waganda escort deluded me with the idea that we would come upon boats by the side of the Nyanza; and Mariboo ordered the

MODE OF CONVEYANCE. 189

march as he liked, halted when it suited him, got tipsy whenever he could, but in the end compensated for all by conveying me safe to his king.

Rumanika had a sort of litter made up, on which the Waganda lads were to carry me; my half-dozen Seedees could not have done it, as the country afterwards proved to be precipitous, and full of swamps and marshy drains. On the morning of the 14th April, when a start was made from Karague, Mariboo came into camp with his thirty or forty men, making a noise and saying they had been starved while waiting for the Unyamuezi doctor and myself during the last fortnight, and were determined to move to-day whether I was ready or not . " Bring out the white man. Where is his bedding ? Let him get into the conveyance." The property, however, had first to be despatched. I lost sight of it for two days, but none of the loads were plundered. On our journey, the stretcher was changed from the head to the shoulder of the Waganda, who went at the rate of six miles an hour, jostling and paining my limb unmercifully. The coach and four, as I may term it, was put down every mile, or less, that the bearers might rest, laugh, joke, and make a deafening noise with their mumbling language, beating their tongues to the roofs of their mouths. They seldom spoke when in motion, only when one stumbled the others would cry out against him, recommending greater care of their charge. Certainly it was not a safe position to be perched such a height on an open frame of sticks, with rocky precipices, small footing for the men, and very often water below. One great difficulty was to make them carry the conveyance so that the country in front could be

190 MARCHING WITH WAGANDA.

seen in travelling; this they, for some reason, refused to do, and persisted in carrying me head first, instead of feet. If a grove of plantain was by the side of the path, it could not be resisted; off all would dash at the fruit, eat, and carry away as much as they were able, sometimes politely offering me a share, or more frequently remaining so long away, as I lay on the stretcher, that it became irritating. The best way was to join as much as possible with them in their frolics; my men did so, and enjoyed the march extremely.

At these groves, a single bunch or cluster of as many as 150 ripe plantains could be got in April, and their juice drunk from them *al fresco*. The large leaves of the tree, green, and soft as satin, were spread on the ground as a table-cloth; a wisp of grass, well softened by rubbing, enclosed a quantity of luscious ripe fruit, and what the men seemed most to enjoy was to bite and suck the fruit through the grass. During the march they all carried some small load on their heads, never more than 20 or 30 lb., rolled in the form of a web of cloth, neatly bound round, and having pipes and flutes stuck into it. Each man had a spear and shield over his back; the latter served as an umbrella when rain fell; and thus, with their bark-cloths kilted up, their dress was secure from rain or boggy ground. On arrival in camp, the march costume was changed for a clean suit of bark-cloth as stiff as silk, or for a set of many-coloured goat-skins, with scalloped, pierced edges, in which they made themselves smart, and strutted about like gentlemen. Those who had been able to find dogs led them with strings tied to their waists or wrists as they ran along.

MARCHING WITH WAG AND A. 191

Very ridiculous they appeared, for the animals (not accustomed to it) always refused to be led in this way. On coming near habitations, the men shouted and sang, as if carrying some object of triumph. Had I been a dead lion, they could not have made greater noise; and on getting near camp, regardless of cultivated fields, they would plunge into them with malicious delight, trample them down, slash away branches or plantain-trees which came in their way, and deposit the litter inside a grove.

When morning again came, the gay Mariboo, always scrupulously clean and proud of his dress, would appear, followed by his drummer-boy and dog, to announce, by beat of drum, a march or halt. If the former, the shouts of his men coming to join him would be heard in the distance, and Mariboo would answer and receive replies, till one by one all rushed up, spear in hand, as if to attack him, shouting allegiance, and causing their " captain" to spring and bound with delight, while I looked on with admiration at the strange and wild spectacle. After several exhibitions of this sort, it became evident that presents were expected, and if the march was to be a success, a little " tipping" was necessary; consequently, the captain was summoned to receive a gift of beads. His delight, as he handled the beautiful small beads, knew no bounds; his spear was flashed up to my face, while his left hand held his shield, and he finished with a number of nimble antics. His arms laid aside, he repeated, " N'yans, n'yans" (thanks, thanks), perhaps fifty times in succession, with a diagonal motion of both palms at each repetition. This over, another mode of thanks was adopted, and was

192 WAGANDA ARE SO JOYOUS.

even more agreeable; he drew his flute from his waist, played some soft music, making his eyes twinkle with delight, and swayed his body as if charmed with his own sweet strains. They certainly are a most joyous race. On our third march from Karague, the ground was so steep, and there was so much danger of my falling off the stretcher, that I was obliged to get out, and be half-carried up the rocky side of the hill, never dreaming that they would run away with my conveyance, which they did on seeing that I was able to put my foot to the ground. For a couple of hours they allowed me to wait there, while they, like a parcel of wicked boys, kept throwing rocks down the precipice, listening in perfect quiet till they heard the last sound of the stones reaching the bottom of the ravine, when all would shout together.

From the capital of Karague to the right bank of the Kitangule, the distance *vid* Meegongo was forty miles over flat-topped bare hills, and across valleys with swamps. On emerging from these to the river plain, the flat country became studded with mounds from six to eight feet high, raised by the ever-working white ants. Thorny shrubs, cactus, climbing aloes, with pink flowers, covered them, or the jungle of grass was varied by circles of brushwood, giving shade to the rhinoceros; the older trees were veiled over with silvery grey moss, which drooped gracefully, like the pendent branches of the weeping willow. The plain extended for ten miles, with several " back-waters" upon it, covered with the thorny mimosa and papyrus, through which we had to cut our way. Emerging from it and going towards the river, we came upon higher landla dry grassy plain three miles across, kept short

THE RIVER KITANGULE. 193

by cattle, and just the ground on which to find a flori- kan. There were several huts, which gladdened the eye after a dreary march. The first sight of the river Kitangule, which had been so often named to us as an old ivory dep6t, and the stream by which wood was floated down from Ruanda, was rather disappointing. Standing upon its steep shelving bank of white gravel, the stream is almost hidden by the papyrus, which lines its sides in a depth of from twenty to sixty yards; but when ferrying it, its majestic flow is seen. The canoes here were of one log of timber hollowed out, fifteen feet long, the breadth of an easy- chair as you sat in them, and capable of carrying fifteen Waganda, with their loads, dogs, spears, and large shields. They were propelled by poles through a winding channel closely shut in by the papyrus, and by paddles when in the stream, a man at each end holding one about five feet long. I had obtained from the Waganda lads several of their neatly spun coils of rope, which they carry on their heads; three or four of these were knotted together and a stone tied to one end as a sounding-line ; but on the ferryman noticing what was to be done, he objected, saying his sultan Kumanika would not permit any stone to be placed or thrown into the sacred Kitangule. A bribe at last softened him ; but Mariboo now interfered, saying, in his superstition, that he had an equally sacred charge from his kinglnamely, that he was to convey me in safety to him, and he would allow no pranks to be played with the river, for " suppose in the middle of it some spirit were disturbed by a stone, and rose to upset the boat, what would his king say ?" In short, after wasting words and time,

194 THE RIVER KITANGULE.

the project was given up, and we commenced the passage of the river at a reach four hundred yards long, having paid beforehand twenty strings of beads for my men, and an extra handful of cowries were given by the Waganda to the ferrymen. Poling for twenty yards through a winding channel cleared of the tall papyrus, and not broader than our canoe, we reached the stream, fully eighty yards across, judged to be five to six fathoms deep, looking as if any man-of-war could sail up, and flowing majestically at the rate of about three miles an hour. The strength of the current was so great that we had to pole up its right bank inside the fringe of papyrus for thirty yards, and then the two ferrymen, with a paddle each, made the canoe glide across diagonally down to the opposite channel in the reeds, which they reached with great precision. Poling for fifty to eighty yards was now adopted, landing upon mire which nearly sucked us into its hold; beyond this, the old line of the river rose abruptly like a railway embankment . At that level the country extended far away in a pleasant grassy plain, giving it the appearance of an Indian parade-ground; but the footing was treacherous, being full of ant-holes, and dotted with cactus-trees, white- ant mounds, with their usual vegetation, thistle-looking plants, and a scarlet-flowering shrub. In the distance to the north were rocky hills.

We observed that the waters of the Kitangule are accumulated from the lakes Karague, Kagaera, Kishakka, Ooyewgomah, and water from Utumbi. This river is, beyond comparison, the greatest body of water met with from the south of the Victoria Nyanza all round its western shore to its most northerly point,

THE RIVER KITANGULE. 195

where the Nile was seen by Speke to make its exit from the lake. It reminded me, when ferrying it, of the Hoogly ten miles above Calcutta. Every other stream entering the lake was walked across, none had to be ferried; and they were so numerous that nine and ten might be forded in as many miles ; this was a daily occurrence when marching on the western shore of the lake. The accumulation of these streams, and the rivulets (no rivers) known from Arab information to be in the eastern or unexplored portion of the Victoria Nyanza, form a boundless sea of 20,000 square miles, never traversed from one side to the other. All these arteries throw in an immense mass of water, and though the greatest of them is the Kitangule, still it is 160 miles distant by water from the point whence the Nile issues from its parent reservoir, the Lake Nyanza, at 21 miles north latitude.

The country between the Kitangule and the Ka- tonga, a distance of 100 miles, is a parallel series of grassy spurs tapering down to the lake's shores on the east. There are many beautiful spots on the route|high grounds from which, for a quarter of the horizon, are seen the waters of the lake, or the country undulating and park-like, covered with tall waving grasses, and overlooked by rocks. The curves, sweeps, and inclines of the hills often blended together in great beauty|never making the path inconveniently steep or too long in ascent or descent. All the cultivation was on these slopes, as the plains between them, sometimes six miles across, were ankle-deep in water and mud in this month of May; or where the valley was narrow, water would have accumulated in a drain four feet deep, across which the Waganda

196 THE VICTORIA NYANZA.

carried me on their necks, or, like a child, in their arms. On some marches we had to cross ten different waters, and, to avoid others, long detours were made to get upon higher grounds.

The now famous Victoria Nyanza, when seen for the first time, expanding in all its majesty, excited our wonder and admiration. Even the listless Wan- yamuezi came to have a look at its waters, stretching over ninety degrees of the horizon. The Seedees were in raptures with it, fancying themselves looking upon the ocean which surrounds their island home of Zanzibar, and I made a sketch, dotting it with imaginary steamers and ships riding at anchor in the bay. On its shores are beautiful bays, made by wooded tongues of low land (or points such as'Boonjacko and Surree Points, guarding the Katonga river) running into the lake, with very often a rounded detached island at their apices. The low islands of Sesseh lie on the western shore of the lake. A deep fringe of the papyrus generally hid the view over its waters. When standing here, the hoarse tromboning of the hippopotamus, wishing to come out to graze, echoed from out these rushes. The harbours of the natives were cleared spaces composed of a spongy mass of seeds, rotten reeds, sticks, and roots. In front, for twenty yards, a short rush with a circular leaf grew, breaking the small surfing waves on the lake from two to three hundred yards, showing that it was of no depth. In the distance, large boats paddled along from the mainland to the islands of Sesseh. One, of five planks sewn together, having four cross bars as seats, was brought to convey me to Uganda; but after four of us had got into it with some loads, theTHE SHORES OF THE LAKE. 197

craft was so cranky that such a voyage would have been madness, the water streaming in. Her bows and stern were pointed, standing for a yard over the water, with broad central plank from stem to stern, rounded outside, answering for a keel, and well adapted for gliding through papyrus.

The flora along this tract did not afford much variety. The most graceful tree on the route was the wild date-palm, growing in clumps of three and four upon the bare green hills: its crested plumes waved in the breeze, giving almost animal life to the silent scene. Birds' nests, or clusters of Indian red fruit, hung in pendants from the branches. We met with a new acacia, whose thin pods were broad and numerous ; on looking at the tree, the crop was so abundant that the leaves were all but hidden by the fruit. Few large trees were seen ; they probably got killed by the different varieties of lichens and parasites which covered them. One acacia with a flat top was netted over with bushes of them, as if they had been planted on the tops of the branches. The north-east sides of trees were observed to have the most moss upon their trunks, denoting that it was the dampest wind at that particular locality and position. On the 14th of May I Avas sheltered from the rays of the sun by the boughs of the coffee-shrub, then with clusters of green berries bowing down its branches till within reach. Each yearly growth or produce could be seen by looking at the number of knots in the branches. No care or pruning was observed, and the roots near the trunk grew very much above the soil. On the grounds facing the lake, 20 or 30 miles south of the equator, quantities must be grown, as some houses there were

198 FRUITS AND FOOD.

found full of sacks containing very large berries of it. The sacks were remarkably stout and well madel somewhat similar to Calcutta rice-bags. Two fruits, new to us, were seen growinglone, the colour and size of the Indian loquat, with several stones, but growing on a lofty tree with sombre foliage and densely-close branches. The other was an underground scarlet fruit, growing in sets of five and six clustered together like bananas, and of the same size. After being peeled, the pulp, with numerous black seeds, tasted refreshing as a lime, and was much enjoyed by the Waganda, who carried them strung as necklaces. The stalk of this plant (an amomum) grows four feet high from a creeping knotted root, like that of many grasses; and the scarlet fruit does not show above ground till ripe, when it forces up the soil like a mole.

Food was abundant, plantain particularly so, and might be had by the king's guests for the mere pulling; but if fowls, goats, or animal food was required, the natives charged almost London prices, preferring cowries, which we had none of, to beads. In the houses different grains were slung, in plantain-leaf coverings, from the posts which support the roofing. The staple food of the people is green plantain, a particular variety, boiled, when the peel comes off freely, and eaten like mashed potato. A piece of meat boiled with them made both very savoury, but plantain alone is not satisfying to a European. The various uses made of this tree surprised us. A chip from the bark was so watery that the hands could be well washed with it, but it was said to crack the skin: thread, wrappers, and stripes like ribbons were taken from the trunks, and the leaves were made into screen-fences, &c.

WINE-MAKING. 199

The wine I have before mentioned; two quarts of it could be drunk without any injurious effect. Every large hut seemed to have a trunk of a tree scooped out like a canoe, leaving a narrow opening. Several of these are collected in the grove when sufficient fruit has ripened, and the plantain juice is put in them to ferment, with some grain, and heaped over with leaves. The scene at opening these, after three days of fermentation, was quite a festive one. The immense gourds of the village were brought to be filled; cups were made from the leaves to taste the new beverage, and all was merry as at a carnival. A species of wine was made by the Waganda boys, very simple in its mode of manufacture, and excellent to drink. A small cavity was made in the ground, plantain leaves were placed flatly into it, so as to make a basin for liquid. Fruit, mixed with leaves, was pressed with the hands, some water added, and the leaves ultimately thrown away, leaving the "togweh" in the basin ready for drinking.

In travelling through this country our Seedees never received any pay as in the southern provinces, for the king of Uganda gave orders to his people to provide and cook for us. This was not always done : it more frequently happened that as soon as our approach was seen the natives fled, leaving almost all their goods and chattels at our mercy. No persuasion would bring them back, they are so accustomed to be surrounded and captured by troops of men sent by the king. Several influential ofiicers in charge of districts were seen on this routelSimjabee, Kittareh, Kuddoo, and some of the Wazeewa or Wahia race. All brought presents of fowls, buttermilk, sugar-cane, and wine.

200 CHIEFS OF DISTRICTS.

Simjabee was a tall, thin, long-faced man, with small beard, and very much marked on the forehead with smallpox. His caste was not a particular one, for he ate honey, boiled beef, goat, sheep, antelope, water-boc, beans, and grains, and drank boiled milk and wine. He was a gentle old man, and begged for wires and large beads, which I did not possess. His present was several fowls and some buttermilk, which I thought strange to see in this part of the world. Kittareh called, bringing a bunch of the richest plantain I ever saw, actually dropping juice. Before presenting it he went through the Uganda custom of smoothing it over with his hands, and rubbing it on his face. We became great friends, and he took me over his neatly- kept premises enclosed trimly with high fences of plantain leaf. In his hand he held by a cord a red pariah dog, and a liver-and-white beagle (?) followed at his heels. This animal was the only one of the kind I had observed. Kuddoo, a fine intelligent young fellow, was my companion up to Uganda : it was his duty to see that the various district officers on our route provisioned us properly. He was very fond of looking at pictures, a hunting-knife, or any European- made article. On my showing him a paper of pins, and strewing numbers amongst a crowd for them to take as curiosities, I was surprised to see all collected most carefully and returned to me, because their king did not permit them to keep anything so strange.

They are under extraordinary control these Wagan- da, and obey their king through fear, making as smart obedient soldiers as any in existence. Two on our march quarrelled one day, and fought in the most manly mannerlnot with spears, knives, or bows and

MODES OF SALUTING. 201

arrows, as an Unyambo, Seedee or Wanyamuezi would do. They planted their spears, tucked up their bark clothes, and wrestled until one knocked the other down, and held him till he gave in. Previous to our leaving the finely-kept grounds of Kittareh (the man owning the beagle), he brought out a stirrup- cup of wine and some boiled plantain-squash for the Waganda lads, who, having finished all, knelt in a body before the old man to thank him for his politeness. This they did by diagonally swinging their hands placed together, and repeating the words " N'yans, N'yans," or " M'wambeea, M'wambeea," in a loud choruslafter which, all sprang up, looking grateful and happy. The upper class are in the habit of making speeches. On a present being put into their hands, they hold it, and talk for five minutes expressing thanks. The Waganda mode of salute on meeting a friend is peculiar: neither party smiles until the words "Nyo, Nyi, Nyogeh," are repeated alternately by each many times, when one makes bold to address a sentence, then resumes the " Nyo " once or twice, and after these formalities a conversation may with propriety commence. When the women wish to show respect to a superior, they kneel before him like the Wanyamuezi women. All these social forms are as scrupulously attended to in Africa as the ceremonies at the most polite court of Europe.

On the march we never knew where we were to halt for the day. The men did not know themselves; they could not tell the probable time of arrival, so that the dinner-hour was always uncertain; and if our baggage was tied up by seven in the morning, we seldom left before eleven : once off, we continued

202 UNCERTAIN LIFE OF THE AFRICAN.

wandering till sunset. They were like a parcel of hungry hounds, darting into every hut, spear up, and shouting at places where they thought they could safely plunder, eating and drinking on the way perhaps five or six times a-day. Mariboo, although in charge of me, would be absent for days drinking, allowing me to get on as I best could; consequently, on several occasions, my conveyance, bedding, and writing materials were nowhere to be found. Some villagers, instead of presenting our party with wine, would in excuse make an offering of half-a-dozen cowries to me, and on having it explained to them that the white man did not exact presents, they would express great surprise. The Wezee doctor (Kiengo) of our party had Rumanika's orders to seize the officer of the Kisuere district for having committed two misdemeanours. The man had been to present me with a gourd of wine, and did so very hurriedly, slipping away from my sight. Soon after, chase was given, a party following him up to his house, but the alarm had preceded him. The cattle that were to have been taken as forfeited to Rumanika, and the wives who were to have become the wives of Kiengo, were both driven to the jungles, but the plunder that fell to the lot of his pursuers was brought into our camp. The case was an illustration of the uncertain life of African men and women. The home they have lived in since the day of their birth, may in an instant, by the caprice of another, be wrested from them, or they may return to find it a ruin. My Waganda were careful not to plunder too much in their own country, for fear of the wrath of their king; but when in Rumanika's territory, or on the borders

THE SHORES OF THE LAKE. 203

of their own, they never hesitated to seize what they could. In the same way the Karague race of Wan- yambo, now that they were of our party in the strange land of Uganda, were the most expert of thieves, making travelling painful and annoying from the cries of the sufferers. On inquiring of an officer whether such plunder was permitted by the king, he replied that the order was that the natives should quit their houses as soon as a guest came into the country, and take to the hill-tops. Numerous instances of this were observed, and on my wandering up a hill to beckon them back, they retired as we approached. On this occasion I had an instance of the taste of the Waganda race. The sun was setting (it was the 13th of May 1862), when one of them, having pointed out to me the various directions of the countries around us, quickly turned, and eagerly directed my attention to the full moon rising out of the Victoria Nyanza, sending its glittering rays over the beautiful placid waters. Here was a lover of the picturesque !

On the slopes looking towards the lake the climate was delightful, quite English ; only once, in a confined valley, did the temperature show a great heatlviz., 97, falling during the night, with the cold damp air, to 50. We had showers, on an average, almost every third day between 15th April and 19th May, and but one severe N.E. storm of wind and rain. On the 14th of May, our Seedees predicted that no rain would fall if Dr Kicngo's magic horn of an antelope were placed in the sun; " for," said they, " is not the M'ganga out ? No rain ever falls when it is in the open." Sure enough, when rain was threatened, the horn was taken in to prevent its getting wet.. The

SECTION 10

204 WAGANDA ORNAMENTS.

contents of these idol horns must be renewed periodically, as the charm within them is supposed to live or have power only for a certain period of time. Some other superstitions were observed on this route : [By the path a pole was stuck into the ground, with a large land-shell or some relic on the end of it; or the same relic was placed on the tallest branch of a tree. In the same way that we sometimes place a horse-shoe behind our front door, they hang a small charm of rush and feathers, or have a magic wand in the house. The Waganda had anklets of seeds, wood, &c., which were supposed to keep away snake-bites ; but few or no snakes were seen. Their other charms and ornaments consisted of tiaras of the abrus seeds, tiaras of large snowberries, necklaces of the scarlet amomum fruit, tusks of the wild boar, horn-tips of antelope, and a square or kidney-shaped pendant round the neck, covered with the skin of a serpent.

The industry and wealth of the Wazeewa or Mohia (a race mentioned in the Karague chapter), amongst whom our camp was pitched for a few days, was very marked. Some of them had migrated from the right to the left bank of the Kitangule, and were now cultivators under the king of Uganda, bringing all the grains of the country for barter into our camp. They seemed a very cleanly race, using little or no grease pomade on their bodies, and never sitting down unless some grass or leaves were placed between them and the ground. Many of their bark-cloths were coloured red crimson, having *zigzag* marks of black upon them. They dressed their cow-skins very beautifully, placing them stretched on a huge upright square frame to be thinned by scraping with a hatchet; this was observed in Bog-

WAZEEWA WOMEN. 205

web. also. One chief amongst them came to see me, leading his fat brindled dog, partly of bull-dog extraction. He wore a silver)" roan-coloured cow-skin down his back, and slung from the neckla most handsome garb, almost lustrous, and of which he seemed very proud. Their women were comely; and although they had an objection to allow me to drink out of their gurrahs or earthen jars of water, one of them, while her husband, an officer in the king's service, was absent, wished to accompany me on the march; but even this pleasure had to be declined, and the pretty Wazeewa had to console herself, as many others did, without even a lock of my straight hair, which was the wonder of them all. These people paid great attention to their plantain orchards. The bunches sometimes contained 200 large fruit, bending the stems, which had to be supported by a forked stick or ropes. On the fruit being ripe the tree is cut down, to permit the growth of the young shoot, which comes from the parent root. All the groves are of bare-poled single trees, which makes the fruit much finer than if the trees were allowed to grow in clusters; and should the leafstalk droop too much from the trunk, the natives bandage it up to prevent rain from beating into the heart of the tree. They use large circular trays, four feet across, made of osiers, and covered with cow-dung, for drying their grain in the sun. An article of diet not seen before was locusts; a number of them were brought in by a woman to be roasted as food. They were one inch long, had two pairs of wings, and antennae 1 inches long. White ants also, when young and freshly fledged, were caught in a framework placed over their mound of earth, to be eaten by the people.

206 A WOMAN MADE PRISONER.

In concluding these remarks upon the country lying between the two rivers Kitangulc and Katonga, which is occupied by Wanyambo, Wanyoro, Wazeewa, and Waganda, it may be mentioned that "Khass Uganda," or Uganda proper, has yet to be reached when the Katonga river is crossed; and as the dwellings, domestic and wild animals, &c., had nothing about them peculiar, we shall not stop to describe them, but cross the arm of the lake at the mouth of the above river.

Letters from Speke announced that the king of Uganda, as well as himself, were impatient for my arrival, and that I was expected to come by water. The king, he said, now dressed in English clothes, and our men were regularly supported by him. Uganda, however, was not a land of milk and honey. Grain could not be had to make bread, and I was, if possible, to lay in stores of flour and pease among the Wazeewa people.

By sunrise of the 20th May 1862, I had packed and was ready to cross the equator at Katonga Bay. Seeing a new face seated apart from, but within sight of, Mariboo's little wife, for the sake of speaking to the downcast-looking creature I advanced and asked her the way out of camp; she suckled an infant, was very pretty, with deep black round eyes, and she smilingly gave the information. She was so interesting that on getting into camp for the day I inquired her history. She had been captured by my Waganda the previous day, and was now their prisoner, for our party was strong, and her relatives, had they come to claim her, would also have been made slaves. She had not been brought into camp : we never again saw her, and my Seedees told me she must have been sold, as the Wa-

CROSS THE BAY OF KATONGA. 207

ganda would never give her up for nothing, or they might have killed her.

On the 20th of May, as I sat on a height admiring the beautiful Katonga Bay, one mile across, and looking at the sweep of richly-wooded land on its other side, with hills in the background, the king of Uganda's order arrived that I was to proceed to his capital by land, and the pleasure I had long anticipated of being conveyed by water was doomed to disappointment. My heart sank within me. I descended, however, to the edge of the bay, where our men were amusing themselves, and where five or six canoes were ready for the party. The Waganda and our Seedees got into them to splash and duck each other. The fowls belonging to the ferryman were seized and killed previous to crossing over, because, if the hippopotamus heard them crow, the canoes would be upset! Hours of *larking* were spent, and at last fourteen of us, with ten loads, sat in my canoe of four paddles, and we emerged from the winding channel of tall rushes into the bay ; here we were joined by two other canoes, all well laden. Racing commenced, the paddlers facing to the front, scooping the water with all their might as they sat on the *sides* of the canoe, and, for a marvel, not splashing us, for three-quarters of a mile over rippled water. Here, for the first time, I met with a plant whose leaves looked very beautiful in the water, growing by those of the lily of the Nilelnamely, the *Trapa natans,* the roots of which the Waganda eat. There was no shore to land at; a floating mass of tangled grasses prevented the further progress of the canoe, and we had to jump out into the water. One leg went down four feet to hard sand, while the other

208 AN AFRICAN LUNCHEON.

had to be pulled out of the grasses. A mile of this disagreeable wading, with a mid-day sun on the equator, was dreadfully fatiguing. On getting out of the swamp, we found the country flat and grassy, with cleared cultivated spots and huts. Here, in the shade of some plantain, while resting till the loads arrived, I saw Mariboo's wife enter the houses, quite alone, bringing out a large bundle, which she placed on the ground, and she was immediately surrounded by her servant-girl and two Waganda. I also made one of the party. The bundle contained boiled plantain, sweet potato, and a species of solanumlthe dinner of the people whose house she had entered! All seemed to enjoy it so much, eating it in such a refined way, with a leaf in their fingers to prevent them getting burnt, that the little woman, without any Hindoo ceremony, enticed me to join them, and I never made a better luncheon. Everything was cooked in the most savoury way, and I learned that African cooking is as cleanly and quite as wholesome as our own. It seemed strange that we should be so calm and unconcerned, when the tall spears of the inhabitants watching our movements were seen in the distance; but Mrs Mariboo must have known that the natives dared not attack any party belonging to the king.

The journey from Katonga Bay to the capital of Uganda|named Kibuga|was without exception the most disagreeable I ever made. Climbing over hills is bad enough for a lame person, but when a broad miry bog runs between each range, and there is no means of getting through it but by sinking into mud and water at every step, disgust is superadded. Most of the valleys were a quarter of a mile wide; others were square,

ROADS AND BRIDGES IN UGANDA. 209

and four miles from hill to hill|a dense mass of sombre foliage concealing their swamps, musquitoes, and low grounds. Ravines, dells, and gullies, formed by the waters from- the hill-sides, were veiled with impenetrable thickets; above these the inhabitants dwelt, surrounded by groves of the plantain at considerable distances from each other. Occasional red clay ant-heaps, boulders, and a few trees dotted the middle height of the hills, and the sky-line was a vegetation of waving grass, from three to six feet high. The general elevation of these hills above their valleys is four hundred feet. On their flat tops the air was fresh and delightful. Whichever way you looked, from your feet to the horizon was a sea of these flat-topped ridges and conical hills.

The Waganda make first-rate pioneers; one is struck with the direct cuts they make across the hills: perhaps their duty of conveying messages, or bringing in cattle and slaves to their king, conduces to this quickness of movement. When carrying me, if a hill, however steep, was to be crossed, they went directly over it, or if a bog was to be forded, it was all one to them| they would dash right into it. We had never seen a road in Africa till coming into Uganda; here they were so broad that a carriage might have driven along them, but they were too steep for any wheeled conveyance. No metal was used on them, but the grasses had been trodden down by the constant driving to and fro of cattle and slave-hunting parties. Attempts at bridges had been made, but we found them in a state of dreadful disrepair. Originally, in the late king Soona's time, piles with a forked end had been driven into the bog, and logs of wild date-palm, &c.,

210 THE ENSETE OF BRUCE.

were laid parallel with the run of the valley upon the piles, forming a passage about twelve feet broad. These had sunk and rotted, and walking over them with bare feet was annoying and painful. The trees and deep green foliage in the moist dells were densely thick and lofty, some with straight unbranched stems, towering higher than any ordinary palm. Ferns, mosses, creepers, climbers, &c., hid or covered their trunks and branches, making shade for the wild buffalo and elephant, who, unconscious of a stage erected overhead to watch them, would come to escape the heat of the day.

An extraordinary-looking tree, of the plantain family, was seen growing wild outside a cultivation. I brought home its seeds, and they have been pronounced to be the *Ensete* of Bruce, first discovered by him in Abyssinia. From its similarity to the plantain I had almost passed it unnoticed, but was attracted by its marvellous stoutness of stem and disproportionately low appearance, its shape being as if one big drum were placed over another, with gigantic single leaves growing from their sides. The natives wore necklaces made of its seeds, which were called M'seegwah by our Seedees. At 3N. they were again met with, growing upon broken rocky heights, but they were seen nowhere else. The leaves were much eaten by the goats.

The stretcher which carried me part of the way from Karague had been discarded, as the Waganda saw my only ailment was lameness and stiff knee-joint. Through such a rough country walking was very tiresome and a severe exertion, and it was made more so by the pace these excitable Waganda travel at. But they were very civil in assisting me through difficulties, a

INCIDENTS DURING THE MARCH. 211

sergeant and two privates (if we may call them so) being in constant attendance, leading the way or at my heels. They were Mariboo's chief men, fine fellows, very polite in lending a hand or even bringing water to wash off the pair of black boots of mud I had got in coming through the bogs. The marches varied from 9 to 11 miles daily, occupying from 7 A.m. till noon, or later, according to circumstances. If it was a populous country, and our long line passed through a grove having dwellings inside it, more time was taken. Each hut was entered and ransacked ; cautiously a Seedee or Waganda, musket or spear all ready, would go to the door and call, " Ho, ho!" and, gaining admission, come out with what he had picked up|tobacco, or a good bark-cloth. Every house passed was in this way plundered, while the inhabitants watched us in the distance. Travelling was most disagreeable, and sometimes our men suffered for their rashness. The light-hearted gallant little Mariboo came for the aid of two gun's one day, because one of his men had been wounded on entering a hut . My Seedees were up in an instant, ready to leave the baggage and myself to take care of each other, but no more than the number asked for went, and they returned without a combat. At another camp we were told to have our guns ready in the morning, as the natives were up in arms; a boy amongst them had been, the previous night, captured, and ransomed for two goats and four bark-cloths. Not understanding that Mariboo was the entire cause of such injustice, I ordered the guns of the Seedees to be filled with shot-sized pebbles instead of bullets; but we did not require to fire them. Even my men became as bad

212 MARCHING THROUGH BOGS.

as the Waganda at this trade, their guns making them daring; but it never came to my knowledge till it was too late. For instance, seeing one of Mariboo's boys lead two timid villagers to the grass hut occupied by my Seedees, I watched the result. A conversation ensued, the men afterwards passed me with two naked little girls with strings and tassels to their waists, looking dreadfully frightened. They had been stolen by my men, were the daughters of one of the two villagers, and had no doubt been recovered by paying bribes to Mariboo, his boy, and their captors.

The streams and bogs crossed may be alluded to. All those going towards the Lake Victoria Nyanza were fordable, of white muddy water, rarely brown or mossy, having their bottoms and edges of black mud, the accumulations of decayed vegetable matter. Those which ran north and away from the lake, within two marches of the Uganda capital, had a hard firm footing of sand, with dry edges, and little or no mud. The difference was very marked, and pleasant to observe. The passage of these Uganda bogs is most trying. Imagine a flat valley, a mile across, looking like an osier-bed, but covered with the gigantic papyrus and reeds, &c.; cut a narrow winding passage through it, leaving the roots in the water, and walk through this barefooted. The tears almost came into my eyes, the suffering from the sharp roots was so severe. Being carried was almost impossible, for even the natives, with the soles of their feet hard as leather, bearing their loads, dogs, spears, and shields on their heads, had enough to do to keep their footing. In my lame state, my feet, after having been covered with mud, came out of these bogs red and inflamed, too large to

THE RIVERS MWERANGO AND MOOGGA. 213

wear shoes with comfort; or where the valleys were free from the tall rushes, the chill of walking in such mire with a burning sun overhead was quite stupify- ing; but, strange to say, none of us suffered in health. The Mwerango, twenty miles west of the Uganda capital, was the first large body of water we found flowing towards Egypt. The centre part of the bridge over it had long since fallen into disrepair, and as the river was too deep for wading, we had to swim across about twenty yards of its width, which was from 300 to 400 yards. You could not look up or down the stream, as the reeds hid everything; neither could it be crossed anywhere but at this spot, or at other openings made in the bed of papyrus. In one hour our baggage was all across, and every one was freshened by a bathe. This stream and a sister river, the Moogga Myanza, join and form the Kuffoo, which flows to Unyoro, joining the Nile to the north of Kamarasi's residence. Regarding the rise of these two rivers there were various opinions among the Waganda. The Mwerango, they said, had its rise from rocks one day's journey to the S.S.W. of Namagoma. The other was honoured with a poetical tradition. It was named "Moogga," after one of the wives of the late king Soona. She, on becoming pregnant, was sent, for medical advice, to the S.E. of Namagoma. Accompanying the birth of the child there was a flow of water, which has run ever since, and was christened " Moogga," after the queen ! This river, or rather bed of rushes, was 500 yards across, and breast-deep. As we waded across it, on either side, within reach, the papyrus grew arching beautifully overhead. Its waters were clear, and sounded sweetly as they trickled

214 POKING, THE GOVERNOR.

through the rushes to our left, contrasting pleasantly with the bogs we had previously been crossing. When asked at Namagoma how long it would take to reach the source of the Mwerango, my friend Mariboo replied figuratively by saying, " A pot of plantain would not be boiled by the time you returned from its source," meaning that it would take a very short time.

As my caravan daily shortened its distance from the residence of the king, mes- sengers came to inquire for me, where I was to sleep each night, and to hurry on, because the king had heard I was *beautiful,* and he could not eat till he had seen me ! These parties were sometimes commanded by boys of thirteen years of age‌smart little fellows, who travelled very quickly over the country, never getting fatigued. If they met our caravan on the march, complimentary taps and rolls were sounded by their drummers, and returned by ours. It was not considered etiquette for any of their number to mingle with our baggage-party while moving along; because, if anything should be missed, they might be made answerable for it.

Pokino, the governor of a large territory, was one day announced while I was dressing. His name had been constantly quoted as an authority by Mariboo, and I had a strong desire to see him. On coming out of my hut, he sat surrounded by twenty Waganda in considerable state, and I could not help saying aloud, " Hallo ! is this Pokino ?" At once all grinned at the mention of the name; no one moved from their seated positions, and my iron chair was placed outside the red cow-skin, on which he alone sat,la determined, sly-looking functionary, with a bad expression of mouth, and just the man to have an order obeyed.

THE HABITATIONS OF THE WAGANDA. 215

His dress was the ordinary one of the country, robing him in graceful folds of bark-cloth, salmon-coloured, which harmonised well with his dark complexion. Round his bare head he wore a wreath of creepers *(Coccinia Indica),* which made me inquire whether his head ached. A laugh from him, and suppressed titter from his men at my ignorance, immediately followed, and he wished to see my pictures and lucifer-matches; of the former he preferred the buffalo's head, and one representing some slaves in chains; these amused him more than any of the others, and he soon took his departure, walking away slowly with considerable style, as if proud of his tall stout manly figure.

The dwellings on this route were superior to any we had met with in Africalloftier, better constructed, and more cleanly. Having command of immensely tall reeds, and beautiful grasses for thatching, with, in most places, tall spars, they could readily make themselves comfortable dwellings; besides which, they are a very neat-handed race. A M'ganda has a double roof of reeds to his house, like the two "flies" in an Indian tent. The outer " fly" has a steeper slope than the under, and is covered to the ground with a thick thatch of long broad-bladed grass, a species of wild sugar-cane. This roofing appears when new white and clean from the inside, and is placed with perfect regularity, and supported by more poles than are generally requisite, as there are sacks of grain, dried flesh or fish, &c., to be slung from them. The interior is partitioned off into front and rear compartments, by means of high screens of the plantain leaf. The better class of houses have a raised bedstead in the dark interior,

216 A MAUSOLEUM.

which has but one door as an outlet for smoke, goats, and inhabitants. They also have their summer- houses, generally in a shady spot, where men meet to chat, smoke, and drink. It was amusing to see such comfort in these " barzahs," which only required a table, and to be seated round, to look like a remarkably neat summer-house at home. Two huts on a height appeared devoted to the remains of the dead. On getting over the fence surrounding them, a lawn having straight walks covered with gravel soil led up to the doors, where a screen of bark-cloth shut out the view of the interior. Conquering a feeling of delicacy, I entered one of the huts. I found a fixed bedstead of cane, curtained as if to shade its bed of grass from the musquito, spears, charms, sticks with strange crooks, tree-creepers, miniature idol-huts of grass, &c. These were laid in order in the interior; but no one was there, and we were told it was a mausoleum. These, or similar places less pretentious, might be seen on the bare hill-sides; the latter merely square enclosures or fences of tall reeds, which my Waganda orderlies called " Looaleh," or sacred ground. Occasionally one of their men, to amuse us, went through a strange unnatural antic. Placing both elbows at his sides, with the hands pointing upwards, like a position in the dumb-bell exercise, he commenced glimmering with his eyes, writhing the muscles of his shoulders and back, never drawing breath, and gradually sinking to the ground till he apparently lay dead, as if he had worked himself into a trance, or sleep of death.

Within a radius of thirty miles from the palace nothing is allowed to be plundered, as a number of government annuitants reside there. It was a greatNEWS ABOUT UGANDA. 217

pleasure to get amongst them to see order once more. Sheep, goats, and cattle were safe grazing at the roadside|not one of my escort dared touch them. It must have been very trying to them, for provision was scarce, and could not be purchased. We passed some small lakes, and the residence of the present king when he was a youth|all was now a wilderness, but pointed to with as great reverence as we should regard a sacred or historical spot. When within one march of the capital, Mariboo refused to convey me nearer " till an order came, because all travellers remained there a fortnight and more|it was the custom of the country!" However, the detention was only for one day, and on the morning of the 26th of May a dashing party of Seedees came with their usual joyful demonstrations, bearing a letter and a fore-quarter of goat from my friend Speke! Cheering thought, to have him once more so near! We now heard a great deal of news. First, " there was no food, only boiled plantain, in Uganda, and this could only be had by risking their lives! My arrival would be celebrated by a great deal of bloodshed. Captain Speke was a favourite with the king, because he was not, like the Arabs, particular about having the cattle or goats killed according to Mohammedan rites." This last bit of news led me to ask Frij whether all Mohammedans ate fish. His reply 'was, " They do not eat every fish| only those that have the finger and thumb mark of God making them lawful." They continued: " Baraka, who had been sent to the north with letters for the boats from Egypt, had been seen in Unyoro all safe, but its king would not allow him to come to join us *md* Uganda. The ships were still at Ugani. The

218 THE AMAZON SIMILAR TO UGANDA.

Nile went to Misr (Egypt). The men and women killed daily by a blow on the back of the head are cut in pieces by knives made from the common reed; the pieces are then put into a cloth, and thrown to the birds; Masoongo, the head executioner, reserving for himself all their hearts! Speke had saved the lives of four or five people. If a man is seen being led away with his hands tied in front, he is marked for execution|if they are tied behind, he is under sentence of a fine."

We shall by-and-by see whether this gossip, brought me by the Seedees, had any truth in it. And it may not be uninteresting to mention here, that at a private audience given me by his Holiness the Pope in 1864, when I submitted to him a map of our route, explaining the general configuration of the country upon the equator, he remarked with animation, that my description tallied with what he had observed in the country of the Amazon, where he had passed many years of his life as a missionary,|a fact I had not known before. The Amazon is in the same parallel of latitude as Uganda.

11

SECTION 11

CHAPTER X.

Uganda, May 27 To July 7, 1862|Meeting With Captain Speke | Audience With The King Of Uganda | The Queen's Drawing-hoom|The Detective System|The Executioners|Stick Drill|Ingenious Workmen In Uganda|A Storm.

The day of my arrival at the Uganda capital, the 27th of May 1862, was one not only of intense joy, but deep thankfulness. I felt that my prayers for our safety had been heard. Speke and I had been separated for upwards of four months, and on being led by some of his men to the small hut he occupied, we were so happy to be together again, and had so much to say, that when the pages of the king burst in with the royal mandate that his Highness must see me "to-morrow," we were indignant at the intrusion. The morrow, however, came, and with it the same sharp, intelligent boys, to say that my stool might be brought to sit upon in the presence of the king. Accordingly, the present of a gun and some ammunition having been graciously received by him, at three o'clock, dressed in my best suit|*i. e.,* white trousers, blue flannel coat, shepherd's-plaid shirt, a helmet, and a red turban|I

220 MY FIRST INTERVIEW WITH M'TESSA.

sallied forth with Speke and some Seedees to make the call. It may be mentioned, as a curious custom of the court at Uganda, that when I told Speke that I meant to wear knickerbockers at the levee, he warned me that I should not be considered "dressed" if any portion of my bare leg was left exposed. This costume, because my stockings were not long enough, had therefore to be abandoned for white trousers. In proceeding to the palace we had to make one short descent, cross a bog, with grass thrown over it to keep the feet from being soiled, and rise on a broad road to the top of a hill, on which several hundred houses were built, each surrounded with a screen of tall reeds. The outer gate, having iron bells behind it, was slid aside, and we entered under a cord strung with charms. Here was a wide oblong space, screened all round; one steep-roofed house, beautifully thatched, was the only dwelling visible. Inside its wide threshold sat a single figure; and on the open space in front a mob of bare-headed, well-dressed Africans sat, forming a crescent, and facing " His Majesty M'tessa." Our approach was abruptly stopped, and we were directed to halt. Some minutes elapsed, the court broke up, and the mass of people ran quickly through a wicket that had been opened. We followed, but the doorkeeper closed the gate, and ten minutes elapsed ere we were admitted. We next entered a similar place, but smaller, and stood in the sun, uncomfortable enough, till permitted to be seated on our stools, with our hats off and umbrellas up. M'tessa sat upon a bench of grass, with a dog behind him. His kamaraviona (commander-in-chief) was the only man allowed to sit at his feet; a sister and

MY FIRST INTERVIEW WITH M'TESSA. 221

several women were on his left, also seated on the ground under the shade of the lofty cane-and-grass building. His quick eye detected that part of my hand had been cut of. "How did this happen?" He no doubt fancied that some offence had been committed by me, as it was the custom of his court to maim people by cutting off fingers, feet, or ears for even slight offences. He spoke in whispers to his pages, when Mariboo, the officer who had charge of me from Karague, informed him that I had received the wound in my hand in action; he also told him of the difficulties he had in bringing me to his majesty. The people listened with the most perfect decorum, only once interrupted by a sudden arrest. Maulah, the chief " detective," observing some breach of etiquette |probably a man speaking above his breath|suddenly seized the offender, and dragged him away. The look of anguish of the miserable creature thus apprehended was most painful. No one ventured to show sympathy; and Maulah soon returned alone, looking pleased and satisfied.

Conversation is never interrupted by these scenes ; music from drums and other instruments drown any noise made by a poor prisoner, or it is continued to please the ears of those attending the levee. The mode of testifying allegiance was curious; the mob suddenly stood up *en masse,* with their long sticks balanced in the air, and charged towards the threshold several times, with shouts of praise for their king, who made no acknowledgment. The court broke up, after an hour, by the king walking away on tiptoe, with the most ludicrous swagger, through a screen leading into another enclosure. The doors were222 M'tessa, The King Of Uganda.

opened and shut by men, who watched every movement of the king, for fear they should be discovered off the alert, and punished according to his caprice. A short time afterwards, a third scene was prepared for us. On entering the courtyard, M'tessa leant in a studied, affected attitude against the portico; about two hundred women sat on the ground on one side, and we were told to bring our chairs to within twenty yards of him, facing the women. No men except our Seedee interpreters were present. The remarks of the great potentate, who regarded us with a kindly surprised air, were confined to his favourite women, and seemed to be concerning our appearance. After a time, the thought seemed to strike him that we all ought to remove to some more shaded place. This was the only sensible thing he had done. Making us draw our stools close to the iron chair on which he sat, the conversation turned upon sport, our expedition, &c. A woman ran to fetch the gun he had that day been presented with; two others held spears beautifully polished. He signalled that I was to show my head uncovered to the ladies; a titter followed, and all of us laughed heartily. Another signal, and I was told to place my hat on; this made us all feel less restraint; and the women were not afraid to return our smiles at the ridiculous formality of the scene. As the sun was approaching the horizon, this " drawing-room " was ended by M'tessa walking away, leaving us to reflect on the strange events of the day. He was a tall, well-built young fellow, sprightly in manner, very vain, his woolly hair dressed with the greatest care; small head, remarkably prominent clever-looking clear eyes, good teeth, and long

WOMEN SENT TO EXECUTION. 223

nails to his hands and feet; the instep of the latter was, as in most of the Waganda, highly arched, indicating a well-moulded sinewy leg. His bark- cloth " toga " had not a speck upon it, and was neatly knotted over the right shoulder, concealing his whole body. His ornaments of beads were made with great taste in the choice of colours ; the most minute beads of white, blue, and brown were made into rings and rosettes, which he wore round his neck and arms. Each finger had upon it a ring of brass; on the third finger of the left hand he wore a gold ring, given him by Speke ; with these he played while sitting at his levees, occasionally receiving a golden-coloured gourd- cup of wine from a maid of honour sitting by his side ; after each sip, a napkin of bark-cloth was used by him to wipe his mouth. The only unseemly vulgarity he was guilty of while on his throne was to use his napkin to rub away the perspiration from his person. On leaving the court, and getting outside the last gate of the palace, a woman's screams made us look back; a cord was tied round her wrist, and a man dragged her, almost naked, down the hill to be executed ; she screamed " N'yawoh. ! n'yawoh ! " (Mother! mother!) in the most bitter anguish. A second, similarly tied, followed slowly, but not uttering a sound. A shudder of horror crept over me. Had we been the cause of this calamity ? and could the young prince with whom we had conversed so pleasantly have had the heart to order the poor women to be put to death ?

The road to our hut was crowded by files of men dressed as " Neptunes," in tattered leaves of plantain, their limbs coloured with ashes and vermilion, and

224 KING'S BROTHERS IN CHAINS.

girdles of long-haired goatskin (from Usoga) hanging from their backs and waists. Daily these wild-looking creatures shouted and rushed with all their might along the roads, spears and shields being held high in the air; they were M'tessa's men preparing and drilling for a slave-hunting campaign. The day after my first visit to the king, he came to return the call without giving us any warning. We heard a noisy crowd passing outside our enclosure, and immediately, through the fence, came the young king in a tremendous hurry. He was not the puppet of yesterday, but dressed, like a negro sailor, in an open coat of bed-curtain chintz, loose white trousers or " pyjamas," having a broad stripe of scarlet; his feet and head were naked. He was shown into an iron chair, and seeing some books he turned over their pages as a monkey would; asked to see the picture of Rumanika, and said he would like to know when his own portrait was to be done. His brothers, a mob of little ragamuffins, several in handcuffs, sat behind him chattering very familiarly, and tearing all the while at sugar-cane. I was told to show them my hair by taking off my hat. We were asked if we did not admire the leather wideawake made by one of the brothers?land the vulture, the dove, and the horn-bill his highness had just shot ? This scene over, the king rose, ordered Speke to follow him, and, led by the mob of brothers, all rushed madly away. On following them, the chained lads, escorted by two servants, were very much in the rear, and hobbled along, poor little fellows, in perfect good-humour, looking as strong, healthy, and contented as any of the others. It was said that the king, before coming to the throne,

INTERVIEW WITH THE MOTHER OF THE KING. 225

always went about in irons, as his small brothers now do. Where could they have got this custom ? Wishing to know what had become of Speke, I went in search of him, and found on the way a *flight* of pages lthere is no other name for it, as they always go at full speed, their robes flying, when serving the king. They were going with torches to light his highness home; but they knew not what route he had taken. It afterwards appeared that he had entered a house to dine upon boiled beef and wine, a share of which he offered to Speke; then, taking a suit of clothes out of the tin box he had got from us, and which was carried to this picnic, he cast aside his torn and dirty suit for another, and went home by torchlight and drums.

My introduction to the king's mother took place on the 1st of June. Captain Speke and myself went with five or six Seedees carrying pads of grass (stools not being permitted), with our gourds of pombe", our sucking-reeds, and umbrellas. The dowager lady had been informed of our intention, but took her time as to seeing us. Walking over one hill to the top of another, in three-quarters of an hour we were at her royal highness's gate. On getting as far as the second courtyard, we were told to wait, with the other visitors, in the drum or ante-house. Here for an hour we were left to smoke, drink, and doze. A musical instrument in the place was new to mela harmonicon of twelve blocks of wood, which, on being struck, gave out notes as glasses do when played. They rested upon the trunks of plantain, and were isolated from each other by thin reeds. We took our hats off on approaching the old lady, who laughed

226 CONDESCENSION OF HER MAJESTY.

most heartily, and welcomed us with great cordiality, telling us to sit in front of and near her. She seemed to me like a Tartar woman, being fair-skinned, stout, and short. Her head was shaved, and had a cord tied round it. Conversation was kept up briskly for an hour or so, during which she fondled in her lap a plaything the size and shape of a hedgehog, studded with cowries and beads. She sipped at wine, looked at herself in a small mirror, smoked, and, like any housewife at home, gave orders to her domestics. Quantities of plantain neatly tied up and arranged in line, several basketfuls of boiled beef also tied round with leaves, were laid out as a present for Mariboo and myself.

Each basket of beef was tasted by one of her officers tearing a bit away with his teeth, and we took our leave, very much pleased with her good-humour and homeliness. Many other calls were made upon her by invitation; but although we sat waiting the dowager for hours amongst steaming natives, she did not always give us an interview, saying she was too busy or too tired. Her brother, Katoon- zee, an officer of high rank, and with a most *distingue* Uganda air, pointing his toes and showing off his high instep as he walked, was treated with as much ceremony as ourselves, generally being obliged to sit so far distant from her that he had to bawl out to make himself heard. However, the dowager would allow him to whisper jokes into her ear, and be familiar enough when few were present. Any wine intended for us her majesty always tasted before it was presented. This was a condescension on her part not shown to every one.

The people of Uganda require to have the pennisSpeke's Influence At Court. 227 sion of an officer before the barber can use his razor. The women seen about the queen's residence had no hair, neither had she; all were shaved, and only a few in M'tessa's court were allowed to dress their hair in the same aristocratic fashion as the king. One of these women, in the bloom of youth, we one day saw led to execution. She was the fourth female victim that had passed that day. Her back was covered with scars, and blood appeared on her neck. She wept bitterly. Notwithstanding this circumstance, when we went and had an interview with the king, we found him as gay and cheerful as ever. His detective Maulah lived next hut to ours, and the shrieks of poor people, night and day, were quite heartrending. Not only were their cries heard, but each lash of the stick was distinct; and being in such close proximity to the place of torture was a severe trial. When Maulah captures women, they are asked, " Will you live with so and so ?" if they object, the rod is applied, and consent in this way is forced upon them. He and other chief officers were very jealous of Speke's influence with the king, for they knew he could at times obtain an interview, while they had to wait for days. On seeing us return from the palace, Maulah would inquire, " Have you seen the king ? " and when we wished for an interview, and asked how it could be brought about, he would coarsely reply, "Are you kings, that you always expect to be received ?" Certainly our influence had a most beneficial effect. Not only did Speke save the lives of many, but men about court got him to intercede with the king on several occasions. The executioner Konzah had a favourite son, who was under sentence.

228 THE KING'S LOVE FOR SPORT.

The boy, through Speke's intercession, was pardoned, and it was thought he would never again be punished; but on Bombay asking this high functionary "how the son was; had anything more been said of it ?" the father replied, "My boy was killed yesterday for another offence." A child-page whom we took an interest in, and whom Speke had dressed up very gaily, named Loogohie (or cloth), got into a dreadful scrape one day for coughing while the king was at dinner. It was thought his little ears would have been cut off, and he laughed very much when he found he had escaped, but he did not expect to live long, as he was always getting into hot water. On my asking what the king had killed when out shooting, Loogohie's reply was that, " As his highness could not get any game to shoot at, he shot down many people."

The king had become so fond of the gun, that, like a young sportsman, he seemed to dream of it . In the early morning his gun or the rattle of the diminutive drums which always accompanied his movements was heard. Interviews were difficult; his whole time was occupied. He had received so many presents from us, he had made so many promises to open the road, and his pages had stolen for him so much of our ammunition, that he at last was ashamed of himself, and suddenly permitted us to leave. For several days neither of us could visit him, being unwell, but Bombay, by showing some pictures to his servants, conveyed such accounts of us that communication was sometimes obtained. In a book he had received from Rumanika, 'Kaffir Laws/ his highness wished all the birds he had shot to be painted in imitation of our sketch-books. His pages pestered us, and became

NO COINAGE IN THE COUNTRY. 229

bold and insolent, walking into our hut, taking up anything they saw to examine it, or coming with the king's orders that our very beds, chairs, guns, shoes, &c., were wanted by the king, and saying there must be no delay about sending them. The union-jack which we had got from Admiral Keppel was also demanded. All these indignities, added to the brutal treatment of the women, made us feel that Uganda was not the "garden of pleasure" we had heard it called, and that the conduct of the king was a worse form of plundering than we had experienced in the Ugogo and southern territories. Here, by robbing us of our ammunition, they had placed us in a defenceless position; and though we did not want their offered hundreds of women and hundreds of cattle, it induced our Seedees to become mutinous, saying, " Although *you* don't take them, we will, for as yet we have received nothing but broken bones for the 2000 dollars' worth of property given to M'tessa." They refused to march with us until they obtained sufficient ball-cartridge. This occurred just previous to our departure, up to which time our men had been gathering a precarious existence from what could be plundered from the gardens.

No beads were allowed to be taken here by the natives, although privately they would always purchase sufficient provision for ourselves and men. Cowries were a more current coin, one hundred of these shells making one string = a bunch of a hundred plantain=the skin of a goat; and a single large gourd- ful of wine cost a sheet of bark-cloth. We fortunately received goats now and then from the king, and sweet potatoes from one of the gardeners in exchange for

230 THE PUBLIC EXECUTIONEBS.

beads. There was no flour nor milk used in the country, the natives living entirely upon plantain boiled, or made into wine, which they called " m'wenge"." There was very little drunkenness visible. Cattle were rarely seen : the hills all round were such a mass of tall reeds and grasses that they could not penetrate them; even a dog would have had difficulty in hunting through these thickets. Pleasant walks were cut through them, and kept from being grown over by the constant transit of slave parties. Katoonzee returned from one of these during my stay at Uganda. He had captured 130 women, chiefly old, and only fit for weeding the fields. Some few, fitted for wives, stood apart, to be given away to men thought deserving, or whose services were to be rewarded. Each woman of this class was worth three cows. An instance occurred of the king having given a single slave to one of his officers for some service performed, and the man being bold enough to ask for another, was cut to pieces with the usual reed knife. His limbs were carried away openly, while the trunk was wrapped in a cloth. There were several executioners, men of rank, who were the privy councillors of the king. These men had numbers of followers, distinguished by wearing their mark of officela short turban of cordland sometimes carrying a peculiarly- shaped bludgeon. Konzah has been mentioned; another, named Oozoongoo, was always carried to court in a litter, being an invalid. On meeting him, he would stop to speak, and in expression had nothing repulsive; but when seen with a wreath of black fringe encircling his head, hiding his eyes, and hanging down to near his mouth, his appearance was com-

STICK PARADE. 231

pletely changed, and he reminded one of a black Highland bull looking fiercely through his forelock . Both these executioners were really polite men, always frank when met at the palacelmuch more so than the kamaraviona (commander-in-chief), who was a proud, haughty young fellow. One day I had the curiosity to follow a poor woman who was led by a boy to be killed. She carried a small hoe, balanced upon her head. No one told me she was under sentence, but the cord on the wrist was sufficient; and after travelling for half a mile, I followed her down to the executioner's gardens. Waiting outside for some time, not a sound was heard, nor a person seen. A lazy, yellow-beaked vulture, the cannibal of Uganda, sat perched on the stump of a broken tree; others hovered high overhead, looking on the scene below. This circumstantial evidence was enough for me, and I returned.

One of the sights at the capital of Uganda was to watch the crowds of men on the highroad leading to the palace; all were under officers, perhaps a hundred in one party. If wood is carried into the palace up the hill, it must be done as neatly as a regiment performs a mameuvre on parade, and with the same precision. After the logs are carried a certain distance, the men charge up hill, with walking-sticks at the " slope," to the sound of the drum, shouting and chorus- sing. On reaching their officer, they drop on their knees to salute, by saying repeatedly in one voice the word " n'yans " (thanks). Then they go back, charging down hill, stooping simultaneously to pick up the wood, till, step by steplit taking several hourslthe neatly-cut logs are regularly stacked in the palace

232 YOUNG GIRLS PRESENTED TO THE KING.

yards. Each officer of a district would seem to have a different mode of drill. The Wazeewah, with long sticks, were remarkably well disciplined, shouting and marching all in regular time, every club going through the same movement, the most attractive part of the drill being when all crouched simultaneously, and then advanced in open ranks, swinging their bodies to the roll of their drums.

At every new moon M'tessa went through an examination of his idol horns; but I should not suppose him to be much of an augur: he was too light-headed and fond of field-sports, of boating, swimming, and music, to give much attention to making rain, &c. He left all these things to the Witchwezee race who were about him, and seldom denied himself to visitors at the time of new moon. On the very day that four of his women were going to execution, at an audience given to ourselves and in our presence, some maidens were offered for his harem. He had detained us in an outer court for a long time, and probably brought us in to enjoy our surprise at the poor naked offerings. Each held by the upper corners an open napkin in front of her, and all were smeared with grease and decorated with girdles and necklaces of beads. After being reviewed without a smile, they were told to face to the right, and march to the " zenana." As was customary, the king then sat on the knees of the matron-like woman who had presented the maidens, and, having ordered all away but ourselves, the interpreters, and some young lads, a conversation began about men and women in general. It is, however, worthy of remark, that M'tessa never behaved indecently by word or deed while women were present;

THE DRESS OF THE WAGANDA. 233

his language was uniformly correct. On his complaining of sickness, medicine was brought him by a page, one of our men having first to taste it. In all probability the page was made to swallow the pill instead of the king! He and all his people were less suspicious of us than of any traders; our presents were received without the usual form of preparation; whereas, when Dr Kiengo, the native of Unyamuezi, gave his offering of five giraffe tails, a mould of Kittara copper, &c., all were dipped into plantain wine or " mVenge"," which had to be drunk by the Doctor to show there was no impurity connected with the presents. A pill, having great virtues, was licked all over for the same reason by Kiengo.

The ingenuity of the Waganda in imitating our chairs, mode of walking, dress, gun-covers, &c., was very striking. Having seen so many of our pictures, they at last took to drawing figures of men in black upon their bark-cloths.

At light work they are highly ingenious. Their spears, knives, drums, shields, ornaments, houses, &c., are made with great taste and exactness. Their bark- cloths are cut from several varieties of ficus, beaten upon a log with a mill-headed wooden hammer, and sewn beautifully together into large shawls, ranging in uniform tint from salmon-colour or maize to a brick red. These are very becoming on an African skin, and when worn by our Seedees as a turban, the harmony of colour was pleasing. Our men in Uganda could not be distinguished at a distance from the natives; for their Zanzibar clothes being worn out, they dressed like them in bark-cloths, or the skins of cattle and antelope prepared by leaving on the hair.

234 THE FOOD AND CLIMATE OF UGANDA.

The skins of small antelope, made white and soft as kid, are put together so well that the sewing with banana or aloe fibre is scarcely observed. They have not attained the art of the brazier. The habits of the people are so simple, that the fresh green leaf of the banana serves them as a plate. Wine they drink out of a corner of their cow-skin coverings; shoes, hats, and gloves they have not yet obtained; and a strip from a reed is their knife, as we have often seen when the palace guards were at their excellent meal of good boiled beef, mashed plantain, and wine. Their dinner was a strange good-humoured scramble, the strongest keeping meat from the weakest by snatching it away or tossing it about. They are excellent cooks, cutting butcher-meat up into very neat joints, wrapping them with fresh plantain leaves, and boiling all in a large earthen pot full of plantain, to which, by this process, a rich flavour is added. Our Seedees miaap.fl many a good dinner by not partaking of this fare, on account of their profession as Mussulmans. They could not eat plantain that had been boiled with unlawful meat.

Lightning was said to be very much dreaded at Uganda, but no cases of death occurred from it during our stay.   One of the king's houses was burnt down, the accident causing a great commotion, because on the occurrence of such a calamity it is every one's duty to render aid. We did not call that day (the 30th June), because an interview would have been impossible. The storm had commenced by rain at 1 P.m. ; during a lull we had thunder, lightning, and hail; by 5 P.m. all had cleared away, and .82 inch of rain had fallen. During June, misty showers fell

THE CLIMATE OF UGANDA. 235

almost every day, but not enough to measure in a rain-gauge. The valleys were veiled every morning by a dense fog, and very often we had no sun the whole day. The heaviest shower noted was in the following month of July (4th), when 1.04 inches were measured.

12

SECTION 12

CHAPTER XI.

UGANDA TO UNYORO CAPITAL, 7TH JULY TILL 9TH SEPTEMBER 1862|FIRST STAGE, CAMPS UNITED, UGANDA TO KAREE|THE CATTLE AND SPORT OF THE COUNTRY|ONE OF THE SEEDEES KILLED BY THE NATIVES|BUDJA, THE CHIEF NATIVE OFFICER|MUSICAL INSTRUMENTS | CAPTAIN SPEKE PROCEEDS

TO THE LAKE NYANZA|ANTELOPE-SHOOTING DIFFICULTIES

IN THE WAY OF THE AUTHOR'S ADVANCE|SPEKE RETURNS, AND THE CAMPS ARE UNITED | ELEPHANT - HUNT IN UNYORO.

Although the distance from Uganda to Unyoro by a direct route was reported not much above eighty miles, we were not confident of the fact. The marches given by the natives can seldom be depended upon. A M'ganda without a load will march the whole day, stopping at every hut where he can get anything to eat or drink. A laden Seedee thinks six miles, or even less, a day's work. How, therefore, could we anticipate that Unyoro was so near to us as eighty miles ? The journey may be divided into three sections: the first, from Uganda to Karee, when Speke and I travelled together; the second, when Speke tried the water route and I the land; the third,

WE MARCH TOWARDS UNYORO. 237

when we joined our forces and marched into Unyoro headquarters.

I. Uganda To Karee, Four Marches; Camps United.

The country at first was hilly. As we proceeded north, it gradually assumed the appearance of parks and grazing grounds, dotted with trees and clumps of bushes, favourable for stalking. Water was abundant in the sandy-bottomed streams and miry swamps. With this change of outline, we had no longer the gigantic reed of Uganda; it was replaced by a waving grass three feet high. The trees were small, the same as those species met with 5 south of the equator. Scarcely one-tenth part of the route was under cultivation. Plantain groves were more abundant than fields of sessamum and Indian corn; and in the houses we occupied, bundles of seeroko and jooggo (a pulse and bean) were found. It was a disagreeable march in one respect; for as soon as our caravan halted at a grove, the cultivators fled, and when we entered their houses we found the fire burning, with earthen pots, grain, and vegetables, and their beds and bark-cloth bedding undisturbed. All the etceteras about their snug little domiciles lay at the mercy of our men. Knives, shields, shells, beads, skins, pipes, tobacco, &c., hung from the roof, or were stuck into the rafters; and, on our leaving, it was not a rare occurrence to find that our men had ruthlessly burnt some of the supports of the hut to make themselves a fire to cook their food. This they would do most wantonly, although they had the best of the country, paying nothing for the plundered goats and other property per-

238 THE CATTLE OF THE COUNTRY.

mitted to be taken by M'tessa. The dwellings were not different from those already described, but each had over its doorway a diamond-shaped charm of rush, hung horizontally, and generally stuck with feathers.

The cattle seen in the low grazing country were almost "prize" animals. They were made hornless when young|not by sawing off the horns of grownup animals, as still barbarously practised in Scotland, but by searing with a hot iron. They were most docile, handsome creatures. The general colour was grey, their faces and inside the ears black; they had little or no hump, and were larger in bulk than an Ayrshire cow. The cowherds were the lanky Wa- huma, called here Waheema, who might be seen tending herds of several hundreds at a time. These people were never afraid to come out and look at our caravan, even when it passed their ring fences in a secluded tract of country several miles away from any cultivation. The Waganda, on the contrary, on meeting us, would fly off the road, leaving whatever they might be carrying to be plundered by our followers. This difference in the two races is accounted for by the Wahuma never being made slaves, although their women are very much prized for their beauty as wives. M'tessa had given orders that we and our escort were to receive sixty cattle and ten loads of butter. Half-a-dozen cattle were first brought as an offering. Those made over to our Waganda disappeared the first night, and as ours, having been tied up, were all safe, we were called magicians. When the number was completed, our share was marked by squaring their tails, so as to distinguish them from those taken by the Waganda. During the night they

TRAPS FOR LIONS. 239

were placed within a fence made to surround the only door of a hut occupied by a M'nyamuezee, Manua, who constituted himself their guardian. On receiving an order to slaughter one, our table-knives were called into requisition because the common country knife had no guard to it, and was not considered lawful. The Seedees, though knowing nothing of the Mohammedan religion, the majority not being circumcised, were much more particular on those occasions, and offered more opinions than a "moulvie," or Mussulman priest, would. "The animal must lie facing a proper direction;" "a certain man must officiate," &c. The tracks of elephants and buffalo were numerous, but none of the animals were seen; neither did we shoot any lions, but we heard them at night. It was not a roar, neither was it the sound a lion makes in a menagerie; at the time I considered it to be no more alarming, even to a novice, than if one were to blow through a cow's horn. Two zebra were shot by Speke, and eaten by the Waganda escort, and the skins, being the property of royalty, were simply left in a hut, the proprietor of which was bound to have them conveyed to the palace. Pallah, hartebeest, and other antelope were seen or shot, and might have been hunted on horseback at certain seasons. The n'jezza, whose horns curved over the brow, was new to us. None of these animals were ever seen in herds; a dozen together would be considered a large number. As it was also a great cattle country, the natives tried to trap the lion by means of a number of logs raised high on end. When the animal came under them for the bait of a live goat, all the logs, guided by piles on either side, fell in a mass, crushing him, somewhat after the

240 INGENIOUS FOOT-TRAP.

fashion of the triangle of sticks and stones adopted in the Himalayas to kill tigers, leopards, or bears. Never having seen the contrivance in this form, my curiosity was raised to enter; luckily some Seedees called out in time to tell me of my danger. Three of our cows were less fortunate; one was killed, becoming food for our Waganda escort, because the Seedees would not touch it, and two were dragged from under the logs much bruised. The natives were eager sportsmen, netting the smallest or largest antelope, which they ate or conveyed alive to their king. Nets were made of beautiful soft and strong fibre, from the aloe generally.

A most simple, ingenious foot-trap for wild buffalo we observed here for the first time. It was set generally at salt-licks, where these animals were known to scratch the ground, and consisted of two small circles of wood, placed immediately one over the other; between them a quantity of stout acacia thorns pointed to a common centre; all were lashed strongly together, and the trap, when completed, was several inches larger than a buffalo's foot. This was fitted over a hole made in the ground, and a noose (attached to a block of wood) laid over it, and concealed with earth. On the buffalo putting his foot upon it, the trap fastens, and the more he struggles the tighter the noose becomes. The former king of Uganda was said to have kept a large menagerie of animals caught in this way.

Birds were not numerous; the cannibal vulture of Uganda, now that we had left the capital, was a rare bird. Guinea-fowl and florikan were the only game- birds observed, the grass being too tall to discover partridge, &c. An owl of very handsome plumage, weighing six pounds, was shot. A graceful bird on

FIRE IN CAMP. 241

the wing|a new goatsucker|with a single feather of each wing twice his own length, and since named *Cosmetornis Spekii,* skimmed amongst the plantain trees at night. These long feathers probably sweep up flies as they float behind him.

Fish were not to be had on this route, although cruives or basket-traps, the shape of an Egyptian water-jar, and made of flags or papyrus, were constantly found in the houses of the people. The way of placing them was as follows:|Two long parallel ditches, six feet apart, were cut in a swamp ; here and there their waters were made to communicate. At these points the baskets were laid on their sides, and the fish driven into them, whence there was no escape.

While detained at Karee receiving a portion of the cattle ordered to be given us by the king, we had several exhibitions of the temper of the people. As was customary, we took possession of their houses, and dwelt in them for eight days. This so exasperated them, that, on our Seedees going to fetch water, or leaving camp, they were threatened; a spear was thrown, and one of our men, named Karee, was killed. No redress could be obtained till the king had been communicated with. His reply was, " Allow it to pass over for the present, and when the villagers have returned to their houses I will send a party to seize them all." The night previous to our leaving, two huts occupied by Seedees were set on fire|the natives throwing in a bunch of burning straw at the doorway. Egress through the flames was impossible; but, having secured their guns, they cut their way through the side of the hut, losing a bayonet and their bark-cloths. Precautions were taken against any further alarm;

242 THE ARMS OF THE WAGANDA-

and, on leaving in the morning, after they had fired the hut, our Waganda escort took a delight in burning down all the houses they had occupied. The spear that had been thrown at our men was brought in as a trophy; its handle was 7 feet long, having a blade of 16 inches. This is the size of the common Waganda spear; and one wonders that they ever throw it, as you can always see it coming, and get out of its way. With guns unloaded, no ordinary Seedee would have a chance with a M'ganda, his movements through the tall grass are so rapid. Our men got to know this after the death of poor Karee, who had been the spokesman of the camp. He .was a tailor by trade, and had made several suits, after English and Arab patterns, for the king, who never paid him his bill|namely, four cows. His body was buried by moonlight, in a grave dug with bayonets,| the men remarking that they never saw such a march as ours was, we did not even carry a hoe. The truth was, they had lost or thrown away all our pioneer implements. The men were very crestfallen on the night of this death, the younger Seedees being afraid, to carry the body, and the older remarking, "Suffr maqueesha," " Oh, the march is now done for."

The villagers had a dread of keeping anything left behind by our men. An old bit of calico was brought us by a woman, accompanied by two servant-girls carrying m'wenge" and plantain for us. She sympathised in our loss of Karee, and, having accepted a present of beads, thanked us in the most gentle way by moving her hands and slowly repeating in a soft low tone the word " n'yans," thanks. Her attendants then fell upon their knees, and bashfully, with down-

NATIVE TOBACCO. 243

cast eyes, went through the same form of acknowledgment. Another instance of the honesty of the people may be mentioned. Manua, the cowherd, wished to return to the last camp for a cloth he had forgotten. On telling him that it would be brought to him, he hesitated, but the wild strains of a tambira were heard approaching the camp, and the rag was produced by the party, along with a gourd of wine for the Mazoongoo. In this case the instrument was played as a token of truce, to show that the arrivals were friendly. On the other hand, the natives often betrayed fear. If a few huts were passed by us while out shooting, first the children, then the women, and afterwards the men, armed, would fly from their houses, and conceal themselves in the plantain groves. This order was invariably observed the children were the first care of the parents. Once, on calling to some men running away, a single man came up and sat by us; others became equally bold, and did so also, till a mob gathered round us, and the women returned to their several vocations in and out of the houses. To test their hospitality, I asked for as much tobacco as would fill my pipe. A handful was given me with the greatest readiness. It was like the coarsest- grained black tea in appearance and consistence; and, after obtaining information about the game to be procured in the country, we parted excellent friends so much so that the day following they paid me a visit at my hut, and brought me some more tobacco, for which they received a present of beads.

Budja, the chief officer or M'koongoo, whom the king had sent in charge to deliver us over to the king of Unyoro, was a very handsome, intelligent man,

244 BUDJA, A KING'S OFFICER.

clean in his dress, and never sitting down unless a carpet of cowskin was laid for him by one of his attendant boys. Like all his race, he was impetuous ; if sent for, he would come leisurely with the haughty airs of M'tessa, sit for a moment, pretend to listen to what was said, and before any business about the march could be negotiated, would rise abruptly, making some silly excuse, that the cattle must be looked after, &c., and then disappear. He travelled with three wives tall, fair women and about twenty young lads, who anticipated his every wish. One amongst them always looked after the ladies, whether on the march or in camp; another had both ears and fingers cut off for adultery. These men without ears had a very curious appearance one old man in particular, his head looking like a barber's block, with black holes bored in it; not a fragment of the external ear was left. Whether the operation ultimately affected their hearing we could not ascertain, but apparently it did not; they had the sharp look of pug dogs. As Budja and party will accompany me into Unyoro while Speke goes to look at the exit of the Nile from the lake, his name will appear often in this chapter. He was a great authority on the road, being the mediator between the kings of Uganda and Unyoro. On asking him what relation a certain man was to the queen-dowager of Uganda, he replied by placing his left hand on his own right shoulder, thereby signifying that they were full brother and sister. I had never before seen any race that adopted this mode of expression, and it would imply that they, like ourselves, think the right hand of more importance than the left Budja, however, could use either hand equally well.

MUSICAL INSTRUMENTS. 245

On his arm he carried a reed-whistle three inches long, but it seemed to be more for ornament than use.

In Uganda were both wind and stringed musical instruments, and the natives excelled in whatever they attempted. Night and day, in the palace precincts, the sound of drums was heard from the hill-sides. Every officer who commanded fifty men was allowed a kettle-drum. These were neatly made of wood, and when carried were slung on the back by shoulder- straps ; the short drumsticks were stuck in loops outside, and a loose cover protected them from sun and rain. Each party of men had its regimental drum- call. Budja's was a certain number of taps in quick time, which we all soon got to distinguish from any other. But none sounded such a loud tenor " doogoo, doogoo, doogoo," as the king's small drums when he was out for the day. They were beaten so as to make the sounds swell from double piano to forte, and *vice versa*. At all levees bands of reed and bugle players attended, and also danced. The reeds, held like flageolets, were never without decorations of blue, white, and scarlet beads, with hair at their lower ends, and they sounded sweet and pleasing. Sometimes an enormous kettle-drum, slung over a stout Waganda's neck and shoulder, was allowed to join the wind instruments. It was profusely decorated with shells, beads, brass bells, bouquets of long goat's hair, &c., and beaten by single taps, the drummer throwing back his head and body, and giving a deep long " Bah!" after each tap. The harmonicon has been mentioned, also the stringed "nanga" or tambira, their most elegant instrument, looking, while laid in the lap to be played, like a harp in miniature. The queen generally

246 OUR CAMPS DIVIDE.

had a blind musician performing on the harp, and the king was most expert at all these instruments, sitting for hours playing or listening to others. There was not much singing among the Waganda, though a great deal of instrumental music. During the march they sang in a quivering voice, slurring the notes and words in an odd manner, only heard in Uganda. They could all whistle through their fingers, and snapped them curiously when wanting to speak with emphasis. On parting with M'tessa, he gave rather indefinite orders to Budja, who was in charge of our march, to take us to the exit of the Nile from Victoria Nyanza, nearly east of his residence. This route was not adhered to by Budja, and for four days, in the most obstinate manner, he led us more north than east . Having got so far out of the line, it became a question whether it was really of importance to visit this point. Speke did not see any great advantage in it, and many would have been of the same opinion, because we had seen the lake daily from above our quarters at Uganda, and knew, from all accounts, that after making a few more miles we should come upon an immense river, with which we were now running parallel. However, in order to avoid any reproach or charge of indifference at home, we resolvedlBudja being overruledlto see the river issue from the lake, and thus leave nothing undone. Speke asked me whether I was able to make a flying march of it along with him, while the baggage might be sent on towards Unyoro. At that time I was positively unable to walk twenty miles a-day, especially miles of Uganda marching, through bogs and over rough ground. I therefore yielded reluctantly to the necessity of our parting; and I am anxious to

OUR CAMPS DIVIDE. 247

be explicit on this point, as some have hastily inferred that my companion did not wish me to share in the gratification of seeing the river. Nothing could be more contrary to fact. My state of health alone prevented me from accompanying Speke to set at rest for geographers the latitude of the interesting locality, as to which we were perfectly satisfied from native report.

II. CAMPS SEP ARATED, FROM JULY 19 TILL AUGUST

On the 19th July Speke left with a light equipment for what he afterwards named the " Ripon Falls," where the Victoria Nyanza discharges itself to form the main waters of the White Nile. He intended to have joined me at the headquarters of Unyoro by proceeding there by boat, but was repulsed in the attempt. Budja, the majority of the Seedees, the baggage, and myself, struck away in the opposite direction towards the capital of Unyoro. The chief incidents of the first few days' marching have been embodied in the previous part of this chapter. But I will now, to vary the narrative, give the events as they occurred daily during Speke's absence.

22d July.|Marched N.N.W. through nothing but meadows of tall grass from 7.30 till 10 A.m., seven miles|from cultivation to cultivation. Rain during the night. The district is in charge of the queen of Uganda's brother. During the march a large black animal, looking back at us, glancing in the side way that an elephant does, ran fearlessly past some huts occupied by Wahuma in charge of cattle. No one turned out to give chase or showed much alarm ; on

248 CORPOEAL PUNISHMENT IN CAMP.

this account I fancied that elephants are not uncommon in these parts. Manua, who has charge of our cattle, came crying, and bleeding from a jagged cut on the back of his head. A Seedee, twice his size, had struck him with a bludgeon for refusing to give up his hut. The offender, who generally was well-behaved, expressed great penitence. The truth of the story could not be arrived at; and after threatening the Seedee with confinement in irons (which we hadn't), all seemed satisfied except Manua, who could not brook the insult of having been taunted for being " only an Unyamuezi." Blubbering most bitterly, he said, " It is not the wound that pains me, but here, here," violently beating his heart. Poor little fellow ! he felt his honour at stake, and swore he would take the other's life; but nothing further occurred.

We were to receive the remainder of our present of cows from M'tessa at this ground, which is on the borders of Uganda. Some cows are brought, but Budja pronounces them no better than goat. A particular favourite of mine, Ooreymengo, the goat-boy, reported having seen a herd of Waganda villagers sweep away all our goats. I ordered an armed party of men to proceed in pursuit. Half an hour afterwards our goats were discovered grazing close by camp; no one had stolen them|the boy had invented the story because he could not find them! He was sentenced to receive twenty lashes, having lost three goats for us some time before. On his hearing my order, he exclaimed, " I don't want to be flogged ;" but Mabruk tied him to a tree and gave it him well with a long switch. On asking the latter, whose duty it also was to keep count of the cattle, how many cows

WAGANDA MODE OF COOKING. 249

were now left, he took a half-inch rope which he wore on his head as a turban, and told me to count the knots upon it; " Chumsa-thillatheen "|35|all right.

23d.|Halt. Budja, on seeing the baggage packed for a march, says that if I go without receiving the complement of cattle, his king will kill him for not obeying orders. One of the women of camp being unwell, this is also brought forward as an excuse for halting. The district officer pays me a pleasant visit, and afterwards sends a gourd full of m'wenge". Went shooting from 9 till 12, wading up to the knees through bogs after elephant or buffalo (Bogo): plenty of their spoor, and several large game-traps were seen |also fish-cruives set; but nothing was bagged. We had a cow killed to-day. Although all its "joints " were at my disposal, the Seedees cut them so small, and into such cross-grained-looking pieces, that when served up they were very uninviting; there was no carving them, because the meat was cut up while warm. The Waganda, on the contrary, cut as neat joints as we do at home, the Seedees calling their cooking " Kissoongoo," or " a l'Anglais," meaning that solid j oints are always cut. When boiled they are surrounded by plantain leaf; a layer of peeled plantain is put in a bundle at the top, and all placed in an open earthen pot, which is covered with leaves as a lid. I took to this cookery, and found it answered admirably.

24 *th,* A.M.|*Halt.* Cattle not yet arrived. Chief officer presents another gourd of wine. Thunder, lightning, and heavy rain about noon. Leopard and lion must be common about here, as one of the former was seen by our men while fetching water, and there are three lion-traps (of logs) within a short distance.

250 DIFFICULTIES IN MARCHING.

The dogs kept by the Waganda rarely run loose after their masters; they are tied to the elbow, hand, or toe (when seated) with a cord, which cannot be bitten through, as a stick is generally attached. If they have to run through grass, however long, even with a basket of chickens swinging at their backs, the poor dog is dragged after them in the most ludicrous way. The breed would be shot down in England, but here they value them very much, castrating them as at Karague. Our goatherd was offered 250 cowries for a playful dog he had picked up, but refused every offer under 300 ! .

Some cattle arrived by 3 P.m., and a march was ordered ; but Budja said, " There are no habitations; nothing ahead but jungle full of lion ! We will march early to-morrow." A meeting took place to discover who had stolen some property at our last ground; until this is settled, I am told, we do not move from here. My men quarrel with Budja about the unfair distribution of the cattle; we were given not only all the bad ones, but were short of our number.

*25th.|*By daylight I had everything ready-packed for a march, to avoid disputes about the cattle. Budja came saying we could not march till evening: the cows must be looked after. " We must go now," said I. An hour passes, then I am told we cannot move, as the men have just commenced cooking. A second hour, and Budja's drum will sound the advance. It now looks cloudy, and a M'ganda comes to say, " After the shower we will move off." Not being able to stand this any longer, I walked off hastily to Budja's little camp, got a guide, and we all marched together for five miles; they refused to go farther, camping in a

SPORTING COUNTRY UNYORO. 251

grove, fenced round to protect it from wild animals. By noon I was shooting in a swampy meadow of tall grass, and succeeded in bagging a beautiful red buck, the " n'soono " or leucotis, which we christened afterwards the " noble buck." Plodding through the deep water, full of a network of grasses, was uncomfortable; the wounded game was lost, and no other species could be seen. The proprietor of the house I put up in came timidly to get out his large game-nets, in order to save them from being injured by my men. About his house were the spoils of eland and "phongo" or bush-boc ; so that this is a sporting country.

26th.|Marched nine miles, getting into Unyoro territory immediately after leaving camp. Nothing marked the boundary between Uganda and Unyoro. The country rolled in waves, had many pretty glades, and was covered with tall grass and trees. At the fourth mile an arch of boughs was thrown across the path, seemingly the work of the previous day. My Waganda did not pass under it for some unknown reason, probably because they suspected treachery on the part of their bitter enemies, the people of Unyoro; but nearly all the Seedees and myself did, as we took it for the Unyamuezi sign that dwellings and water were not far distant.

At yesterday's camp a native fell upon his knees to Budja, and presented him with the lid of a tin canister, and a rag of cloth which my men had purposely thrown away. This was the third instance of their returning things through fear of their king M'tessa. Being now in the kingdom of Unyoro, it was considered necessary to halt here, and send some men in advance, to obtain permission to proceed further.

252 WE ARE CONSIDERED CANNIBALS.

Two Seedees quarrelled, and fought with sticks for the heart of the cow just killed. I tried to separate them, but made matters worse, as the whole camp took up the quarrel. My side won; and the two were placed in different huts, but unfortunately not sufficiently apart to prevent their abusing each other. The result was, that they challenged each other to fight it out alone in the forest with sticks ; and I saw the silly creatures march away with a bludgeon each to have their round out. No one followed, and no damage was done.

27th.|*Halt.* Budja and five of my men have gone on a march to ask permission to advance. The rule will be very different to what we experienced in Uganda. If the people desert their houses, there will be no one to take payment for anything; but should they remain, everything, even plantain or sweet potato, must be purchased, and nothing plundered. The day was a weary long one of expectation; but by three o'clock in the afternoon the taps of Budja's drum in the distance were recognised, and we went to meet him returning from Unyoro.

All the villagers except one man had run away at the sight of the Waganda; but this person told them " to return for orders to-morrow, as the district officer was absent; they must not advance, otherwise there would be a fight. When they reach the king's, the white man, as he is a cannibal, will have an albino to eat, and the Waganda the back-bones of an old cow !" It seemed odd that they should consider us cannibals; but my valet Uledi told me that in his native country of Uhiao the people there imagined that "all foreigners eat human flesh; and that cloth was dyed

THE NATIVES OF UNYORO. 253

scarlet with human blood." It seemed to be a favourite joke against the Waganda," the bones of a cow "| they are so constantly plundering the people of Unyoro of their cattle that it is not to be wondered at that this taunt should meet them.

28th.|Halted by order; probably for several days. On requesting a certain number of my men to proceed and find out whether we could advance, they refused through fear, and lecturing them was the only remedy. Appealing to Mabruk, who had some months previously been sent to Kamarasi as an envoy, whether *he* would go, he replied that, although the king had called us names, such as "cannibals" and "butter- eaters," &c., he would willingly obey orders; therefore he and some Waganda went, returning in the afternoon. They had seen a MTcoongoo, or district officer, who said we must remain where we were till orders arrived from headquarters. He particularly inquired, " What could have made the other white man go by water while I proceeded by land ? for it looked as if he was approaching the country by a forbidden route." This made me anxious about Speke, of whom I could hear nothing. The natives were laughing and shouting during the night, and in the morning three of them, with spears covered up, came to call, begging for some beef; but my Waganda were very angry with them for appearing armed in camp, though they seemed poor harmless creatures. The Wanyoro I have seen are all dull, stupid-looking men, with heavy foreheads and eyebrows, without the gentlemanly appearance or smartness of the Waganda.

New moon was seen to-night. Seedees uttered their prayers as they looked at it.

254 MODE OF PURCHASING PROVISIONS.

29th July.|*Halt.* Coarse, rainy morning and afternoon. This month, when no rain is falling at 5 south lat., we have had several heavy showers; rain seems to fall here every month in the year, which accounts for the continuity of crop. A dozen armed Wanyoro, with capped spears, pay us a visit, their chief bringing me two bunches of plantain as a present. They get some beef and beads, and say that Speke will never be allowed to proceed by the water-route he is trying. He will have to return and approach by the regular beaten track on which I had travelled. On my appealing for aid to Budja, he says it is impossible to communicate this information to Speke; he will find it out himself, and there is no fear of him.

My valet, whom I considered honest, I found helping a brother Seedee to some m'wenge". On reprimanding through an interpreter, he begged pardon for the offence, while lolling on his bed with a quid of tobacco in his mouth. These Seedees are not to be trusted unless the most rigorous discipline is enforced.

Two of my men start with their guns, carrying beef and cowries with which to purchase plantain or potato from the villagers. They meet a party of Waganda there, who say to them, " You fools! what do you mean by paying for food, when you can get it like us for nothing?" The custom was for the Waganda to go to the Wanyoro and make a polite request for provisions, which were generally given free.

An infectious disease has broken out amongst the cattle. One of them has the roof of its mouth so affected that it cannot eat. Its tongue has become discoloured, and there is an appearance of irritation

THREE SPECIES OF VULTURE.|LIZARDS. 255

between the hoofs. This does not prevent the men from wishing to eat it before it should become worse.

30th.|*Halt.* Rain during the night. We are haunted by three different coloured vultures. The first is the ragged-looking, wedge-headed vulture of Uganda notoriety, the "m'saega," easily caught in a trap by a bent bough and two nooses. His plumage is a dull sepia colour. The whole neck is red and bare, with a ruff of white feathers circling the root of the neck. The second, probably the female, is a much bolder bird, larger, and of a dun colour, with a bare, dark grey, or black neck, called " m'foongoo " by the Seedees. The third was a very shy bird, quite as large as, and plumper than the last, and much handsomer than either. His plumage was jet- black, with the rump, thigh feathers, and rear half of the wings snowy white.

The hut I am in is full of small lizards about six inches long. In fighting, two chased each other round and round, with intervals, in a small circle, keeping their tails everted, for fear of being bitten off. The largest got hold of the other's foot, held it most viciously, while the other, struggling, made its escape. They live by stalking up to flies, and suddenly pouncing on them. At night they have the power, like flies, of sleeping while on the ceiling of the hut. After rain, when small red centipedes were on the ground, I have seen these little animals make a rush at the insect, shake it as a dog would a rat, leave it there, and run back to the hut. On examining the insect, which remained motionless, its head was found to have been eaten off.

31st.\Halt. I was roused out of a fast sleep by
256 A HYENA STEALS A GOAT.
shouts and screams from my men in the hut. My first thought was to look whether a fire had broken out; and finding this was not the case, I inquired whether Wanyoro had attacked us. The bleating of a goat disclosed the fact that a hyena had carried away the fattest of our flock. Torches were lit and search made, but nothing was recovered till morning, when the paunch and one kidney of the poor animal were the only traces found. He must have been a bold hyena to have broken through so strong a fence close to where we all slept, and in size he must have been a monster, for his spoor was as large as my hand. The Seedees complain that all the plantain and sweet potato about the place have been eaten up|" they are starving;" although every third day a cow is killed for them!

Not far from this hut there are three caverns dug, looking like the hold of a ship, in which the natives secrete their grain, &c., from their plundering neighbours, the Waganda, but at present they are empty. The Unyoro M'koongoo sends a message, bidding us not to be impatient for the king's reply, as it will certainly arrive to-day or to-morrow; but I am more anxious about Speke, who should have joined us by this time, and nothing has been heard of him.

A storm of thunder, lightning, and rain, blew in gusts from the south, then veered round to N.W., dashing like waterspouts upon the ground. It began at 4, with an interval at sunset, and lasted till 8 P.m. About two inches of rain fell.

1st August.\Halt. A bait of a cow's head was placed last night for the hyena that had stolen the goat, but no shot was obtained, as it rained. In the
WAGANDA GIRLS. 257
morning, however, it appeared, from the tracks of the animal, that he must have been dancing about it on his hind legs like a bear. Our cattle, though in a perfectly open fold, the hyena never attacks, as the cows would kick him out of the place.

My men, without permission, went to Budja, requesting him to get vegetables in exchange for the beef of a blind, lame old cow, that was killed to-day. He sent some of his boy-pages with them to the villagers, with an order that two loads of potatoes for each mess should be made over to them without payment. This was done.

I sketched the two Wahuma girls belonging to my camp. The prettiest, " Sikujua," is young but very black, and her history is curious. When at Uganda, Spoke's men had to forage, seizing what food they could lay hands on. One man got his head broken, but he succeeded in making a prisoner of this little girl, and took her home with him as *his* mode of redress. No one ever came to claim her, and she remained his property. She had the pretty oval face and large ears of the Wahuma; and no doubt, as those with a dark skin thrive best at Zanzibar, she is considered there a great beauty. The other sketch was of a younger girl given to Speke by the queen of Uganda, and now the property of Bombay. She had a yellow skin, fine eyes, and a rather droll face and figure.

2d and 3d.\Halt. A man who had gone from Unyoro to Kawalogeh for salt, brings intelligence that Speke had gone far up the river. This afterwards proved to be quite true. No tidings from him or the king of Unyoro. Slight shower about noon. Leg stiff again. One of Budja's men, who had been to sell

258 ATTACHMENTS OF SEEDEES.

women near Karee, confirmed what we yesterday heard about Speke's movements. This man had obtained ten cows in exchange for two women kidnapped on our march. At Uganda capital they would have fetched only five cows. We have a few of the African tribe, called Mukooa, in camp. They are marked on the forehead with a stamp resembling a horse-shoe, called " real" or dollar, and three horizontal cuts are made with a knife on each temple.

Being out of smoking tobacco, I sent a man with half a brisket of beef to purchase some from the villagers. In exchange he brought back four packets, each the size of an egg. Others were bought for ten cowries each, or its equivalent, a single necklace of common beads.

Seedees have strong attachments. Separated from their parents in childhood by slavery, they are cast upon the world, and become devoted to some one\it may be their first master\whom they look upon as their protector and adviser for years, or even for life. Instances of this often occurred. On my directing that a party of five should proceed ahead for orders, one man stepped forward and volunteered ; his pupil, child, or " m'toto," at once made another, as he would not see his patron risk his life, or be put to inconvenience, without sharing the danger himself. A story told me by Frij also illustrates this attachment: Some years ago he was proceeding to sea from Zanzibar, when four boys were placed under his charge by their relatives, to learn their duty. A storm struck the vessel while a boy of his was aloft in imminent danger. Frij went up the rigging, tied the lad to a rope, and lowered him down all safe, but the difficulty now was

JEWISH NOTIONS. 259

with himself. The mast had that day been greased, and while lowering himself by a rope it gave way, and he fell upon the spare anchor, and from thence, much cut, overboard. Two of his boys threw themselves after him. Frij had gone down, but they succeeded in tying him to a life-buoy, to which all three clung till picked up exhausted. He added, that for their devotion the captain gave them 15 and 11 dollars respectively.

One of our men became possessed of a devil, as was believed, for several hours. He was seized with fits so violent as to require being held down. In this insensible state he was asked where Speke was ? Would this march end successfully ? To which he replied, that " Our journey would be prosperous, but there would be delays." All Seedees believe most firmly that devils have this power, and that there are a great variety of them, some English, some Abyssinian, others Mombas, &c.|in fact, every country or district has its devil, some more difficult to get rid off than others, the English being about the worst. Is this African idea a remnant of tradition ? It has some resemblance to the Jewish notions mentioned in Scripture.

The moon shone bright and inviting to-night, though we had a shower during the day, and the men till 11 o'clock made a playground of the space in front of my hut, singing, mimicking, and acting with considerable grace and great humour. The operatic song of the Unyamuezi, from the gesticulations and perambulations of the performer, who invented words as he proceeded, was highly amusing. They were chiefly in compliment to myself|that God had sent

260 INCIDENTS IN A STANDING CAMP.

them the white man, or " Mazoongoo," who gave them beef to eat, and did not, like Dr Kiengo, make use of divination by the horns of antelopes and the entrails of fowls to procure food.

ith.|Halt. Started a second set of men ahead for information. The reply we received from them was, that Kamarasi was a great king, and that it took many days before a question could be referred to him. Such is the way that travelling is delayed in this country! However, I sent a message to say that two days hence we meant to march to the north, even without permission. Heavy rain, thunder, and lightning in the afternoon. Guinea-fowl crying all round camp. I went shooting them with ball from the trees in the forest, and succeeded in getting one. The grass at present is too tall to see beyond twenty yards; and no antelopes have been seen. Water is a mile away from our huts, in a puddle surrounded by rushes, in the low part of a glade running to the north.

6th.|Halt. Sent a party ahead to inquire why we are detained. A portion of them return, saying they had met a number of armed Wanyoro, who asked why we were parading up and down the road everyday|we'll get a thrashing one of these days! By noon of the 7th, the remainder of the men returned without further news. Their commander, Mabruk, had seen a lion in a trap last night. The Waganda threw their spears into the dead animal; while the brave Mabruk discharged his gun at it, to show its effect upon the Wanyoro, who immediately dropped their spears, and ran, never having heard the report of a gun before.

8th.|Halt. By noon a king's messenger arrived,

ORDERED TO LEAVE THE UNYORO TERRITORY. 261

with followers having their spears capped with leather and tufts of hair. He informed us that the king did not wish to see the white men because they had insulted him by approaching his country by two different routes; they had also come *vid* Uganda, the king of which is an upstart. If they choose to return a year hence, with a recommendation from Rumanika, he will see them with pleasure. No remonstrance would be listened to; we might march back as soon as we liked. This was startling, but I still had hopes.

dth.|Halt. A meeting, which lasted three hours, was held to-day to discuss the subject of our visit, and whether we could advance. There were present Wanyoro, Wanyamuezi, Waganda, Karagues, Wung- wana (Seedees), and myself. Every possible argument failed ; entreaties and presents were of no avail; and my most valuable possession, a double-barrelled rifle by Blisset, presented to me by a kind old friend, Blanshard (formerly governor of Vancouver Island), |even this was refused as a bribe to the king. He had sent his messenger merely to see the strength of our party, and to ascertain, if possible, whether we were in the habit of stealing cattle and men, and ultimately to desire that we should retire to the Uganda frontier, where, after eight days, we should have a reply. This appearing to have considerable reason in it, and all supplies having run short, I reluctantly gave my consent to retire next day, but only to the Uganda frontier, where I should wait for my companion. To show the wicked spirit of the men, and their utter want of sympathy at this critical time, a few commenced wantonly cutting down some sorghum which was growing close to my hut, saying they were

262 A FIGHT|AN OFFICER IN THE STOCKS.

hungry. The only notice I took of it was to prevent the further waste of the crop. The same men had often exhibited symptoms of mutiny, and not many days elapsed ere they finally deserted.

*10th.|*March back nine miles to Uganda frontier, agreeably to Kamarasi's orders, though much against my inclination. Two Seedees were speared by Wag- anda villagers while taking possession of houses. We in return took four prisoners, chased and kept at bay others ; and, to prevent a sudden alarm, cut down all the plantain-trees growing within thirty yards of our huts; but except seeing numbers hovering around us, we had no further annoyance. The wounds were slight, but made much of by the Seedees, who said that one of the women prisoners was necessary as a nurse. This was a mere ruse to be allowed to keep the woman, whom I had made over to Budja, and I would not hear of it.

llth.|Halt. Fever and ague all night. Fifteen armed villagers came to pay their respects, but they had no sooner entered Budja's camp than he demanded what right they had to come there carrying spears. A row, in which my men joined, at once took place, and all were disarmed. I saw here the male prisoner of yesterday, a district officer, in the stocks. Perfect torture the creature seemed to be in; he sat upon the ground, with two long sticks, forked at both ends, between his feet and hands. The neck and waist were tied tightly to a post, so that all night long he could not lie down, nor have the use of either hands or feet. However, in the afternoon Budja released him, on promise that the men who committed the assaults should be surrendered, otherwise his wife,

SEND IN SEARCH OF SPEKE. 263

now our prisoner, would never be given up. What a mode of coercion! But ever since Budja has had charge of affairs he has shown very great tact, doing his duty most conscientiously. His defences, in comparison with the slovenly ones put up here by the Seedees, really seem erected with the eye of a general. He is very proud of his position, will not associate with his own or my men, neither will he eat meat that has been killed by Mohammedans. All his cattle, I may remark, are killed by a blow on the back of the head.

12th.|Halt. Sent eight Seedees and eight Wag- anda to inform Speke of my compulsory retreat. They did not know where he was, but had orders not to return without having seen him. They all returned at sunset, giving us a surprise. An officer had told them their errand was useless, for Speke had gone to Kidi, far, far away. Budja was infuriated with his men for being such poltroons as to return; besides, what would his king say if Speke had proceeded to Kidi, where he had no permission to go ? He (Budja) had been imprisoned three times by M'tessa, and thought if a fourth offence were committed he certainly would not escape.

After sunset, cries came from Budja's camp, about 200 yards distant. I found that the cries were those of one of his good-looking wives, beaten on mere suspicion for having been outside the house after the sun had set. Such severity to guard the honour of the wives is not unlikely to have a quite opposite effect; and, so far as my observation went, the husbands had no great cause to complain. Adultery is severely punished; mutilation is not uncommon ; and

264 CAMP GOSSIP.

the Wakoongoo, or officers in charge of from fifty to several hundred men, have power to order these punishments, and even to put the offenders to death.

13th.|Halt. Twelve men are sent in search of Speke. A Seedee had fever from bathing after noon, which is thought by them an unhealthy time. Out shooting after " noble buck," with a dozen villagers as guides. The animals were very wild; and the bogs, with a broiling sun overhead, were disagreeable.

1ith.|Halt. Fever and ague all night. Frij and all Seedees believe that the Jews, or Yahoodee, living in Calcutta, seize people, and tie them up by the heels till blood falls from them into a dish, when they are released, but rarely survive. The blood so obtained is prepared, and sold as a most valuable chest-complaint medicine called Moomeean. Frij had, while in Calcutta, once been seized, but escaped while the Jew went up a ladder. Also one of his comrades he had seen tied up by the heels, gave evidence to the police, and had the Yahoodee put in prison for eighteen months. These silly stories helped to pass the time.

The cowherd Manua knows his duty thoroughly, for the day he herds the cattle he brings them home full and sleek - looking, being acquainted with the grasses the animals like best|those that are green and succulent, in deep shade. The other herd, not knowing a cow from a horse, drives in the cattle from their grazing as lean in appearance as when they went out. '

We lost three cows some days ago; and Mabrak, who keeps count of them, now stands every night, with his rope in his hand, at the door of the cowfold, passing a knot as each cow goes inside; in this way

COULD NOT COMMUNICATE WITH SPEKE. 265

he counts easier than by the usual enumeration, and the animals walk in to enjoy the volumes of smoke rising from the fire in the centre of their fold.

15th.|Halt. Feel anxious for news; by noon it came. Speke could not be found; he had gone up the river. The chief Wahuma officer would not give an audience to my

Mussulmans, in case the sight of them would make his cows run dry; and men who sat upon chairs before kings|meaning the "white men "|would not be received in Unyoro.

Shot two guinea-fowl with one bullet, and also two "n'soono," or noble bucks, accidentally with one ball . The second one could not be found, although he went away dangling his broken leg, followed by dogs. I stood in admiration of the villager who, with his spear-head, skinned and cut up the animal into saddle, brisket, leg, and other joints, laying them on the pure leaves of plantain as quietly and cleverly, and with far less mess, than is to be seen at the abattoirs of Paris.

16 th.|Halt. The time has arrived for Kamarasi's reply, and none has come. My men all press me to retire. There is not one in the camp who wishes to go the north or Egyptian route; and I long most anxiously for Speke. Here we are, not more than seven days, it is said, from the place where boats lie to take us down the Nile; yet nothing will move those around me to push on. It is most tantalising. I asked Budja to join me in forcing the road, but he could not be induced to leave his country. " Let me then communicate with Captain Speke, *wherever he is."* It was impossible, as his men had no permission to visit Oogoongoo, on the other side of M'tessa's,

266 KING OF UNYORO PREVENTS OUR ADVANCE.

where my companion was; but if I retired for two marches, and halted there, he would ask leave from his king. In the afternoon he anticipated my wish to send ten men into Unyoro to demand a reply from Kamarasi. To dispel the anxiety we both felt we went out shooting | Budja having dressed himself very smartly in cow and antelope skins.

At night I assembled all the men to explain our difficulties, and to intimate to them that our rations of butcher-meat must be curtailed, otherwise there would be disgrace and starvation for us. They agreed to my proposals.

11?th.|Halt. Having now been twenty-two days without a message from the king, as a last resource I sent a dozen men ahead, carrying some wires as a bribe, to ask why we had received no definite reply. In the mean time I went shooting some distance off, and had a shot at a leucotis buck standing knee-deep in water|the tall grasses almost concealing him. This animal is always to be found in ground of that nature, though he has not the hoofs of a waterboc. Rain commencing, we returned shortly before the sun had set, twenty-five villagers having accompanied us, and been entertained by my burning some powder in the bare palm of my hand. They told me it was no use sending men so often to Kamarasi, as he had determined on not seeing us.

18.|Halt. My men all return from the Unyoro frontier, bringing back the presents of wire I had sent. The district officer said, "How can I receive these gifts if the king, my master, refuses to see the white man ?" and he added, that if I stayed ten years where I was the road would not be open to me. So,

OUR CAMPS UNITED ONCE MORE. 267

after a dismal day, I determined|having been attempting this route since the 26th ult.|not to stay a moment longer, but to make search for Speke, whom we had heard nothing of for thirty days, and to try the route to Unyoro *vid* Karague.

*19th.|*Marched eight miles south, crossing a bog five hundred yards wide, and knee-deep, and camping on the second crest of land beyond it. No sooner settled down than Bombay and three Seedees arrive with a note from Speke, who had that morning reached the ground we passed! I at once walked joyfully over to his camp. He had gone out shooting. His servants were got up like M'tessa's pages|heads all shaved, except cockade-like tufts left to grow above each ear, giving them a knowing look. In the absence of their master they gave me a cordial greeting. I waited in the camp till Speke arrived, and I need not attempt to describe our joy at meeting once more.

III. Our Camps United.

Each of us had met with a reverse. But Speke had accomplished his object, and seen the first cataract of the Nile at the point where it flows from the Victoria Nyanza- He had been attended by only a dozen Seedees under Bombay, himself a host, and a few Waganda. Our further plans could not now be decided upon without a conference with Budja. It was proposed, if everything else failed, to induce M'tessa, by enormous bribes, to give a thousand men, and with this force try the Kilimanjaro route to the east coast.

20th.|Return to my yesterday's ground along with Speke. Having discussed whether we could again send messengers into Unyoro, the plan was considered

268 PROSPECT OF ADVANCING.

impracticable, as the natives had threatened us. Besides, we did not know what impression had been produced by the fight on the Nile with Speke's men, where several of the natives were killed. Probably their king was enraged at this disaster. In our difficulty we are saved by the arrival of Kamarasi's factotum, who brings us an invitation from his king. The relief and delight experienced at the moment were inexpressible|everything had happened for the best. We had evidently been on trial, closely watched, and, most probably, the fact of our having been so submissive obtained for us the royal favour. The king had ordered that our Waganda escort should quit us as soon as we entered the Unyoro territory. They refused to obey, thinking the order was insulting to them ; but I considered it a very wise policy, as they are such a wild plundering race, and apt to quarrel.

On the march I struck a zebra with a bullet, which made him, curiously enough, rear twice in the air. A second ball did not take effect, but he separated from other three, and went away limping through the long grasses, which hid him from our view.

21st.|Halt. Something stops the way. We cannot move as we should, but in Africa no one ever can. Budja distrusts the Wanyoro, and does not want to give us up to them. The Seedees get up a complaint, refusing to march because they have not enough of powder ; they observe the Waganda leaving their heavy baggage here, and suspect treachery on the part of Kamarasi, who is said to be enraged at having his men killed on the Nile by Speke's party. All this was a mere pretence, and they were distinctly told that they might go back to Karague if they chose,

WE MARCH NORTH|SHOOT A BUCK. 269

but their guns must be surrendered. Their cool reply was that they would talk it over in the morning, treating the matter as if time were of no value.

22d.|Hurrah ! we march again some miles nearer England, and encamp on the northern boundary of Uganda- Seventeen of the mutineer Seedees delivered up their guns, their names were noted, ammunition was served out, and they had the guns returned|a very simple expedient, accomplished without any further misunderstanding.

Went shooting in a swamp. My first shot was at a leucotis buck, but he bounded away untouched. Again we came upon him lying immersed in water, all but his noble head. On being alarmed he stood for a shot, which penetrated both shoulder-blades, and lodged under the off-skin. Budja was in such ecstasy that he jumped through the water up to him, with all his lads following. A Seedee got well butted before he could cut the buck's throat; but after the Waganda had talked and laughed over the powers of my rifle, eight of them raised the animal with the greatest care out of the water, preventing his beautiful skin from being soiled, and placed him upon a bed of clean grass, where he was left to be cut up *d la* Waganda. Budja's eyes glistened when told that he might have the skin; there was no end to his "nyans, nyans," thanks, &c. We heard elephants screeching and trumpeting near some acacias to the far north, but my Waganda dreaded going within sight of them, and stole away home. We could not find them, but during the night heard their musical cry as they browsed in the moonlight.

Between the 23d August and 2d September we only

270 MARCHING IN UNYORO.

made four marches, but fortunately they were all in the right direction. The country waved in gentle long swells of land covered with tall grass and thin forest, with a few low conical hills. The clearances for cultivation, generally fenced against wild animals, were few; and in the low grounds sweet potato, ooley- zee, and a few plantain were grown. The houses were of grass, perfect domes, but dirty, ill-made, and without door-screens or frames to their single entrances. The people, as we marched past, appeared inanimate and unconcerned; they stood listlessly gazing at us, so different from the reception given to a regiment passing through an English town, when every handkerchief waves a welcome. The natives deliberately carried away everything out of their houses and allowed us to take possession, but at the same time showed sullenness at our intrusion. Our Waganda did not mind this. Wherever they go they know how to enjoy themselves, living always like a party of jolly brigands, by plunder. Numbers of natives came out to see the Wazoongoo, and never having seen boxes before, they believed that the white men were carried in our japanned tin cases!

The Wanyoro would seem to be penurious. The cowries which circulated amongst them were generally covered with earth, as if they had been hoarded up, and kept concealed under ground. This coin had reached them through Karague j and Kidjweega, an officer not more than thirty-five years of age, recollected the time when ten cowries bought a cow, and thirty secured a woman. Times have changed. It now takes half a load to purchase a cow. Here, at the division between the commerce coming up the

BROTHERHOOD AMONGST THE WANYORO. 271

Nile and that of the east coast of Africa, beads were little used, and cloth and coinage were unknown. But Kamarasi had received, four years previously (reckoning five months to the year), some beads from the traders on the Nile, and it is to be hoped that, the road having once been opened, trade and civilisation may advance. The natives manufactured ornaments of ivory for the wrists and ankles. These, and rings, were split at one part, not formed in entire unbroken circles, probably for the reason that they could be slipped on more easily by being divided. The price of their smallest ring was twenty-five cowrie-shells, which I considered expensive. They had also spear- blades, two spans long and two inches at their greatest breadth. The Waganda purchased several of them at five hundred cowries each, and one cow would buy ten, or bark-cloth would be taken in exchange. While here a good deal of business was done, the natives purchasing meat from our men; but if any butter had been used in cooking it, they would reject it as food. Men and women wore anklets made of hair covered with twisted brass, iron, or copper wire.

Manua made brotherhood with the officer Kidj- weega, as he had done with Bombay at Ukuni, but after a different fashion. A Wanyoro made a slight incision to the right above Manua's navel. His blood was tasted by Kidjweega, who had the same done to him by a Seedee, and Manua partook of his blood. These brotherhoods arc synonymous with our masonic institutions, and do a great deal of good, as from that time forward friendship is sworn; and I must say that until the last moment these two men remained excellent friends. The work of civilisation may be

272 MORNING DEWS|MESSAGE FROM M'TESSA.

promoted by this means, as the natives have no objection to make brotherhood with Europeans.

We had not much rain during the last week of August. After a shower one morning, upon the space cleared in front of our hut appeared hundreds of white maggots with black heads, curling themselves into an arc, jumping and throwing themselves over the ground as if set upon springs. The morning dews, as we marched in Indian file through grasses higher than and thick as a field of wheat, made everything uncomfortably damp. The Wanyoro, fearful of getting wet, or having their rags of skins and bark-cloths injured, carried in front of them an immense broom made of plantain-leaves to brush the dew off the grass, which they considered injurious to health, causing the itch. At first we could not understand why unclad natives should carry about these besoms, and the sight of so many of them by the side of the path perplexed us.

M'tessa had sent a large party to inquire how we were getting on. Imagining this was all they wanted, we thought they might disperse; but their leader produced four little pieces of wood, saying with emphasis, one was for a double-barrelled gun that would last the king his lifetime; a second was for gun-wads; a third for strengthening medicine; and a fourth for anything the " Bana" (meaning Speke) liked to send. We returned our kindest regards to their king, and told them that all they asked, and even more, would be sent from Ugani should an opportunity ever offer.

A touching incident occurred here. A woman of the village recognised amongst our Seedees her brother,

STRANGE RECOGNITION. 273

whom she had not seen or heard of since they were children at their home in Uhiao, fifteen hundred miles distant to the south-east. Both had been captured as slaves in infancy. On seeing her brother the poor woman burst into tears, but did not, through timidity, make herself known the first day, merely leaving a message that he should be asked whether his name was not so-and-so when he was young. The following day her owner came for the brother (called by us Barootee, or Powder), and led him away. Several Seedees went to witness the scene, and I felt much inclined to be equally intrusive. They reported that the girl, who was very like her brother, fell at his feet, got into hysterics, but could not communicate with him, as she had forgotten her native language, and Barootee did not know that of Unyoro. This was the only interview they had. She would willingly have followed him, and she sent him all she could to show her affection|namely, an immense dish of porridge and three fowls boiled into soup! Her husband or owner accompanied us on the march for several days; but Barootee said he had no present to give his sister, and she therefore was left behind.

On the 31st August, a party of Waganda came with an important message from the king that we were to return at once to him, even if we had got within a march of Kamarasi. He had something very particular to say to us, and would allow us to proceed by whatever route we chose. Budja said the order could not be disobeyed, it was imperative; but after four hours' consultation, neither side would yield, except the Seedees, who said, "We go to Uganda whether our masters like it or not." On being told

274 ELEPHANT-HUNTING.

they were welcome to leave, but they must not take their guns, as they were Speke's property, they got up abruptly, saying, " The guns are ours, and we march to-morrow with Budja to M'tessa." They insolently beat the drum at night for a morning's march. Kamarasi seems to have had information of this, for nearly two hundred men, all armed, were collected and gathered round our hut next day to resist, if necessary, any attempt made by the Waganda to take us forcibly away. However, they were not required, as by six o'clock of the morning of the 1st September twenty-eight Seedees deserted with Budja, who took with him the rain-gauge as a present for his king. Thus we were well rid of all the disaffected of our camp, and left simply with Bombay and our best Seedee servants.

2d to 9th September.|The great events of this week were elephant-shooting and our arrival in sight of Kamarasi's residence.

Let us note the former. A number of Wanyoro led the way out of camp to a forest covered with tall grasses like wild oats, and with ordinary-sized shady trees. Mounds of earth, the formation of white ants, were here and there visible. After a time the boughs bore marks as if lightning had struck them, they were broken so wantonly; the grasses underneath were trodden as if they had been passed over by a roller. All the spoors were fresh, so that every moment we expected to see the herd, and not a little excitement prevailed. A low whistle from a sharp-eared Wanyoro made us all exchange glances. He had heard the cracking of branches, and soon, sure enough, about three hundred yards distant, in the open grass, were

ELEPHANT-HUNTING. 275

the blue backs of about forty elephants. I had never seen such a sight, and Speke wished me to have the first shot; but another herd appeared in an opposite direction, and I preferred going alone, with a single follower carrying a spare gun. Here, whichever way we looked, for three-fourths of the horizon, elephants were seen, all grazing quietly, perfect "lords of the forest," and so unconcerned that I walked boldly upright through the grass to a tree within fifty yards of twenty of them. It was a beautiful sight; all were mothers with their young; none so large as the Indian breed, but short, stumpy, handy-looking animals, with small, long, and uniform tusks. The most game point and the most striking about them was the peculiar back-set of their enormous ears. While waiting to get a close shot by their coming nearer me, I looked round for my man with the second rifle. Master Seedee was nowhere! so putting up my

Lancaster rifle, and aiming behind the shoulder of an old female with long tusks, I fired: she merely mingled with her comrades, who stood around in stupid alarm. In an absent fit of gazing, I forgot to reload till they were approaching me. I then changed my position to another tree, within thirty yards of a full-sized animal, whose shoulder-blade wrinkles I could trace distinctly, and brought her down on her hind-quarters with a small bullet. Up she got, rushed in amongst some others, who, with tails erect, commenced screeching and trumpeting, dreadfully alarmed, not knowing what was taking place. At last, some head wiser than the others took the lead, and off they all scuttled into thicker cover. I ran after them, but the jungle got so dense that there was some fear I should lose my way, as no one was within

276 ELEPHANT-HUNTING.

hail. Returning to more open cover, a female elephant was coming diagonally towards me, and she passed so close that I saw her wink her eye; but the bullet behind the shoulder, though delivered at eleven paces, only frightened her into a bowling amble with her tail half cocked. A low whistle now announced Speke close by. He had been trying their heads as well as shoulders, and had no better luck than myself. The "Wanyoro guides joined us, as all the elephants had left, and kept saying to us in compliment, "Weewaleh, muzoongoo m'saeja"!You white men *are* men. The same compliments on our bravery awaited us on our arrival in camp, where we were looked upon as wonderful sportsmen for having gone so near elephants. During the night we heard their wild music, first to the west, then to the north, gradually dying away in the distance. The herd had very wisely marched, taking their wounded along with them.

SECTION 13

CHAPTER XII.

The Capital Or Palace Of Unyoro, September 9 To NovemBer 9, 1862, Latitude 1 37' North, Longitude 32 19' East |Topography Of The Country|Its Climate, Soil, And Animals|King Kamarasi And His Wives|Class Of MenDicants|Arms Used By The Wanyoro Their Food And

Drink|A Blacksmith's Shop|Amusements Of The NaTives|THE EXPEDITION EMBARK ON THE NILE.

The country, for a few marches before reaching the residence of King Kamorasi of Unyoro, was gently undulating and evergreen, with tall grass and trees. On the light and higher grounds the grasses grew six feet high, with large panicles which adhered to one's dress. Where the richer soil had been washed down to the low grounds the vegetation was shorter but more luxuriant. Nothing could be more desolate than our encampment at the capital of Unyoro. I can only compare it to a bare and dreary common|not a tree nor a garden to relieve the eye or afford shade from the equatorial sun. The vast plain was covered with tall grass, through which at this season we could not walk without wading, so that we were completely hemmed in by water. The northern half of the horizon

278 THE RIVER KUFFO FERTILITY OF THE SOIL.

presented a few small detached hills, the most interesting being in Kidi. They sloped away to the north from a high bluff" point at their southern extremity.

Our huts were within a few yards of a sluggish stream, the Kuffo, from Uganda. Its depth, its mud- coloured water, and the tall rushes with which it was fringed on each side, prevented us from seeing the crocodiles with which it is said to swarm. In the third week of October its waters had swollen immensely, and bore along with them islands of the papyrus which it had torn away in its course, and on which I often wished myself embarked, as they were on their way to Egypt. Several times, when a gleam of sunshine broke upon the hills of Kidi, we could see from a height near camp the river Nile, looking like a mirage, but we were prohibited from going nearer it- While fishing upon the Kuffo I was rather surprised to find that its bottom was pebbly, while its banks were formed of retentive clay, about ten feet in depth, through which no water seemed to percolate. The soil upon the pathways, after it had been thoroughly washed with rain, became of pure white sand, without gravel, and formed a pleasant walk. It was a loam, with from 40 to 70 per cent of clay, and, if closely drained, would make excellent land for growing wheat. Of the surrounding countries we obtained a good deal of geographical knowledge; for the people here were not afraid, like those about M'tessa of Uganda, to state what they knew. We had fully expected to receive letters from Egypt, but saw only some beads quite new to us, which must have been brought from thither. Until Bombay should return with a letter from a parly of Egyptian ivory-traders to the north,

THE NILE AND LUTA-NZIGE LAKE. 279

we did not feel that the two hemispheres had been thoroughly united by our efforts. Our first move was to make the junction with these traders at Faloro. We were told that the water route was impracticable, and we afterwards found this to be the case, owing to the cataracts on the river between Chopeh and Madi. Were it not for these, our informants told us we might proceed the whole way by water. This intelligence, together with our own observations of the level nature of the country, enabled Speke to map the bend of the Nile, which we were not able to visit, it being entirely off our direct route, and within the province of a rebel chief.

One of the king's officers had travelled to the Masai country, to the east of Kama-rasi's, and he said we might do the same, if his king gave us a particular horn filled with charms to be carried at the head of our party. This, with 600 iron hoes, giving two to each chief of a district, would enable us to get through the unexplored country without molestation.

This man also spoke a good deal about the Lweet- an-zigeh (the Luta-nzige" of Speke), an immense body of water some marches away to the south-west, and extending back towards Karague. He thought we should take twenty days to reach it; but a M'ganda would go the distance in half that time. This is the lake whose position we expect the enterprising Sam Baker to ascertain, as we gave him a map of its general direction, and he would also be enabled to verify the latitude and altitude of that portion of *our* journey over which he might pass. When last heard of, he had manfully gone back on our track and reached Kamarasi's. God grant that he may be spared to return.

280 THE CLIMATE OF UNYORO.

Far to the north-west of our position, at Unyoro, are people named Ooreea-Wantu|translated eaters of men, cannibals|the Walaega, perhaps. We saw some of them, but were told they had drunk or tasted the blood of Kamarasi in the same way that Kidjweega and Manua had made brotherhood.

We had a considerable quantity of rain during our stay here. The showers were very partial, appearing to fall from six or seven different points of the heavens at the same moment, while the small river by our camp had been rising for three days, though we had no rain. There were no regular prevalent winds at this season; three violent storms, all from different directions, the north, south-west, and south, were noted.

An observation of the weather, from sunset of the 7th November to 8 P.m. of the 8th, is here given :|

Sunset.|A bank of clouds collected in the south-west .

Night.|Still and fair.

7 A.m.|Perfect calm ; the grasses arching with the weight of dew.

9 A.m.|A breath of air. Last night's clouds rising. Clear horizon

from north to east.

Noon.|Heavens fleeced over with cloud. Gentle breeze. 3 P.m.|Breeze increased to freshness. Temperature, 82 in the shade. Sunset.|Wind dying away. Heavy clouds over the south horizon.

8 P.m.|Still and calm. Sky half covered with watery clouds.

Every morning and every day seemed alike, only varied by occasional falls of rain. The mornings were dull, with fogs hanging low, the paths wet, and the tall grasses dripping with dew. A fire was very comfortable at night, particularly when the rain trickled through the roofs of our small grass huts. We suffered no inconvenience from the heat, being always sheltered.

DOGS AND CATTLE. 281

We had no sport while here. The king was such a morose autocrat he would not allow us to go beyond our dwellings; but this was no great loss, the country being mostly covered with water. It had been said of this country that the fences of the huts were made of elephants' tusks; but we found that the natives rarely killed the elephant, and when they did, used only the rudest uncertain methods. No pitfalls were seen, merely a heavy wedge of iron suspended from a tree. A leopard-kitten was one day brought us; he had been caught in the rushes, and Speke desired to buy him and make a pet of him, but his owner would take nothing for him in case he should happen to die; if, however, he survived, a present would be acceptable. The little animal seemed to pine away for want of its natural food, and died in a few days, when it was given back to be eaten by its original owner.

The king had a large coarse breed of dogs, foxhound colour, although he never seemed to employ them for any purpose. He wished us to give him a medicine to prevent disease amongst cattle; but our own soon became affected, and we knew of no remedy. The complaint attacked grown-up animals of all ages; they became thin, with a staring coat, refused food, sometimes frothed at the mouth; and as certain as they were attacked, although showing no signs of actual distress, their death was inevitable. The natives always ate the carcass, but the meat looked fly-blown and discoloured.

Calves appear to suffer from a weakness in the limbs. Our cowherd came, with a five-days-old calf following him, to our door, asking for a thread to tie round each of its hocks. On being asked what charm this had, the reply was, " Don't you see

282 FISHING ON THE KUFFO.

that he cannot put his hoofs flatly on the ground; that he is walking upon his toes ? This thread will give him strength !" The calf actually did become strong. We found that some meat would not keep beyond a single day; this was not attributed to the heat, but to the man who had performed the operation of killing the cow. "He must be a dirty fellow, sleeping cuddled up with his hands between his knees." "If Baraka had been there to kill the animal, the meat would have kept for four days." Goats were never healthy; the soil stuck between their hoofs, making them foot-sore, dejected, and unable to graze with any apparent satisfaction.

We were unsuccessful in fishing with the hook. The natives had a better system; they set creels, into which they drove the fish in numbers. At the Ripon Falls, while Speke was there, the Waganda plied to considerable purpose a barbless hook, baited with roasted plantain cut in dice. On trying the fishing in the Kuffo, first with entrails, and afterwards with worms from the mud on the banks of the river, none would take properly, and the stream was too muddy for the fly. Four loads of dried fish, as black as tar, were sent us by the king. Our men did not recognise them, but called them " mamba," the name for crocodile, because they had large teeth, and were supposed, from the rounded form of two of their fins, to suckle their young. Manua, on being asked to have some, replied that he had never tasted fish, and did not see why he should begin then; our men also had some objection to them; and when the women of the country were shown them, they ran away. In fact, some of these very species were purchased at the

RATS AS FOOD LIZARDS. 283

Ripon Falls, but the women refused to cook them. I tasted both a bit of the tail and shoulder; the former had been dried to a stick, and the latter was tough and tasteless. All had been caught in the Nile, and were eaten by the male population alone.

On my asking some of our Seedees, four in succession, if they had eaten rats, all pleaded guilty, saying, " We have eaten every living thing except hippopotamus, dogs, snakes, and cats. Rats were better food than beef, tasting sweetly, like tender chickens, and frogs were also very excellent! But now that they had become Mussulmans, they had given up living upon these animals." None had ever eaten human flesh, but they stated that when a person in their country of Uhiao dies from having been bewitched, the wizard eats part of the body to complete his incantation. In our huts the number of rats and lizards living on friendly terms together was immense. Every house had two or three traps, but these did not keep them down, or prevent their annoying fowls, in consequence of which the latter could not hatch on the ground, and were suspended, like flower-pots, from the ceiling in a tray made from the leaf of the plantain. Lkards fed upon cockroaches and other insects, and much enjoyed picking the bone of a fowl. There were two species ; the largest was dark, covered with bright spots, with a white fish-like belly; the other and more handsome one had a bright stripe down either side, from the arch of the eye to the tail. Rats fed like rabbits on grass, or flour when they could get it. Whenever we camped near swamps the musquitoes were in myriads, working their way even through bed-curtains of net.

284 THE KING OF UNYORO.

Nine days elapsed before the suspicions of the king would permit of our seeing him. Our servants had many interviews before his highness would grant us an audience. But it was at last brought about by informing him that, as he seemed to prefer black to white men, we would shave our heads and beards, blacken our faces, and present ourselves! His messengers at once brought a reply, that we must not do so, for the king was preparing a house and throne where the reception would shortly take place.

His excuses were, that he had heard many bad reports of us through Waganda, who said we required several men and women for our daily food; that we drank up rivers and ate up mountains; that he did not know exactly what to believe; but we must have patience, and we should be gratified. He had some Wanyamuezi guests whom he made swear, by stepping over their arms (bows and spears), that we did not do these things. They became answerable for us, consenting, as a punishment, to be circumcised if we should commit a fault. Although the king, from suspicion and timidity, took these precautions, he would daily inquire for our health, sending provisions occasionally; and on being asked what he would do if the Waganda carried out their intention of rescuing us from him, he replied, seizing a stick and holding it like a spear, that he would not allow them to touch a hair of the white men's heads. If they came, he would put us in boats, and send us away to our own country. He was lost in admiration of our hardihood in coming to such a far-away land. We must be devils; we must fight his rebel brother, and also fight the Kidi la race of people who constantly annoyed him.

THE KING OF UNYORO. 285

His highness's residence, for the last seven years, had been where we now saw him, in a naturally strong position, on the point of low flat land between the Nile and the Kuffo. About three hundred huts of grass stood here, covering an area of two square miles. One dwelling was conspicuous amongst the rest, from its size, and in it his highness resided, with his cattle and followers around him. This station had been chosen in preference to his proper residence, three marches south, as a greater security against the attacks of his rebel brother Reonga, living upon an island down the Nile.

In appearance the king was fair for an African, of slender figure, nearly six feet high, and about forty years of age. His features were good, with soft gentle eyes; in sitting he would often rest his head upon his hand, with his elbow on his knee, and having long arms, this position did not seem constrained. As was the custom of the natives of his country, all the lower incisors and eye-teeth had been extracted in his youth, and the dentist to his father received the handsome sum of one hundred cows for the operation. The teeth are probably taken out by the head of a spear or small knife, as no more refined weapon, such as a dentist's key or pinchers, was observed in the country. His forehead was disfigured by black patches where it had been burned or cauterised for headache or other ailments; on his nose he had a similar mark, which he wished us to take off because it disfigured him. We never saw him wear any calico or silks; a bark-cloth covering, tied round his body tightly from above the waist to his heels, was his only raiment. It was the usual salmon colour, but had

286 THE KING OF UNYORO.

small pieces of black bark-cloth, sewn very neatly with a looping stitch, dotting it all over. His head was periodically shaved, scissors being unknown; and small tufts of wool, the size of black pepper-corns, were the only protection. A single necklace of beads, worn very long, was his most conspicuous ornament. By his side a spear rested against the wall; its blade was neatly capped over with leather, laced like a shoe with two long strips from the skin of a leopard.

Our presents of beads, boxes, guns, cloth, &c., were received by Kamarasi very coolly, with no sign of pleasure, only an occasional remark. He sat, as Bombay said, " like a cow," showing neither astonishment nor delight. A pair of spectacles put on by Bombay created a titter amongst the men, but he remained perfectly solemn. Nothing was examined by him, or handled with that eagerness which all other Africans were in the habit of showing; all was affected indifference. None of these things were new to him; he had seen all, except the double-barrelled rifle, and the watch which he saw Speke take out of his pocket. This watch, a valuable chronometer, was yielded to him at our second interview; and whenever he received it, he told us that we had better leavel it was going to rain ! Though he now followed us to the canoe in which we embarked to cross to our huts, and stood on the shore, spear in hand, till we had landed on the opposite side, he neither bade us adieu nor smiled; and even the natives accompanying him squatted or stood unconcerned. However, we paid him every honour, standing up in the canoe, with the union-jack floating high over our heads.

At the other interviews it was constant begging;

THE KING OF UNYORO. 287

he must have table-knives, musquito-curtains, our pots and pans, our medicines, finger-rings, &c., and most of them had to be rendered up. Once, when we had got into our boat after an audience, he followed and ordered us out into one with water in it, because he required the best canoe for himself. All was done so roughly, and with such a total want of grace and hospitality, that, at the moment, I felt inclined to throw myself into the river and swim across it, but the effect would have been lost upon such a coldblooded mortal.

On his sending to announce that he would pay us a visit, Speke prepared his hut as nicely as our means admitted, by ornamenting it with antelope-horns, blankets from our beds, the union-jack, &c. A japanned tin case was covered for his higlmess's throne, and a donkey-rug placed for his feet. Salutes were arranged to announce his arrival, and all our men had donned their best to pay him every honour. But our preparations were not seen to advantage, for a wooden stool and some leopard-skins were placed for his majesty to sit upon, hiding our decorations. On being asked to change his seat for the one we had prepared, he eyed it suspiciously, and in a coarse voice asked what it waslwhat was underneath ? and on being shown that it was no more than a box such as he had previously received in a present, he sat himself down upon it. The conversation turned upon trade. " Did he desire traffic by opening the road to the north?" With his usual chilling stiff manner, though seeing the advantage to himself, he replied that all the ivory of his country now goes to Zanzibar, because he is constantly at war with the tribes

288 THE KING OF UXYORO.

to the north : two days he is at peace, and five days at war (curiously enough indicating the division of time into weeks). Changing the subject, lie commenced to scold a swarm of boys who were naturally peering in at the door. He ordered all but a few listeners to withdraw, and now commenced begging everything he saw in the hut. Pointing to his cheek, head, and back, he said that all his children after a certain age die; we must give him a cure for this. A quantity of medicine was tied up in a veil, and he left abruptly, saying to his men, " Erokh togendeh " |Let us go. Although we accompanied him to his canoe, he took no notice of us, and was paddled across by some naked boys. No influential persons were around him, and when one of the scullers fell overboard the canoe was not stopped. The creature swam ashore, and commenced to scrub himself without any ceremony before his highness the king of Unyoro.

With all his apparent rudeness, Kamarasi was not unkindly. Though his neighbour, M'tessa, ordered his subjects to be butchered, no such savage custom prevailed in Unyoro ; men were admonished, and told how fortunate they were under the king's lenient rule. Murderers, however, were flogged or speared, and their bodies thrown into the river Kuffo. Scarcely a day passed that we did not receive a little flour, some drink (very coarse and bad), sweet potato, or other remembrance; but the great present was made soon after our arrival, when we each had ten cows and five fowls sent us, with an explanation that the king thought it necessary to send us separate presents, as we had approached him by different routes. Before

ARRIVAL OF VISITORS FROM UGANDA. 289

leaving, we solicited, and were presented with, a few more cattle, and a tusk was offered to each of our head-servants. In return for his presents, Kamarasi received English and foreign goods to the value, in England, of $150 sterling; this included a double gun and rifle, a chronometer, &c. Besides these, he obtained a considerable quantity of property left behind at Karague; so that it is confidently hoped he will treat all future white men with due hospitality.

Kamarasi was constantly visited by men of far countries coming to trade with him for cattle, slaves, and ivory. By his permission, the Waganda who had accompanied Speke to the Bipon Falls arrived with a message for us from their king. When they appeared, in their beautifully clean dresses, our hearts quite warmed towards them as old friends. Their orders, they said, were to accompany us through fire and water as far as we wished, only they were not to go to England! Kamarasi would not hear of this, telling them, until he heard farther from M'tessa, he would not risk their lives amongst the wild people of Kidi and Madi; so they had to return to their king with a messenger from us in the form of a tin-lid, which was supposed to convey our kind remembrances. We gave them some salt, which they licked like sugar. Unfortunately they would not eat our beef, as it had not been killed by one of themselves, and had been boiled in our pots ; however, they got some porridge, some m'wenge", and a cow. Before leaving, after having knelt to " nyanzig " (return thanks) at our door, they expressed themselves devoted to us; " their lips had been sweetened and their hearts

290 THE WAGANI EATING RAW MEAT.

wanned in our society." The skins on which they had been seated in our hut were smartly bundled up by boy-pages, their court-dresses exchanged for marching costume, and away the merry creatures went back to their king. I learned with regret that my good friend Budja had died from the fatigues of marching back and forward between Uganda and Unyoro. The report was that the " black art" had accomplished his end. A thorough soldier the poor fellow was, with good tact and spirit.

People from Gani to the north often paid Kamarasi visits : they and the Kidi were similar in one respect Ineither, in their own country, wore any covering around the loins, and their language was a perfectly new one to our men, as well as to the great majority of the people of Unyoro. They used to come with strange presents : for instance, a small tusk, the skin of a tippet monkey, a string of handsome beads procured from Egyptian traders, and the tail of a giraffe, formed one present received by the king while we were there. They returned to their homes with a few cattle in exchange. The Wagani had conveyed and brought back Bombay from the camp of Nubians, and for this service they received a cow. After it had been skinned, the muscle that lies on either side of the back-bone was neatly taken off in a long ribbon, the meat scraped off, and eaten before us without being cooked. A portion of the entrails was also eaten raw at the same time. It seemed quite a *bonne bouche* to them after their journey; and on the following morning, when they were seen wearing the fat of the animal twisted in a coil round their bare necks, they looked fresh and well after their dinner of the

THE WIVES OF THE KING. 291

previous day. This custom of eating a little raw meat from an animal immediately after it has been killed is not an uncommon one, but I do not think they are fond of it after the meat has been allowed to become cold; they then have it cooked.

The language of Unyoro, as spoken by its natives, although it differs but slightly from that spoken in Karague, was not understood by our Seedees until they had been some weeks in the country. It had not the mumbling sounds of the Uganda dialect, where their d, g, k, &c., and most consonants, are doubled in pronunciation. The dialect of the Chopi, Kidi, and Gani was perfectly unintelligible to our Seedees. They said it sounded in their ears like English; but there was no resemblance, every word uttered being guttural, and not thrown smoothly out from the lips, but kept in the mouth by closing the throat with the root of the tongue. Many of the names of our Seedees, such as M'kate, Uledi, and Sirboko, all coast words, were heard in Unyoro applied to men of the country. We also found this in Uganda; and Kamarasi is the name of an Indian Bunnea, or corn-dealer, living at Pangani on the east coast of Africa. These names are diffused over the country by means of the slave-trade.

The wives of the king lived upon milk, and were of enormous proportionsIdrinking the milk of from five to fifteen cows daily. They were slovenly and listless, not able even to make butter, or assist in any household work, and never appearing at any audience given us. In the fields, while at work, the women wore a neat kilt of bark-cloth to the knees, and had nothing on the head or above the waist. One came

292 A CLASS OF MENDICANTS.

to our hut while it rained, saying she feared being seen if coming at any other time, and wanted medicine. They are of an average height, and appear healthy, though their husbands complain that their offspring do not survive many years. An officer made a sad complaint to us, saying that if his wife had a child to a servant it always lived, but any she had to himself died. An extraordinary little old man, not more than three feet in height (correctly drawn in Speke's 'Journal'), paid us a visit. He was perfectly sensible, though very restless while sitting for his portrait, constantly moving his head or holding up his fingers close to his one eye. In contrast to this dwarf, the king had a man who looked a giant in strength, though scarcely six feet in height. He was employed in conveying messages to us, and could go through all the motions of a warlike attack, wielding his spear with grace and agility, struggling with his enemy, planting his foot triumphantly on the dead body, snorting, and finishing off by wiping his spearhead upon the grass to free it from his supposed antagonist's blood.

A class of mendicants or gentle beggars called "Band-wa," allied to the Wichwezee, seem spread all over these kingdoms. They adorn themselves with more beads, bells, brass, and curiosities than any other race, and generally carry an ornamented tree-creeper in their hands. Many of their women look handsome and captivating when dressed up in variously - coloured skins, and wearing a small turban of bark-cloth. One man amongst them wore, from the crown of his head down his back, the skin of a tippet-monkey, to which he had attached the horns of an antelope. They wan-

THE ARMS AND HUTS OF THE WANYORO. 293

der from house to house singing; and are occasionally rather importunate beggars, refusing to leave without some present. A set of them lived near us at Un- yoro, and seemed to have cattle of their own, so that they do not entirely depend upon begging for subsistence. The natives all respect them very much, never refusing them food when they call, and treating them as religious devotees. Any one may join their number by attending to certain forms; and the family of a Bandwa does not necessarily follow the same occupation. I knew one of them the captain of a band of soldiers. This whole country was once occupied by people of this class, called Wichwezee, who, according to tradition, suddenly disappeared underground !

The arms used by the Wanyoro were the poorest we had anywhere seen. Bows and arrows are unknown, although their neighbours at Karague make them their chief weapon. The spear is small and weak, with a thin six-feet-long handle of ordinary wood. Excellent spear - heads are hawked for sale in the southern borders, but the Waganda, a richer people, buy them up. A party of soldiers, wretched representatives, dashed into our camp one day to rescue us from the Waganda. They wore each a handkerchief of bark-cloth tied round the head, high in front like a Highland bonnet, and dirty rags of the same material covered their loins. Bead ornaments round the neck were worn by such as possessed means to obtain them. Others wore flattened pellets, larger than garden-peas, made of polished iron or ivory, and strung round the ankles.

The huts or hovels of the country were wretched; but there was this excuse for the people, that no wood

294 THE PRODUCTS OF UNYORO.

grew in that out-of-the-world cornerland most of the habitations seen by us were temporary. Their floors were never swept, but bedded with grass, which, when it became soiled, was left there to rot like a dunghill, and fresh grass laid over it: vermin of every description swarmed.

The cultivation is carried on chiefly by women, who cut up the stiff soil with an iron hoe, and plant the various crops. We missed the shady plantain- groves of that garden of African neatness|Uganda. No fruit of any description is grown near the palace. Coffee is brought from Uddoo. The vegetables are pumpkin, sweet potato, and the grains sorghum, sessa- mum, ooleyzee, and the other ordinary varieties. The bread and porridge made from these grains are miserable; and butter being scarce, and no plantain to moisten the flour, we had very poor fare. The cowries were the chief coin of the country; two hundred of them bought a small bag of flour; and in selling the meat of a sick cow to enable us to buy fowls (for thirteen cowries each), we obtained ten foondo, or one thousand cowries. The natives were sometimes induced to sell butter by our making up necklaces with alternate-coloured beads. A string of these five times round the neck purchased three-quarters a pound of butter, which was brought neatly tied in the broad fresh green leaves of the sorghum. We had fallen upon the man who procured this treat for us in a simple manner. Seeing him pass, his body glistening with grease, we accosted him, and gave him the commission which he executed so well. Our men killed a cow as food for themselves and us every third or fourth day. The natives, on hearing that meatA Blacksmith's Shop. 295

was for sale in our camp, would bring their flour, tobacco, or sweet potato to barter. In this way sufficient variety was generally to be had, and both parties vere accommodated. We could obtain milk daily from our own cows, though they were but poor milkers.

The intoxicating drink sent us pretty often by the king was called m'wenge", and made from the millet murwa. Kamarasi's officer, on presenting a jar of it, vould say, he " had brought it with the king's compliments," and that " we should find it as pure as water," tut it tasted like the dregs of a beer-cask, and I wonder how his highness could get tipsy upon such coarse spirit. The person who brought the jar always went through the form of tasting it, and the vessel was never required to be returned, as was the case in Uganda. Near the king's residence a market for this " grog," and for meat, fowls, firewood, &c., was held almost daily, our servants calling the place a bazaar; but we were never allowed to cross over the Kuffb river to inspect it.

A visit to the blacksmith's shop in any country always repays one, and there the gossip is usually heard. In Africa it seems to be the same, and idlers always lounged about the Unyoro blacksmith's. The " shop" was a ten-feet-high awning made of the stalks of sorghum. One lad sat on the ground and blew a double-handled and double-nosed bellows, the air from which passed through a detached earthen tube upon the live charcoal. Two men squatted naked all but a leathern waist-cover, hammering, talking, and smoking all at the same time. Their anvil was a flat boulder, and the hammers bolts of iron, the shape of large

296 AMUSEMENTS AND SUPERSTITIONS.

chisels. The only other instruments were bent sticks as pincers, and a wooden handle like that used at home for a firing-iron. One man had three iron hoe& in various states of preparation; the other was making needles. When the bellows-boy forgot his duty staling at me, and allowed the fire to get too brisk, the smith gave him a lecture, and some water from i brush of straw damped the flame.

One of the commodities which, being rare, we mucl enjoyed, was salt, brought from Kivro, a place to the north-west upon the Lake Lweet-an-zigeh, and whicl was perfectly pure in colour and taste. The natives there are said to extract it from the soil by boiling and evaporation.

The amusements of the people are few, but our See- dees remarked that the dancing of Unyoro was superior to what they were accustomed to see at Zanzibar. We had the opportunity of seeing a few of their dances, at which the men wore all the beads and shells they seemed to possess, and, forming a circle, sang and clapped their hands while going through some graceful figures. The nights were often enlivened by soft-sounding duets coming from the harmonicon and drum played across the river.

Superstition is prevalent, from the king to his lowest subject. Some straws out of the thatch of a house occupied by an enemy of Kamarasi's were to be brought us, that, bewitched by our supernatural powers, they might bring calamity upon their owner, who lived miles away. When our rain-gauge was missed, at the hour for observing it, the theft was communicated to the king, who sent a one-eyed man with a cow's horn in his hand to detect the thief. The horn was capped

VARIOUS SUPERSTITIONS. 297

over with a rag of bark, and had an iron bell tinkling from its top. This instrument was shaken roughly in the face of each of our Seedees as they sat down ; all seemed to change colour at the suspicion, and the old man proceeded to the spot where the gauge had been taken from. He found it lying a short way off. A hyena had removed it, as his tracks were visible. This did not shake the faith of our men, but only the more strongly confirmed their belief in the "black art." Manua wore wood tied round his ankle, which he had received from some of his Waganda cronies, who told him it was a charm against snake-bites. Upon Bombay ridiculing him, he sharply replied, " Why do you take medicine from the Bana or Sahib ? my charm answers the same purpose." At cross roads we several times came upon a dead frog or fowl; and in such places, if the party is wealthy enough, a goat is laid. The animals are split open, with some plucked grass beside them, and are placed there for the purpose of curing any sick member of a family. Wonderful stories were related of a dog having a single horn, and of the horn being long preserved by one of the king's officers, and used, when war broke out, to be stepped over by the troops as a good omen previous to going into action. One superstitious belief struck us as very remarkablelthat Kamarasi, if he chose, could divide the waters of the lake ! It seemed a long-enduring and far-spread tradition from the time of Moses.

No funeral was ever seen by us in Africa, and human bones were remarkably rare. The dead are buried somewhere near the house or under the cattle-fold. The body is wrapped in bark-cloth or the skin of a cow. The king's corpse is dried with heat, and the

298 OUR SOLITARY SITUATION.

lower jaw-bone ornamented, buried, and a tomb-house built over it. The hands and hair of kings' officers are preserved in a similar manner. The umbilical cord of male children is buried inside the doorway, and those of females outside, as was the custom also at Zanzibar. We had not much sickness while at Unyoro, but there were some cases of tertian fever and dysentery. Amongst the inhabitants there were no remarkable diseases; the only complaint of the men was that their progeny did not always live; they could not have the number of children they wantedl a fact which can only be explained by the poverty of their diet and the abuses of polygamy.

Our situation was little better than that of a prisoner in a solitary cell. We certainly had our " morning post" after breakfastlthe king's messenger lbut there was seldom any news, and the day hung heavily. No one was allowed to visit us but these postmen coming to ask how we had passed the night. Natives from interesting countries all round would visit the king, but *we* could not see them! Dances and parties went on, and we could not attend them. Rain was felt as a relief, as it employed one in reading the gauge every morning. The insects at night were interesting, particularly a species of glowworm half an inch long, seen amongst the roots of the grasses. If placed upon the hand or sleeve, it travelled quickly, throwing out a constantly twinkling light at shorter intervals than the firefly, which also was numerous. We slept in separate huts. Mine was occupied by my two servants, who, though only screened from me, talked incessantly to themselves or to me, and sometimes got up to eat in the middle

PREPARATIONS FOR LEAVING UNYORO. 299

of the night. The head-servant was an intelligent Seedee, named Uledi. On asking his opinion as to copal, which is used as varnish, he said it was not the production of an insect, although an insect is always seen inside; but is a formation from the roots of decayed trees, called " nango," plentiful in Utumbee.

The march to the north from the capital of Unyoro was effected, as before mentioned, by sending Bombay and Mabruk in charge of some northern men, with a letter to find out whether Petherick was upon the Nile with boats for us. Kamarasi would not hear of our accompanying them : besides which, he said that, when we did leave, he meant to keep five men of each of the three races we should pass through, as hostages, till he heard of our safe arrival ! After many days of suspense, on the 1st of November, when working at some lunars, a gun was fired in the direction of the king's house, then another was heard. In the distance a man, it was reported, was seen with trousers on. It was Bombay; and his dress was hailed by us as a substantial proof that he had come in contact with civilisation. For a moment there was a feeling of disappointment, as if we had nothing further to do. Our expedition seemed over, and we tried to scan or predict the far-distant future. What would be our next duty ? What our destiny ?

In gratitude to Kamarasi, we sent him everything we could possibly give away, asking whether he had any objections to our leaving. He replied that a couple of our Zanzibar Seedees, with their guns, must be left with him, as he required them to deceive his enemies into believing that we were still his guests. Many other excuses about the unsafe state of the road

300 WE PADDLE DOWN THE KUFFO.

were laid before us, but Speke's *suaviter in modo,* no less than his *fortiter in re,* won the day. A parting souvenir of two spears was sent him by the king, and on the 9th November we glided down the river Kuffo. The banks of the river were lined with crowds shouting and waving adieus as we shot down the stream. Amongst them was a woman conspicuously dressed, and recognised by our men as a maid of honour, who generally sat at the feet of the king. She was the only female of rank we had seen, and she seemed plain and flat-featured. Her dress of yellow bark-cloth was striped with black, and her hair was dressed in a ridge-like form, after the fashion of the Uganda court. We enjoyed excessively the boating down stream, going at the rate of four miles an hour, and driving fish before us. The Kuffo was so broad that two "gigs" might race abreast of each other. The sides seldom admitted of landing, being margined with rushes and reeds, hiding completely the country behind them. Delightful to us was the prospect of the water route!

14

SECTION 14

CHAPTER XIII.

JOURNEY FROM UNYORO CAPITAL TO AN EGYPTIAN CAMP, NOVEM-
BER 9 TO DECEMBER 3, 1862 | FLOATING ISLANDS ON THE NILE | RIVER
SCENES AND CANOE CHASE | THE PEOPLE CIVIL AND HOSPITABLE|DWELLINGS
AND ORCHARDS OF THE NATIVES|WATERFALLS AT KARUMA|FISHING
AND HIPPOPOTAMUS TRAP | FERRY THE NILE, AND CROSS AN UNIN-
HABITED FOREST|JOIN AN ENCAMPMENT OF TURKS.

My first sail on the *river* Nile|the White Nile|was made upon this journey, but my
companion, Captain Speke, had sailed on it at Urondogani. We entered it on this
occasion in a log canoe, a few miles below Kamarasi's residence, at the point where
the Kuffo joins it; and we floated upon its sacred waters during a portion of four days,
making the rest of the journey to the Falls of Karuma by land, along the left bank.
Though the mode of transit was not dignified, the water route was extremely pleasant,
from its novelty and interest. Having emerged from the channel of the smaller stream,
we suddenly found ourselves in a large lake, to all appearance without an outlet, being
surrounded by rushes; and without a pilot it would have been hard for us to guess
which direction to take. After

302 FLOATING ISLANDS IN THE NILE.

proceeding for an hour the scene changed: we were upon a river a thousand yards wide, and in certain parts so large that we had a sea horizon. The waters struggling past myriads of moving and stationary- islands, made the navigation very exciting, particularly when a strong head-wind blew, and hippopotami reared their heads in the water. Having passed these, there was no perceptible current; but by watching the floating islands rolling round and round like a tub in the water, we saw that the stream moved about a mile an hour. These islands were perfect thickets of growing ferns, creepers, small trees, &c., hiding one-third of the stems of the lofty papyrus rush. It occurred to me at the time, seeing such masses of these islands, some being twenty yards in length, that the delta of the Nile could easily be accounted for by an accumulation of their sediment. During a smart breeze, with all their vegetation yielding, and lying over to the wind, they looked like a fleet of felucca-rigged vessels racing, and continually changing their relative positions. No sight could have been more striking as the crests of the waves dashed against them, and the sky looked black and stormy. It was a beautifully wild picture; the slender stems of the tall papyrus, with their feathery tops, now erect, then waving to and fro, or crouching before the sudden blast, as if prepared for a spring.

By the third day all the islands had disappeared ; they had melted away into floating fragments, or had got ashore, and lay over|wrecks|the leaves and fronds drooping in shapeless disorder.

Where the river was above 500 yards wide, the colour of the water in the centre was quite muddy from the freshes ; that of the sides a clear brown. The

RESPECT PAID TO AN OLD CANOE. 303

greatest depth was eighteen feet, which it preserved, with a hard bottom, till within a boat's length of the side, where it became nine feet deep, with a bottom of mud. As it narrowed between steep banks to 200 yards, there was no impediment to landing; the waters then became of a uniform dark colour, and were shallower, flowing with a current of about half a mile an hour. We landed daily to sleep ashore, and had to pass through a long channel of water vegetation, as the sides in most places where the river was of such immense width were walled in by a depth of reeds, rushes, and convolvuli. An interesting custom amongst the boatmen was observed as we paddled past an old pensioned canoe of huge size which lay in the rushes. A boatman patted my shoulder, and then sprinkled water upon the veteran boat. I did the same, which pleased the natives, who never pass it without paying this mark of respect.

Many fine scenes were come upon at reaches and bends of the river. One with a precipitous double- coned hill called M'kungurru, on the right bank, was remarkably pleasing, the river sweeping majestically round its wooded heights. This hill was reckoned to be 800 feet above the water, and for a long distance it served as a prominent landmark. The Kidi side of the river was undulating, wild, and uninhabited, covered with handsome trees overspread with a network of flowering creepers, then, in the month of November, in rich bloom, and presenting every contrast of colour. It was the hunting-ground of the Wanyoro and Kidi people.

We had some exciting chases after canoes seen on the river, the king having given the officials who were

304 CHASING CANOES ON THE NILE.

in charge of us orders to procure food by seizing any provisions they might find. Immediately any canoe came in sight, all our energy was applied to the oars. The " chase" on seeing us would double and race with all his might, till, finding it hopeless, he would strike his colours by standing up in his canoe, when a yell of delight burst from the conquerors, though still several hundred yards from the prize. No sooner did we come in contact than the prize was at once rudely boarded. Bark-cloths, liquor, beads, and spears were taken and concealed by our Wanyoro followers, while the poor owner looked on powerless. The sequel, however, was delightful: the Seedees, of their own accord, recovered all the stolen property from the hands of the Wanyoro, and restored it to the proper owners, who then laughed with ourselves at the joke. The largest canoe carried a ton and a half, and was hollowed out of the trunk of an immense tree|not made of planks, like those on the Victoria Nyanza. Our kit was placed in the centre, or formed a seat for us at the bow or stern. Some cows we had received from the king were sent by the land route, and had to pass through a boisterous people, who twice tried to plunder them. While a few goats were in charge of my valet Uledi, four Wachopeh threw their spears at him. He could not see the men coming on account of the long grass, but he captured a spear and a stick, losing none of his herd, thus showing his tact and bravery. He carried an unloaded gun, with ten rounds in his pouch; also a spear, which he broke by throwing at the enemy. We fortunately caught another, thief driving away our goats to the jungle. Two of our men brought him into camp with his arms

WARNINGS DURING A MARCH. 305

tied behind, and a rope round his neck . On seeing him each Seedee took a savage delight in slapping his face, and then covering his body with a mixture of mud, ashes, and water. They also tortured him by binding his body tightly with cords; but .during the night, though the door-screen was fastened, his comrades came and released him.

When marching across country, we required aid from the inhabitants as porters, but they showed great unwillingness, never agreeing until their women or cattle were seized. Kidjweega had the king's orders to collect a force of forty men as our guard. He had, however, much difficulty in procuring even half the number, the natives making excuses that the country of Kidi was dangerous to pass through. Our route was thus rendered circuitous, as we had to zigzag from village to village in order to obtain relays of porters. Even when the distance to the nearest village was only a mile or two, most of them insisted on being relieved, and the more refractory were compelled to carry loads by our seizing their spears. On the line of march they were lively and polite enough. When any obstacle occurred on the path, such as a sharp rock or hole, they, with their disengaged hand, would slap their thigh to warn those behind them to look out. No remark was made, merely this simple signal given. The Seedees had a different mode of giving warning: they called out " M'wiba,"|that is, thorn; " cimo," hole; or "jiwee," rock.

To return to the Nile, its scenes and sports. One day's journal notes " four hippopotami, two crocodile, two dead fish, and numerous small gulls," seen in and

306 BEASTS, BIRDS, AND FISHES.

over the waters as we glided down the stream. The hippos required sharp shooting, as they seldom gave us time for an aim, sinking their heads the moment the boat was steadied. The natives harpoon them with barbed irons stuck loosely upon heavy poles longer than capstan-bars; and use trimmers of "solah," or pith-wood, attached by long ropes to the barbs. It must require expert swimmers to get up to a hippo in the water and deliver the thrust. We saw small gulls flitting about and darting at them. The dead scaly fish upon the water were about seven pounds weight, the shape of a thick short cod, but with a well-forked tail, above which, as Speke observed, there was a small rounded fleshy fin, like that seen on salmon or trout. The boatmen eagerly picked those up that floated along, even though they were stale. We could not account for their being found dead, except that they had been poisoned by the decayed matter which filled the river. At every place where a creel-trap was set, our men pulled in to extract the fish, but got little for their trouble. One morning we had some " Macquareh" for breakfast, and enjoyed them very much; they had as little bone as a sole, and tasted like trout. Where the banks were high and covered with trees, monkeys occasionally jumped from bough to bough, and did not seem alarmed even within sight of habitations. They were grey, with long tails, white beards and eyebrows, black faces and ears. The largest birds were the Batteleur eagle and the Buceros: the former, when seen soaring and circling in the heavens, resembles a bat in figure, and has a black body, with the wings white underneath; the Buceros is a large black bird, walking awkwardly about

MODE OF ADDRESS. 307

the cultivated grounds, having short legs, and his three toes almost of equal length.

The people were generally civil and hospitable, sending us small presents of their produceǀplantain, or perhaps a goat; but they did not relish our passing through their country, and they gave up their houses with great reluctance. This was no wonder, for our Unyoro escort plundered wildly like the Waganda, and escaped capture by running away. On one occasion they cunningly got up an alarm in camp, and took the opportunity, when the inhabitants were in a state of fright, to seize their property. But in districts where the population was numerous, all turned out to look at us, rejoicing most heartily, leading the way in a crowd, shouting and saluting. Some of our men became so drunk from their good wine, taken while resting in the middle of a march, that the natives tried, by applications of water, to bring them to their senses. They actually wished to carry one man, and never attempted to rob him of his clothes or gun, which he kept brandishing about. We were addressed indiscriminately as Wazoongo (white men), M'kama (sultan), Nyans- wengeh, and Witchwezee. Those who knew us best used the two former titles, while others spoke of us as Nyans-wengeh, meaning, probably, strangers, sailors, or Nyanza men.

The women wore a sort of double kilt, as if a short one had been put over a long one. Some had tight- fitting leggings of iron beads, as bright as steel, and very becoming on their fine limbs. The quantity of brass wire round some of their arms surprised me. It seems that their husbands take ivory to the mart of Karague, and exchange it with the Wazeenja or people

308 USEFUL PLANTS AND TREES.

of Usui, which is on the road to Zanzibar. This metal was more commonly worn than copper; being an importation, it seemed to be in greater favour.

The dwellings were detached grass huts, generally in the middle of plantain orchards, and forming three sides of a hollow square, with some charmed poles outside.
A store-hut raised upon piles is built in the centre space, to contain their grain, hoes,
&c. The bark-cloth tree, or ficus, which we had not seen for several months, abounds
in the district, but never grows to any great size. The people collect the flat linear
leaves of a rush growing on the river-bank, and extract salt from them. After being
dried and burnt the ashes are washed, and the water, which becomes impregnated with
salt, is used to boil potato or plantain. Some leaves of this rush measure fourteen feet.
The papyrus is here converted into door-screens (like a hurdle). Strips from its stem
bleach white in drying, and make beautiful fish-creels, while its pith is converted into
wrappers or coverings for jars of wine. The pith-wood supplies floats, door-bolts,
and oval-shaped shields to the people. A tree with compound leaves was an object of
Phallic worship|the only instance of the kind we knew of. These, with the universal
bottle - gourd, were amongst the most useful plants we observed.

We found fresh eggs placed in the forks of trees
near houses, said to be put there as medicine or M'ganga. None were rotten, though
several placed similarly in the ceilings of the huts were shaken, to try them, and then
replaced. The spoil of hippos, their skulls, tusks, &c., lay in small heaps near the
houses of those who possessed tackle for killing them. It was not thought

EFFECTS OF EXPOSURE. 309
lucky to throw these away, and a beautiful convolvulus *(Argyreia sp.)* with immense
mauve flowers, was planted by their side. With a branch of this plant in the hand of
the hunter, it is believed that he is certain of sport.

The millstone in use here is a slab from the brick- red, rough-grained granite seen
along the pathways, and it is placed inside a hut, embedded in and edged round with
clay. Any round stone in the hands of a woman, who kneels to her work, rubs down
the grain. These stones had not been seen in Uganda, as the people there seldom grind
corn. Another slab, with irregular fracture, seemed of hornblende, as waving lines ran
through it.

In our short experience we did not observe much disease amongst the people, and
the country, where it sloped down to the Nile with an eastern exposure, appeared very
healthy. Wens on the forehead and behind the ear were noticed upon some men; and
a woman, whose hand had been cut off, probably for some misdemeanour when in
Uganda, was the only maimed person we saw. She appeared to be an old vixen.

Exposure in an open canoe during the heat of the day is very trying, and told on both
of us, causing sick headaches. There was nothing, when the river was broad, to rest
the eye upon but its glassy surface, consequently we were glad to come upon cataracts
and proceed by land. On the eighth and ninth days from the time we embarked, both
of us had attacks of fever, sickness, and dysentery.

After a severe day of illness during the march, I arrived in camp exhausted, at dusk
of the 19th November, and found Speke also unwell, but with

310 THE KARUMA FALLS.
the delightful sound of a cataract on either side of his position. The night air
conveyed this sound to us distinctly, and when morning came, after a night of fever,
vermin, and musquitoes, the noble sight of the Karuma Falls quite revived us. It was

health and joy to convalescents! There were three cataracts upon less than a mile of the river at this point, and each had its own music. Seated upon the rocks of the central fall of Karuma, we were strongly impressed with its grandeur. The cloudy sky tinted the river a mossy brown, and the water was broken into white foam by a fall of six feet over three channels worn in the rock. On the centre block a hut has been daringly placed to commemorate some event. Below the falls, upon an island, other huts are erected, but they are uninhabited, and approachable only with considerable difficulty. They may have been placed there as stores for grain, as the Kidi people on the opposite shore are constantly plundering. The trees upon the island had their branches connected by cords, on which were slung the wings and feathers of birds, giving it the appearance of a charmed spot. Looking up the river from this fall, there is a long reach, broken by foam in two places; but what gives enchantment to the scene is the view of the steep banks densely covered with tree foliage, forming a frame to the picture, and recalling similar scenes on our wildest Scottish rivers.

Immediately below the Falls, where the water eddies amongst rushes, we observed several baskets suspended from trees; they were put there to contain fowls as a bait for hippopotami, or rather as an inducement for these animals to come and fall under a trap placed not

AN ALARM IN CAMP. 311

far off. Across their track a cord is placed, with creepers twined round it; and over this a short log, shod with iron, is suspended from a bough. On the cord being touched, this weight falls upon the animal, transfixing him till the arrival of the villagers, who come for -water. We tried to catch some fish with Palmer flies, moths, and hooks dressed with red rags, but nothing would take; although, however, we were thus unsuccessful, the natives brought us large fish they had caught in their creels.

We were not sorry to be detained here by the officer of the district for three days, as ferry-boats "were not ready for us, and supplies had to be laid in for a journey across the Kidi forests. *As* I was one diy trying to sleep after breakfast, the natives outside ccmmenced shouting with excitement. On going to 863 the cause, Frij coolly told me to " Nenda indani"| *i.L,* Get inside|get inside! Two distinct parties had collected for a fight|the Seedees, with their Tower rifles at the "ready," with bayonets, &c., and their adversaries with spears, shields, and sticks, in position for attack. All were on the point of fighting, but a gun going off in another part of the camp caused them to disperse, and we heard no more of the intended battle. A woman, it appeared, had been insulted, and the men got excited on the subject, but the affair was soon over. We constantly had these little alarms.

In the afternoon of the 22d, the loud sounds of the stringed tambira (a large harp) announced the arrival of visitors, and it was not long before the Kateekeero or governor arrived with a squad of rather well-dressed Wanyoro. This official had leprous hands, looked dull and stupid, and would give no direct reply to

312 WE FERRY THE NILE.

our questions. He *was* muffled up all but his head in a yellow bark-cloth with black horizontal stripes. He presented us with a small bull, some flour, and three jars of m'wenge", for which on the following day he received some beads and pills, with the promise of a handsome necklace when we reached M. de Bono's camp. On his second visit this governor wore a different costume, and another variety of beacs, thereby wishing to impress us with the idea that he was a man of importance. He was commander-ji- chief of the district, and constantly fought his men against Reonga, the brother of Kamarasi, residing 01 an island one march below the Falls. The interview was not over when it was reported that a large party of travellers were walking down the opposr bank of the river. Through the grass we could see a line of people going like a train, each one with a losd on his head, and some wearing white skin coverings. They were Kidi going to assist Reonga in fightiig against the governor with whom we were conveis- ing, and they marched along with perfect security, as a wide and rapid river divided the belligerents, and the distance prevented the possibility of an arrow- reaching across the water. No one proposed to have a shot at them, as we were to ferry the river, and cross their track as soon as the party had passed. We issued orders that our twenty cattle should be first sent across, but Africans always reverse everything. The cattle were not over till after the sun had set, and we were put across in the first canoe. The canoes were of hollowed logs, eighteen inches out of the water, very rotten, and obliged to be caulked with the roots of the papyrus. We had three men pad-

WE FERRY THE NILE. 313

dling with spoon-shaped sticks, who worked hard to get us across the one hundred yards of stream, as delay on their part would have caused us to miss the landing-place, and probably carried us down to the next cataract. Kidjweega, who had charge of us, brought over a small goat as a sacrifice to the rocks, and to propitiate our march. A " M'ganga," having some boughs in his left hand, killed the animal, and spread it out upon the path, with its head laid in the direction we were to take. Speke was then asked to step over it, in order that we might have- a prosperous journey, and all followed his example. Another goat, I understood, had been similarly sacrificed on the left bank. While waiting for the cattle being brought across, we ascertained the altitude to be 2970 feet above the level of the sea. The manner of swimming the cattle was very simple. Men in the canoe held ropes tied to their horns, and those wanting horns were tied by the lower jaw. There was considerable delay on account of the tricks of the ferrymen, who, had they chosen, might have taken four cattle over at each trip; but when about three-fourths were crossed, a message came that, until we gave them one cow for their trouble, over and above the amount of their agreement, which they had already received|namely, a hatful of beads|the others would be detained. This was acceded to, but another messenger arrived saying they must have a larger one in exchange. On getting this, they brought us a quantity of ripe plantain for our liberality, and we encamped for the night a mile from the Falls, in the middle of a forest of tropical vegetation. A storm of wind and rain blew with violence, making the boughs above us creak, and our

314 OATH OF ALLEGIANCE.

unprotected camp-beds became pools of water. But notwithstanding these and other discomforts, in the midst of vivid lightning and bursts of thunder, our Seedees kept up a cross fire of shouts and songs. A sudden cry that our cattle were wandering away, put every one on the alert, as the beasts were to be our mainstay for the journey of six days which lay before us, through a country destitute of habitations. A fire was lit for the poor animals, and they enjoyed it like ourselves, till moonlight and the break of day.

The evening before we ferried the Nile, our Wan- yoro escort got very tipsy, and came to salute us with presented spears, after the manner of the Wa- ganda, but not with such grace; neither did they find such ready use of their tongues. After laying down their spears, they stepped over them, and back again, as much as to say that they were prepared to die for us ! This over, while Kidjweega hopped a dance on his tiptoes, all his followers performed a Highland fling round him, to the music of a humming song. The effect, as seen by the light of a blazing grass fire, was ludicrous and wild.

Kamarasi sent us, as his last request, that we should go and fight his brother, who was not more than a few hours' walk off our track; but Kidjweega, his messenger, was not very pressing, and we marched under the guidance of an active little man of Chopeh, called Luendo. For three days we were in forest, broken occasionally by a serpentine bog, along which the path was a gutter with grass eight feet high, and so close on either side that we had to push our way through it. Emerging from this forest, the country to the north was covered with tall grass, undulating

THE BEND OF THE NILE. 315

from our feet to the horizon, where the low hills of Gani were visible twenty or thirty miles off in the far distance. It was a cheering sight, for there we expected to come upon civilisation. My field-book, dated 27th March 1862, at this point notes: "From a red-clay ant-heap saw the Gani hills to the north. Country to the right a plain of withered waving grass, without trees. The same kind of country lay to the west, in the direction of the river." This note I look upon as important, for it may be held to be a proof that the chord of the arc to the bend of the Nile, which we actually followed, was a plain, offering no hilly obstacle to the flow of the Nile from the point where we ferried, till reaching it again ninety miles farther north. Marching through this tall grass was harassing and monotonous; the tread-mill could hardly be worse. If you held up your head to look for trees, none were to be seen. If you looked for the man who walked in front of you, he was generally hidden. If you walked in your ordinary manner, without stooping, the sharp grasses went into your eyes and nose, blinding you for a moment, or drawing blood ; and if you did not keep your eyes and ears open, and take the warning of the hole, rock, or log ahead, you hurt your limbs, or tripped and stumbled in the most vexatious manner. Several times we lost our way, but little Luendo would good-naturedly jump upon an ant-mound, take his bearings, and put us right again. In going through bogs he was most careful in taking off his sandals, which he slung upon his wrist; the Wagani, whose only covering was the skin of a kid in front, also took this precaution. As the journey was nearly at an end, and a prospect before us of

316 WILD BUFFALO SHOOTING.

renewing our wardrobe, we were becoming extravagant, and walked through everything with our shoes, socks, and trousers on; but this was a mistake, as sand got into our shoes, and the grass cut our socks or gaiters. When we came to a pool, the scene was like that of a number of boys bathing. The Wanyoro first plant their spears upright in the ground, thea take the load from their heads, doff their small coverings, and proceed joyously to splash each other in the water. Older stagers sit on the banks enjoying the sight, smoking or eating meat cut with their spearheads. This lasts for nearly an hour, and then we move off again through the tall grass, till we arrive in camp, where arbours or huts are made wherein to sleep. Huts left by previous travellers were sometimes met with, their fires still burning; and we were informed that the people of Chopeh and Kidi came there to sport. Speke shot a buffalo, which afforded great excitement. On his wounding him, the natives, with spears erect, rushed at the animal, who charged and drove them away like flies; at last, however, several shots and spears pierced him as he lay wallowing in the water. Not an inch of the buffalo was wasted: though the Wanyoro had our loads to carry, all was brought into camp as food. Many of their spears were broken and bent, showing the softness of their iron. Afterwards, in our march, we saw a knot of elephants, heard the lion, came across some hartebeest|here also called " gnamoera"|and were informed that the people of Chopeh can creep up to the wild buffalo and spear him while he is asleep. This is strange, but is quite credible.

On the 29th of November our party of eighty souls

THE NATIVES OF GANI. 317

stood upon the face of a rock, large enough to form the site of a garrison. Here we had the satisfaction of seeing in front of us another height, on which houses were actually discovered. All our rear men and cattle having come up and refreshed themselves from a cool spring in the rock, after half an hour's walk we stood by cultivated ground, and in sight once more of habitations. How delightful the feeling after the monotony of the forest! I could not resist a " hurrah," and had a strong inclination to bound forward and see this new race of the " Gani," amongst whom we were that night to sleep. Patience, however, was requisite. Our men walked along in Indian file, led by Luendo sounding his small horn to convey the tidings that we were upon a friendly mission. Knots of natives appeared on the heights above us, and we halted under a tree, waiting permission to ascend to the village. Although we had had men of their own race to guide us from Kamarasi's, and they had burnt grass on the downs the previous day to intimate our approach, and that they might prepare pombe" and lodging for us, we had to wait till the "lord of the manor" invited us to his residence. By-and-by relief arrived. Two naked young fellows, their faces whitened with ashes, came rushing like mad "jogees" or devotees down the hill with spears balanced, and pulled up beside us. Their bodies had two coats of paint|purple and ash colour|the latter scraped as a painter imitates mahogany | and this colouring gave to their thin tall figures a very grotesque look. They were soon joined by others, no two painted or ornamented alike; and some of them vermilion all over. Even boys affected gay colours,

318 OUR RECEPTION AT A GANI VILLAGE.

and dressed their heads with single feathers of jays, &c., floating like a vane in the wind. Brightly polished iron rings were worn round the fleshy part of the arm, a pendant of iron-wire hung from the under lip, large rings of copper and brass were in their ears, and all of them carried spears with bamboo handles. Bombay and Mabrook, who had passed through the district some weeks previously, were gladly welcomed with " Verembe", verembe"," sounded in a guttural tone of voice. They had stools offered them to sit upon, and after some delay permission was given us to advance.

Having mounted the side of the rocky height to its top, we were surprised to come upon a flat cleared space, surrounded with huts of bamboo and grass. In the centre stood a single "miloomba," a bark-cloth tree, with two idol-huts of grass, and horns of wild animals on the ground by its trunk. An aged man with grey hair advanced, with other "elders" and women, carrying a white chicken, some m'wenge", and a handful of a plant with a white flower. This old gentleman was Chong'ee, the chief of the place. While holding the fowl he addressed us, then waved it over the ground, and passed it to his chief officer, who did the same. The body of our guide, Luendo, who had conveyed us from the Karuma Falls, was now rubbed over with m'wenge" from the plant; the liquid was also sprinkled on us, and we were invited to sit upon the cow-skins placed in the shade of the miloomba tree, and were presented with m'wenge", called "water," to quench our thirst.

The first impression made by the appearance of the little colony was very pleasing. Their beehive-looking

WOMEN AND CHIIJ)RJEN OF GANI. 319

huts were cleanly swept and tidy, and their stores of grain were raised upon rough pillars of granite, smaller, but resembling those circular erections in our own country known as Druids' temples. These grain stores consisted of an enormous cylinder made of mud and wattle placed on the top of the stones, and covered with a roof or lid of grass and bamboo, which could be raised sufficiently with a pole to admit of a man entering them. A rough ladder or stick with forks enables the women to get to the top for the purpose of taking out grain.

The women, married and single, old and young, wear only a bit of fringe suspended from the waist in front, and a pendant of chickweed, or a bunch of long leather thongs like shoe-ties, behind. They have no other clothing. Enormous heavy rings of iron sometimes ornament their ankles, and a few beads their necks; and they are not nearly so smart in appearance as the men, who may be seen sitting upon the rocks in the shade of trees dressing each other's hair with shells, beads, feathers, or turned-up queues covered with fine wire. Their whole employment would seem to be ornamenting their persons; and they are generally seen standing in conceited and ridiculous attitudes. The women carry their children on their backs, tied by straps, and the mother has thus the free use of her hands. The infant is shaded from the sun by a gourd placed over its head and shoulders. This custom is said to be common also with the Watuta race. Here also the people sleep upon the skin of a cow or goat placed on the clean-swept floor of mud, and have no covering. The doors of the huts are so low that ordinary people would have to go upon their

320 THE COLONY OF GANI.

knees to enter, but the natives are so supple that they can bend their bodies until within two feet of the ground, and still be able to walk. The women make a superior description of basket, of close workmanship, from osiers or wands brought from the rocky dells. It may be mentioned that we had not seen the bamboo tree growing since we were in the seventh degree of south latitude, and we were gratified to come upon our old acquaintance again. Many of the trees gladdened the eyes of the botanist of the expedition, Manua, who knew most of them, as the same species grow among the rocks rising out of the forests in his native home of Unyamuezi. Again Bruce's *ensete* was found here, of a small size, greedily eaten by goats; also several plants hitherto undescribed or unknown to science, giving a double interest to the colony of Gani. Strolling along amongst its ravines, and wandering far in search of plants, I came upon traps set with slabs of rock and cord: only small animals, such as weasels or birds, could get under them, and the circumstance shows that all races are fond of trapping. A native from the heights above shouted and beckoned to me; in return I beckoned to him, and though we could not understand each other, he was most polite in leading the way, knocking down the thorns and branches that obstructed us, or lending a hand over the rugged rocks. He understood my sign that he should accompany me into the camp, but before doing so he left his spear in a hut, probably for fear his chief should find fault with him for appearing armed. In return for his kindness I presented him with some beef. Chong'ee, the morning after our arrival, harangued the people of the village, telling

THE BEER, CROPS, AND CATTLE OF GANI. 321

them they must be kind to his guests: and that whatever we wanted|meat, drink, house-room, &c.| must be provided.

The beer made by the natives was strong and pleasantly bitter, so that Bombay and others showed the effects of it, becoming rather noisy towards night. The beverage is manufactured from Murwa, roasted, pounded, soaked, sun-dried, and boiled. When cooling it ferments slightly, and it is more agreeable to the taste in this lukewarm state than afterwards when entirely cold. It appeared to us a wholesome, though coarse, heavy drink. The other grains here were ses- samum, *Hibiscus,* and *Hyptis spicigera.* The last is called " neeno;" we had never seen it before, but the natives cultivate it, eating its seeds roasted, or making oil of them. Although the fields were well weeded the crops were poor, and often appeared full of the *Crotolania glauca,* or "m'caewae," of whose inflated pod, leaves, and flowers, the natives make a dish resembling spinage. We had entirely lost the plantain- tree of Uganda, and rarely came upon Indian corn or ground-nut, which up to Unyoro had been always procurable.

Like the crops, the cattle are poor, and of a small breed, rather dirtily kept. It was amusing to see the odd way in which our two Gani men, who accompanied us from Unyoro, and who had received a present of some small cows from the king, drove the stubborn animals along. Simple driving they did not understand ; one of the horns and the tail were caught hold of by a man who walked alongside, and in this way the cow was urged along the road. Of a morning, when all the cows are brought to the space in

322 APPEARANCE OF THE COUNTRY OF MADL

the centre of the village to be milked, the calves tied alongside the mother, the cow, on seeing her milker arrive, makes water into his hands, when, having scrubbed them, he commences to take her milk in a neatly-made oval basin or tureen of wood. The other domestic animals about the village were stupid-looking, long-tailed sheep, with reddish-brown hair. Goats jumped about the rocks, feeding on the leaves of the Indian jujube tree; and dogs were occasionally met with.

Ten hours' marching in two days brought us from Gani to a camp of Egyptian ivory-traders, whose acquaintance Bombay and Mabrook had made some weeks previously. The small quantity of baggage we had left was carried from village to village, after the manner of the " Begaree " system of India. Our Seedees could have done this, but the villagers, coming forward voluntarily, generally enjoyed the labour. On arriving at a palisaded village where porters were to be relieved, we usually gathered under a tree waiting for the relief. The head man of the place, when wishing to show politeness, had the skin of a wild animal spread, and upon this he placed a wooden stool or two; liquor of the country or sour curd was offered, and after enjoying his hospitality we proceeded on the march. The appearance of the country, with its forests and undulations of grass, and with clusters of habitations every three or four miles, was very pleasing, particularly as it was often intersected by running streams from the hills. Some of these were torrents, and the largest was a river knee-deep, with steep banks and bed of gravel. All flowed to our right.

ARMS AND HABITATIONS OF THE MADI. 323

We met with two new trees, both handsome, and one of them, the Sheabutter, called " Meepampa" by Manua, resembled an oak in girth and general outline ; its flowers scented the air and were covered with the honey-bee. The other we found to be a new species of *Boscia,* with long lanceolate leaves and terminal inflorescence. The people here, though differing very little in their mode of painting themselves from the Gani, are called "Madi." Their women have the same small fringe in front, and the same appendage behind, formed of fresh green weeds, plucked daily from the edges of water, and hanging from their waists to their knees. Their arms are spears seven feet long, bamboo bows, bound round with leather thongs, and arrows of reed. As many as ten arrows, each with a different-shaped barb, are sometimes carried by one man; their peculiarity is that they have no feathers, and their barbs are as straight as a nail, lance-shaped, or like a broad arrow having hooks; and though none of those we saw were poisoned, all were cruelly notched, to make them more difficult of extraction. The interiors of their palisaded villages are kept very clean; idol horns and miniature huts, near which grow medical plants, such as *Bryophyllum calycinum* and *Amaranthus* (love lies bleeding) are always to be seen. The houses are cylinders of bamboo wicker-work, plastered inside to make them warm, and have steep roofs of bamboo and grass. Game-nets, arms, two-feet-long horns (made of gourd, the shape of a telescope), buffalo foot-traps, slabs for grinding grain, &c., are in the interior. The mode of roosting hens is novel; a five-feet-long stick, having three prongs, is stuck into the floor of the

324 WE REACH A CAMP OF EGYPTIANS.

house, and the hen hatches upon grass placed upon the forks. A custom which we had not before observed was, that in the early morning a jar of hot water was sent us to wash with; and along with this came a present of some beer of the country.

De Bono's ivory - traders had selected Faloro, a favourable position, for their camp, situated on the concave side of a hill, with a stream below. Our junction with them at sunset of the 3d December was one of those happy epochs which can never be forgotten. We announced our approach by firing guns when within a few hundred yards of the settlement, and a very lively scene ensued. Turkish banners flew, welcome guns were fired, and an army of well-dressed men, "fezzed" or turbaned, turned out with drums and fifes to greet our arrival and escort us the rest of the way. A procession was formed, with music and colours in the van, the two commanders with drawn sabres went next, and then we followed in our rags of clothes, the soldiers bringing up the rear. As we passed outside the village enclosure others joined, kissing our hands; women shouted shrilly with delight, and *we* were told to be seated upon a bed covered with leopard-skins placed for us in front of commander " Mahomed's " door. The traders all knew Petherick by name, but they either could not or would not tell us anything about -him, excepting that he was twenty marches away to the north, and that our letter sent to him from Unyoro had not been forwarded.

Everything around us looked strange; we had become such " roughs " that the most common object in this semi-civilised life gave us pleasure. Every one seemed so well dressed, they had all shoes, regular

CAMP OF EGYPTIANS. 325

bedsteads, crockery, &c., none of which we had seen for more than two years. The scenes also in a camp of Egyptians were new to us. Mahomed, the commander, seated on a low stool, while being shaved by a barber, excited the wonder of the Wanyoro. A white napkin being placed on his chest, the boy strapped the razor with the rapidity of lightning, and, standing with extended arms, passed his instrument over the whole head and beard at a frightful pace, handing his master a gilt frame looking-glass when the operation was completed. Donkeys were ridden at a sharp amble, without saddle or bridle, driven by a long stick, and the rider seated in the native fashion on the animal's haunches. Riding-oxen, with halters and ropes through their noses, were exercised about the village by negro lads, who made them go at a fast trot. Our bedding and cooking utensils not having arrived, we requested Mahomed to have some dinner prepared for us. At once he offered a cow, but it was late, and we did not wish to wait till it was killed. Coffee in true Arab style was served, and an attendant stood by offering occasionally tin mugs full of native-made beer. "When dinner was ready, a crowd squatted beside us, and a woman stood with water to drink. The'. repast was minced meat in balls served in a tureen, a roast leg of goat in another tureen, honey and thin cakes of sorghum; all looked inviting, and we longed to begin. We found, however, that there were no spoons, knives, or forks; and we made the most of it without them, and enjoyed an excellent dinner, which we had not done for many a day. But the greatest treat was to comelwater was brought us to wash our hands, and, luxury of all luxuries, soap !

326 CAMP OF EGYPTIANS.

After the repast was finished, we were gratified to find that the remains were placed before our Seedees; Mabrook was so surprised on receiving a cup full of honey, that he inquired whether it was to be eaten ? and after having dined, they all had soap and water served to them by one of the Nubians. A large open shed was made over to us, but we could not retire to rest without a prayer of thankfulness to the Almighty for having preserved us through so many difficulties, and at length, by His all-protecting arm, brought us in safety to the boundary of civilisation, after twenty-six months of unceasing toil and anxiety.

15

SECTION 15

CHAPTER XIV.

FROM DECEMBER 3, 1862, TO JANUARY 11, 1863|FALORO, LATITUDE 3 15' N. | THE TOORKEES OR TURKS | REGIMENTAL PARADE|MOONLIGHT DANCE|PRODUCTS OF FALORO|WILD ANIMALS|MIANI'S TREE AT APUDDO|AUTH● HEARS OF THE DEATH OF CAPTAIN SPEKE|PREPARATIONS FOR ENTERING THE BARI COUNTRY.

At Faloro we found upwards of a hundred men of every Egyptian caste, colour, and costume. They were called by the natives of the country "Toorkee," or Turks; but there was not a true Turk amongst them, and only one or two European countenances. Curly locks were exceptional, and wool predominated. They were adventurers without homes, born in the most northern Egyptian dominions from negro stock. We afterwards ascertained that the bazaar at Khartoum was full of such idlers ready for any employ. The merchants there engage them to go into the interior for the purpose of collecting ivory; guns are put into their hands, an intelligent native is placed over them, and they are sent up the Bahr Abiad (White Nile) as ivory-hunters, not to return perhaps for several years. These were the men we were so glad to meet, but from

328 OUR LIFE AMONGST THE TOORKEES.

whom we found it difficult to get away, although they had been at Faloro for nine months previous to our arrival.

The obstacles offered to our departure were many and vexatious. The rivers ahead, we were told, -would not be fordable for two months, and we could not cross them without using force; besides which, a party was expected to arrive soon from Gondokoro with ammunition and means of carrying down the tusks in store, and it must be waited for. This we could not assent to. As the streams were getting dry and a march was quite practicable, our Wanyoro men were ordered to be in readiness, but they had deserted to their homes, and we were helpless. Seeing that delay was inevitable, we proposed a trip to the west, in order that we might have a look at the White Nile, which we had left at Karuma Falls. The reply, however, was, that there was no use looking at the river there, because we should see it two marches ahead on the way to Gondokoro. This information was afterwards confirmed by our standing on a rocky height, from whence the river was seen marked by a long line of mist hanging over its course, which ran from the west in a north-east direction. The next event that startled us was the announcement that a party had to go to a district where a quantity of ivory had been accumulated, and that on their return we should all leave together for Gondokoro. There was nothing for it but submission. While we kept their camp eighty started on this razzia or raid, bringing back about a hundred tusks, a herd of cattle, and several slaves. Our importunities to get away were treated as the cravings of children, and we were told, " Do not fear,

A TOORKEE PARADE. 329

you'll get to Gondokoro before next moon." We surprised them, however, by packing up our luggage and preparing to start with our remaining twenty Seedees. Our residence amongst the Toorkees reminded me of a military life, for at break of day the *reveilU* was sounded regularly with drum and fife ; at certain fixed hours we had more music; and at night sentries were placed the same as in a cantonment. But the grand spectacle was their parade every Friday, which was equivalent to our Sunday. We were once requested to attend and see them manoeuvre, and anything more ludicrous can hardly be conceived. All were drawn up in line, but no two were dressed alike, neither had they uniform guns. Captain Mahomed stood in front, with drawn " shumshere," in a red jacket and loose Turkish trousers, fez, and silk turban. His second in command had adopted the rifle uniform of green jacket and black braid, loose pyjamas, gaiters, and tasselled fez; he also carried a drawn sword. Speke was the reviewing officer, and I stood on a height in the distance. Bombay, looking very dissipated, thought it his duty to stand alongside of his master; but his appearance, bare-headed, with a dirty shirt worn outside his dress, and holding a spear in his hand, betokened a pretty hard morning's carousing. Our second interpreter, Frij, was also decidedly tipsy, but had not the sense to remain quiet. While the men were marching he would rush wildly at them, flourishing his sword-bayonet, then attempting to show them how to march, blow his boatswain's whistle, repeat the commands, and interfere with the commander, who took it all good-naturedly. The series of manoeuvres embraced file-marching, forming

330 TOORKEES AS SENTRIES.

square, and open columns of companies|moving in these formations to any flank, over rough ground, to drum and fife music, in slow and quick time. The " general-officer," who had served with Turkish troops in the Crimea, was, of course, obliged to compliment them on their discipline, as their marching and shouldering passed muster; but the commander seemed to be of a different opinion, as any man who lost distance was at once cuffed and shoved out of the ranks, and when one side of the square faced inwards, I thought he would have cut them all down.

After parade, the standards were planted in the open space inside the village, and were there saluted by the men marching round them with drums ; or a cow was killed and the colours consecrated by putting some of the streaming blood upon them or on their staffs. This custom was known to our Seedees, who had seen it done by the Sultan of Zanzibar's Mohammedan troops. During the night sentries were posted all over the village, and they performed their duties very regularly, never sleeping, although they sat the whole of their turn of duty upon a stool or stone. This is more than most men could do ; but I watched some of them and never saw one fall asleep. Had we asked our Seedees to do this, they would have laughed at us, showing the difference which discipline had made between these two classes of men. The Nubians were seldom idle, employing themselves in curing skins, looking after their cattle, or conducting household matters; seeing this, our men at first were very shy, appearing like savages amongst them, but after ten days the restraint wore off, and they had their usual dances and sport. We could not keep

TOORKEES AS PLUNDERERS. 331

them from getting drunk and quarrelling, until, at the end of a week, we refrained from speaking to them, and then they desisted. One day I saw Fry riding with another man upon a bullock, and he offered me a ride, thinking I should enjoy it after the long journey on foot. There were numbers of riding donkeys and bullocks in camp. On the detachment making a flying march in quest of ivory, &c., the line was paraded with a colour on either flank. At the signal of one gun all moved off, with the three commanders each upon his donkey|the baggage, beads, and ammunition on the heads of natives. Before they returned from this trip, a native brought us information that three villages had been ransacked of their cattle and ivory, and that one more was to be swept before their return. This was pleasant news for us, their allies, as we now felt we were nothing but spies in the camp of a set of land-pirates! A circumstantial proof of this was that their chief banner, embroidered in two characters, " Andrea de Bono," had been left in camp with us. They could not conceal this fact, though they tried to keep us in the dark about their movements ; neither could they drown the cries of a girl they had captured. The story of this young captive was curious. Her father had heard and recognised her cries, and brought a tusk to offer for her release, apologising for the people of his village having fled, instead of hospitably entertaining the traders as they passed. The child was returned, and a cow given along with her. They had many more female than male slaves; but there were numbers of captured boys, who, being of naked races, would all their lives be ashamed to return to their homes because they had

332 THE WIVES OF THE TOORKEES.

been marked by circumcision. Grown-up women, generally the best-looking, were prevented from deserting by having a few rings of solid iron tied between each ankle, the links so short that, in fetching water from the stream, they could only advance a few inches at a time. There were about twenty women in this camp of the Unyoro race, distinguishable by all the lower incisors being extracted. Our Seedees could talk with them, and by this means obtain information for us. Some boys also, who were considered more trustworthy than the Nubians, were placed by them over their property of beads and ivory. No doubt they, as well as many other races, were destined for Cairo, and through them information regarding the Nile could at any time be obtained.

The wives of these soldiers were natives of Bari, Madi, &c., and very industrious. They might be seen, in their only dress of a single petticoat, on their knees cleaning what was equivalent to our doorsteps, in the early morning, by covering the space with a preparation of cow-dung. They kept the interiors of the huts very clean, and employed themselves in grinding murwa, making beer, baking cakes, or tending their infants. The women of the villages carried a small knife in their girdle, or stuck into the rings of iron worn above the elbow. This was a curious practice, but not so Amazonian-like as what was told us of a cannibal race nine marches to the north-west, where the women carry ten small knives with leather handles in each side of their girdle. These they hold by the tip of their blades, and throw them at their adversary. Our informant remarked, that after his party had obtained sufficient ivory, and wished to

NURTURE OF CHILDREN. 333

leave this cannibal race, they were told, " No, you are our food, and must not leave us;" but one shot dispersed them, and they escaped being eaten! He further added that they were not a nude race, neither did they keep cattle, but they wore the skins of goats. A knife which he had brought from Koshee, three marches to the west, was formed of one piece of iron, and had a round spoon as the handle to its dagger- like blade. He probably exaggerated when he said that the people gouged eyes with it. When a birth took place in the Toorkee camp, drums were beaten violently from break of day; and women assembled to rejoice at the door of the mother, by clapping their hands, dancing, and shouting. Their dance consisted in jumping in the air, throwing out their legs in the most uncouth manner, and flapping their sides with their elbows. One would have supposed the whole to be drunk, but it was their mode of congratulation. When the mother sufficiently recovers, a goat is killed, and she is asked to step over its body, and return again by stepping over its throat ; this operation is repeated. Mothers nurse and tend their children with the greatest care, washing them daily with warm water, and licking their faces dry as a dog would her litter of puppies. After this, the body is smeared with a vermilion-coloured pomade, and the infant is laid upon its back on the skin of a goat, which forms its cradle. The four corners of the skin are then knotted together, and the child is sung to sleep while slung in the hand or over the shoulder. When the mother is otherwise busy, the tender burden is hung upon a peg in the same way that we hang a cloak. A wife of the commandant's went through a

334 PECULIAR MARKS OF THE TRIBE.

strange custom with a handful of burning grass. She passed it three times round her body from hand to hand, while she walked to the left of her doorway. The grass was re-lit for her, and the same operation was gone through as she walked in front and again to the left of her door. The whole was performed with perfect solemnity until she saw herself observed, when she returned our smile. This ceremony was connected with the birth of her child. The women of the Bari race cut three horizontal lines on the cheeks of their children, and a black oily paste is rubbed into the incisions, which are kept open, looking raw and inflamed for ten days. I watched the operation upon an intelligent child of two or three years of age. Three deep scars were cut on its plump cheeks; fever seemed to ensue, as the little thing lost its wonted playfulness and its amusing imitation of the mother in her household duties. Ultimately these marks become lines of raised skin, and are cut in different parts of the body according to the race or district. Some have them in horizonal lines on the top of the arm-sockets; others have half-circles on the buttocks; and a very common mark seen at Faloro amongst the natives, was having the temples disfigured by barb-like cuts pointing to the eyes.

The people of Madi, to whom the village of Faloro belongs, did not seem happy under the yoke of the Turks. Their head men only showed contentment when presented with Arab gowns, pyjamas, &c., and they walked about the villages with canes or whips of buffalo-hide, like the Turks. However, they had their enjoyments of dancing and drinking. Their most pleasing performance was when a band of young

THE DANCES OF MADI. 335

men, usually about thirty, each with a hand-drum and a single stick (looking like kangaroos), danced in a circle to a lively quick tune, closing to a centre and retiring again at particular parts of their music.

By moonlight of the 5th December, we witnessed a most extraordinary dance in the village above where we resided. Some three hundred nude men and women were assembled. Six drums, of different sizes, slung upon poles, were in the centre; around these was a moving mass of people, elbowing and pushing one another as at a fair, and outside these a ring of girls, women, and infants, faced an outer circle of men sounding horns, and armed with spears and clubs, their heads ornamented with ostrich-feathers, helmets of the cowrie-shell, &c. Never had I seen such a scene of animated savage life, nor heard a more savage noise. As the two large circles of both sexes jumped simultaneously to the music, and moved round at every leap, the women sang and jingled their masses of bracelets, challenging and exciting the men facing them to various acts of gallantry; while our Seedees joined in the dance, and no doubt touched many a fair heart. But although these night scenes are enjoyed by the inhabitants as well as the Turks, they are during the day oppressed by their masters, and compelled by the lash to labour. Instances of this were constantly seen: a Toorkee thought nothing of giving a woman a cut with his cane if she stood the least in his way; and to escape such cruelty, we saw the people removing the *materiel* of villages for a new erection on a spot more distant from the Toorkee encampment. Any information regarding the neighbouring countries

336 MODE OF CARRYING ELEPHANT-TUSKS.

could not be obtained, because the natives feared the Turks, who in turn were jealous, and asked us what business it was of ours to interfere with their subjects ? They had also their guests who came on private affairs. These affairs were generally connected with razzias for cattle and ivory, which it was their object to conceal from us. Having been at Faloro for three successive seasons of nine months each, the Toorkees had collected an immense store of ivory, purchasing it with plundered cattle, and occasionally with a few beads|sixteen pounds of ivory fetching but two strings of large blue beads with cut sides. During this their third season, about one hundred monster tusks, and three hundred small ones, called karashas at Zanzibar (averaging sixteen pounds weight each), had been gathered together. All these were easily distinguishable from the eighteen that had been shot by the party, as they were red, and blackened with the flames of fire, applied by the natives in extracting the tusk from the elephant's head. When about to march, sets of tusks were securely lashed together with thong, cut in a single continuous stripe from the hide of a cow. One man could carry from fifty to sixty pounds weight on his head, and when the load was heavier, two men carried it slung to a pole between them.

In discharging our Gani guides by payment of beads at Faloro, we gave one of them, in addition, a pair of trousers. He at once put all his small beads loosely into the pockets, but on sitting down, in his usual native manner, the beads kept dropping out, causing much laughter amongst us. To make him still more happy, Frij tied a turban of red rags round

KNEE DISEASE IN MADI. 337

his head, which was much admired; but the knowing African rubbed his arms, as much as to say, " Where is the coat ? " This man's father, Chong'ee of Gani, a decrepid old man, with wrinkled skin and dull eye, had received some small beads in return for a cow he presented. They did not satisfy him,|he must have others, the ingenious excuse being that he was too old to see such small things! Other beads much less valuable, but larger, were instantly given and accepted in exchange.

A common disease amongst the natives was a large permanent swelling or growth below the knee-cap of one leg or both. Though the size of a cricket-ball, it was soft, and did not incapacitate the person from sitting, kneeling, or walking, and grown-up women seemed more liable to it than the male sex. Dr Murie (whom we met at Gondokoro) imagined from my description that it might have been brought on from exposure to cold. The only death that occurred while we were with the Turks was that of one of their own number, arising from fever and general exhaustion. His funeral took place at sunrise inside the village ; a silent mass of soldiers surrounded the grave, which was dug within the shell of a hut accidentally burnt down a few days previously. And on the occasion of this fire, I may remark that we were all saved providentially by the stillness of the day. The huts being made of grass and bamboo, huddled close together|ammunition and property in every one of them|and water half a mile distant, the alarm was frightful. No one knew what to do, as the unmanageable flames burst through the roof, or kept creeping onwards for more prey. Nude men

338 CATTLE AND PROVISIONS.

could not approach it; in their attempts to quench the flame, they held skins of animals to screen them from the heat, which we in our clothes could hardly bear. Its further progress was happily stayed, but the hut with all that it contained was soon a heap of ashes.

In December, the people burn down the grass on the hills and dales. The black ashes fill the air for some days till laid by rain, serving the purpose of manure for the following season. The dews are very heavy at this time of the year : one night my knife was left on a bank, and next morning it appeared rusted all over. After eight in the morning it was too hot to walk out with comfort before the afternoon; and although no musquito troubled us, the place was infested with flies, which stuck to our faces and clothes during a morning walk. The small stream below the village dried up as our rivulets at home do in summer, and, during January, scarcely afforded sufficient water for the cattle. There were nine separate herds, and probably fifteen hundred cows, to be seen daily. They belonged chiefly to the Turks, but the country being overstocked, the animals were small and poor, and many of the calves were not able to follow the flocks. While housed in the villages, each animal was tied to a peg in the ground; and when released, in order that they might be taken to graze, all rushed to a salt bank of earth which had been scooped out by their tongues. We obtained provision here by sending our men with a cow to a neighbouring village, where they killed it before the natives, who exchanged their grains or vegetables for the beef. Very often, when a fowl was required, the

HANDSOME TREE-CLIMBERS. 339

natives, though they would not take beads in exchange from us, were obliged to submit to see the Turks knock them over with sticks, and walk away without payment. The vegetable products were tobacco, murwa, a few sweet potatoes, and the stringy seed-vessel of a species of mallow, called here *bamea*. The cultivations were all at least a mile away from where the people dwelt, probably to allow a cleared space for their cattle to range. The field-hoe had a handle as long as the English one ; it was large and heavy, but preferred to those made in Unyoro, which were refused here when offered in exchange for sweet potatoes..

As has already been mentioned, the situation chosen at Faloro by the Turks was a very pleasant one. We were surrounded by low hills, the country afforded delightful rambles by rocky streams, through forests, and over downs, with distant prospects. The plants gathered were many of them new and interesting. A plum-tree, having fruit larger than the green-gage, was found in the woods, and large black caterpillars of great beauty, armed with rows of white porcupine- like spikes, fed upon its leaves. A species of silver bush *(Protect, sp.),* its flowers spread out like a silvery sunflower, with its scaly calix a pink colour underneath, was interesting. A tree-climber *(Landolphia florida ?)* lay with its trunk winding like a huge snake, and then serving as a bridge to the stream. If traced further, you found it had mounted a lofty tree, and spread itself into innumerable branches, covering with luxuriant white flowers the highest foliage. The natives of Uhiyow convert its milk into playing-balls, like those of india-rubber, and consider the rubber

340 SUPERSTITIOUS OBSERVANCES.

superior in quality to that obtained from another tree, M'pira, which has not such adhesive properties.

A very handsome branched lily *(Crinum sp.)* was one day brought in by Speke, who had found it on the bank of the stream-bed. We could find no other in flower, but succeeded in preserving and bringing home this single specimen, which is now in the Kew herbarium. Later l probably by February l their bulbs would throw out fresh shoots for the year. A variety of resinous trees were also foundl*Boswellia, Balsamodendron, Khaya, Soymida,* &c.

Trees of the " Sheabutter," and others of similar dimensions, sometimes had diminutive seats placed against their trunks, with the ashes of fire alongside. The seats had been placed there for some idolatrous purpose, to produce rain or probably to remove sickness. The only other trace of superstition we saw was in front of the chief entry to the village. Here a slab, two feet out of the ground, with a circular hole across, faced the entry in an upright position. A pole with a branch of the meelalla palm *(Borassus)* flying from its tip, was planted alongside it.

We had no sport at Faloro, killing only one bush- boc, which we found feeding in the jungle of sweet pasture and shrubs by a stream. Further up, amongst rocks, we saw two descriptions of monkeyslone the Lungoor, with black face and bushy head of hair, which barked angrily at us; and the " Yanee"lso called by our Seedeesla smaller monkey, red behind, and said to be so vicious that he will return a spear thrown at him! Both were wild, and changed their ground so often that we did not obtain a shot. The way the Turks have of inflating a sheep or goat after

BUSTARD AND OTHER GAME-BIRDS. 341

it has been killed appeared strange to our Zanzibar Seedees. A rattan was passed, from an incision in the hock, to the stomach; air was blown in, not with a bellows as in France, but from the mouth, till the animal became distended. Where the air had not reached, a passage was made for it by striking the part, and the skin by this method was drawn off with greater facility.

The bustard, or "cock of the woods," was occasionally marked down. On starting him he would get up with the usual hurried flight and noise,make a majestic sweep over the woods, and disappear in low ground, or, folding his wings, alight on some cultivated spot. He is a noble bird, with rich game plumage, and nearly the size of a vulture. The other game-birds were chiefly quail and guinea-fowl, but our supply of shot being almost finished, we-did not disturb them. Flocks of guinea-fowl were running in the fields three marches north of Faloro. I had never before seen them so numerous; but they were wild, being killed by the inhabitants with bow and arrow. A few rooks, with peculiarly short tails, were now and then observed. They took swift cutting flights from tree to tree, calling like crows, and cleverly evading the darts made at them by kites.

We left Faloro on the llth of January 1863, our loads being carried by our remaining Seedees, twenty in number. We then travelled without the Turks for a few days to the north, and were joined by their headquarters on the 31st. In this interval we employed the time in shooting over the desolate-looking undulations of grass jungle. Rhinoceros, buffalo, gnamaera, n'soono, &c., were killed; and elephant,342 GiraffelCrocodile's Eggs.

giraffe, eland, pig, the white-eared antelope of Peth- erick, and other smaller fauna, were observed. The natives would not eat the rhinoceros. Giraffe were numerous, but very wild, they being in open cover, over which they could, by means of their long necks, see the sportsman. Nothing is more handsome than their bright-yellow black-spotted skin when seen shining in the morning sun; but as you approach to shooting distance they canter away like camels and lash their sides with their tails. Gnamaera or hartebeest are also most provoking animals to stalk; they allow you to approach within three or four hundred yards, when they wheel round with a whisk of their tails, take a canter, and turn back to look at you. The Turks shot a crocodile, and carried him into camp to extract his teeth, which are used by the natives of Madi as necklaces. They are like the long incisors of a sheep, and being pierced, are strung to be worn on the neck. Most of the Turks ate of the crocodile, but our Zanzibar men regarded it with disgust . We ate their eggs to breakfast; and although they were sweet and good without any particular flavour, we had no desire to try another. Ninety-nine of them had been found buried a foot under ground in the sandy bed of a stream, all laid in very neat order. They were longer and larger than the eggs of a tuAey, pure white, and uniformly shaped at both ends, with one-third of them an air-chamber.

The stream below the village of Apuddo, where we encamped for several days, had cut a wide channel through the plain. Observing some shining scales on its sandy shore, they so much resembled gold that I thought I had made a discovery, and washed the sand

MAGNETIC IRON ORE. 343

for several hours. The result was, glistening black sand resembling iron filings, and a mixture of these gold scales, probably mica, but which remain to be analysed. (*Vide* Appendix B.) While at this operation cf digging, a number of bees of the ordinary size came lound me, and I could observe them alighting on the sand to enter burrows they had made. They were of two colours, green and yellow, the latter predominating, and barred with black stripes. A few inches underground, a cocoon of the tender leaves of the *Stereospermum sp.*la tree with pink-white blossom lwas found neatly wrapped round some scented yellow substance, having the faintest taste of honey. It may have been liquid wax, as the natives told me that the bees ultimately transport this preparation to their hives. But the curious thing was to see it lying in the wet sand, and almost in water, probably put there to keep it cool from the hot winds. The natives dig wells in the sand and take their drinking water from them. At first we imagined they had been digging for gold, as numerous little pits were in the ground, each with a tumblerful of water; but we observed that the natives filled their earthen " gurrahs " from them in preference to taking water from the running stream close by.

The strong barricade of sticks and logs placed round the villages had numerous openings for en- ' trance. At night these were closed by pulling thorny bushes into them; and during the day one had to stoop to gain entrance. Even their women, when carrying a pitcher of water on their heads, were obliged to go on their knees to pass inside the village. The huts had not room for a camp-bed, not being of greater diameter than seven feet; but, luckily, at this

344 THE PEOPLE CONFIDE IN US.

season, quantities of ripe grass were stacked for thatching purposes, and we could always get a temporary- shed made to shelter us from the sun. The inLabi- tants of Panyoro, on seeing our small party arrie, showed a disinclination to admit us inside their vi- lages, and the Turks tried to dissuade us from living there; but in our previous travels we had always fraternised with the natives, and wished to make no difference in the present case. The consequence was that the people confided in us, bringing their property to be placed in concealment under our beds lest the Turks should come and rob them. They also gave us small presents of milk, flour, ears of grain, &c.; and one chief kindly brought us a basin of soup and a mess of porridge. The soup was very nitrous in taste, too much salt of the country having been used. Another dish they had was a mixture of uncooked flour and water, savoured with the fruit of a date-sized plum, the *Balanites JEgyptica, Dal.* The chiefs had a singular mode of salutation, which the common people did not venture to copy; they took our hands successively in theirs, lifted them up as high as they could, and then allowed them to drop. This custom was never seen in Unyoro, Uganda, or south of the equator; and although the hands of the chiefs were not very clean, we were glad to submit to the ceremony. After the natives had become familiar with us by our shooting animals for them, they got up dances similar to the Madi " quadrille." The men held spears over the heads of the women, pointed their elbows at them, and bent their heads to the right and left in time to the drum-music. The Toorkees did not join our men in these dances; they were encamped outside

LETTERS CUT ON A TAMARIND-TREE. 345

the villages, and thought it was too much like savage life, and beneath them, to participate in the festivities.

As there is no conveyance in the country except by porters, the Turks found it very difficult to get their two hundred loads of ivory carried. The natives on several occasions refused to aid them, saying they were not slaves to be made to carry their property. Resistance being continued, active hostilities were resorted to, and disastrous results ensued. What between the firing of guns and discharge of arrows, three Toorkees were wounded, fifteen natives were killed, and seven made prisoners, the village was burned to the ground, and about one hundred cattle captured! This was told us by some Seedees we sent back to find why the Turks were not coming to join the party. The women captured on these occasions remain the property of the captor, while all cattle and ivory must be shared by the master and his soldiers.

Within sight of Apuddo stands a tamarind-tree, three or four miles from the right bank of the Nile, at 3 341' N. lat. and 32 E. long. The Turks informed us that a European had, two years previously, accompanied them from Gondokoro as far as this point, and had returned to Egypt from hence, because the rains were heavy, and he had not sufficient escort to push further south. They did not know his name, but they described him as having a long beard, and said we should find his name cut upon the tree. My notes on the 1st February 1863 are as follows regarding it: "I visited the tree on which a European had cut some letters, but they were so indistinct, that I walked twice round it before I could distinguish them,|they were grown over with a thorny creeper and bark, and

346 MIANI's TREE.

had been merely scratched in the wood. They appeared like|AIA A ; the centre letters were I and A, and the outer ones either A *without the stroke,* or part of W. Nails seem to have been extracted, and to read it properly, I had to stand upon some lower branches." I at once concluded that the traveller was not English, because his letters were not deeply cut into the tree as an Englishman would have done it, and also because the letters were curiously formed. The illegible letters without strokes were scored in thus|M,|as a foreigner writes the capital letter M. Not until we reached Khartoom did we find out for certain who this traveller must have been. His name was Ml AN I (Miani), a native of Venice, who has protested against *our* Nile being the proper Nile, because we have placed his tree in a position of latitude and longitude (obtained by daily observations) different to what he made it, without scientific instruments. His assertion is bold, considering the above evidence; but as M. Miani is trying to organise another expedition, I have no doubt he will discover,and perhaps ultimately acknowledge, his error. In the mean time, Mr S. Baker will in all likelihood have passed the spot, and taken the exact position of the tree and river. The Nile at 3 N. lat., had quite changed the wild character it possessed at Karuma Falls. Its banks were tame and flat, with but few trees. The opposite, or left bank, rose into three blocks of lofty bare hills, almost mountains, called " Jubl Kookoo." Round their north-east bluff end the majestic Nile made a sweeping turn from the west to the north; and looking down the stream from this point, the scene appeared wild and romantic like the Highland Pass of Glencoe.

AUTHOR HEARS OF THE DEATH OF CAFT. SPEKE. 347

At this point of my narrative I was arrested by startling intelligence: the first dark cloud connected with our African journey had suddenly appeared. In a moment, without warning, the devoted leader of the expedition was cut off in his prime, and just as he had told the wondrous tale of his adventurous life ! On the 17th of September, when engaged as usual in transcribing from my Journal, my apartment was entered by my brother-in-law, the Kev. Peter Mackenzie, whose countenance wore an unusual expression of grief. It was to break to me the sad news that my fellow-traveller|poor Speke|had been shot by the accidental discharge of his own gun. I could not realise the fact. Could he possibly be dead ? Was there no hope ? The telegraph gave us none. A few days only had elapsed since he and his brother invited me to their home in Somersetshire to be present at the meeting of the British Association at Bath, and had I gone thither and been with my friend, this calamity might have been averted. Innumerable such thoughts hurried through my mind on the first shock of the melancholy tidings. It was hard to believe that one who had braved so much had thus fallen, and that his career of usefulness was run! I reproached myself for having silently borne all the taunts and doubts thrown upon his great discovery, the truth of which will ultimately be acknowledged by all but those determined to

CAPTAIN SPEKE.

cavil. We had corresponded on the subject, and agreed that controversy on my part was to be avoided. Any attempt of the kind might only weaken his cause, and I felt that no assertions of mine were necessary to bear out the facts which he had recorded. Truth in time would conquer, and bear down all gainsayers, while that grand reservoir of twenty thousand miles|the Victoria Nyanza, with its fountains and tributaries|would speak for itself. Knowing that on our travels my attention was more directed to the habits of the people than to the geography of the country, he expressed a wish that I should write an account of our camp life in Africa. I complied, and part of this narrative lay on his table on the day of his death. It now goes forth without his revision or suggestions I a public loss; for my fellow-traveller had a thorough knowledge of the country, loved its inhabitants, was a practical ornithologist, and would have aided me with his views on all topographical questions. Added to a singular adaptation for the work he had made choice of,Iarising partly from his imperturbable temper and great patience,ICaptain Speke was, in private life, pure-minded, honourable, regardless of self, and equally self-denying, with a mind always aiming at great things, and above every littleness. He was gentle and pleasing in manner, with almost childlike simplicity, but at the same time extremely tenacious of purpose. This was

CAPTAIN SPEKE.

strikingly displayed in his recent efforts to prosecute his work in Africa, which, had he lived, he would ultimately have accomplished. But God has ordained it otherwise. His will be done! To Captain Speke's mourning relatives and friends, there remains the consolation that though he died in the prime of life, he had attained to immortal fame, and now rests in his own beautiful native district, lamented by all who knew him, and a brilliant example to the youth of future generations. His remains were laid with those of his ancestors in the family vault of the parish church; and had the toll of the funeral bells reached the shores of the Nyanza as it touched the hearts of those in the valley of Ilminster, there is one at least Ithe King of UgandaIwho would have shed a tear for the untimely death of the far-distant traveller who had sought and found his protection. I must now resume the course of my narrative, which has been so painfully interrupted.

At Apuddo gales blew hot and powerful enough to melt any number of glaciers. The "Kousee" wind from the N.E., carrying dust with it, blew as if through a funnel during the latter half of January; it was no doubt reflected with greater violence on account of the proximity of the Jubl Kookoo range of mountain to our N.W. While sheltered from its blasts we perspired profusely ; but by sunset it had lulled away, and we

350 VILLAGE OF APUDDO.

were able to walk about with comfort. A coat was then bearable, and during the night we wore sheets of serge to keep us warm. Rain was noted in my journal on the 12th of January from the N.E., and another note mentions at this time, wind "all day N.N.W., blowing with great freshness."

ProvisionsInamely, koonde, murwa, and jowariI were scarce and dear in the villages opposite Jubl Koo- koo during the month of January, which was their winter season. Large figs, called M'kooyoo, though thick- skinned and full of seeds, were now sweet and palatable. No crops were seen growing I all looked desolate wastes and covers. Even the stream which flowed past Apuddo, for three miles up its tortuous course had not a thicket to mark its windings through the plain. The banks dropped straight down fifteen feet to its sandy bed, which was sometimes broken by grass- topped and fissured rocks, and in places by ridges of rock, making a cataract or waterfall. Above this, in one reach two hundred yards long, the water lay deep and almost still, teeming with fish two and three feet in length. We had no means of catching them, and the natives did not use nets, but most likely they had basket-traps.

The people dwelt in villages surrounded by palisades. Some of these villages contained two hundred souls, young and old. It would not be considered safe to have a much smaller settlement, as their neighbours to the east, the Kidi, would come down to plunder them of their herds of cattle. We observed a leper with white hands and limbs. Whether he had succeeded by right to his position of "M'koongoo," or head of a district, or whether from being looked

CURIOUS NECK ORNAMENTS. 351

upon as a favoured man lie was elected president, we could not say, but the latter is not unlikely ; for the natives of Africa have a respect for men with spotted skins. The Turks generally applied to us for medical advice. One day a tooth had to be drawn; a rag was tied round each half of a pair of scissors, and I had to make these answer all the purpose of a forceps. Again, a disease which very much resembles diphtheria, and which was said to be fatal unless cut, was treated in an odd way. The patient had a white abscess in the throat, and it required to be cut. They had no instrument for the purpose, and we had only a penknife, and there was further the difficulty of reaching the seat of the disease. The natives, however, are ingenious; they pulled out the tongue so far that a hair noose could be put round the abscess, and it was then cut, much to the poor man's relief, who speedily recovered.

It has been mentioned that the people of Madi wear the teeth of crocodiles as neck ornaments. The natives of Bari do the same, and the pearly white colour of the teeth is most becoming to their deep bronze complexions. Another ornament seen here was new to us: the thigh-bones of sheep and rats were pierced at one end, and slung from the neck. I had seen nothing like this since leaving Delagoa Bay, where the Zulu Kaffirs, called in Central Africa "Watuta," wear bones, bird's-feet, &c., as charms round the neck.

On the 1st of February 1863, we marched in a caravan or troop of no less than three hundred souls from our camp at Apuddo to some villages fifteen miles distant on the route to Gondokoro. Having to

352 FORDING THE RIVER ASUA.

cross the river Asua, a wild rocky torrent, the journey occupied six hours and forty minutes, our escort consisting of two hundred ivory-carriers, the Toorkees, their wives, women, slaves, donkeys, cattle, &c. The route lay above the right bank of the Nile, and although the country was uninhabited, I do not recollect ever making a more interesting march. At the fourth mile, and to the west, we heard from the heights on which we stood the White Nile sounding below us, like the ocean, but we could not see it until we had proceeded two miles further. The beautiful noble stream was breaking now and then into foam upon hidden rocks; or running at the rate of about four miles an hour past islands so laden with trees and vegetation that we could only partially discern the opposite bank, and obtain occasional glimpses of the river. On our side we had several species of acacia, the double black thorned and the white; with other trees in lilac bloom, wild figs, &c.; and, had the underwood of thorny scrub been cleared away, the place might have been deemed a paradise. The ivory-carriers marched steadily onwards, but I longed for the halt, that we might have a drink of the water that appeared so inviting. At the eighth mile a happy break in the thicket gave us this opportunity; and we who had traced the stream from the Victoria Nyanza were so glad to see our Uganda acquaintance once more, that we addressed it in the language of that country, exclaiming, " Awangeh ! awangeh !"l old friend ! old friend ! While resting on the rocky bank, the views across, up or down the river, were of great interest. At our feet, by the side of a foaming rapid, fish rose like porpoises, showing their backs in

THE RIVERS NILE AND ASUA. 353

a whirling black pool, where reeds, rushes, branches, and logs floated about, making it impossible for any but an adept to attempt fly-fishing The shore was strewed with fish-scales, and remnants of fires showed that the natives had been enjoying dinner at an appropriate spot. Looking across, an island, covered with grass and aquatic vegetation, hid the other branch of 'the river. For a quarter of a mile at this point no boat could live at any season; it would be dashed to pieces on the bed and sides of sunken rock; and the immense body of water is so strong that no boat could sail up it. Looking down stream, the river ran in a deep one-sided gorge, the left bank being the Jubl Kookoo range, forming a straight barrier of escarped hills, probably two thousand feet in height. They were bleak and barren, diminishing in size and breaking into cones as they receded into the blue distance to the north. At the ninth mile of this march, we suddenly dropped into the bed of the Asua river, and crossed to its right bank. Our first remark was, " Is this the Asua we have heard so much of?" The fording was fifty yards across, waist deep in the strong middle current over sharp slippery rocks, painful for bare feet. The water was good, though not refreshing nor transparent; it ran through five- feet-high rushes *(Cyperus longus)*, on the right shore. During December, this river, judging from the appearance of sand lying above its present water-mark, must be a wild torrent, impossible to cross; but we were disappointed with its small appearance when we came to ford it. Our large *cortege* amused themselves for two hours in crossing the cattle and laden donkeys, and in bathing. At this place I saw the brutal

354 THE NILE AT 3 47' N. LAT.

nature of the ivory-traders. One of them, in getting upon his laden bullock, mounted so awkwardly, that he tilted the load over to one side, and the animal would not start with him. He belaboured it on the head with a loaded life-preserver, till the poor animal sat down. Immediately he dismounted, and in rage put a bullet through its head; and the men around Vn'm cut off the hump and legs to carry with them as food, while the owner sat gloomily apart looking on : anything more revolting I never saw. Having forded the river we encamped in a village, the inhabitants flying at our approach. We had been from sunrise to sunset on the road, having passed several deserted villages and a jungle of thorny wood. The path along, which we had travelled was on the top of vertical strata, pointing to the north-west. It was of slaty blue rock, cleaved into loose squares and oblongs, with quartz veins.

One morning I walked, along with three of our Seedees, due west for two hours, to have another look at the Nile. We tried to get guides from the villages, but after promising they generally slunk back into their huts. However, when approaching the river, past the dwellings, I induced a native to give me tobacco, when an escort of about forty men, well armed with bows, spears, and handfuls of arrows, accompanied me to the water's edge. For two miles the calm river ran in a straight reach, unbroken, as far as I remember, by rock or cataract. Its breadth appeared to be about eighty yards, and the current four miles an hour; both banks were dead-level, and of stiff clay. Beyond these, rather barren hills rose abruptly. While sitting on the bank, my feet almost touched the water; and the level ground was dotted

CORPORAL PUNISHMENT. 355

with tamarinds, fig, palm, plum, and jujube trees, the soil itself being then, in parts, lying under cultivation. The people had a ferry-boat|that is, a log of wood scooped out to form a boat; and they tied together large bundles of the jowari straw, and ferried over upon them. I had never seen this before, but further down the Nile it is a common practice. On my way back from this excursion, the villagers at several places invited me to partake of milk, and the guide, on being rewarded with a single string of beads, in a coaxing and familiar manner asked for another. One of the Seedees whom we had picked up in the heart of Africa, was convicted at this encampment of Madi of having stolen a cloth belonging to a Toorkee with whom he lived. The offence was a grave one, bringing dishonour upon our Zanzibar party; he, therefore, was awarded fifty lashes. Bombay administered forty with a whip of buffalo-hide, and Frij the remaining ten. The offender, after receiving the first few lashes, cried, " Kill me ! kill me !" meaning that death was preferable to the pain; but little Bombay, who was flogging him, said, "Are you a woman that you scream in that way ?" The fellow was at once silenced; but though his back was scarred, he ate his dinner before us and carried a load the following day. He was a hardened culprit, and deserted from us in Egypt, after being detected in stealing from a comrade.

The sick of this district of Madi were not allowed to reside within the enclosure of the village; but huts or hospitals were erected outside for all who were diseased. It was curious to find such a civilised precaution taken in Africa. But the huts were also remarkable for neatness and cleanliness ; bamboos were

356 SHELLS, THE COINAGE OF THE MAPI.

numerous, so that they had the material for making themselves comfortable. The floors were of red clay, packed hard, and the thresholds of the doors the same, but paved or macadamised, with fragments of earthenware neatly inlaid. Many of the doorways had gateposts, with bamboos as movable bars, which prevented goats or cattle entering. Upon the grass tops of the huts in Barwudi numbers of large univalve shells lay bleaching; they were the same large, spiral species as those seen five degrees south of the equator. The natives cut them into circles the size of shirt-buttons, and string hundreds of them to be worn as ornamental white girdles round the waist. They formed the ordinary coinage, and if beer or fowls were required they were used in the purchase. The value of labour was estimated in cows. The porters engaged by De Bono's party to carry their ivories were paid one small cow each for a journey of four marches, and they were expected to carry a return load; so that travelling in these parts is a difficult matter, unless you have plenty of camel and donkey carriage: the hire is always paid beforehand. It was amusing to observe the distribution of the cattle, but it presented much the same scene as that witnessed at home in a cattle-market. Here the naked natives, mingling with the well- dressed Toorkees, as soon as they received their " one- cow hire," chased it away to be tied up in some secure place till their journey was completed. On arrival at one of the villages, I asked the Sheikh what his beer was like; he made no reply, but at midnight he stole into our camp, passing our Seedee sentries, who were fast asleep, tapped Speke on the head, and then shook his hand to awake him. Speke immediately called

CONSEQUENCES OF COERCION. 357

Frij, to find what the old man meant by coming at such an hour, when it appeared that he had brought us a taste of his beer. It seemed raw and spiritless, but as soon as the sun had risen, the old Sheikh generously brought us a large jar full of the beverage.

The country was populous: but in this month of February, though displaying pretty undulations or downs, dotted with shady tamarind and fig trees, and though the double-coned hills have wooded tops, all had a parched appearance. The brooks were dry. During several of our marches we met with no stream, and what water was obtained was procured by digging holes in the dry and rocky beds. Sometimes wild- fruits would refresh us, such as the fig; it was the size of a strawberry pippin, and tasted excellent. The natives gathered quantities of the fruit of a *Cucur bitacece,* the size and shape of a fowl's egg : its yellow rind was dried and eaten by them. Their grain they stored in separate houses from their dwellings, and built or placed them upon a few piles of wood or rough pillars of stone. On arrival in a village the Toorkee always made his way to these stores for the purpose of pillaging. On my desiring one of them to desist, he coolly laughed; but Bombay succeeded better with him. As soon as our caravan arrived at a village for the day, the Turks formed camp outside of it by removing the roofs of the houses, and making their owners carry them for them! If resistance was shown, the butt- end of the musket was applied to the poor owner, or the muzzle of the gun was presented to his stomach. One consequence of this system of coercion and plunder was that, whenever the people of Mad i or Bari had the opportunity, they retaliated and stole from the Turks freely.

358 GAME|WEAPONS|EARTHENWARE OF MAPI.

The country was too open and populous for game. Along our route we saw none; but the men often wore ornaments of the wild boar's curved tusk. This was tied with a thong above each elbow, and looked very jaunty on their well-formed arms. Their spears were some inches taller than most men can stretch., with handles of bamboo and handsomely-shaped iron blades. Each was shod with a sharp point of iron, or had its end like the leaded end of an Indian hog- spear. Their iron weapons were of superior construction, and were chiefly made on the spot, as there were traces of smelting. The earthenware was very ordinary; but we remarked an unusual article of luxury, a strainer actually of earthenware|the only *civilised* bit of crockery we had seen since leaving Zanzibar: it was chiefly used for straining beer. The perennial cotton-bush grew 8 feet high, without irrigation, close to the houses; the pods, thick and numerous, were now ripening. Three or four bushes give sufficient cotton to each family for all the use made of it; the women dye it brown, and make their scanty dress| waist-belts and tails|of the fibre. The men practised archery a good deal, placing a number of the large seed-vessels of *Kigelia pinnata* on end and aiming at them at 40 and 50 yards' distance. They must be practised shots, as a villager was, brought us in a sinking state with an arrow-mark in his side. The wound was covered up, and plastered all over with leaves|their remedy for everything. He had, in all probability, been struck by a poisoned arrow, as they sometimes use these in Madi.

We had very little sickness, and all were in high glee at the thought of going to Egypt in boats. SomeManua's Plans For Retiring. 359

men tad arrived from Gondokoro reporting that three boats were lying there; we concluded they must be those of Frith, Petherick, and De Bono, and we were delighted at the prospect of meeting Petherick. The time we were detained by the Toorkees, because they had difficulty in procuring porters to carry their ivory to Gondokoro, was occupied in botanising or gossiping with our men. Manua, the " Man of the Moon," was forming his plans as to what he would do after he got paid for the journey. He said, very truly, that Zanzibar life would not suit him ; he could not afford it; because if he retired there, he would have to pay for water, food, drink, clothing, and house-room. His plan, therefore, was to purchase beads and cloths and take them for sale to his native land of Unyamuezil a resolution which shows the mercantile nature of his race. This little fellow was very intelligent, and a great traveller. He talked in high praise of his late king, Foondeekeera, and was quite in raptures when he mentioned his name. It seems that before the king's death a man and woman were suspected of having worked an enchantment upon him, and they were slain; but the king died nevertheless; none of his wives were buried with him, and a house was built over the grave. The chief of Wakeembwah, to the west of Unyamuezi, is laid in the bed of a small stream when he dies, and fifty living women (his wives), and fifty men, are tied to frames and drowned in the same stream to commemorate the event. Their race practise the rite of circumcision, which is exceptional in Central Africa.

Between the district of Madi and Gondokoro there is a tract of country 40 miles long, inhabited by the Bari,

360 TRAITS OF SEEDEE CHARACTER.

who are the terror of all ivory-traders, as they are an independent and powerful race of people. In passing through their country we were told that our *guns* should always be at hand, that we should not drink any water, as it was poisoned, and, above all, that we should move across the country in a compact body, and not in procession. On seeing the nipple of Bombay's gun blown out, I inquired how he was to ger through the Bari ?lwas the gun safe to fire in its patched state ? Oh yes, he'd fire it, because the gun was stronglit had stood the proof of three cartridges ! How was that ? " It's some time ago now; but Ubede, Abdulla, and a man who deserted, had a spite at me, and each of them put a cartridge into this gun, thinking it would blow my head off, but the nipple was only blown out." He was such an excellent little fellow that he never told us this when it happened; and when asked whether he had suspected his enemy Bar- aka to have played him this trick, he generously replied, "No, I never suspected him." One other instance of the Seedee character may be mentioned before giving an account of our travels through the Bari people. Our cook boy, M'kate, a very tall good- looking lad, ever obliging and good-humoured, one day left a cooking-pot twelve miles behind. He was admonished by Frij, and took the matter so much to heart that he travelled back for it alone that same day and returned during the night, having recovered the old pot, which was certainly not worth the journey. It only proves what men will do with kind treatment ; he was not asked to go back, and had walked by himself thirty-six miles through a strange country.

SECTION 16

CHAPTER XV.

PASSAGE THROUGH THE BARI|POISONED STREAMS|GONDOKORO |MEET-
ING WITH MR SAMUEL BAKER|MR AND MRS PETHE- RICK ARRIVE AT
GONDOKORO|TRADE AND TRADERS|THE NILE AND MODE OF FERRYING
IT | EMBARK IN BAKER'S BOATS FOR KHARTOOM.

The Bari country was a series of gently swelling downs, sloping to the Nile a few
miles to our left. The downs were covered with grass now ripe and only a foot high.
During the bright mid-day sun, with a fresh, hot breeze, the grass, when set on fire,
burns with alarming rapidity; but in the darkness of night, when the air was still, it
burned quietly but brilliantly, and we dined by its light: no theatrical footlights or
exhibition of fireworks could compare with the brilliancy of the consuming flame.
Densely foliaged tamarinds covered with ripe fruit, wild plum, sheabutter, and several
other umbrageous trees scattered over the landscape, gave it the appearance of an
English park, for here no palms nor other tropical genera were to be seen. We had
to step over numbers of running rivulets whose channels and banks were generally of
rock. In the rainy season these torrents must be difficult to cross, as they have all
  362 BARI MEN AND WOMEN.

worn deep beds for themselves; but now in fording the largest they only reached to the knee, and -with bare feet we enjoyed the wading. Their waters were rather insipid and tasteless.

We dared not rest at any of the Bari villages, as the Toorkees distrusted the people; but Bookhait, the second in command of the traders, beckoned to a Bari, and he frankly joined us. He was a tall, erect, thin man, naked from head to foot, but with all the airs of a well-dressed beau, for his body was smeared with a red clay pomade. Above each elbow he wore a massive ring of ivory, upon one shoulder he carried a diminutive stool of one piece of solid dark wood, and he had a rope-sash which possessed a five-finger-like charm; he was unarmed. Next morning he brought into camp a very fine tusk, for which he received in exchange a female goat and its kid|cheap ivory certainly. The women wore each a long apron of leather to the knee and a separate broader one of sewn leather behind : these skins they colour with clay, and they seem to wear no ornaments; however, there was not much opportunity for observation on our part, as they ran away on observing us watch them. It seems strange that these people, who for the last thirty years have been only from twenty to thirty miles distant from the Austrian mission-station at Gondokoro, should still be so wild; but the missionaries state that the ivory trade has spoiled the country for civilisation, and whenever the inhabitants see a foreigner, white or black, they look upon him as an enemy, come for no other purpose than to seize cattle or whatever else he can.

In travelling through the Bari our large caravan

THE BARI POISON THE STREAMS. 363

was astir at the rattle of the drum in the morning, and marched the whole day, except the three hottest hours, which were spent under shady trees. During the march the colours led the way, no one was allowed to precede them, and a complete cordon of armed Toorkees surrounded the moving mass and kept order. In this way we proceeded across country at a smart pace, allowing no straggling, but making many halts. Sometimes, at several fields' distance, or outside their palisaded huts, or under trees, knots of the people watched us. A favourite position with them was to stand on one leg, resting the foot of the other leg against the standing limb above the knee. A spear balanced them more firmly, but the posture would be most uncomfortable to a European. We passed through one body of the men, and they showed no fear till they saw our white faces, when they ran wildly away. While halting to drink and refresh at a stream, after I had quenched my thirst, seeing some large branches of the *Euphorbia antiquorum* placed in the water with stones over them, I inquired what could be the cause of the branches being so placed, when they replied, " Oh! have you drunk of the water ? that plant has been placed there to poison it." The Toorkees laughed when told that I had been drinking heartily, but as the stream ran as clear as crystal I had no hesitation in partaking of it again, and felt no bad effects. The natives preferred digging holes in the sand of the stream, and drinking from them. The Bari are no doubt a dangerous people. We had two porters wounded by their arrows, of which they carry numbers, and they showed such a front on the occasion

364 PREPARATIONS FOR AN ATTACK.

of my umbrella being accidentally left behind, that, although thirty of our men went back to recover it, they thought it prudent to abandon my old and trusty friend!

Our most serious affair with them was on the night of the 14th of February 1863, the day before getting into Gondokoro. A most anxious night it was: we were all lying encamped upon a grassy slope round a large tree within a mile of the Nile, when, having dined, Frij came to us, saying, "Have you heard that the natives are coming to attack us ? Mahomed says we must be prepared with our guns for a fight." "Do you hear that, Speke?" "Yes," was the calm reply. On reflection, we remembered having, shortly after our arrival, seen the porters and Toorkees go to the village and take away a quantity of palisading, and whatever other articles they could carry. The smoke of two guns had also been seen; but whether any natives were killed, the Toorkees would not say. The people had fled at the time, and their return accounted for the present alarm. Darkness soon fell on the camp. We ascertained that the sentries were unusually alert, so we retired to rest; but about ten o'clock my servant Uledi awoke me, saying that "the natives were about to attack us. Do you not see their fires?" Sure enough one-third of the horizon was a flame of burning grass, and my first impression was that we should immediately be surrounded by the spreading fire. The natives screamed, and beat drums, and men carrying torches made of grass collected from other villages. We now dressed, placed our rifles by us, and sat watching the scene. Dances in circles were performed to drum-music beaten in the most furious manner, and the women's

WE SEE GONDOKORO IN THE DISTANCE. 365

shrill voices sounded loud amidst the bargoma and other horns. Overcome at last by sleep we lay down again, and at daybreak awoke to find the rest of the night had passed without further disturbance. This was very fortunate, as had the maps, journals, and collections of our expedition perished on this occasion, the loss to us would have been irreparable. During the night, Captain Mahomed was asked to send them by a bearer to Consul Petherick at Gondokoro, but he replied that no one dare travel at night, and that the fires and dancing we saw were only an intimation that we would be attacked in the morning. Twice the enemy had come up to our camp, but the click of the sentries' gunlocks frightened them away.

We all moved off in a compact mass by daylight of the 15th February, and were not molested, though we passed villages, outcropping rocks, and jungle of low trees, all favouring attack. After proceeding seven miles the features of the country completely changed from highland to lowland. As far as the eye could reach, there was to the north a dreary plain, dotted with the Punjab madar, growing upon firm and heavy sand. As we approached Gondokoro, a white speck was pointed out to us as the keneessa, or church, the spot where the Austrian mission-house stood. Afterwards we could see the masts of Nile boats, the appearance of which increased our excitementlI could have flown to them ; and when our band of Toorkees drew up a mile from them to form line and fire a,feu- de-joie, I had great difficulty in submitting to the delay. However, Speke was tolerably cool, and we all marched in together. Entering the first respectable hut we reached, we inquired for our friend Petherick,

366 OUR MEETING WITH BAKER.

and were informed that a gentleman had been there only a few minutes before. The inmates offering to conduct us, we proceeded in quest of the gentleman referred to, and soon had the happiness to see a sturdy English figure approaching. With a hearty cheer, we waved our hats and rushed into the arms, not of Pe- therick, but of Baker, the elephant-hunter of Ceylon, who had bravely come in search of us. All England, he saidlnay, all Europelbelieved that we should never get through the tribes! Here we were, however, grateful for our preservation, and grateful also for the sympathy of our kind friends and countrymen. Baker led us to his " diabeah," or Nile pleasure-boat, and we found him surrounded with many of the comforts of civilised life long denied to us I tea, sugar, coffee, bread, wine, &c. We had had no English news later than August 1860, and now it was February 1863; so that there was much for us to hear of national affairs, as well as matters of private interest. But where was Petherick ? Had he made no preparations for us ? or, finding we had not been able to keep to tune, had he despaired and given up the search ? A handsome diabeah and luggage-boat of his were here, but there were neither letters nor instructions for us. He himself was not at Gondokoro, and had never been there. Instead of co-operating with our expedition, he had gone to his own ivory depot in the west, and only arrived at Gondokoro four days after ourselves. We learned from Baker that kind friends in England had placed $1000 in the hands of Mr Petherick for our succour, and were doubly surprised that he had made no effort to meet us. It was to M. de Bono's men, and not Mr Petherick's, that we were indebted for our

THE CLIMATE OF THE WHITE NILE. 367

escort. I feel it due to the memory of my companion to state these facts, and to say that I had the same feeling of disappointment which he had, and that our meeting with Mr Pctherick was by no means the cordial one we anticipated. Having been previously supplied with all necessaries, and three return boats by Baker for conveying us to Khartoom, we required nothing save a few yards of calico to replace the bark- cloth rags of our twenty Seedees, and this we obtained from the stores of Mr Pethcrick.

We halted at Gondokoro from the 15th till the morning of the 26th, so that Speke might find the moon in lunar distance for the longitude, which he ascertained to be 31 46' 9" east, and latitude 4 54' 5" north. During this dry season it was very hot, the thermometer ranging from 94 to 100 in the shade; but it was thought a better climate and more pleasant residence than Khartoom, there being only two hot months, January and February, during the year. Between Gondokoro and Khartoom the White Nile is reported unhealthy; and amongst its many European victims was a distinguished French naturalist, Dr Penny, who had explored farther south than any previous traveller. His loss was deeply felt at Khartoom. Many of the servants of the traders were suffering from ulcers, having been in swampy countries; and on the tenth day of my arrival at Gondokoro I had an attack of fever. Nearly all our Seedees had tapeworm disease, contracted on the journey. The animal generally appeared in single white portions, one inch long and one-third of an inch broad. It gave them no pain, nor did it reduce the men in flesh, but it was very inconvenient. Bombay vomited one, which meas-

368 THE NILE AT GONDOKORO.

ured six to nine inches in length, with pointed head and tail. This happened several times to him; but he thought that until he got rid of the great one, which he called their " mother," the disease would stick to him. On our arrival at Khartoom I prescribed half a tumbler of salt dissolved in water; but having once tried my remedy, the Seedees pronounced it too nauseous to try a second time. Speke, half-a-dozen of our twenty Seedees, and myself, were the only men of our expedition who escaped this disease.

The Nile at Gondokoro is in two branches; the main one lying on the right, and a small low island, on which cattle feed, divides it from the left branch. The old banks were at this season fifteen feet above the alluvial deposit of the river, which again was four feet out of water. There seemed a greater body of water, because it was spread over a larger surface, than when we had seen it thirty miles farther up. Here the strongest current, bearing to the right, was about three miles an hour, and the breadth a hundred and fifty yards. Standing upon the bank, and looking around, the country presents a flat Egyptian aspect, with the solitary hills of Rujub, Beeleenja, &c., to the N.W., S.W., and S. The water was full of lake debris, making it muddy and disagreeable to drink until allowed to settle. All day long parties of three and four natives swam across, resting upon a log of the pith tree or ambadj. They do not swim as we do in England, but stretch out their arms alternately over the water, crowing loudly "ow, ow," as they go merrily across. Although there were small canoes on the river they were not often used, even when produce was to be conveyed from one bank to the other. They got

ANIMALS GONDOKORO AS A PORT. 369

sooner over by swimming, and when a cow was killed on the opposite bank, its meat was placed inside the inflated skin, and propelled through the water by the man swimming behind it. Crocodiles were no doubt numerous, but we saw no accident; they must be frightened by the number of people who daily cross at this point. We heard from Petherick of crocodiles as high as a table, and twenty-five feet long. At night the stillness was often broken by the trumpets of the hippopotami, which sound softer and more musical than when heard during the day. Baker had an excellent fishing-net, with which, in a jolly-boat, his men would cross the river to still water, and in a couple of hours bring back half-a-dozen species. Some resembled herring in shape, but the best for eating was a large flat fish. Of birds, the most interesting was a scarlet and green fly-catcher, which nestles in the perpendicular banks of the Nile like a swallow. We had not met with it on the journey. It took short flights, rapidly skimming the air, and then resting for a moment on the brink of the bank. From the Nyam Nyam. country to the west very handsome black goats are brought, remarkable for their small size and long hair. It may be worth mentioning that we here saw leeches, which we had not met with in any previous part of our journey; whereas, in the Himalayas, one cannot go through the grass returning from a day's sport without having a dozen of them fastened on one's legs.

Gondokoro presented quite the appearance of a seaport, there being twenty large boats anchored there. We had understood it to be an outlandish placeldangerous and almost inaccessible. But for the last five- and-twenty years or more it has been a mission-station370 Koorshid Aqa's Hospitality.

and place of trade. For about fourteen months previous to our arrival, it had never been without Egyptian boats and boatmen. A sailing boat, " diabeah," or a " naegur," leaving Cairo in November, can reach Gon- dokoro, with a north wind, in three months. On the 19th February, Baker received English news dated 1st November. The return journey to Khartoom is made so as to insure arrival by June, with the advantage of the south wind; but we made the voyage much earlier, and landed on the thirty-third day from Gondokoro. To give an idea of Nile travelling in these regions, I may mention that a boat which conveyed Baker, with his crew, attendants, and four horses, was hired by him at Khartoom at eight pounds per month|a most comfortable boat, with two cabins. The pay of his sailors was lower than what we paid our Seedees for the journey|namely, two dollars per month, and the helmsman and carpenter seven dollars each. Their food, "doora," grain|*i.e.,* jowari|would cost, say, ten dollars monthly; so this, altogether, was cheap travelling on the Nile. He had also brought up several camels and donkeys; and the former gave an Oriental look to the scene around his encampment. Koorshid Aga, a Circassian gentleman, lived here for some months, and was noted for his hospitality. Plainly dressed, and living in the most simple style, he would produce to his friends sparkling wines and other luxuries in profusion, for which we could make no return. Here he remained in security, with his guard-ships at anchor in the Nile below his premises, while his three or four hundred dark Nubians, armed with beautiful, though cheap, percussion guns, were on their beat for ivory in the interior. He had his tract

THE WHITE NILE TRADE. 371

of country or "preserve," like all other traders. " Latiffe's beat," " Petherick's beat," " Koorshid Aga's," "De Malzac's,"| all were known by these names, just as we know the "Black" or "Braemar" forests. A trader who attempted to go upon another's beat was considered a poacher, and a fight would certainly ensue if this etiquette were violated. Events taking place in these wide ranges of country are little known, as every party is a world to itself, and all are jealous of one another. But if the stories of " White Nile trade" be true, it is considered disreputable for any European to engage in it. The " Blue Nile trade," on the other hand, is esteemed respectable; but here also there is some jealousy when a new competitor enters the field. The reports we heard at Faloro of Mahomed's men attacking villages by surrounding them at the hours of deepest slumber, and capturing their people and cattle, &c., were here confirmed to us, and these raids had taught the men of Gondokoro the most lawless habits and practices. Life was unsafe, guns loaded with bullets were constantly fired out of bravado close to our boats, the consequence of which was that fatal accidents occurred, and there was no government or police, and no river steamers to stop the slave-trade. Consul Petherick was looked on as an interloper; he tried to put down this illicit traffic, but he was opposed by a clique, and his men saw no advantage in his service or that of any European. They could not keep slaves, so there was great discontent.

We saw with Koorshid a splendid and well-shaped old tusk, which weighed one hundred and thirty-five pounds, and which at Khartoom would fetch 114

372 THE MISSION-HOUSE AT GONDOKOBO.

dollars. Every country has its own particular quality: and I should imagine the ivory produced *from* the tall reed grasses of a forest country like Uganda would not be so favourable for forming huge tusks as the vegetation in a lower and more swampy country, although the ivory would be of firmer texture. We were told that the ivory of Kitch on the Nile, at 6 49' N., was of a superior description; the country there is swamp and covered with reeds to the horizon.

The mission-house at Gondokoro had been built some thirty years ago. Dr Knoblecker, a very eminent man, had long laboured in it, but now it is a mere shell, and its garden of lime, pomegranate, and orange-trees is a waste for cattle to graze in. We met a kind hospitable gentleman, Mr Moorlang of the Austrian mission, on his way to Khartoom :)as station had been at Kitch. He gave a mournful account of his labours, and was now recalled because the influence of the traders had checked his endeavours to propagate the Gospel. He had found the natives always civil, but if they or their children were not presented with clothes and beads, they kept aloof from him, and ultimately looked upon the missionary as having paved a way for the Nile trader to traffic in slaves.

In walking about Gondokoro, the natives always addressed us with " Adhoto," which may mean Good- morning ; some got as far as to say, " Salam alek." They were all nude like the Bari, and carried a small basket, in which were a few pieces of charcoal with which they lit their pipes. A baron, very highly spoken of, was killed by them a few years ago; his men had accidentally, when firing their guns at ran-

PREPARATIONS FOR LEAVING GONDOKORO. 373

dom, shot a native, and as no redress was given, the men were attacked, and sixteen of their number slain. The poor baron was away shooting ducks at the time, and, returning in the middle of the tumult, was killed. A missionary, whose boat was close by, was not touched. At Khartoom it was not expected that we would ever succeed in crossing Africa, but Madame Tinne, her sister the baroness, and Miss Tinne, had more hope of us, and in the most philanthropic manner, braving the malaria of the White Nile, they reached Gondokoro in a steamer expecting to aid us. The natives will long remember their humanity and generosity ; but the deadly swamps have since proved fatal to poor Madame Tinne, and also to a medical man of her party, and several European servants. Mr Baker, too, was full of hope, and had told the people of Khartoom that, as Bruce had discovered the source of the Blue Nile, our party would decide that of the White. At length it was time we should leave Gondokoro. By the 25th of February 1863, Speke had found the moon in proper position for taking lunars. We had heard all the English news from Baker, we had shared his hospitable table during our stay, seen his spirited sketches, and listened to his animated conversation. Our boats were filled with the necessaries and comforts of life, and everything was prepared for our starting with the stream in the morning.

17

SECTION 17

CHAPTER XVI.

GONDOKORO TO KHARTOOM, FROM 26TH FEBRUARY TILL 3OTH MARCH 1863|LEAVE GONDOKORO BY BOAT|THE SHIR COUNTRY|AUSTRIAN MIS-SION - STATION AT KITCH|THE

RIVERS BAHR-EL-GHAZAL, BAHR-GIRAFFE, AND SOBAT THE

SHILLOOK COUNTRY|BANKS OF THE NILE|ARAB SETTLEMENT OF EL EIS|ENTRY INTO CIVILISED COUNTRY|ARRIVAL AT KHARTOOM.

Ottk Seedees were divided among the three return boats furnished by Baker to convey us to Khartoom. Two were naegurs or baggage-boats, made roughly of the *Acacia Arabica* or soonud, and having each an unwieldy sail, without awning or cabins. The third was a diabeah, which we and our private servants occupied. Her build was lower in the water than the others, the hold was neatly boarded over, and upon it was built a poop-cabin. She drew three feet of water when unladen, and had the peculiar Nile rig, with twelve rowers, a helmsman, and a captain or "nakhoda" named Diab. Two of the other hands were not forthcoming, preferring to lead a roving life with their former master, Baker; but at two in the afternoon of the 26th, having bade adieu to all, we shoved off, and floated down with .the current. The oars were rudely

THE PEOPLE OF THE SHIR COUNTRY. 375

tied with rope to the gunwales, and the men only required to keep the boat in the stream and prevent her getting ashore on banks of sand. When any exertion was required, they rose from their seats, laying the weight of their bodies on their oars, and joined in a pleasing monotonous song, led by the " stroke " of the party. Proceeding in this way against a slight headwind seemed no labour to them; they rowed, joked, sang, or munched dry " dooro," bread and garlic, from sunrise to sunset. By noon of the third day we had made great progress|namely, one degree of north latitude|notwithstanding that we lay-to during the night on account of the shallows. We had reached a station of Koorshid Aga's in the Shir country, and passed through a corner of the Berri country. The banks were grassy and flat, and the trees were covered with creepers, giving them the appearance of old towers or abbeys. The river was divided by islands into four branches, and it required all the knowledge of our captain to decide which of them to choose. Some of the islands were covered with cattle, which ran off as they saw our boat approach. In the dry season, the natives bring down their cattle to graze and water them near the river. Their rustic settlements, of a conical form, with numerous people about, were built upon the very banks of the river, and were so small that a single man could hardly lie at length in them. The people sometimes spoke to us, wishing to get beads; but possessing so many cattle, they certainly were not objects of compassion. Nearly all of them were covered with ashes, as if they had lain in them during the night.

Sitting on the poop-deck, we watched the scenes on

376 SCENES ON THE NILE.

the river. Pelican flew in solemn procession, or marked the water's edge by a line of white. Myriads of the Indian paddy-bird perched upon the trees. There were cranes, divers, and sometimes a fish-eagle. At one time I counted the heads of twenty-two hippopotami, a perfect shoal of them, packed as close as they could swim together, looking like monstrous retriever dogs in the stream. Some were spouting water, others dipping, others snorting, and others rearing their heads and shoulders; but as we got near them, all dived to come up again scattered. This packing seemed common, as at other places we came on them in the same order, with cranes perched on their heads.

We saluted Koorshid's colours with two guns from our deck at a Shir village where we lay-to for some hours. Two of his soldiers, holding possession of the place, were posted with a supply of beads, &c., with which they purchase ivory. The village chief came to call on us; he was dressed like a Turk, with a fez and long-sleeved gown of pink striped calico, but the crowd of natives who sold commodities on the bank were nude, only that their skins were covered with wood-ashes.

They made here an excellent basket, shaped like a finger-glass, from the fronds of the doom palm. Its fruit and flour, tasting of gingerbread, as also tobacco, were exposed for sale, in exchange for our men's provisions of doora-grain. Many of the nude natives had been circumcised, and all had their lower incisors extracted like the Wanyoro. On entering the village we found it clean and tidy; the part before each doorway plastered as a space to sit upon. Here, sitting by some standards, three women received us

WOMEN OF SHIR|RACE OF ALIAS. 377

graciously by shaking hands and saying, "Adoto." They were the last race that we saw wearing only fringes and switch tails of corded fibre. They smoked clay pipes, in shape like a reversed cone, -with two resting-prongs, each holding half a handful of tobacco; and their long stems had mouthpieces of iron, quite fashionable in comparison to those seen in Uganda. The young men sported a two-feet-long piece of solid Dalbergia wood, the shape of a marline-spike, but tapering at both ends, and often nicely milled longitudinally. There was nothing further to remark about this Shir village, but that the cattle were comfortably housed under sheds made of the fronds from the doom palm la tree we had not seen since leaving the Zanzibar coast.

The next race we came among were the Aliab, known at once by their women being partially dressed. Here they slung a goatskin over the shoulder, like the Wanyamuezi, to hide their chests, and two other skins were tied round their waists, depending in front and behind. We were told, however, that only married women were allowed to wear all this clothing. The men were also distinguishable by a tuft of wool on the crown of their heads, a circle of very white mud plastered round it, and their faces and bodies covered with ashes. They did not seem at all afraid of us, for they assisted in pushing off our boat. Their diet is said to be almost entirely a milk one, and they have numerous herds. We put in to the left bank at the settlement of Shenooda, a Khartoom merchant, and found the latitude to be 6 5' 9" N. Another station, where there were forty men and a boat, was low and unhealthy, the musquitoes at night being in myriads.

378 DUR PARTY ARE FIRED UPON.

Our crew were somewhat lazy, and stopped nearly a day at this point under pretence of laying in wood, but in reality to talk with the people, and kill a cow. However, we were rewarded for the delay by getting a favourable breeze near the point where we again joined the main stream.

From thence to the Austrian mission-station of Kitch the banks did not present any landing-place ; we were hemmed in by reeds, and not a tree was to be seen. The station consists of a few round huts, with doors and glazed windowsla miserable place for the clergyman, the Rev. Mr Moorlang, who had there spent three years of his life. To land we had to be carried through swamps which lined the banks, and as we touched the tall grasses, clouds of mus- quitoes rose from the vegetation. Here was the good Christian's little glass-roofed chapel, surmounted by a cross of wood; there was his schoolhouse too,lbut all desolate and forlorn, for not a native would come to learn. The mission was therefore about to be forsaken, as Mr Moorlang had informed us at Gondokoro. On his passage down to Kitch, the natives had fired poisoned arrows into his boat in open day; one man had been wounded, and was since dead. This story elicited from our men mention of a similar incident. They also had been attacked while in rear of our larger boat, but it was during the night, and the arrows and spear fell harmlessly into their boat. To remedy such evils, I should say that the frequent visits of a river steamer would be highly desirable, both as protecting the natives from being plundered by the followers of traders and travellers, and as tending to civilise the people themselves.

TORTUOUS COURSE OF THE NILE. 379

Mr Moorlang, in the fulness of his heart, was unbounded in his kindness and liberality. Candles, wine, and goats were pressed upon us by the generous Tyrol mountaineer. He was to be in our wake to Khartoom; and Speke having taken the latitude of Kiteh, we roused our crew, asleep on the shore, and rowed during moonlight to Abu Kuka station. Here was another miserable swampy spot; not above six huts of grass, closely surrounded by water; not a tree, only high grass and reeds. The place was unworthy of the name of a station. From this point Consul Petherick had gone across the country to his trading depot of Neambara, in Moro. We came upon another station in this Kitch country, known as Mr Binder's, late De Malzac's; its latitude was 7 8' 18" N. It was rather pleasantly situated on flat ground, and consisted of a dozen round huts, plastered outside, and having a neat thorn fence surrounding them : but the natives were about the most wretched I had ever seen. They brought us their small loads of firewood to exchange for grain, and seemed like living skeletons. They had bead ornaments upon them ; but of what use were they ?—there was no grain for them to purchase. Before reaching this point the river had been winding in the most fantastic manner; a gentle breeze blew; and over the tops of the tall reeds we could perceive by the sails of our other two boats that we three were sailing in a circle, or that the stream ran in the shape of the letter S.

From the 5th till the 9th of March, while passing the Nouer country, we lost sight of our two other boats. The wind had been contrary, and the hands were reduced by sickness. A breeze luckily came

from the south, and brought our fleet together again. They had been alarmed, and expressed a wish for gunpowder, as the tribe of Shillock had lately killed a trading party three hundred strong, and were bent on attack. Some traders' boats we met " kedging " up stream conveyed us this news. It must be extremely tedious going up the Nile where the shores do not admit of landing to tow the boat. The plan adopted is this,—ten men being engaged, a row-boat goes ahead with a cable and anchors, and the large boat is then pulled up to the smaller, much in the same way as they " kedge " on the Ganges. We observed that the huts in the Nouer country were numerous and large; they lie in open plains, which are dotted with cattle and goats, at some distance from the river bank. The papyrus, the .pith-tree, or ambadj, and reeds, line the sides of the river, and beyond them was a forest of acacias, which afforded us an opportunity of laying in a supply of firewood. The tracks of elephants were numerous; and the damage done by the gigantic brutes in eating the pods of the trees and breaking down the branches is very great. While in the Nouer country we had the extreme pleasure of seeing the polar star for the first time after nearly three years, as bright as ever, and in the old place!

On reaching the Bahr-el-Ghazal, an affluent of the Nile, our boatmen fired a single gun as a salute. They told us this was done both on the up and down voyage. Our river, which had lately been averaging eighty and a hundred yards wide, kept its course, not mingling its waters with the Bahr-el-Ghazal, which here was without debris or apparent current, looking more like a back-water or still pond half a mile square. After their junction there was an evident increase in depth and breadth; the waters, also, were less like a sewer in colour,|they had become clarified to a certain extent, and the rate of current was estimated at two miles per hour. The sides were rushes to an unknown depth ; indeed, from the accounts given by our captain, the Ghazal must at one time have been almost choked with water vegetation. He mentioned that the first explorer of it took three months to penetrate through reeds a distance which can now be reached in five days. I expected to have found it looking more like a river; but instead of this, had we not been prepared for it, we should have passed it without notice. The White Nile was at once pronounced by our captain to be the nobler stream; and he added that, with a favourable wind, it takes ten days to reach the Ghazal from Khartoom, and one month more of fair wind to reach from the Ghazal to Gondokoro.

While waiting at the junction, our cook, M'kate, discovered a crocodile's nest with seventy-seven eggs. They were nearly all presented to us; but their taste being disagreeable, we made them over to our boatmen. Rowing for nineteen hours almost due east, at the rate of two miles per hour, brought us to another stream, the Giraffe, coming from a south-east direction. It seemed to flow with rapidity|probably four or five miles an hour|was from fifty to sixty yards across, and bore down with it quantities of the pretty rosette called *Pistia Stratiotes L.,* which was first gathered in the Karague Lake. Our captain, who was an authority, said of this river that it had received its name from the circumstance that cameleopard abound in the

382 THE RIVER SOBAT.

country through which it passes. " It is a large river, and if you were to sail up it for fifteen days, you would only be half way to its source in the Bhor country." The character of the Nile changes soon after the Giraffe joins it; the current becomes scarcely perceptible, the width increases from one hundred and fifty to two hundred and fifty yards, and you can generally land, there being acacia trees on the right bank. We observed on both sides of the Nile distant mole-like solitary hills, the first seen since leaving Gondokoro, which may give some idea of the flatness of the land. There were several large islands also,| one in particular, to our left, dividing the stream above the junction of the river Sobat, which joined us from the right almost at an angle of ninety degrees. The Sobat (lat. 9 20' N.) was a hundred yards across from bank to bank|a large body of water, its surface undisturbed by current or weeds, and sweeping round to the left in a remarkable manner as you looked up its stream. The left bank of the Sobat was abrupt, and from twelve to twenty feet high, with a few acacias. Its right bank was lower|say eight feet| had more slope, and down to the water's edge grew a dense thicket of reed vegetation. From general appearance, I judged that the body of water thrown into the Nile by the Giraffe during four-and-twenty hours was equal to that contributed by the Sobat in the same time. The distance between those two rivers was calculated to be sixteen miles. We had rowed it in 9 hours, not including the time we rested while a gale blew from the east. These gales came on suddenly, and detained us generally from nine till three o'clock; the boats stood them well;

HIPPOPOTAMI BECOME MORE RARE. 383

but, from the impossibility of quickly lowering the yard, to which the immense sail is securely fastened, the boat was often very unmanageable. The crew found the yard so unwieldy, pivoted as it was on the top of the mast, catching the wind and nullifying their rowing, that it had to be finally lowered, the operation taking three-quarters of an hour !

Our course improved after we were joined by the Sobat; instead of sailing east, we were going north-east. The river varied in width from two hundred and fifty to five hundred yards; sometimes it branched round long stripes of islands, or a beautiful reach of water was presented. We had no longer the low swamp on either side ; the banks rose boldly ten feet above the water ; we could land anywhere,|either in the Shil- look country, which was a plain clear of all vegetation, or on the opposite or right bank, the country of the Denka, where firewood might be obtained. Hippopotami in such a locality were scarcer than where there were reeds, but they were met with even here ; and at night, between those steep walls, their lowing reverberated pleasantly from bank to bank. An oarsman by chance struck one while sleeping in the water. The sport it afforded caused quite a commotion in our boat, for after being touched, the animal arched his back in self-defence, sending himself half out of the water.

On the wooded banks of the Nile, about 10 N. lat., opposite the Sultan of Dainab's territory, we found thirteen boats at anchor. They had come to demand redress from the sultan, and to settle some political matters regarding the annihilation of a whole zariba, or station of Arabs, in the interior. Their commander, we understood, was one Ibraheem. He and his party

384 ENCAMPMENT OF BAGARA CAVALRY.

of three hundred soldiers, foot and horse, formed a picturesque encampment under some beautiful large soonud trees\Acacia Arabica. The Bagara Arab horsemen re- minded me of the wandering tribes we read of in the Bible; the listless way all walked about in their long gowns, the docility of their pony horses, the Oriental-like saddles, the women grinding corn, all camped so close together looking in amazement at the white men, wondering where we could have dropped from, and smiling as we walked amongst them. These boats had been two months on the voyage from Khar- toom, and had been joined on the route by upwards of a hundred Bagara cavalry, who with fifty camels travelled by land, keeping pace with the fleet. The Bagara wear no covering on their heads; their hair is straight, black, and silky, worn off the face in long broad plaits pinned flat down behind. Their horses, though small and thin, were well cared for, having no galled backs, as might be supposed on looking at their awkward-shaped saddles. With these animals, and their long-handed, broad-bladed, glistening spears, wonderful feats are said to be performed by them in elephant-hunting, although no guns are used. At night, their camp was guarded by sentinels, who called out at intervals, instead of our custom of going the rounds. Music was indulged in to a late hour by incessant beating on drums. An interesting funeral scene took place in this camp, on occasion of the death of one of the Khartoom natives. The body, veiled in white linen, was laid on the brink of a grave, and a line of well- dressed Arabs stood over it reading prayers from a slip of paper held in their hands, all in the most devout and solemn manner.

THE PEOPLE OF SHILLOOK. 385

The canoes of the natives are small, and made of planks, with pointed bows and sterns. Raffcs of grass or ambadj are used for ferrying the Nile, the natives standing up to their knees in water while paddling or propelling them with a stick. After coming out of this raft, they place it on end to dry on the shore. The Shillook men, residing in a large tract of country about 10 N. lat., are nude, and, looking at them from behind, the hair is so trained that it resembles a black fan. We took one of the men as a guide to conduct us in searching for our two rear boats that had not come up, as we believed, and had caused us some uneasiness and alarm. Sailing up stream, he landed to speak with the people of Shillook, who immediately flew away in fear of us, commencing to drive off their cattle. Our boats had passed us during the night unobserved, and we found they had preceded us twenty miles. This may give some idea of the size of the river. The guide was not satisfied with two yards of calico, saying," If I were not alone, you dared not offer me so little;" he was very impertinent, and before leaving the boat exchanged his calico for a spear. We had now got to about 11 N. lat., where the territory of the true original Shillook race ends, and that of the mongrel Shillook and Bagara horsemen begins. On the left bank was an Arab station called Kaka, its two hundred huts being fenced and ditched against the hostile natives. For the first time we came upon irrigation in the true Egyptian forml a large pole weighted at one end, with a leather bucket at the other. Indian corn, tomato, onions, and plantain were grown here in great luxuriance. The native who commanded at this post was carried on board of our boat to be treated for a

386 CURIOUS SMALL FORMATIONS.

swollen limb. From our remnant of medical comforts we were able to give him some plaster, and he went gaily away on one leg, so pleased, that he sent us a plate of rice and some tomato. I have a recollection of seeing strewed on the broken ground about Kaka, curious formations, which may have been ancient relics, or concrete ; but, in order to direct attention to them, I may mention that Dr Falconer, the fossil authority of the day, suggests that they may have been fossil remains. The whole depot of Kaka turned out to greet our captain, calling him by name " Diab." They intrusted him with messages, billets-doux, and money, till he seemed astonished at their number. Even after we had sailed, two men ran along the shore with letters, which were thrown at our boat, and cleverly caught by one of the crew.

The evening before our arrival at Kaka we saw twenty boats at anchor in a river said to be a branch of the Sobat, on the right bank of the Nile. They lay one mile up its stream, and the people were on their way to punish some Denka, having with them camels, donkeys, and ponies. I could not learn the name of this unexpected river, but our captain assured us that it was not a branch of the Nile, which, indeed, it did not appear to be. Hence Captain Speke has written of it as a second Sobat; while Consul Pethe- rick asserts that it only exists in Captain Speke's imagination. The windings of the river in this latitude, about 12 N., were very eccentric: sometimes our " head" was west, at other times direct upon the polar star, as when passing a solitary hill, a strange sight in the Denka country. The heat was excessive l94 in the shade, making the bilge-water very dis-

WATER-SNAKESlFISH-EAGLE. 387

agreeable, though causing no sickness. Indeed, the native sailors considered the smell to be healthy. Our boat was full of cockroaches, climbing about at all hours; musquito also abounded. Our crew were sometimes put into a flutter by seeing a harmless water-snake making for the boat with head erected out of the water. These creatures steer along so direct that they seem to see nothing before them; but the natives imagined that they were purposely making for the boat to get on board! The shores were often lined with thousands of black and white geese, or the solitary fish-eagle might be seen standing apart. He is a bird of remarkable beauty; his general colour is black, but his head is white, and the shoulder-tips and feathered thighs are a glossy red.

Although highly favourable for cultivation by means of irrigation, not a single field or village is to be seen as you glide down the splendid, almost lake- like stream some 400 yards wide. Either side is a flat dry country of alluvial soil, covered with natural bowers of climbers connecting the trees. The banks reminded me of the beautiful Garden Reach on the Hoogly at Calcutta. One evening, in the distance, I thought a range of swelling hills was visible, but their outline seemed suddenly to change into a cloud! This mystery was soon explained: the forms I had seen were myriads of finches covering part of the horizon : the creatures were migrating, and resembled swarms of bees in the air, quite darkening the sky. A day or two afterwards, one night on deck, I was startled by a sound as if wind blew through a forest, and was about to beat upon our boat; but we had only disturbed the birds, which in their flight had

388 BEAUTIFUL COUNTRY SIGNS OF CIVILISATION.

rested for the night in the tall reeds of an island ; the wave of air caused by their motion and their twittering reached us, though we could not see them in the darkness.

We travelled without an accurate chart of the river, and the beautiful parts of it cannot therefore be mentioned by name; but about 13 N. lat. five hills ("Jubl Denka," or "Jubl Nyamat'ee" of the maps) appeared three-quarters of a mile from the right bank. Some were ridged with vertical strata, and descended to the river; but none appeared above water. From this point we may say that civilisation was fairly entered upon, for we were addressed in friendly Arabic from both banks. Boat-building went on in the forests of " soonud " or acacia, and hundreds of camel and cattle stood upon the receding banks of white sand, or drank the waters of the Nile. Women were clothed from head to foot, and carried water- pitchers on their heads I forming a peaceful and pleasing sight after the hardships and anxieties we had endured. The last trace of our jungle life was seen in the acacia forests, where trees lay prostrate, and where occasionally some antelope, new to us, with large horns bending over their shoulders, browsed on low bushes with the camel. A flight of wild geese, a host of monkeys, and a brood of guinea-fowl gave warning to the antelope, and none of them fell to our rifles. Domesticated animals now took the place of the denizens of the forest, and the trading-boats had driven away the wild inhabitants of the water. The sound of the hippopotamus was rare after we had passed the hills of Jubl Denka. Small grey duck no longer flew in line skimming the water; and the

WILD-FOWL BECOME SCARCE. 389

black duck with yellow bill, said to be very palatable, no longer stood packed in hundreds on the banks. The myriads of monster black and white geese were left behind. The familiar quack of the mallard was seldom heard at night. The pin-tailed duck shot past the boat, seeking less busy scenes. The crocodile had been scared; he had lost his boldness, but still watched for a victim. Against his attacks thorn fences enclosed portions of the river, where cattle or goats might drink in safety; and it was remarked that in these more frequented regions wild-fowl were seldom seen upon the water; the Egyptian goose, which floated in scattered coveys near the sides, was the only species which showed no fear amidst the sounds of human voices : he fell an easy prey to the sportsman. These, and sundry other familiar sights and reflections, gave warning that our journey was fast drawing to a close.

El Eis, or the Well, at about 13l N. lat., is an Arab settlement on the right bank, on the highway between the countries of Sennaar in Abyssinia and Kordofan. Its houses are not seen from the river, but the shore is lined with troops of camels, a mounted guard or herd being over each batch, denoting that the country is well peopled. Khartoom, we were inform ed, could be reached from here on a donkey in six days. The river at El Eis is five hundred yards in width, but increases to a mile of shallow water, with islands, as we float down its stream to Shellai and Al'aga; farther down, when opposite Jubl Musa on the left bank, it becomes narrower, being only twelve hundred yards wide, and sluggish as a mill-pond. The next feature in the flat landscape is Jubl Broame, a table-topped solitary hill,

390 THE BANKS OF THE NILE AT EL EIS.

three hours' row from Jubl Musa; and the object last seen before arriving at Khartoom is Jubl Aolee, so called because it is the first hill observed when ascending the White Nile from its junction with the Blua It is not above a quarter of a mile from the right bank, and rises two hundred and fifty feet in a barren, mass of rock, which sends a spur down to the brink of the river and crosses it in a N.W. direction, showing one small peak in the stream. The country is finely varied about this hill; the verdure of the shore recedes under small acacias, or the bush euphorbia dots the streaks of white sand.

The banks of the Nile at El Eis shelve gradually into the water: the soil is so rich from the quantity of floating sediment brought down by the White Nile, that it was no uncommon occurrence to see the goats, which had gone to nibble the short sweet grass and drink the stream, sink up to the knees in the soil, and remain there bleating, quite unable to extricate themselves. Beyond this green line the soil becomes cracked, and strewn with several species of shells, some of which we had seen in the interior. Drifting sand, conveyed by the north winds, spread itself over the rest of the shore, and there the walking is firm, and forms the highway for Arabs proceeding upon ambling donkeys to or from their capital of Khartoom. A curious line of sand-hills margins the river almost the whole way between El Eis and Jubl Aolee. There are none upon the left bank. It is naturally an abrupt wall eight feet high in the alluvium of the country, and these violent north winds, bringing the sand of the desert with them, have given it the appearance of sand hillocks; at Gutoena, this is particularly obser-

THE CULTIVATION OF COTTON. 391

vable where the sand has not perfectly covered them. The consequence is, that wood gave way to sand; and the voyager has to lay in his last stock of logs from the woods above El Eis. Below this all firewood must be purchased, or stolen from the walls and fences on the banks of the river.

We were all much struck with the industry of the natives, who are called " Hassanyeh Arabs," and are fine powerful - looking men. Though differing from the Bagara who live higher up the river, and not having so many horses, they arm themselves with the same broad-bladed spear, and have few guns amongst them. The chief dwellings and cultivated grounds are at some distance from the river; they reside there during the rainy season, and migrate with their flocks to the edges of the Nile for the dry season. Temporary abodes are erected, and they trade in salt made from the subsoil of the river. In March we observed bareheaded, good-looking men, with a sheet covering their shoulders and with loose " pyjamas," pulling the ripened pods of the cotton. Towards the equator women would have been employed in this occupation, but here, with a Mohammedan population, they are kept indoors cleaning the cotton, making butter, or out drawing water from the well. The cotton bushes are eighteen inches high, planted in lines a yard apartl very luxuriant, in consequence of the rich clay soil being shaded by drifted sand from the rays of the sun. By this provision of nature the soil does not cake, and the roots are kept cool, and free to send out their branches. The islands vary in length from three hundred yards to that of Marda, which is estimated at five miles. All are strips cleared of their natural

392 WOMEN DRAWING WATER.

vegetation, and flourish under a hard-working people. In the brightest of suns we observed two men, harnessed to ropes, pulling a toothless rake, guided by a third man, over the soft mud, preparing it for seed; and, unlike the Africans, the Egyptians never cease to work while a boat passes them. The islands in March were not less than three feet above water; no houses were upon the smaller ones; straw was stacked; a few plough-oxen might be seen; and a small boat lay to ferry the labourers to the mainland at night.

The operation of drawing water from the wells dug in the shore is interesting. Two women, a boy, and a donkey are required: the wells are five feet deep, thirty inches across, and only half-a-dozen yards from the ripple of the river. We saw a fair woman stand down the well and pass the water in a gourd to another, who filled it into a goat's skin. Her beautiful black hair was parted in the centre, and braided in small plaits, which hung over her flushed cheeks and neck. Though her bosom was bare she showed perfect innocence. On my asking for her cup to drink from, it was at once given, apparently without any fear of its being defiled by the touch of a Christian. The water, in comparison with that obtained from the filter on board of our boat, was warm and not refreshing. Two goat-skins or " mussocks " having been filled and allowed to rock about in the river, they were placed on the donkey, the boy jumped up nimbly behind them, and with one hand held the water-bags steady, and with a wand in the other he guided the unbridled donkey to the huts.

The people were listless and indifferent to us if we went near their poor abodes, but their dogs at once

BATHING SHEEP IN THE NILE. 393

challenged the intruder. This struck us, because in our journey through Africa we had rarely heard the voice of a dog. We now found that we could no longer purchase produce with beads or cloth. Money was the mode of exchange. We were amused with Bombay going amongst these Arabs to buy fish with an iron hoe: the honest fellow thought, from their simple mode of life and appearance, that we were still amongst a wild set of people; and so they were to a certain extent, for beyond the produce of the soil, and their cattle, sheep, and goats, they seemed to have no other desire. Great care was consequently taken of their flocks. The large lop-eared breed of sheep are bathed in the Nile by their owners. They are carried into three feet of water and dropped on their backs or sides, then scrubbed to the tail, and allowed to run back to join the flock. The goats are tall, generally black, with immense udders and long hair; they are clipped with a knife, and their hair, with that of sheep, is made into a coarse blanket or bernoose by the women. Powerful smooth greyhounds, indigenous to the country or to the western parts of Abyssinia, are used as we use sheep-dogs, and seem to guard carefully the habitations as well as the flocks.

Our captain, Diab, was known to many of the people along the river's bank . The Arabs would call out eagerly to him, asking after their brothers or husbands far in the interior ivory-hunting. I watched several of these interviews. Once an elderly woman called him by name from the shore while our boat moved down the stream. Without asking for our permission, he landed, and they saluted by each placing the right hand on the other's shoulder, then a solemn shake of the hand

394 COLD NORTH WINDS FROM DONGOLO.

took place, and Diab for a moment left her to go and sit upon a dry spot of sand. She followed, sat by him and told her tale, while a boy joined them, and was kissed by Diab on the cheek. Master Frij seeing what went on, thought he had better join the small party, and listen to what they had to say to one another. Taking his place close by them, he sat there with the greatest coolness, without introduction to the lady, or any previous knowledge of her. The Africans are generally a free-and-easy race, and despise the formalities of society. When Mr Moorlang, the Austrian missionary, was pressing upon us the acceptance of some delicacy, Frij, too proud to confess our poverty, found a reply by saying that our larder was full to excess|we did not require anything! He was the Caleb Balderston of the Nile Expedition.

Our passage down the Nile from El Eis to Khar- toom, though only one hundred and fifty miles, occupied us eight days. The stillness of the current, the head wind, and the enticements offered to our crew by the bazaars at Shellai and Gutoena, prevented our reaching sooner. Although the diabeah was all that we could wish for in comfort, yet knowing the distance to be so short, the delay was vexatious; the more so as we were told that at that point, or more particularly at Gutoena, the north wind coming from the Dongolo direction sometimes, at this equinoctial season, detained boats for eight days, or even a month. I was astonished with the coldness of the atmosphere, even after the sun had risen, occasioned by these northern winds from Dongolo, and I asked Diab, the captain, regarding them; his reply was, that they and the Cairo winds are colder than any ever ex-

TOWING, TACKING, AND SAILING. 395

perienced at Khartoom. We had to lay-to so often that walking on shore was resorted to as a pastime ; and we were glad to renew our acquaintance with the Persian wheel, driven seemingly by the same old bullocks and the same drivers as are seen on the plains of Hindostan; even the squeaking music from the wheels was there to complete the parallel.

The management of the diabeah was left entirely to the captain, who, with his crew, tried every possible means of progress|towing, tacking, sailing, and rowing ; but all generally failed. The truth is, they were waiting for a fair wind, and preferred a little quiet society on shore every evening, to making any great exertion to get to their journey's end. When they rowed, the boat was held with its broadside in the direction we wished to take; and when they tacked from shore to shore across the river, which was a mile broad, we stuck as regularly as the tack was made, not getting off till the crew jumped into the water and pushed the diabeah. Instead of making progress by these movements, we generally lost ground, in consequence of the awkward way they had of making the boat wheel a complete circle, or fall off the wind at the particular moment of changing the tack. Towing was willingly adopted by the crew, who harnessed themselves to ropes, and walked at a staid pace on the hard part of the shore. However, at this operation it was often very disheartening to find the wind blow, retarding, and finally stopping their advance. We generally put up for the night by the shore, to enable the crew to eat their dinners, and we were on the move by daybreak. When at ShijrNagara (literally, tree-drums) we were told that, if we stood by a solitary tree on the

396 KHARTOOM IN VIEW THE BLUE NILE.

island, we could hear the drums of Khartoom. We did not make the experiment, and doubt the truth of the saying, on account of the distance. On the night of the 29th March, having rowed for Shijr Nagara till the moon was well up, we lay-to, our captain not wishing to enter the port of Khartoom at so late an hour, because all *eclat* and firing of guns would thereby be lost. Accordingly, on the following morning, we saw, when looking across a plain as bare as a table, at two miles' distance, a single conspicuous minaret, with an extinguisher top, numbers of mud houses, and groves of the date-palm. This was Khartoom‖lat., 15 36'. Our route was down the White Nile for two miles, and then up the Blue Nile or Bahr Azrak for another mile. Wishing to take particular notice of the junction of the two rivers, Speke and I were both on deck by daybreak. As the main branch of the White Nile approaches the junction, the current gets strong and rapid, showing a broken surface, with a dangerous sunken rock in its right centre. The crew got excited, and shouted ; but in an instant the danger rock was past, and we were carried a dozen yards beyond the junction of the Blue Nile. The sail was here spread, and we soon recovered our lost ground, and proceeded up the Blue, whose waters now, in March, had scarcely any flow, and were so shallow that we had to pole a good part of the way up-stream. The colour of the water at once attracted our notice, being some what like the Mediterranean ; it was a green-blue, and, on being disturbed, was lively and sparkling in comparison with the muddy waters of the White Nile. The junction of the two rivers, the sweeping curve, and both shores of the Blue river, are not unlike what we had seen at

ALI BEY WELCOMES US AT KHARTOOM. 397

the place where the Sobat joins ; but the right bank of the Sobat is of gigantic grasses, while here the Blue river is of shelving, drifted sand. Their left banks resemble each other in being an abrupt break of twenty- feet in the alluvial soil. A pier of stone lies unfinished near the confluence of the rivers; and after we had passed it by sailing and poling slowly up, the left bank was enlivened by boat-building operations, irrigations, gardens, date-trees, walled enclosures, &c. Two of De Bono's men, to whom we had given a passage from Gon- dokoro, fired a salute in our honour from the shore. We had not anchored when Ali Bey, the "Wukeel of the Governor,Musa Pasha, arrived with a friend in his boat, and stepped on board. He embraced us in the most affectionate manner before we had even time to learn who it was that had thus welcomed us. We proceeded on shore in his boat, which was shaded with an awning, and carpeted. Ali was very nicely dressed *d la Turk,* in a claret-coloured cloth suit, quite a contrast to the ragged clothes we wore. There was no such thing as a pier or platform. We stepped ashore and ascended the steep incline of the river bank, and then stood upon the level of the town. Proceeding at a great pace, our hands being held by our kind conductor, down lanes and round corners, every one we met on the way showing him great respect, we at last reached a house and garden. A white Arab horse stood eating from the same bundle of grass as a caparisoned donkey, and we were directed to sit upon a charpoy (four-poster) covered with carpet, while the Wukeel bustled *off* into the interior of the house. During his absence, the friend who had accompanied him to the boat told us (native fashion) that the Wukeel who had taken us by

398 ALI BEY DRESSES US.

the hand was a man of great influence and importance. As yet we had no interpreters, and it was difficult for us to guess what was ultimately to be done. However, the Wukeel soon rejoined us, and, more mysterious than ever, he beckoned and led us into the first or outer room of his house, where we were shown a quantity of seedy old-fashioned clothes, and told that we must put them on,|they were his. I don't know what possessed me|whether affection for my own tatters, or a natural repugnance to put on clothes that had been worn by another|but I shrank from wearing the garments, and objected strongly to a thick cloth sur- tout, stating that it was too hot for 94 in the shade. The Wukeel then commenced to put his fingers into the holes and rents of my ragged old flannel friend, and said, that I must really oblige him, because these holes were " ibes" or blemishes, which the expected visitors would observe. I accordingly submitted to being stripped by Bombay and our host, who seized my arms, pulled off my old coat, and replaced it by an extraordinary sky-blue paletot. Speke's costume was ludicrous; he looked as if dressed up for some boyish frolic. His trousers, in front, though short, were passable, being of English blue cloth and cut; but when he turned round we saw an immense piece of calico let in, so as to enlarge them for a figure of twenty stone. The next difficulty arose from his unwillingness to change his comfortable plaid waistcoat for a chintz jacket, which buttoned to the throat and had tight sleeves. He objected, because there was no watch- pocket, but one was found, and he yielded. Over this garment a tight-sleeved frock-coat was pulled on by

ENTHUSIASTIC RECEPTION. 399

the good little Wukeel. There was great trouble in squeezing him into it, but it was effected, and I thought all was completed. No ; Ali Bey took the wideawake off, and placed instead a tasseled fez on the back of Speke's head ; and then, fully equipped, Ali Bey stood back, examined him from top to toe, clapped his hands, and pronounced the whole get-up highly becoming! The ingenuity of the Wukeel was not yet over. Tying a knot on each leg of the cast-off trousers, he crammed into them coats, waistcoats, wideawakes, &c., making a decapitated Guy Fawkes, and bundled them over to Bombay. I thought I had escaped all further dressing, but my toilet was not considered complete until an attempt was made to fit a fez upon my head; and this proving hopeless, we were ushered into a room with sofas all round, to partake of coffee, brandy, and cigars. About twenty fashionably-dressed gentlemen in European and Turkish costumes then came rushing in to welcome us. They had heard of our approach the previous day by a letter which we had forwarded from Gutoena, and they had already despatched the message that first reached England regarding us, announcing that the " Nile was settled." It was the intention of these gentlemen to have ridden out on horseback and camels up the bank to bring us into Khartoom in triumph, but their messenger had failed to find us, and they politely expressed regret at being taken unawares. However, their welcome was most enthusiastic. M. de Bono, commonly called Latiffe by the natives, whose trading depot we had found at Faloro, took the lead in offering us hospitality. We all adjourned to his beautifully fitted-up house, and enjoyed the " chi-

400 RESIDE AT THE BRITISH CONSULATE.

book" amidst animated conversation, interpreted by Bombay, who stood looking as great a rough as one could well imagine. M. de Bono generously offered us his house as a home during our halt at Khartoom ; but there being a British consulate, we considered that it would be more correct to reside under its protection, and therefore we proceeded thither.

18

SECTION 18

CHAPTER XVII.

KHARTOOM, FROM 30TH MARCH TILL 15TH APRIL 1863|THE BLUE NILE|NATURAL PRODUCTS|ALI BEY|KHARTOOOM A CANTONMENT FOR TROOPS|ITS BAZAARS AND MANUFACTURES |THE COPTIC CHURCH|THE AUSTRIAN MISSION-HOUSE| EGYPTIAN REMAINS|DEPARTURE BY BOAT FOR BERBER.

Half a century ago no town existed where the present Khartoom stands, at the confluence of the Blue and White Niles; but, in the days of Egypt's greatness, a city stood on the plain, on the right bank of the Blue river, not ten miles from the modern site. The origin of Khartoom forty-four years ago was a military post on the Egyptian frontier. Previous to annexation it belonged to Abyssinia: now it is a place of considerable trade, governed by Musa Pasha, and held by fifteen thousand Egyptian troops. The point of land on which the town is built is so low, that every season the streets are flooded by the overflow of the river, and still its locality is not changed, though all agree as to its unhealthiness. The derivation of Khartoom is most probably from the samower *(Cartha- mus tinctorius L.),* called here " Gartoom," cultivated all over Egypt for its oil, used in burning. Except

402 THE BLUE AND WHITE NILES.

where irrigated, the country everywhere presents an arid, uninteresting aspect; drifting sands cover the land; there are no trees or anything green to relieve the eye from the glare. In the distance to the north, about seven miles off, there are a few bare hills|those of Dongola, and a small range to the left. It is truly a land of banishment, cut off by deserts and a river of cataracts from the civilised portions of the world. To this Soudan, or country of the blacks, many whose conduct is questioned by their government are sent to pine without hope of release, unless their shortcomings should be forgiven, or a change of rulers take place, when they might hope for pardon, and permission to return to their homes in Egypt proper.

In April the Blue Nile was twenty feet lower than it is during the months of July and August; the snows in the mountains of Abyssinia bring it up to this height; and I suspect this flood has more to do with the inundations of Lower Egypt than the more constant flow of water from the White Nile. The latter river we saw at its maximum height in November, and it has another flooding season in April. Where do these waters go ? A great portion is lost in overrunning a space of perhaps 1000 square miles of lowland; and the White Nile thus robbed, as it were, never displays those sudden changes in height that the Blue Nile, more confined to its bed, presents.

The waters of the two rivers are very different in taste and appearance. Neither is considered first-class drinking water by residents at Khartoom ; but after their waters are mingled well together, the mixture is esteemed excellent. Opposite the town the Blue Nile is two hundred and fifty yards across, and of a

FRUITS AND VEGETABLES OF KHARTOOM. 403

greenish colour. Six miles up stream it narrows between steep banks to one hundred and fifty yards. The town being on the brink of the river, and every year its houses getting cut away by the falling in of the bank, there is no room for walking along|no quay, as it were, for the exports and imports. You are obliged for half a mile to brush past the walls of houses, the wells, goods, and animals|a most uncomfortable state of things. During our stay at Khartoom the sun was very powerful, and we had but one shower in a fortnight. Bathing in the Blue Nile was much resorted to by men and women, who appeared to enjoy it thoroughly; but I only attempted it once, because the river was so low that I had to walk thirty yards before getting into water deep enough to enable me to swim. Fish were generally to be had in the town. They are caught in various ways ; some by nets nearly fifty yards long, with large meshes and short floats of wood. Irrigation from the Blue Nile is effected by cutting narrow channels in the bank; or the Persian wheel, with its hanging earthen jars, overhangs the river, and so raises the water to the height of the fields and gardens. Fruits and vegetables thrive at Khartoom. The former include a small variety of grape, oranges, limes, custard apples, pomegranate, plantain, dates, and figs; the vegetables are beans and pease, onions most luxuriant, lupin, nole kole, bamea, lettuce, &c. The tobacco grown was different to what we had met with in the interior; here it was the low bushy description called *Nicotiana rustica L.*, that of the interior being *N. tabacum L.*, which grows with a longer leaf. Senna is one of the herbs cultivated, also saffiower, already mentioned. The harvest of bearded wheat

404 THE HOUSES AND VICINITY OF KHARTOOM.

is cut in March, and the grain is large and rich in colour. No pleasant walks had been made in the neighbourhood ; the few groves of date-palms, affording the only shade that existed, are generally walled round; and if you proceed into the country, with one exception there is nothing but a desert of sand. This exception is a " cottage in the wood," belonging to M. Bartolemy. It had been surrounded by a belt of the fast-growing yellow-blossomed *Parkimonia aculeaia L.,* and, when within the grounds, the flowers and vegetation looked so green and fresh, that one might imagine he had been transported to a quiet retreat at home. The other European residents lived in the town. Their houses, generally of one storey, are large flat-roofed structures of mud and brick, surrounded by walls, having a single gateway guarded by a doorkeeper. They reminded me of the serais, or stations made for travellers upon the grand trunk-road of India. In their courtyards tame birds or antelope walked; wild animals lay chained; camels, donkeys, cattle, goats, or horses stood about; lumber and store rooms filled the space; and a corner perhaps was devoted to a shady retreat under the vine. Each consulateland there were French, Austrian, American, and Britishlat Khartoom had its elliptical signboard over the main entrance. The principal room of the house is the hall; there business is transacted, and visitors are received in the morning, which is entirely devoted to calling, smoking, and drinking coffee. It has been mentioned that we chose to reside under the British flag, although at that time the consul was ah- sent at Gondokoro. The attentions we received from the various gentlemen residents were such as are per-

TRAVELS OF THE BARONESS CAPELLEN. 405

haps only met with in a foreign countrylso friendly, free, and unrestrained. Unfortu-nately neither of us could communicate with them, except through Bombay or Frij; but they had become great adepts at interpreting, and we succeeded pretty well. However, a lady, the Baroness Capellen, sister to Madame Tinne, could speak English fluently, and we enjoyed her society frequently. She had been a great traveller, had reached Gondokoro, and had seen the miseries of sickness amongst the slaves of the ivory-traders. Smallpox had broken out amongst a party when opposite Jubl Denka, and the shocking remedy of throwing the slaves overboard when attacked by this disease was resorted to by these native traders. On making our first call upon the Baroness, we were astonished to see Frij and Uledi follow us into the room, both the worse for drink, and each carrying a rifle and spear. We all laughed at their ignorance of European customs; and having asked them to place their arms outside the door, we were amused at their advancing, rather unsteadily, to the lady, kneeling and kissing her handlthis being the most polite mode of salutation known amongst the inhabitants of Zanzibar. We brought her the three young girls of Uganda, to let her hear their language, and see their mode of sitting and of returning thanks. They were highly delighted, received great kindness, conducted themselves very gently, and gave great satisfaction, making friends with a servant girl whom the Baroness had rescued from slavery. While calling upon another occasion, a steamer arrived from the Bahr-el-Ghazal, having made the passage in fourteen days, and bringing news of Madame Tinne and her accomplished

406 OUR RECEPTION BY M. DE BOXO.

daughter. The Baron Von Ablaing was on board, and was to return with stores and baggage-donkeys, to enable the party to prosecute their journey as far as Fernando

Po. Since then we have learned how fatal has been the result of this expedition. Poor Madame Tinne has died, and their labours at exploration have thus been suddenly arrested.

We were hospitably entertained at a large reception by M. de Bono, whose ivory-hunters at Faloro were the first to welcome and render us aid on the Egyptian side. There were present four ladies and upwards of twenty gentlemen, French, Italian, Austrian, German, and natives. After dinner our health was proposed, and a toast by M. Thibaut, French consul, " The alliance of France and England," was cordially pledged and applauded. Our twenty Seedees were introduced, and, to amuse the party, went through a number of antics they had learned in Uganda.

Ali Bey, Effendilor, to give the address written by himself, Ally Fud(h)lee bek, Wakeel, Hokumdariut, el Soudan bil Khartoom (minister, Government House, country of the blacks, Khartoom)|was most constant in his attentions to us. He was the first to receive us and the last to part with us|showing us over the Government House, the schools, manufactures, and magazines, giving us horses to ride, parading the troops for our amusement, and doing numerous other acts of kindness. He had a white Gulf Arab, the most docile, at the same time fiery, creature I had ever beheld. When caparisoned in blue velvet trappings, richly embroidered in gold, and a Busserah bridle of silver chains and hanging tassels, the animal looked the most perfect and picturesque of steeds. The bit was

AM BEY'S CHARGER|A REGIMENTAL PARADE. 407

a circular ring placed round the lower jaw. If the ribbon-like rein was slightly pressed, the animal, from the utmost speed, was in an instant sent on his haunches, and continuous working of the bit put him into fits of high spirit. I thought from this instance of horse-management that we have still a good deal to learn in England; for there was no pace or figure that this animal would not go through, even if a child were upon his back. We were brought by Ali Bey to see his private house and family. The ladies, however, did not appear. Ajim carpets and luxurious couches filled his suite of upper rooms; all had been brought from Cairo by boat and across the desert. In his Turkish politeness, he said whatever we fancied was ours! He paraded five hundred troops in line one morning for our amusement. They were black sturdy young men, out of mixed races from the Soudan, and were armed with flint-muskets. The uniform was a white suit, jacket and loose trousers, cross-belts covered with calico. In putting them through the platoon exercise, the officer in front stood giving the commands, which were repeated by another officer in the ranks. They went through the exercise with perfect uniformity, quite as well as any sepoy regiment. Their passing in review and forming squares required considerable practice; but these were mere lads, recruits, Ali Bey remarked; and the old trained soldiers, from ten to fifteen thousand in number, were at present on a tour with the governor of the Soudan, Musa Pascha. Every Saturday, Sunday, and Monday morning they parade for exercise, and march through the town, headed by an excellent bugle or drum and fife band.

408 CURIOSITIES TO BE SEEN AT KHARTOOM.

Another gentleman, one of the oldest residents in Khartoom, was kind and attentive. This was Micha- eel, commonly called Lutfullah, a highly respectable banker and merchant . In advancing us funds", lie would not accept the rate of exchange, so glad was lie to serve the English Government!

Khartoom being upon the highway to Abyssinia and the countries of the White Nile, it is quite an emporium for the trade and products and animals of those regions. At the residence of M. Thibaut, we saw a happy family of black and white geese, guinea- fowl, a Koodoo antelope, ariel, a Soakim long-horned goat, a Nyam Nyam goat, with immense long hair and short legs, and other genera. In his drawing- room, a chetah, a species of leopard, played with a pup-dog; and in the garden a striped hyena, not thought fit company for those in the yard, was amusing himself on his chain. At the British Consulate two ostriches walked solemnly about the yard picking up sand; they had no feathers upon them, having been plucked as bare as the dead fowls in a poulterer's window. At the premises of a Marseille Mussulman, who had been in Khartoom for thirty years, we recognised a great assortment of arms and curiosities brought from the southern counties of Ilyria, Bari, and Shillook, but none of the Uganda weapons had reached him. The most remarkable shield we saw was in the possession of M. de Bono, who said it was used hi Ilyria by the "rain-makers." It was of iron, diamond-shaped, three spans long, and above one span broad, with a handle of wood. Of M. Miani, whose name we had seen cut on the tree far up the country, we heard an amusing account. Having proceeded

SIGKIOR MIANI MR AIPPERLY. 409

farther up the Nile than any previous traveller, his information was always sought for by gentlemen arriving from Europe. Four Frenchmen asked for counsel and advice; but Miani gave them such an unpromising account of the country that they said they would defer their journey, and returned to Europe. Another traveller sent for M. Miani, and told him he wished to go up country; " Very good; but you will find the monkeys up there very savage." " Oh, then," replied the other, " I shall not go." The Signior, I suspect, is somewhat of a "character," or original. In his native town of Venice, one room, with his name in large characters upon the door, is entirely devoted to his collections of arms and curiosities, and the wall is hung round with sketches of his battles, as he has designated them, with the natives. He himself is made to figure very largely in his collection of sketches.

We were much interested with the honest frankness of a clergyman belonging to the Pilgrim Mission from the Swiss Protestant Church, Mr Aipperly. He was under middle age, and seemed to have great determination of character and kindliness of disposition. He had come in from his station at Galabat, Blue Nile, riding upon his handsome camel, to transact business in Khartoom, and, knowing English, he came frequently to visit us. His labours were amongst the Dacrooree people, who originally settled in Galabat, in preference to returning from their Mecca pilgrimage to their own country in Kordofan. These people clothe themselves in coarse " damoor," or calico, made into long "jungeers," somewhat like the trousers worn by the handsomest of races|the Seikhs of the Pun-

410 CONVEYANCE OF COTTON.

jab. They cultivate jowari (or doora), have numbers of goats, but few sheep. Weekly markets are held by this race, at which about 250 camels, laden with cotton for sale, are seen; also cattle and goats. Each camel-load of cotton costs three dollars, and, as there are no Europeans to purchase it, all goes into Abyssinia, where it is made into country stufis, such as the damoor. Mr Aipperly expected to receive from England a machine for cleaning the cotton. From the market it might be carried by camels a few miles to Aboo Kharaz, on the Blue Nile, and thence, when the Nile is at its height in August, to the Mediterranean by water. This worthy Swiss interested me very much, living, as he did, such a contented and happy life with a single missionary companion. Two servants (a native Christian and a Mussulman) formed their entire establishmentlone would not eat a forl or goat killed by the other, but neither had any objection to eating them when killed by his master. For the last year these two missionaries had together only received $43. Mr Aipperly had learned blacksmith's work, and made friends with the natives *by* assisting to put up their irrigation-wheels, and other carpentry. I was struck with the docility and obedience of his camel, which he had purchased for fifteen dollars in the Galabat market; a single word from him made the animal kneel, and there was no roughness on his part, as with an Indian Surwan, and no reluctance shown by the camel. He described the wine made from honey as remarkably good. Bees abound; they are kept in trees or houses, and the natives do not kill them, but smoke them away froffl the honey. The Dacrooree people pay tribute to both

FRIJ GETS MARRIED. 411

the Egyptian and Abyssinian or Mokad'a Governments, as their territory lies between both. Their country is hilly, stony, and cool; the hills of Abyssinia are seen in the blue distance, and the minister's station is on the postal route between Khartoom and his fellow-labourers of the Pilgrim Mission in Hubeesh or Abyssinia.

Our Seedees had been living a life of freedom ever since their arrival in the capital of the Soudan. Ma- nua and the Uganda girls had never before witnessed such grandeur. Bombay and Frij were seldom sober, and went about smoking cigars. The clothes in which Ali Bey had dressed Speke and myself were given to Bombay and Frij, with instructions that it would be indelicate of them to wear them while in Khartoom ; but they forgot the injunction, and Bombay paraded the town in a blue frock-coat and fez ! Frij contemplated marriage, and on the same evening that he announced his intention, the ceremony was performed by a " Fakee," or clergyman, who was paid the fee of one dollar. The lady had been the property of Bombay, and was given him by the king of Uganda, but, for a trifle of twelve dollars, promised to be paid at Zanzibar, she was made over to Frij, who told me that the clergyman exacted a promise from him to protect her and be a faithful husband for life. However, there was a clause in the contract that, should he tire of her, she was again to become the property of Bombay.

Nearly twenty years ago Khartoom was a cantonment with twenty thousand troops. The regimental officers led a gay social life, and the town increased greatly. In 1863, it had rather a decayed look, with

412 TRADE OF KHARTOOM.

few or no troops; but there were shops kept by Europeans and natives, where nearly all commodities might be had, including such varied articles as guns, ready- made clothes, wines, Bass's pale ale, groceries, hardware goods, &c. All manner of trades are carried on in Khartoom; and on the streets water-carriers and people selling pigeons and fowls plied their vocations. Old Turks sat playing chess and backgammon; and in the uncovered streets and open spaces stalls for cooked fish, trinkets, sweetmeats, and vegetables, were laid out as at a market. One is surprised where all these things come from in such a desert country. Except the irrigated parts, and the senna-plant growing as a weed, Khartoom does not yield a single natural or manufactured export. The river presented a busy scene; all the firewood, corn, earthen jars, bricks, grass and palm-leaves for matting and rope, stones and lime, Berber salt, and European goods, were being landed from boats for the use of the inhabitants. Gum (the best coming from Kordofan), ivory, bees'- wax, cotton, and sesamum (called sin-sin), are brought thither, but merely pass through on their way to Egypt. The White Nile is said to have 250 boats trading upon it yearly, including those on the Sobat and Bahr Ghazal. The Blue river probably has as many more; but we saw only forty-five boats lying off Khartoom, and ten on the stocks, of which the largest measured twenty yards in length. The only manufactures we observed at Khartoom were a few for oil and soap for home consumption. The oil-press was a heavy millstone placed on edge, and pulled round over sesamum - seed by a bullock with blinders. After being well bruised, the grain, now looking like a mash

THE BAZAAR OF KHARTOOM. 413

of bran, *was* removed to a screw-press, made of wood (without a nail), cow-hide, and grass. The oil, so expressed, dropped at intervals into a receiver below. At the soap-factory belonging [to Shenooda, an ivory- trader, we saw two boilers busily at work. The lime and sesamum-oil used in the manufacture were both from Azrah. Ali Bey, who kindly showed us over these places, brought us also to the gold and silver smiths' shops. The artificers are celebrated for working in filigree, similar to that of Delhi or Cuttack, and must originally have learned the art from Easterns. Cups with stalks, made for holding the Turkish cofiee-cup, are formed of the purest soft yellow gold, found as a dust in the Soudan. Napoleon or sovereign gold would not answer for such fine workmanship, having too much alloy; consequently, when cups are ordered, gold-dust is given to the workman. At the two shops we visited several youths were busy, sitting on the ground, each with a small anvil before him, hammering at threads of pure metal. Handsome small drinkiug-cups are turned out of the rhinoceros- horn, which has this advantage over the horns of cattle, that, in a hot country, it retains its shape, and does not crack.

The coinage of Khartoom was puzzling, on account of the variety of pieces and their names. The following re some of those in circulation :|

1 para, equal to one-fifth of a pice.

8 pice or 8 five-para pieces, equal 1 piastre (copper silvered over).

2j piastres or groosh, 1 thick sixpenny piece of silver.

4. shilling

19$ 1 Egyptian dollar or five-franc piece.

20 1 Maria Theresa dollar.

77 1 napoleon.

100 1 sovereign.

414 GOVERNMENT HOUSE|BARRACKS.

Besides these there were small coins of gold valued at 4 and 8| groosh or piastres. In Abyssinia, where the smallest coin is a bit of salt, the five-franc piece is valued at 28 piastres; at Galabat, Mr Aipperly informed me, its value falls to 18 piastres; but at

Cairo it rises to 34. On Speke drawing $150, the account was as follows, the banker (Lutfullah), with great liberality, remitting the charge for exchange :l

Piastres. Pam

100 napoleons, at 77 piastres each, ... 7700 0

379 francs or Egyptian dollars, at 19-10 piastres each, 7295 30

4J piastres, 4 10

Total, 15,000 0

There is but one public building in Khartoom, the Government House, which overlooks the Blue Nile, and is a substantial brick edifice. A flight of steps leads up to the reception-hall, which is lofty and handsome, hung round with engravings of naval engagements, &c. In the courtyard Lubach-trees (*Acacia lebbefy* give shade to orderlies and officials. Baths and all conveniences are attached to the suites of rooms, and comfortable stabling is provided for cavalry and horse-artillery. We were shown through the powder-magazine, a mile distant from the town; it contains an immense store of ammunition, neatly arranged in cases. A barrack, simply walled round and almost smothered with drifted sand, is in the vicinity. The minaret we had observed on first approaching Khartoom is part of the mosque of the town; it is protected from the houses of the city by a high wall of stone, and sentries guard the gateways.

Walking through the streets with AH Bey, lie *led* us into a walled enclosure, where there were from

THE CHURCHES OF KHARTOOM. 415

twenty to thirty tombs surmounted by crosses. The fumes of frankincense met us, and we began to wonder what sight was in store. We entered an arched building ; a man in spectacles read aloud from a volume placed on a desk in the centre, and around him were men wearing large turbans, their shoes placed on one side, and several children, all sitting on a carpet listening devoutly. On the walls were draperies and pictures of our Saviour, and within a doorway was the high altar covered with a cloth marked by the figure of the cross. We were in a Coptic church. As the service proceeded in Arabic, a handsome old man entered, bearing a staff surmounted by a golden cross. He proceeded to the altar, and knelt at each of its four sides, after which he returned to where we stood, and conversed with us. By his invitation we left the church to have coffee at his house. I have seldom seen a finer face than that of this venerable Copt. His name, we found, was Gabriel; he is at the head of the Coptic church at Khartoom, and has a congregation of about five hundred persons. He showed us his copy of the four gospels, printed in Arabic and Hebrew characters; and on our taking leave of him, he thanked Ali Bey and ourselves for having visited his church.

The Austrian Mission has a large and long-established station at Khartoom. It occupies a few acres of ground upon the river bank, and is surrounded by a wall ten feet high. The main gateway faces the town; it is handsome, and built of sandstone from the Rao. Their temporary church is small but very neat; the front pews are occupied by the men, and those in the rear by the women. Through the kindness of Mr

416 BAPTISM OF A NEGRESS.

Moorlang, we took our Seedees to church, in order that they might be gratified with the sacred music from the harmonicon. It was a Sunday, and many other natives were present. Mabrook became greatly excited. On seeing the bleeding figure of our Saviour upon the cross, he held his mouth with his hand; he wished to touch the figure, thinking it was real. While at Khar- toom Speke was asked to be godfather to a grown-up negress, a servant girl in the Mission establishment. His being a Protestant did not preclude him from officiating in this capacity. The ceremony took place in the morning, and there was an immense gathering. The liberal-minded Ali Bey, though a Mussulman, was present, also the Baroness Capellen, who was godmother to the girl. Another christening took place at the same time, when Madame Bartolemy and M. de Bono officiated as godmother and godfather. During the ceremony loud reports took place outside; probably the fellow - servants of the girls were making merry by firing guns in honour of the event!

The ruins of Soba, on the right bank of the Blue Nile, though as yet not much excavated, repaid us for the trouble of a visit, as we had not seen those of Thebes or Phylae. Ali Bey kindly arranged a picnic for us, and in our old diabeah, Mr Aipperly, M. Angelo, a moullim or secretary, Speke, and I, rowed and sailed up the Blue river for three hours in the afternoon, accomplishing about six miles. We were then opposite Soba. There were no houses on the bank, and the country appeared flat and dreary. Sometimes the ground swelled up, marking the spot where houses or temples were still entombed. Arriving too late to paj the ruins a visit, we delayed till morning, and had

THE RUINS OF SOBA. 417

dinner on deck. Ajim carpets were laid out, candles were lit, and we sat round six brass saucers full of pastry, cutlets, and stews, which were eaten with the fingers. The usual coffee, liqueurs, and tobacco followed, and we rested for the night under variegated rezzais or counterpanes on the top of the cupboards. Next morning on the shore there was a curious collection of riding animals brought to convey us to the ruins of Soba. None looked inviting, but we were allotted a horse each, while others rode camels and donkeys. The moullim, a sedate fat little man with black turban, had by no means a dignified appearance sitting on the donkey without a bridle, and the animal soon dropt down on his knees, allowing the functionary to slide over his head. The first mound we examined had been a room ten feet square, floored with square bricks; at each corner stood a round pillar of granite, seven feet between the capital and square base. The capitals were of three different designs; the most conspicuous being marked with the cross between acanthus leaves. All were now in ruin : the pillars were sunk, and the capitals lay separate. This excavation had been open for some time. The next we visited was opened by Dr Dumichen, a Prussian gentleman, whom we met upon the ground, and who kindly gave us an alphabet of characters. It was a small square building of stone, with two-feet-thick walls very neatly built, having two opposite doors, and its floor four feet below the present level of the country. The next and last excavation was a scaly sphinx lying upon a plinth, which, though considerably broken, was written over in Coptic characters, which consist of figures of men, beasts, and birds. The head of the sphinx, and some

418 PREPARATIONS FOR LEAVING KHARTOOM.

ornamentation on the chest, had been broken off. The measurements werel Shoulder to plinth, ... 60 inches.

Centre of chest to tail, . . . 115
Greatest circumference of neck, . 122
Over the saddle part, from plinth to plinth, 140
Over the rump, do. do. 145
Length of the tail, ... 60

Although there were other ruins about Soba, we were informed that the above were the only remains worthy of note; so we re-embarked at noon, and returned to Khartoom.

Preparations were making for our departure by boat to Berber, and thence by desert upon camels to Korosko. It was necessary, on account of the poverty of Berber, to lay in supplies of food at Khartoom for both these journeys. Ali Bey procured us a small diabeah which belonged to Government. We had only to pay the hire of the crew to Berber, namely, twenty-eight dollars. We had twenty Seedees, and each required to have two goat-skins, or "girba," to carry his drinking-water; Speke and I had two "rey," or cow-skins, each, for the same purpose, and water-bottles to hang from our camel-saddles. All these were purchased, the small ones for seven, and the large for thirty-eight koorsh each. It was necessary to grease and test these skins before setting out on the journey. A number of lads, each with the skin of a goat, blew into them with all their might, and then tied up the inflated skins for our inspection. Having arranged everything, we intended sailing at noon of the 15th April; but the hospitality of the Baroness, the Austrian missionaries, M. de Bono, and

ADVICE TO TRAVELLERS. 419

other gentlemen of Khartoom, delayed our departure till the afternoon, when about a dozen of our kind friends came to bid us farewell. The advices we received as to crossing the desert were numerous, and I may here mention them for the benefit of future travellers:|Have a list of the stages by land and water, mentioning what supplies are procurable. Always sling a water-bag and bag of biscuit to the pommel of your saddle. Ali Bey recommended a thimbleful of nun in a good deal of water as the best thing to keep one awake, and prevent tumbling off the camel during night. Always take a sleep for a few hours from nine in the morning. Water is more requisite than food; next to this, abrey (or dry unleavened bread) and hard biscuit are the best. See that your men do not steal your water, or the sailors your ropes. The camels, too, are apt, from thirst, to bite through the water-bags, which must be taken care of, and also covered during the night, to prevent the wind drying them up; and always have something under them. We found all these advices excellent; and I have nothing to add except that a "Hadjeen," or riding camel, is indispensable to comfort.

19

SECTION 19

CHAPTER XVIII.

KHAUTOOM TO CAIRO|THE GHERRI PASS|RUINS AT SCENPI| THE PYRA-
MIDS AND RUINS OF MERGE|THE RIVER ATBAKi |THE TOWN OF BERBER|SCENES
ACROSS THE DESERT| THE VILLAGE OF ABOO AHMED|THE FALSE SEA, OR
BAHS BELAMA|NATRON WELLS|EXTRAORDINARY NATURAL TCS- NEL|KOROSKO|

We rowed down stream till midnight of the 15th April, and lay-to for the remainder
of the night at Halfaya. Here Ali Bey and the sheikh of the platf appeared, bringing
us a present of two sheep. Ve all dined together, and afterwards our generous friend
Ali Bey took leave of us, and returned on horseback to Khartoom, having left an
aide-de-camp to escort us to Berber. Our crew rowed incessantly till sunset About
Halfaya the banks are either of hard shelving sand or perpendicular clay, and low,
solitary hills are generally in sight. The river was again mud-colour, and surprised us
with being so narrow|not more than a hundred and eighty yards wide. On the left bank
grew tamarisks, a species of willow, and several other plants we had not met with on
our previous journey. While at Khartoom I had an opportunity

PASSING A CATARACT. 421

of seeing a collection of plants from the Bahr Ghazal, made by Dr Steudner (since
dead) of Madame Tinne's expedition; they were nearly all the same as those luund

upon the Nile, but some auricularias were interesting. The sunset view of Mount Roeean and tbe low chain of mounds to its right, as we looked down a rocky reach of the river about four miles in length, was striking; the slopes of the hills became purple, and the bushes on both banks were lit up in gorgeous tints. The river had quite changed its character; numbers of rocks at the sides and centre of the stream stood out of the water, making the navigation dangerous, and impossible at night. Our rowers had to pull very hard to escape the sunken rocks, which we avoided through the aid of a pilot from the shore.

17th.|Having passed the island of Roeean to our right, the river ran through a narrow pass of hills called "Gherri." Nothing could be more desolate- looking : splinters of black rock lay on their sides, like refuse thrown from a quarry. The river branches on making its escape from these hills. Our boat took the right channel, and had scarcely entered it when we had to pass through a rapid and dangerous cataract, known as the Sixth Cataract of the maps, and called by the natives Cibleoga- It was so narrow, that while our oars were poised, and we shot down the sluice, guided only by the helm, the oars almost touched the rocks on either side. The pilot, steersman, and boatmen saw that one false move would have dashed the boat to pieces, so they did not breathe freely till the difficulty was over. No more rocks were met with till reaching Murnat at

422 VISIT THE VILLAGE OF SCENDI.

sunset, where it was considered desirable to rest for the night.

18th.|There are only two large places, or "bunders," on the route by water to Berber|namely, Metamma and Scendi. Nearly the whole distance is flat, bare, and uncultivated, without villages; but numerous flocks of cattle, camels, sheep, goats, and sometimes horses, are to be seen upon the banks. The people were civil in offering us milk and garden vegetables. To-day, although the mainmast of our boat had been taken down, the north wind and storm of sand blew so hard from nine till two o'clock that we could make no progress. We were not, however, troubled with rocks in the stream, and by sunset had made as far as the tame-looking district of Bowalat From this point we had no rocks, but rowed steadily down, at two and a half miles per hour, as far as some wells and cultivations on the right bank at Go(n)cil Ihu A native of this place, calling himself a Shygeea, had three lines cut upon each cheek, similar to the custom practised on the Nile at 4 N.; but though an aborigine, he was a Mussulman|converted, probably, at the time the late commander-in-chief, Ibrahim Pasha, conquered the country. The district was reckoned exactly half-way between Khartoom and Berber; but we anchored for the night at the left bank of Metamma. There were no antiquities to be seen; and, having gone down stream for an hour, we lay-to on the 20th at the town of Scendi, a straggling, dusty, miserable place, but which afforded liquor to our sailors, and fresh bread to ourselves. There were mounds of ancient remains in abundance; and three miles to th south-west some buildings and figures in stone were

THE STORY OF ISHMAEL PASHA. 423

said to exist. In the town there had been a deep shaft dug for a well|evidently ancient, for it is not now in use : a deep stratum of pebbles, with concrete above, forms its sides. There appears to have been a canal or watercourse at this place, for its windings, flooded with water and covered with grass,, are still visible. The women, as they carried water on their heads, struck us as having a singular way of dressing their hair; but our Seedees remarked that a race of Central Africans, called the Wabeessa, near Lake Nyassa, adopt the same fashion. The Scendi women, like those of Abyssinia, have a tuft of hair on either side of the head and one behind, and the Wabeessa aave the same, but add another tuft, like a high comb, to the top of their heads.

Scendi is a place of some note, being the locality where Nimur (tiger), the former governor of all the blacks, planned the death of poor Ishmael Pasha. The story was related to us as follows:|After Ishmael Pasha nad conquered Khartoom, &c., he returned to Scendi, and asked Nimur what he was to give him. The reply was, " I will give you whatever you name, silver or gold, for I am anxious to make friends with you." After a time Ishmael with some followers became the guest of Nimur, who heaped quantities of provisions and straw for cavalry around the dwelling where Ishmael lived. No suspicion was excited ; but the straw was set fire to one windy night. Ishmael, it is said, was too proud to attempt an escape. His followers shielded him as long as they could from the flames, ind one arm only was burned, but Ishmael perished ancler the ruins. After great difficulty a European recovered the body from Nimur, and it was sent for

424 THE PYRAMIDS OF MERGE.

interment to Cairo. A bad imitation of the mosqne at Khartoom marks the place where this tragedy K"as enacted.

We left for Meroe, the ancient capital of Ethiopia, before sunrise of the 21st. Date-palms, we observed were here more frequently irrigated, and the doom- palm grew wild. The bunder, or port, from wlich Meroe (called by the natives Tarabil Kobosheei, or Pyramids of Kobosheea) is visited, may be either Ko- bosheea or Budjerewa; we chose the latter, as the wind was not favourable for landing at the former. The pyramids are seen two miles across a plain, *upoi* the right bank, near some low elongated hills. T visit them during the heat of the day it is desirable to have riding donkeys, which, with common woodei saddles, may be obtained at either starting-point . A man carries water, and you make straight for the ruins over a plain strewed with small pieces of clay of curious shapes and lustrous colours. There are three groups of pyramids. The first group consists of fifteen, dismantled to half their original height, and built apparently, as to site, without any regular system or order. A pyramidal shell of masonry 24 feet square, built without lime, and eight feet thick, had been filled with the rubble of the country. The sandstone blocks with which they had been faced were now so soft that a knife could cut them. The second group, consisting of 18 or more, half a mile farther east, are in a better state of preservation, and have their figures of meu and animals wonderfully complete. We ascended one having ten tiers, each tier a span and a half high. and diminishing in breadth as you reach the summit- The porches or entries into several pyramids of this

THE RUINS OF MERGE. . 425

group were arched over with stone, and handsomely ornamented with bas-relievo figures chiselled out of the sandstone. These figures consisted of men driving slaves, carrying sheep, or seated on lion-faced dogs, funeral processions, women carrying palm-leaves, and representations of birds, lizards, and elephants. The third group of five pyramids was across a death-like valley covered with withered grass. Having seen all, and made some sketches of the curious figures, we next visited three sphinxes very much defaced, which remain amongst the ruins of the city. They were not marked with scales like the Soba sphinx; they had been cut out of a rock with slaty stratification, and were defaced by the laminae having split off". In the city, several old walls and pavements, built of immense blocks of sandstone, are to be seen ; but everything is in utter decay. On returning to our boat we found a considerable number of people wishing to dispose of curiosities they had gathered. These were relics of stone and copper, some representing the scarabaeus, and others human figures, but no corns were produced, for they said the coins were too valuable to show us. 22cZ.lA considerable number of palm and acacia trees were growing upon the banks we passed to-day, and we saw Jubl Ag'edah on the left bank six hours' distance above the port of Damur. We called to get a letter of introduction, and orders for camels from the Mudir, Ibrahim Bey, to the Mudir of Berber. There are upwards of one hundred flat-roofed comfortable-looking dwellings near the river, shaded by acacias. A market is held every Friday, when cotton, salt, baskets, mats, ropes, cattle, &c., are exposed for sale. The Atbara, a river navigable for a long dis-

426 THE BLACK RIVER OR ATBARA.

tance, is not above a *few* hours' sail from this port. We lay for the night just above its confluence with the Nile, because there were sunken rocks in the bed of the river. In the morning we saw the Atbara, Bahr-el-aswad (Black river), the Astaboras of Ptolemy lthe last great feeder of the Nile. We liked the brown appearance of the stream. From bank to bank it looked one hundred and fifty yards across, but now there was not more than sixty yards of water flowing slowly in its bed, with a low rock at its junction with the Nile. It joins the latter with even a more graceful sweep than we observed at the confluence of the Blue and White Nile. For a distance of two miles below its mouth there are sunken rocks very annoying to the boatmen, but at this dry season of April they are generally visible. While detained below the Atbara on account of contrary winds, Bombay brought his wife up to Speke, saying she was very unwell; but as she was too diffident to speak, we could do nothing to help her. An hour or two elapsed, and Bombay came, grinning with delight, to announce that his wife had presented him with a child! One of the girls in the boat had told him of it, but he did not know whether it was a boy or a girllhe would go and ask This was the second child born to Bombay upon the journey; but both died, and he regretted very much that there would be no keepsake of the journey for him to take back to Zanzibar. The infant was buried on the shore.

Our journey by water had now for the present endedlwe had anchored off the bunder or port of Berber. There was some show of trade, and twelve large boats lay alongside ours. The population of

EGYPTIAN MODE OF THRASHING WHEAT. 427

Berber and the neighbouring villages is probably five thousand souls. The houses are built in irregular streets and lanes, chiefly near the Nile. A handsome embankment has been constructed around Berber, which forms a pleasant walk at all seasons. On the outskirts of this is the unenclosed burial-ground. The tombs have upright slabs at either end, with white shingle laid between, and a few are built of bricks and lime. From the number of graves and the extent they cover, it would be supposed that the locality of Berber is unhealthy, but the natives prefer this latitude to Khartoom: provisions, also, are only about half the price. Wheaten bread, milk, meat, oats, onions, water-melons, tobacco, salt, fish, &c., are abundant in the market every morning, and other articles can be obtained and work executed in the bazaar. The operation of thrashing wheat is performed in the true Egyptian style. A man sits on a frame drawn by bullocks, and resting upon three rollers, each furnished with iron discs; the bullocks eat all the while, and the grain is well thrashed, but the work is overdone, as the seed gets bruised in the process. In the bazaars the boys discovered that our Seedees had arrows and other weapons to dispose of, and came offering money. The exchange was very easily arranged, for the Seedees were eager to purchase the Egyptian dates. The inhabitants of Berber are proverbially honest, and their servants are considered superior to those of Khartoom. I went to the market to buy food, and saw the rude way it was managed. The butcher not having sufficient weights and measures, a sheep's head and two broken bricks were put into one scale, and my meat in the other. Having weighed it, he said

428 THE TOWN OF BERBER.

its price was so much. Upon which, trusting to the reputed honesty of the Berberese, I put into his hand more than the amount, and he told me to come back for the change, as he was too busy to give it me then. This I did, and received the balance. The few troops here were a tidy set of men, in clean quarters, below the town. Their arms were flint-musket and bayonet; their uniform, the fez, white jackets, knee-breeches, long white socks, and red shoes. At a short distance from their barracks there is a magazine with four high walls, a single gateway to the south, a few trees in the interior, and towers with embrasures.

Berber became Egyptian at the same time as Khartoom, about forty years ago, when the army advanced from Wady Haifa. The present Governor- General of the Soudan, Musa Pasha, is the man of whom the story is told that when he was sent to conquer the country he circumcised every one of the Bagara Arabs, and so brought them under his subjection. We were not fortunate enough to have an audience of the Governor-General; he was absent on a tour of inspection, and our friend Ali Bey acted for him. The Vakeel of Berber, Rehan Aga, came to call upon us : he had lived twenty years in Constantinople, and, to my surprise, he had more of the features of a M'ganda than a Turk. He has a comfortable house, well furnished, and he kindly showed us every attention. The Sheikh of the desert, a dark, stout, middle-aged man, we saw more of, as it was through him that we were to obtain camels for our journej. He was handsome, with a long black gown and high white turban. He thought we might get off in a couple of days; and, in the mean time, he would get

WE MOUNT OUR CAMELS FOR KOROSKO. 429

us a house to live in during the heat of the day. We were accordingly put into a dark inner room without a window, but it had a high verandah outside where we could sit during the day. We engaged thirty baggage-camels, at ninety piastres each, to carry us to Korosko; the party consisted of twenty-six souls'in all, and the spare camels were for carrying two guides and two loads of water for Speke and myself. Every other man had to carry his two water-bags on the camel he rode. We tried to get a pair of

Hadjeens or riding camels, but failed|all were as rough as they could possibly be. .
The majority of our Seedees had never seen a camel before, and were somewhat afraid
to mount; however, once seated, their pleasure was excessive. All was good-humour
and fun the first day's march to El Chore, where we arrived at sunset of the 27th April.
El Chore, "the Lake," had no water at this season, but the Nile, which is within a
quarter of a mile, overflows the grassy ground immediately below the few inhabited
houses. The people were civil in selling us milk, bringing us water, and giving us
small cots to lie upon during the night. In the desert, amongst Egyptians, a traveller
may always expect to be treated with civility.

28th.|To-day we divided the march into two stages, making one in the morning
to El Ab'idy, and the other to Gin'ceneet'a|the latter name as sounded by a native is
peculiarly Italian. The journey occupied seven hours, generally over a hard road of
gravel. Although never far from the river, we saw low hills upon the opposite bank,
and travelled amongst tall grass, madar, and palms. From this grass the people make
a coarse description of rope. The nights were

430 THE RIVER OF ASSES.

cold, owing to north winds; but, sheltered by the walls of the small flat-roofed
houses, we rested comfortably on the cots lent us by the people. From Gin'oeneet'a
we made twenty-two miles in eleven hours, two stages to a point in the desert beyond
Aboo Ban, resting during the heat of the day at Wadi Khumar|the bed of a stream then
dry. Here there is a bend in the Nile, and we were able to fill all our water-sacks afresh.
This route was over ground strewn with splinters, and ridged with quartz and clay-slate
dykes. Some of the rocks were cobalt blue, ringing when struck, and bearing marks of
having been combed down with rain. Wadi Khumar (which signifies the river of asses)
derives its name from being the spot where wild donkeys and zebra come to drink. We
rested under some palm-trees in rich foliage, beside the Nile, which, at this point, runs
rapidly over a bed of rock, divided into several courses. After leaving the river the
march became dreary and desolate ; not a sign of a human being; all a waste of heavy
sand, dreary valleys in the hollows, and splintered black rock on the heights. We lay
down at night in a country filled to the tops of the hills with white sand, not a tree nor a
drop of water to be seen, and a kind of fearful stillness everywhere around! However,
there never was a desert that had not some living thing to show|some insect, bird, or
animal. Several tiny ariel appeared as we passed the peaked height of Aboo Ban. In
the morning we set off over the sand on foot to keep us warm, but it proved such heavy
plodding work that, after some miles, we mounted the camels and descended from the
plateaux of sand to the Nile at Bagcere, where we made our

CAMEL-RIDING. 431

noonday halt . The river may be called beautiful at this point, for it runs at a rate
of from three to five miles an hour amongst myriads of rush-covered islets, with high
banks aboiit five hundred yards apart, and on the opposite side densely covered with
tropical vegetation. The people of Bagoere allowed us to occupy a shed roofed with
the leaves of the doom- palm. They brought us milk, and for their attention we made
them a present of a lantern. Travelling as we all did upon camels, not in file as in
India, one camel tied after the other, but like a herd of cattle gently driven by men
walking behind them, there was always considerable jostling; and if a camel wanted

to pluck a mouthful you could not prevent him, as there was no ring in his nose, only a rope tied round his head, which gave the rider no command over him. Their pace was slower than that of a man, and so rough, that the saddle, assisted a good deal by the cold wind every morning, chafed the skin. The march in the afternoon to Wadi Shiroeg (another dry bed of a stream) was over rough stony ground, to the brink of the Nile, occupying us only two hours, when we encamped under date-palms, and amongst houses, near one of which a rudely-made loom was at work. On this march we passed several cairns of stones four and five feet above the level of the country; our camel- men could not say who had formed them, they were of so old a date.

1st May.|The route to Aboo Hasheem, " the Father of Hospitality," was so smooth and pleasant that one might have ridden, driven, or walked the whole distance, which occupied us more than four hours on our baggage-camels. It lay on the outskirts

432 SUPERSTITION AMONGST CAMEL-DRIVERS.

of wheat stubble-fields on the banks of the Nile, and on our right roae the variously - coloured rocks of the desert. The river is about three hundred yards across, and has a current of two and a half miles per hour. When passing a roadside house about halfway, we halted to go through a superstitious ceremony. A burial-ground was close by, with cups upon many of the graves, said to be placed there for receiving offerings of frankincense or money. We all dismounted at the hut, which had no appearance of being regularly inhabited, and found several jars of drinking water, which a boy served to us ; the skull of a lion was stuck upon a pole, and stood high over the hut. Our guide received from the boy two hand- fuls of sand, some of which he strewed over his person, some he put into his pockets, some he licked, some he put on the camels, pistols, and saddles, and he finished off by putting the last grains carefully into the bag slung from his riding animal. This odd custom is common over the desert, and is adopted by camel-men to insure their safety on a journey. We came upon old acquaintances as we made for the north: the white kite, raven, sand-grouse, and stone- finches were recognised after we left Berber, and became the most common birds of the desert. At Aboo Hasheem we were allotted a two-storeyed house to rest in. We observed that here six or eight donkeys in a knot are used for treading out the wheat, and are prevented from eating it by a band tied round the lower jaw, crossing the forehead, and fastened behind their long earslan artful contrivance. The afternoon march, made to Gcegee, on the Nile, occupied us till 11 P.m. We had not seen the river the whole way;

ABOO AHMED BY MOONLIGHT. 433

the track was over heavy sand, strewed with fragments of rock and pebbles. The hill of Burgul Anak was passed when we were four miles to its left, and on arrival at Gregee we could look back upon it seven miles off in a south-east direction.

2d.|Starting off across the plain at sunrise, our beacon was a pyramidal mass of quartz a few miles distant. We passed a tomb erected by Latiffe Pasha to the memory of a Liverpool gentleman, and at length, picking our steps amongst the splinters from the blue and grey slate rocks, we arrived at Musra Jahoesh, upon a bend of the Nile, which here flows in a westerly direction. There were no people nor houses on our side of the river. To avoid the heat we lay in the deep shadow of the doom-palm, and changed our positions as the sun veered round. Starting again at five in the afternoon, we ascended to a wild dreary plateau, but which became interesting from the colours of the rocks. Every moment I was tempted to dismount and pick up specimens in which blue was contrasted with pure white quartz, or pink was marbled with white, or all three colours would blend together. By seven o'clock we had descended from this plateau by a sandy tract, and reached the high gravel bank of the river again. Here the moon lighted up the rippled blue water and the palms and green vegetation on the opposite bank. The village of Aboo Ahmed looked beautiful in this light, but on reaching it we found it ankle-deep in sand. My camel, which for the first time I had pressed ahead with a cane, showed his fatigue by squatting down without warning, upon my stopping to ask for the Deewan's house. He knew that his journey had come to an434 Manua's Cure For Cold.

end, but the proceeding would not be pleasant were he to try it in a desert. We rode past a large caravan from Berber|traders conveying young camels and home-made camel-cloths for sale to Korosko, whither we also were journeying. They were anxious to know whether we had commenced to stint our camels in water, previous to putting them upon the desert allowance of none at all; they had done so, and were ready to march next day; we had not, and therefore our march must be delayed. I may here remark that travelling in the desert on a baggage- camel is far from being comfortable. The usual seat is the same as that of a lady on horseback, but without any kind of stirrup, consequently the legs get chafed, the dry wind chips your hands and nails, and you get cold in the head. Manua, an old and experienced traveller, sat always upon his camel with his nose in a sling, which, he said, was a protection against cold; he had a cloth shutting up both nostrils, and tied on the top of the head.

3d and ith.|Detained training our camels for the desert journey, and getting ropes and other necessaries. The station of Aboo Hamed is upon the right bank of the Nile, with the island of Mokrat opposite. An oblong wall of mud, with a tower at each corner, encloses the few huts that are there, and other abodes are placed outside the walls in a straggling line of misery. Sand has nearly banked up the whole place|walls, fort, and all|and the majority of the people live upon the island and opposite shore. We had a call from two gentlemen travelling (not for their pleasure, but till further orders) to that Siberia of Egypt, the Soudan, with a line of camels and horses carrying their

MEET TRAVELLERS FROM CAIRO. 435

worldly effects. They had been fifty-one days coming by land from Cairo, and were the first Egyptian travellers *we* had met. They could not make out where we had come from, and asked us a number of strange questions. Was it true that the Governor-General of the Soudan, Musa Pasha, had made prisoners of us ? had we been serving the Abyssinian Government ? were English officers fighting for the Abyssin- ians ? was Queen Victoria to resign in favour of the Prince of Wales ? were we the remnant of fifty Englishmen who had left Zanzibar to cross Africa ? These interrogatories were all put to us by an Albanian gentleman; the other traveller was a priest, a very intelligent man. He went so far as to say, when told that we had come from the source of the Nile, that the Koran had always said that it proceeded from a lake; but what was the size of it? Had we seen cannibals ? What did we pay for these five Seedees and the little girls we had with us ? Having answered all these queries to their satisfaction, we saw them depart for Khartoom. In the afternoon we had *a* visit from a fortune-teller. He sat at our feet, smoothed with his hand the floor of sand, and asked our names, which we did not tell him; however, he commenced to span the sand and to mark it in his own cabalistic way, after which he pronounced the opinion, that the fatigues of the long journey weighed heavily upon Speke's heart.

5th.|Intending to start across the desert at noon, we had prepared for the journey by keeping our camels without water for two days, and we now gave them as much as they could drink before setting out . Several of them had pieces of goat-skin sewn to the

436 LIFE AND DEATH IN THE DESERT.

horny part of their feet to prevent the sharp pebbles or rock from making them foot-sore. We killed a sheep for ourselves, and hit upon an excellent plan of preserving the meat, by cutting it up into portions the size of a mutton-chop, and boiling all in grease : when cooled, it was put into a leathern bag, and being cooked, it lasted us during the journey. Our caravan consisted of twenty-nine persons, including two guides, all mounted on camels. Each camel, besides grain and baggage, also carried, slung on either side, two girbas or water-bags. We had three men and a couple of lads, over and above the experienced guides, for the purpose of driving on and attending to our camels. They wished us to hire more carriage, saying, our water was insufficient, but we found that we were amply supplied. Setting out soon after noon, we passed to the right of a hill, called Moogeran. The route was as firm as a gravelled garden-walk, not a shrub nor tree upon its whole extent, and grass only where water had coursed after rains. I had always fancied a " desert" to be drifting sand, as is seen in the Overland route, but here it was perfectly level, and swept by the wind. Several doves passed us; a jet-black swift skimmed in front of our troop of camels, and alighted on the ground without fear, as the Mother Carey's Chicken alights on the billows; sand-finches and sand-grouse, &c., flew about. We had two species of lizard to interest us while proceeding on our march, and the ground was riddled with rat-holes. These may be said to have represented life, and we had skeletons of camels representing death. The latter were in every state of decay and position. Few seemed to have died here (at the close of their journey from Korosko) with-

A DUST-STORM. 437

out a struggle. While crossing to the hill above mentioned, we saw at its base what seemed a lake with boats upon it; our Seedees at once said, " Let us go for water, let us fetch wood." It was a mirage, the Bahr Belama, or false sea, seen about two in the afternoon in the most fantastic shapes, wherever there was a hill to obstruct the current of air. There was a good deal of bantering amongst the Seedees after the mirage was discovered, each trying to dupe his neighbour into walking over to it. We had been in the saddle from noon till sunset, when we dismounted for two hours to allow our camels to eat their corn, and then we proceeded again, sailing over the plain of gravel till near daylight. This was our first severe night. I felt as sleepy as if I had been drugged ; even walking now and then at a brisk pace scarcely kept us awake.

6th.|We had rested well at Aboo Inteh Shurrut, with the glorious heavens for our canopy, and jumped up off our blankets light and joyous, and were saddled by sunrise, having, with the aid of some of our firewood, got a luxurious cup of coffee. We had two severe days' work before us. First, we had to reach Furoodh, a four hours' morning ride across a hard plain, with solitary hills in the distance, and mirage near them. Then we had an afternoon march to Ta- boon, or Taban (trouble), where the camels were baited. Here, the place, true to its cognomen, gave us the benefit of a dust - storm: the bank of cloud rolled on from the eastlevery one lay upon his face; the camels turned their backs and rested their long necks on the ground; the lights were blown out, and for a minute, while we were pelted with sand and gravel, all was dark. The blast, however, was soon over. We

438 IPSEHA, OR THE CLOUDS.

were off five minutes after it, making for the pass called Durb-wait, or Udder-a-waep (signifying narrow- road), and entered it after passing two hills, named Gorebat (solitary) and Abnoogara (the drummer). The pass wound very much, and varied in breadth from three yards to a thousand, being sometimes so rocky that our camel-men cheered up the spirits of the animals by calling out to them " Abdil Ka-a-dr," as much as to say, " God preserve you from harm over the rough stones." But when the sandy level bed of the valley widened, and rugged mountains imprisoned it all round, there was something wildly-grand about the scene. The natives had christened this place Ipseha, or the clouds. We encamped some distance up the valley, where a few acacias, having pods like earrings, grew upon the plain of sand. We had been for ten hours on the move, and we left again at one o'clock, keeping still in " Udder-a-waep," or the pass, for six miles. Waves of drifted sand almost buried the higher hills, up whose sides it lay like snow- wreaths. Here, curious enough, were some dead trees which we might have earned in as firewood, but the Seedees were too apathetic. The desert we were about to enter was our first genuine sandy desert; all the preceding had been firm and hard. Nothing but miles of heavy sand, as deep as a lake, was now seen. The camel-drivers and guides again shouted " Abdil Ka- a-dr " to give heart to their camels, and with this short prayer urged the animals quickly over the danger. There was no trace of a path, and the night was coming on, but the sky was clear. The Seedees knew no danger; all were jolly; and as there was no chance of a dust-storm, we lay down for two hours. We then

KATRON WELLS OF MOBAD. 439

resumed, and continued the journey till three in the morning, not feeling so sleepy as we had done the first few nights. It seemed extraordinary that the Sheikhs could find their way in such a desert in the dark, without the aid of hills or trees as landmarks, but they do so unfailingly. They are extremely careful, and when any of our men lay down for a moment's sleep, the ever-vigilant Sheikh would report him for being so indifferent to his own life as to linger behind for an instant. However, by midnight of the 7th the danger was past, and we walked upon rocky ground where the Morad valleys commence, and where there are springs of brackish water.

As we approached the natron wells of Morad, the country appeared to open, though covered with slaty rocks bristling above ground. Hills and valleys, patched with drifted sand, presented the most dreary, waste-like appearance. The heat was relaxingla crow appeared, and the Sheikh informed us that it was a good signlwe should certainly find water in the wells. A turn in the road suddenly disclosed a long valley below, running from east to west, with camels, donkeys, goats, and sheep standing languidly around five or six wells. Carcasses of animals were numerous in this valley of death. Our camels showed no anxiety for water, although they had been without it for three days; but they seemed eager to have a roll upon a clear patch of sand in view. The well our party took possession of was protected from sand by a wall on its upper and lower sides. It was dug ten feet below the surface, and had only six inches of water. After having been used all day it had not run dry; but the water was like saltpetre in taste. In this

440 NITROUS DRINKING-WATER.

dreary valley several huts built of matting axe inhabited by Arabs and their flocks. Who else could live on the spot? Where do their small long-haired goats get a single blade of grass to feed upon ? It- would seem as if they could not exist; yet before us is a flock of sixty, which are brought to drink at the well every third or fourth day, and though living on this brackish water, no animals ever appeared more healthy. The people residing here are not different from the natives of Aboo Ahmed, and are not more unhealthy; but one of them begged for medicine to cure a chest complaint. Several of their children were pretty, with intelligent eyes, and looking wild as colts, with all the hair shaved off their heads except a forelock and long tress from the crown of the head. In this valley of Morad there is not an atom of firewood; indeed, for three days' travelling, day and night, we had not met with more than thirty trees; and, being so rarely seen, we took them almost every tune for a mirage.

9th.|At eleven o'clock we left the wells *en route* for Korosko, still some days' journey without wood or water upon the way; and therefore we carried the brackish water of the Morad wells with us. It was very unpleasant to wash with, as it curdled the soap, and the exterior of the water-bags became powdered as with flour. The camels did not suffer much from drinking it . Our route was across a series of rocky spurs and dykes, all tapering down to the Nile far away to our left. The strata of the rocks seemed reversed in position, as if they had been uplifted by a convulsion in the north. One of the ridges which crossed our road at Wadi Soofoor was four hundred yards long,

INTERESTING SPECIES OF PALM. 441

and so remarkable that it looked as if a waving wall had been built there as a boundary between two properties, standing up in the sky-line like *chevaux-de-frise.* The colours of the accumulated debris and sand in the gorges of the hill-sides were striking. At the top of the incline the sand was flesh-coloured and fiery; lower down the debris was grey and purple, consisting of slate in various shades, and blue rocks like masses of cobalt; bits of spar were also collected. Between each of these are tempting valleys for a ride, the ground being of firm hard sand.

The connection between each valley is formed by a steep rugged path, sometimes, as on entering the valley of Dull ah, with high cliffs on either side; and looking through this vista upon the scene below, the effect is picturesque. There is a line of palm-trees which adds a charm to the spot. At a distance they might be mistaken for the doom-palm; but their fruit, unbranched stems, and leaves are different. We had not seen them before, but Manua had found them growing eight degrees south of the equator, in a country where there are numerous rivulets. Some seeds, brought home by the expedition, were propagated, in Kew, but they ultimately died. Having passed the valleys of Dullah, Wadi Soofoor, and Thillatha Jindeh, with its acacias, we rested between six and eight o'clock on the sands of Wadi Mereesha, and were on the move again till three of the morning.

While riding along upon the march, conversation is continued in order to keep each other awake. The topics are generally upon the natural objects around us, whether it be the hills, stream-beds, trees, or rocks. The Seedees laughed, mimicked, and ridiculed each

442 EXTRAORDINARY NATURAL TUNNEL.

other as they rode along briskly on their camels. We had with us a poor half-witted fellow, or fool, named Mahoka, whom Bombay had obtained for a few yards of cloth, and kept as his servant. He was a hardworking fellow, but would often burst out into fearful rages, refusing to work. There was something of the rogue about his fooleries, and he held his own amongst the men. One night he fell asleep upon the top of his camel, and dropt down upon his back on the ground, his legs, arms, and spear flying in the air. I thought the creature was killed, but he got up, laughed, snapped his fingers, and danced a war-dance. He would not, however, remount his camel for an hour or two. While marching through the picturesque valley of Dullah, a circumstance elicited from Manua in his account of his wanderings, may be mentioned here as noted at the time. I repeated it to Dr Livingstone, who also had received some information regarding it Extract, 10th May 1863 : " While riding along on our camels last night, Manua told me of a tunnel, the work of God, which runs north and south between Loowemba and Ooroongoo (two months' march from Kazeh), which took the caravan of Arab Khamees, with whom he was travelling, from sunrise till noon to march through, and which was as broad as from that white stone to the back hill (a distance which I judged to be four hundred yards). Over this tunnel an unfordable river with rocky sides (here he pointed to the hills around us) runs at right angles to the Tanganyika Lake. If boats were to attempt to ferry this river, the cliffs are too steep to permit of their landing,lthe river is forded by passing through the natural tunnel underneath. As to its height, this

EXTRAORDINARY NATURAL TUNNEL. 443

camel, with me mounted, could inarch through the tunnel and then not touch its top. No water comes through; it is obtained by digging holes in the sand. The reed from which the Waganda make flutes, grows inside it. The rocks are black, and look as if they had been planed (basalt, from his description). White pebbles are plentiful there. Inside it is not as clear as day, but once within it there is sufficient light the whole way. The natives consider it a m'zimo (namely, wonder or worshipping spot). They have no name for it, but the river above it is called Kaoma." On my interrogating him further, as if doubting his tale, and making him repeat it to Speke, he got nettled, and asked with a sneer, " Did not the people of Wambwch take shelter in it, with their cattle, from the attacks of the Watuta ? (meaning a branch of the Zulu Kafir). And if you do not believe my story, because I did not mention it before, ask so-and-so of Unyanyembe, who was of our party." Manua added, that "he went and returned by this tunnel, as it is the regular highway road between Loowemba and Ooroongoo." It will be interesting to know what account was received of it by Dr Livingstone. In the mean time the above description as to size, direction, &c., must be considered vague and general. From Manua's description I understood him to say that this river Kaoma flowed into the Tanganyika Lake.

We went smartly over the Bahr Hut'ab, the waterless sea, in ten hours' marching, and by breakfast-time of the 10th reached Aboo Rakeeb, or father of shade, a shelter-rock of sandstone upon a commanding height. The surface of the country was dotted with black conical masses of sandstone, intermixed with which were

444 PAY TRIBUTE AT THE MOUTH OF THE PASS.

volcanic bombs, single and stuck together, varying from one inch to three in diameter. Those that had become detached lay like round-shot on the expanse of the desert. We next marched, for four hours, across the Bahr Belama, descending to a pass called El Bab, where we dined, and then travelled all night between bare abrupt hills, which, as we advanced, broke up into cones, looking like huge redoubts and batteries. The footing in these valleys is of level sand. On arriving at the pass our cavalcade was halted by the Sheikh in command, and his men immediately commenced to rattle and beat the bones of some dead camels that lay on the spot; the men also screeched and shouted, making a great noise. The cause of this demonstration, we found, was, that we had there to pay a certain footing or tribute, and this being agreed to, we advanced. Frij tells me that the same custom exists on board of an Arab vessel when she is leaving the port for the first time; the new hands amongst the crew are obliged to contribute money, to be expended in a jollification. In ten hours, over firm sand, we reached Oogab Ghowab', where there is a sandstone shelter-rock written upon by foreigners. It protected us during the heat of the day. An efiendi (secretary) had dug a well, and surrounded it by a wall, but there was no water. There was, however, some vegetation, giving us an idea that water was not very distant or very deep: the wild senna was growing, and some withered bushes of another plant blew about in balls with the wind. With two rests on the way, we reached Korosko from Oogab Ghowab' after sixteen hours' travelling. In a few places there were slabs of sandstone, and as we neared

THE SHEIKH OF THE DESERT. 445

Korosko we came upon old red sandstone and conglomerate as hard as flint. Our direction during six days had been mainly upon the pointers to the north star, when they are westerly and horizontal. The cry of the Sheikh to rouse us for the march from our comfortable couches upon the desert sand, can never be forgotten; his "Abdil Ka-a-dr," repeated and repeated till he saw us up and saddling, was at the time provoking, but how very necessary with such a waterless country to pass over ! In my Journal I have noted, with reference to the Sheikh and his followers, that we should never again meet their superiors for civility, their unpresuming modest manner, their thorough knowledge of their work, and their willingness always to serve. They would assist our Seedees in conveying water during the march, picking up for them whatever they let fall, packing and tying up our baggage, and never murmuring or begging. They left us smiling, satisfied with our treatment of them.

The first indication of the Korosko habitations was the appearance of some date-palms, long-stemmed, like the wild date-tree of Uganda. As we emerged from the sandy wastes there was a general impression that the Nile was amongst the hills we saw; and the old Sheikh confirmed this by stating that shortly we should drink of the waters of the Nile. Rounding a hill, the scattered village of Korosko was full before us in the midst of an amphitheatre of hills, their fiery sides of sand nearly killing every living thing around them. There was, however, some shade by the river bank; and we hired a diabeah, and a party of seven men to convey us to Shellal. It was a luxury to get rid of the camelslto experience any changeland

446 THE PASHA SENDS A STEAMER FOR US.

especially to taste a water-melon after such a journey! The effendi gave us every aid; and, as it was not desirable to stay long in a place which he called as hot as hell, with no wood or provisions to be had our crew, glad to escape, ejaculated, " In Sha TJUah!' or " God be praised," and we floated down old Kilns on the evening of the 12th of May. The song and the sailors' mode of rowing were strange to us; the former was powerful, harmonious, and pleasing, and the men stood two feet above the deck pacing upon planks as they propelled the boat; their language also had a strange twang to our earsla regular Nile *patois.* As we glided past the Bar'edy hills, with narrow terraces for cultivation, the country appeared hot and dry; everything was parched and arid in comparison with the green of the Soudan. The present Pasha will, I trust, open up the country of the Soudan, for it might be converted, by draining and irrigation, into a valuable possession. We were beginning -to feel that the tourist's route had at length been reached, for at Korosko we were pestered for " buxees," or money. Our captain also made an extraordinary request: provisions were scarce; and, purchasing a calf, the captain demanded, as his right, the head and fore-quarter of the animal; which we, however, refused, although he said it was the perquisite of all captains who had charge of travellers on the Nile. We landed at the snug harbour of Shellal, below Phylae, and there had the final confirmation of our being on a beaten track, for a host of donkey-boys gathered round us, clamouring and shouting to be engaged.

The day we were to leave Aswan for Cam) ifl a small diabeah, a steamer came puffing up the river.

SAIL FROM CAIRO FOR ENGLAND. 447

His Highness the Viceroy, Ismael Pasha, had sent this vessel to bring us down, and we sailed on the 19th of May 1863. The mudirs or governors on the way were politely attentive, and we anchored at Boulac, the port of Cairo, on the 25th, after a pleasant voyage of six days. Few of our Seedees had ever before seen a steamship, and they viewed it with strong interest. Every day fresh wonders were revealed to them. The ruins of Dandoor, Kalap'shee, and Phylae, with their carvings, paintings, and stone roofs, filled them with amazementl" no one at Zanzibar could make such buildings." On our passage down the river, the windmills, the tall chimneys, the tame buffaloes going about the villageslall they saw interested, astonished, and delighted them. At Boulac the naval commander, Latif Pasha, sent for us; and on parting, after a short interview, he presented Speke with a bouquet of flowers which had just been handed to him. Our Seedees were lodged in the public garden at Cairo, as the people were afraid to admit them into their houses. On the 1st of June we saw them, headed by Bombay, depart by train for Suez, *en route* to Aden and Zanzibar. They took leave of us with affectionate regret and many prayers, trusting they would again see us in their own country. On the same day we had a private audience of his Highness the Viceroy, who showed great interest in our journey, and offered to aid Speke in any further exploration. On the 4th of June we sailed in the Pera, Captain Jamieson, for England, where we arrived in safety after our long and varied journey, and an absence of eleven hundred and forty- six days.

APPENDIX A.

List Of Personal Kit Taken With us From England For The Expedition.

12 blankets (grey Crimean) and 2 pairs scarlet do., from Grindlay & Co.'s ; 73 Ib. weight.

4 leather bags for shooting apparatus, from Grindlay & Co.'s. 1 set of bits in box handle, do.

1 spring balance to 60 Ib., do.

2 iron beds, from Brown & Co.'s, Piccadilly ; 28 lb. each. 2 belts for revolvers, from Grindlay.

2 watering bridles, do.

4 packs playing-cards, do.

2 iron chairs, Brown & Co.'s ; each 12J lb.

1 digester for soup, Grindlay & Co.'s.; 15 lb.

4 eye-preservers (glass and wire). 24 flannel shirts, from Grindlay & Co.'s. 12 pairs flannel trousers, do.

1 large housewife, -do.

4 hats, wideawake and glazed, from Grindlay & Co.'s. 12 ink-powder packets (black and red), do.

India-rubber and India-rubber rings, do.

6 japanned tin trunks, weights 13, 14, and 17 Ib., from do. 8 table knives, 6 sailors', 24 three-bladed (Rogers') for skinning

specimens, from Grindlay & Co.'s. 6 pairs leather leggings, short and long, from Grindlay & Co.'s.

2 pewter mugs without glass.

1 medicine chest, containing Brown's blistering tissue, plaster, quinine,

lunar caustic, citric acid, jalap, calomel, rhubarb, blue pill, colo- cynth, laudanum, Dover's powders, emetic essence of ginger; 30 Ib.

2 mosquito netting. 2 hair pillows.

12 pocket-handkerchiefs.

450 APPENDIX.

t 2 penholders.

6 dozen pencils, Winsor & Newton's, &c.

1 2-feet rule.

2 white serge sheets. 12 pairs shoes, Simnett.

6 dozen socks, half woollen, Grindlay & Co.'s. 2 pairs stirrup-leathers.

4 iron stools, Brown's, and 2 sketching do., Winsor & Newton's.

7 saucepans (a nest of block-tin), Grindlay. 16 table spoons, 8 table do., 8 tea do.

12 sail-needles, large and small.

2 lb. mustard and cress seeds.

2 tents (7 by 7, and 7 feet high).

Toolsl2 hammers, 2 saws, pincers, files, chisels, &c.

8 pairs trousers, drill, unbleached. 2 oval tin teapots.

40 lb. tea, from Sterriker. 2 gingham umbrellas, half carriage size, with white covers, Grindlay

& Co.'s. 4 waistcoats of Scotch tweed, Grindlay & Co.'s.

2 veils (green), do.

4 waterproof sheets (white), about 10 feet square, Grindlay & Co.'s.

1 photographic instrument for collodion, Bland & Long'.

Instruments for Observing ; weight 228 Ib.

3 sextants of 8$ inch radius, Troughton & Simms.

2 stands for do., do.

2 artificial horizons.

1 chronometer (gold), Barraud & Lund.

1 do. (silver), Parkinson & Frodsham.

1 lever watch (B. & Lund), with double-detaching second-hand.

1 do. (Dent), with split second-hand-

1 do. (Jones).

3 prismatic compasses, cardless, with platinum rings, T. & Sinuns.

2 magnetic compasses (pocket), Eliot.

1 telescope, 1 rain-gauge (travellers'), and 1 rain-gauge (Livingstone's).

6 boiling thermometers.

1 maximum and 1 minimum thermometer, Casella.

1 Massey's patent log ; 10 lb.

2 bull's-eye lanterns, with vessels to fit for boiling thermometers, Casella.

Mapping and Drawing Instruments.

2 reams mapping paper, Malby & Sons.

Tracing paper, black and white, Winsor & Newton.

APPENDIX. 451

1 circular brass protractor, Eliott; 1 parallel ruler on rollers, Eliott. 1 case mathematical instruments, Eliott.

1 pocket-compass, 1 50-feet measuring tape, one drawing-board. ream open foolscap, graduated in squares.

2 boxes of water-colours, Winsor & Newton. 4 block sketch-books, 2 Clifford's.

Books.

1 Raper's 'Navigation.'

1 Coleman's ' Nautical and Lunar Tables.'

4 log-books, 12 field-books, and 5 longitude do., F. Gallon, Esq. 4 Nautical Almanacks, 1860-61-62-63.

Tables for measuring breadth of rivers, Galton.

Maps of Africa, all the recent, foreign and English.

Rifles\Arms and Ammunition\Revolvers.

2 single rifles, Lancaster's elliptical, . 40 bore.
1 single Blisset, . . 4 do.
1 do. do. . . 16 do.
1 double do. 20 do.
1 do. smooth do. . . . 12 do.
1 do. rifle do. . . (?) 10 do.
1 six-barrelled revolving Colt rifle.

1 Whitworth sporting rifle.
1 double smooth-bore by . . 12 do.
2 Tranter's revolvers ; 8 Ib. each. 500 rounds for each barrel.
50 carbines, with pouches, sword-bayonets, and belts, Royal Artillery
pattern 1860 ; each 13 Ib. 200 rounds to each carbine ; caps in complement.
Presents.
1 watch by M'Cabe, in sword-belt, for Zanzibar sultan.
3 gold-enamelled lever watches, by M'Cabe.
REMARKS UPON THE ABOVE KIT.
On reaching Egypt we still had a suit of clothes, a single rifle, and some bullets each.
Except the scientific instruments, everything else had been given away as presents or
was worn out. I may remark that we found nothing wanting in this outfit to make it
complete and excellent in every452 APPENDIX.
respect The iron beds and chairs of Messrs Brown & Co. of Piccadilly, were
admirable. The digester, very useful The japanned tin cases stood the wear and tear
of the journey to the last; they are recommended as superior for travelling to trunks or
portmanteaus, made of wood or leather. Crimean blankets, and sheets of white serge,
also sheets of waterproof, are indispensable upon such a journey. The stout lacing-
shoes, made by Messrs Simnett, Bishopsgate Street, resisted the wet even without
blacking. The nest of block-tin cooking-pots, although in constant use, lasted for two
years, so also did our single canvass tents. Our shepherd-tartan waistcoats (both back
and front of the same material) were so strong, that at the end of the journey they did
not appear to have been much worn. The suits of flannel, though comfortable, were
liable to be torn in going through thorny covers.
   The scientific instruments were little damaged by the journey, as they were always
placed in the hands of trustworthy porters.
   APPENDIX B.
   The following is the analysis of the sand found in the Apuddo stream (page 343):|
   " London, *VIA Nov.* 1864.
   " Dear Sir,|In the absence of Sir Roderick Murchison from town, Mr Francis Galton
left with me a small bottle of sand, together with a note from you, requesting him to
get the contents tested. This has been done in Dr Percy's laboratory, and Mr Richard
Smith (Dr Percy's assistant) reports as follows :|
   "' The black sand consists chiefly of titaniferous iron ore (ilmenite), with small
quantities of quartz, magnetic iron ore, and scales of yellow mica. The sand is free
from gold or silver.'

" Trusting that this information will be in time for your forthcoming work, I am, dear Sir, yours faithfully,

"TRENHAM REEKS. " Captain Grant."

THE END.

PRINTED BY WILLIAM BLACKWOOD AND SONS, EDIKBUHOH.

Lately rrni.isnKD,

WHAT LED TO THE DISCOVERY OF THE
SOURCE OF THE NILE.

By JOHN BANNING SPEKE, Captain H.M. Inffim-'Army.
Octavo, with Maps, &c., 14s. $ '

"Every paragraph, to those specially interested in geographical discoverien, will prove eminently attractive, and will tend, no doubt, to lay-tHe-foundation of accurate information concerning a country which, under its natural aspects, is so beautiful and so prolific in its productions, and demands, on many grounds, the attention of the European."*|John JBull,*

" Will be read with peculiar interest, as it makes the record of his travels complete, and. nt the same time, heightens, if possible, our admiration of his indomitable perseverance as well as tact."*|Disjxiteh.*

JOURNAL
OF THE
DISCOVERY OF THE SOURCE OF THE NIRE.

By JOHN BANNING SPEKE, Captain H.M. Indian Army. With a Map of Eastern Equatorial Africa by Captain Speke; Numerous Illustrations, chiefly from Drawings by Captain Grant; and Portraits, Engraved on Steel, of Captains Speke and Grant.

Octavo, price 21s.

" The volume which Captain Speke has presented to the world possesses more than a geographical interest. It is a monument of perseverance, courage, and temper displayed under difficulties which have porhnps never been equalled."*| Times.*

"Captain Speke has not written a noble book so much as he has done a noble deed. The volume which records his vast achievement is but the minor fact|the history of his discovery, not the discovery itself; yet even as a literary performance it is worthy of very high praise. It is wholly free from the traces of book- manufacture. ... It is, however, a great story that is thus plainly told ; a story of which nearly all the interest lies in the strange facts related, and. more than all, in the crowning fact that it frees us, in a large degree, from a geographical puzzle which had excited the curiosity of mankind|of the most illustrious emperors and communities|from very early times."*|Athenifum..*

"This volume of Captain Speke's, in which he establishes beyond dispute his right to the honour of a discovery which had engaged the attention and curiosity of men from the earliest ages, is not only a record of that discovery|it is a monument of heroic persistency under circumstances the most appalling, and a treasury of new and surprising knowledge of many kinds. More enchanting than a fairy tale, more exciting than a novel, its greatest charm is yet that every word of it is true, and its thrilling